Exploring the Nexus Doctrine in International Tax Law

Series on International Taxation

VOLUME 77

Series Editors

Prof. Ruth Mason, University of Virginia School of Law
Prof. Dr Ekkehart Reimer, University of Heidelberg

Introduction & Contents

The Series on International Taxation deals with a wide variety of topics in the global tax arena. The authors include many of the field's leading experts as well as talented newcomers. Their expert views and incisive commentary have proven highly useful to practitioners and academics alike.

Objective

The volumes published in this series are aimed at offering high-quality analytical information and practical solutions to international tax practitioners.

Readership

Practitioners, academics and policy makers in international tax law.

Frequency of Publication

2-3 new volumes published each year.

The titles published in this series are listed at the end of this volume.

Exploring the Nexus Doctrine in International Tax Law

Ajit Kumar Singh

Wolters Kluwer

Published by:
Kluwer Law International B.V.
PO Box 316
2400 AH Alphen aan den Rijn
The Netherlands
E-mail: international-sales@wolterskluwer.com
Website: lrus.wolterskluwer.com

Sold and distributed by:
Wolters Kluwer Legal & Regulatory U.S.
7201 McKinney Circle
Frederick, MD 21704
United States of America
Email: customer.service@wolterskluwer.com

ISBN 978-94-035-3363-6

e-Book: ISBN 978-94-035-3364-3
web-PDF: ISBN 978-94-035-3365-0

To My Parents
Basanti Singh (Late) and Gorakh Nath Singh

About the Author

Ajit Kumar Singh is a member of the prestigious Indian Revenue Service (IRS), with about thirty years of experience and expertise in tax law administration in India. He is presently a Senior Commissioner of Income Tax and a Member of the Dispute Resolution Panel of the Government of India, adjudicating on international taxation and transfer pricing disputes.

He is an alumnus of Delhi University and the University of Oxford and also holds a Doctorate in Law from the National Law University, Delhi. He regularly writes articles on tax law topics for The Taxman, the tax law journal, published from Delhi.

Table of Contents

List of Abbreviations

AAR	Authority for Advance Rulings, India
AG	Attorney General
AIR	All India Reporter (Journal)
ALI	American Law Institute
All	Allahabad High Court
Am Econ Rev	American Economic Review
Am J Intl L	American Journal of International Law
AP	Andhra Pradesh High Court
APTB	Asia-Pacific Tax Bulletin
ATF	Australian Tax Forum
Austl	Australia
Beng	ITAT Bengaluru Bench
Berk J Intl L	Berkeley Journal of International Law
BFIT	Bulletin for International Taxation
BIAC	Business and Industry Advisory Committee to the OECD
Bom	Bombay High Court
Brookn J Intl L	Brooklyn Journal of International Law
BTR	British Tax Review
BYBIL	British Year Book of International Law
Cal	Calcutta High Court
Calif L Rev	California Law Review
Can	Canada
Can Crim L Rev	Canadian Criminal Law Review

Cath UL Rev	Catholic University Law Review
CBDT	Central Board of Direct Taxes
CBLJ	Canadian Business Law Journal
CFC	Controlled Foreign Corporation
CIT	Commissioner of Income Tax
Colum J Tax L	Columbia Journal of Tax Law
Colum L Rev	Columbia Law Review
Com	Commonwealth
Cornell L Rev	Cornell Law Review
Crim LQ	Criminal Law Quarterly
CTF	Canadian Tax Foundation
CUP	Cambridge University Press
DCIT	Deputy Commissioner of Income Tax
Deakin LR	Deakin Law Review
Del	Delhi High Court
Del-Trib	ITAT Delhi Bench
DIT	Director of Income Tax
DOCSer IBFD AC	Doctoral Services IBFD Academic Council
DPN	Discussion Paper No
DRM	Dispute Resolution Mechanism
DTAA	Double Taxation Avoidance Agreement
Duke	Duke University Press
Duke J Comp & Intl L	Duke Journal of Comparative and International Law
Duke LJ	Duke Law Journal
EJIL	European Journal of International Law
eJTR	eJournal of Tax Research
Euro Tax	European Taxation
ExMemo	Explanatory Memorandum
Expl	Explanation
Fac	Faculty
FB	Full Bench
FC	Federal Court of India
FDI	Foreign Direct Investment
Fla Tax Rev	Florida Tax Review
Franch LJ	Franchise Law Journal
Ga L Rev	Georgia Law Review

GOI	Government of India
Guj	Gujarat High Court
Hart	Hart Publishing
Harv Intl LJ	Harvard International Law Journal
Harvard	Harvard Law Journal
Hastings Intl & Comp L Rev	Hastings International and Comparative Law Review
HBTLJ	Houston Business and Tax Law Journal
IBFD	International Bureau of Fiscal Documentation
ICC	International Chamber of Commerce
IFA	International Fiscal Association
IJFL	International Journal of Financial Studies
IJR	International Journal of Research
IMF	International Monetary Fund
Ins	Insurance
Intertax	International Tax Review
Intl J Fin Stud	International Journal Financial Studies
Intl Tax J	International Tax Journal
Israel L Rev	Israel Law Review
ITAT	Income Tax Appellate Tribunal
ITR	Income Tax Reporter (Journal)
J Comp Leg	Journal of Comparative Legislation and International Law
J Dev Stud	Journal of Development Studies
Kar	Karnataka High Court
La L Rev	Louisiana Law Review
Law & Pol Int Bus	Law & Policy in International Business
Mad	Madras High Court
Melbourne	Melbourne University Press
Mich	Michigan
Ministry of Fin	Ministry of Finance
MLI	Multilateral Convention to Implement Tax Treaty Related Measures to Prevent BEPS
MLR	Modern Law Review
MP	Madhya Pradesh High Court

MTC	Model Tax Convention
MULR	Melbourne University Law Review
Mum	ITAT Mumbai Bench
Natl Tax J	National Tax Journal
NLS of India Review	National Law School of India Review
NTJ	National Tax Journal
Nw J Intl L & Bus	Northwestern Journal of International Law & Business
OECD Pub	OECD Publishing
OUP	Oxford University Press
Pak SC	Pakistan Supreme Court
PC	Privy Council
PE	Permanent Establishment
Penn St L Rev	Penn State Law Review
PCIJ	Permanent Court of International Justice
Princeton	Princeton University Press
Pune	ITAT Pune Bench
Rep	Report
RTC	Road Transport Corporation
SB	ITAT Special Bench
SC	Supreme Court of India
SCC	Supreme Court Cases (Journal)
SCCB	Supreme Court Constitution Bench
STN	State Tax Notes
Syd LR	Sydney Law Review
Tex L Rev	Texla Law Review
Toronto	Toronto University Press
TP	Transfer Pricing
Tripathi	NM Tripathi Pvt Ltd, Bombay
TTJ	Tax Tribunal Judgement (Journal)
U Miami L Rev	University of Miami Law Review
U Pa J Intl L	University of Pennsylvania Journal of International Law
UNCTAD	The United Nations Conference on Trade and Development
UN Pub	UN Publication
Universal	Universal Law Publishing
UOI	Union of India

US SC	Supreme Court of the US
UTLJ	University of Toronto Law Journal
Va Tax Rev	Virginia Tax Review
WB	West Bengal
Wm & Mary L Rev	William and Mary Law Review
WPN	Working Paper, No
WTJ	World Tax Journal
Yale	Yale University Press
Yale J on Reg	Yale Journal on Regulation

Foreword

Tax allocation among states has always been contentious. Ideological prejudices and revenue concerns of individual states have led to a multitude of tax disputes in recent times based on the concept of 'nexus'. This book not merely presents a sharp insight into the existing normative principles of nexus in international tax law, but also brings into sharp focus the emerging economic connection as a jurisprudential justification for taxing non-resident's income.

The author, Dr Ajit Kumar Singh, is especially qualified to write this book. He is not only deeply acquainted with the topic academically, but also has a long experience of tax administration in India. This remarkable combination of academics and experience has enabled Dr Singh to offer an incisive description of the Indian and international practices in this regard. The question how the 'nexus' principle in the source rule metamorphosed into a strict physical presence test has not engaged much attention of tax lawyers and academics. The recent tax disputes in Vodafone and other cases have brought out this anomalous bewilderment in greater detail.

This book, thus, fills this gap in tax literature and seeks to address the question as to whether a strict physical presence standard in source rule jurisprudence is an essential legal requirement. This book not merely records the historical evolution of the nexus doctrine, but it also offers a politically informed analysis of the nexus principle and balances the dynamics of physical presence and economic nexus standards, based on judicial pronouncements and international practices in this regard.

This book is a compulsory read, not only for the law students of the universities and their researchers but also for the tax practitioners of various countries as well as for those who wish to foster a better understanding of the constitutional doctrine of extraterritoriality or due process in the context of source rule jurisprudence and solve the question of appropriate tax apportionment under a source rule, founded on a meaningful economic nexus. Dr Singh's book provides us a missing link in the international source rule literature.

Justice Ranjana Prakash Desai
Chairperson, Delimitation Commission of India
Former Judge of the Supreme Court of India
Former Chairperson, Authority for Advance Rulings, India
New Delhi, February 2021

Preface

This book examines the nexus doctrine for jurisdictional tax apportionment and seeks to address the question whether a strict physical presence of an entity in the taxing jurisdiction is a *sine qua non* of source rule jurisprudence. The prodigal growth in cross-border transactions has put additional strain on the revenue concerns of developed and developing countries. The developed nations, who have traditionally canvassed residence taxation, have been exerting pressures on developing nations to reconsider their existing source rule on the lines of a strict territorial nexus or physical presence imperatives. In India, for instance, the doctrine of territorial nexus appears to have been read into the source rule owing to the use of the expression 'any business connection' in India in the Indian statute. There have been fierce efforts by the cross-border operators to exploit these statutory weaknesses, even though the Indian Government has promptly moved to address the statutory gaps by suitable legislative amendments, which have provoked sharp reactions from international tax scholars and stakeholders. Not much research has been conducted into the question of how the 'nexus' rule assumed the form of a rigid 'physical presence test'.'

The object of this book is to fill this hiatus and investigate whether a strict physical presence in a state is a *sine qua non* for its tax rights. Special emphasis is placed on the historical evolution of source taxation in order to investigate whether a strict territorial nexus as a normative principle is ingrained into the source rule jurisprudence. In the process, the theoretical precepts of the source rule, the status of territorial nexus from the standpoint of international customary law and the questions of constitutionality of the nexus principles have been elaborately analysed and critiqued in the book.

Globalisation and e-commerce have intensified the jurisdictional crisis. A sharp decrease in transaction costs has increased inter-nation interdependence among businesses. Further, trans-border business transactions can be effected without a product even physically crossing a national border. The businesses of multinational companies rely heavily upon exchanges of valuable intangible properties, patents, trademarks, licences and other information goods and services to earn income in different jurisdictions. Moreover, the Internet has sparked the rise of new industries and businesses, such as the rapidly growing online advertising sector. With these developments, this strict paradigm of physicality in the territorial nexus doctrine in the tax apportionment is now being increasingly questioned, underscoring and urgent imperative to reformulate these theorisations, which, at present, have hitherto been largely moulded to cater to the needs and aspirations of the developed countries.

The huge increase in tax disputes, based on the physical presence standard, and the governments' reluctance to accept the municipal courts' decisions have, of late, been compelling the cross-border operators to seek the arbitration route. The *Vodafone* and *Cairn* arbitral awards have recently been announced, which the Indian government is gearing up to assail in the appropriate forums. The *Nokia* was another dispute, although India and Finland have reportedly reached an agreement on the high profile tax case under the Mutual Agreement Procedure involving Nokia India and parent Nokia Corp by paying its EUR 202 million dues to the government. Looking to these developments, the jurisdiction foundation of source rule taxation needs to be lucubrated with precise theoretical underpinnings. This book is an effort in that direction.

Doctrinal analysis constitutes the dominant methodology in the present research which would directly focus on legal doctrines as the object of analysis. Terry Hutchinson defines 'doctrinal research' as research which provides 'a systematic exposition of the rules governing a particular legal category, analyses the relationship between rules, explains areas of difficulty and, perhaps, predicts future developments'. It uses 'interpretive methods in order to systematically expose the law and to find out what the law is'. It is normally a two-part process because it involves: first, locating the sources of the law and second, the process of synthesising, i.e., interpreting and analysing the text. The synthesis entails the development of a particular line of inquiry, whether it is conceptual, evaluative or explanatory. The application of such techniques, along with a description of, for example, the use of deductive logic, inductive reasoning and analogy, where appropriate, would constitute the second part of the methodology. Assembling relevant facts, identifying the legal issues, analysing the issues with a view to searching for the law, reading background material (including legal dictionaries, legal encyclopaedias, textbooks, law reform and policy papers, law journal articles), locating primary material (including legislation, delegated legislation and case law) and synthesising all the issues in context are the important steps in the doctrinal process.

However, since the principles of international tax law are not codified in the strict sense of the term, the interpretive process employed in this book will also venture into critically analysing the interplay of tax policy matters and related dimensions of international customary law as reflected through various tax treaties, conventions and protocols in order to capture their influence on legal doctrine. Thus, the binaries of political paradigms, ideological imperatives and developmental dynamics of the developing nations will form the bedrock of this doctrinal probe.

The following features of this book are especially noteworthy in this regard: *first,* the book examines the historical process of evolution of the alternate basis of taxation based on 'situs' or 'source' in order to investigate whether a strict territorial nexus as a normative principle is ingrained into the source rule jurisprudence. This exercise is being undertaken for the first time in this book. *Second*, the book also undertakes a detailed scrutiny of the classical theoretical precincts of the source rule, viz., benefit theory, neutrality theory and inter-nation equity, to probe the linkages of the source rule with the territorial nexus doctrine. *Third*, a comparative critique of the two model treaties, i.e., the OECD Model and the UN Model, is also made with a view to specifically explaining how economic connection as the ultimate jurisprudential justification for taxing rights permeates through the provisions of the two treaty structures. By explaining the underlying rationales through this comparison, this book sheds considerable light on the policies states may adopt when signing new tax treaties, so that any unintended results do not emanate therefrom. *Fourth*, this book also addresses, for the first time, the question whether international law and customary principles mandate a strict territorial link with the source state for the assumption of tax jurisdiction. *Fifth*, this book also investigates at length the constitutional polemic whether the economic nexus-based tax jurisdiction and absence of a physical presence breaches the constitutional doctrine of extraterritoriality or due process. *Additionally*, the book also delves into the question of retrospective tax legislation breaching the principle of constitutional fairness.

Acknowledgements

I wish to extend my deepest gratitude to all the people who contributed in various ways to the successful completion of this book. First and foremost, I sincerely thank Dr Jasper Vikas, Law Professor at National Law University, Delhi (NLUD), whose support and supervision was indispensable for the completion of this book. His expertise, advice, and forbearance have helped me tremendously in the process. I am also deeply indebted to Prof. (Dr) A Jayagovind, former Vice Chancellor of NLSIU, with whom the first draft of this work was discussed, and I greatly benefited from our stimulating discussions and his valuable insights.

The intellectual environment of NLUD, with its rich library and e-resources, really came in handy in this intellectual journey. Particular thanks are due to Prof. (Dr) Ranbir Singh, the NLUD Vice Chancellor and Prof. (Dr) Srikrishna Deva Rao, the then Registrar and the present Vice Chancellor, for providing me with the opportunity of undertaking this project. I must also acknowledge the contributions of two of my very erudite professors at NLUD – Prof. GS Bajpai and Prof. Sitharamam Kakarala. While Prof. Bajpai provided a very detailed and comprehensive exposure to the methods and tools of research, Prof. Kakarala gave a very deep grounding in its philosophical bases. I also thank the academic staff and library staff at the University, whose doors were always open to me as a pupil and researcher. I particularly thank Dr (Mrs) Priya Rai, Deputy Librarian and Dr Akash Singh, Asst Librarian for facilitating access to the e-resources of the library. Special thanks are also due to Divya Ghai, a Delhi University student, for assisting me in this work. I also thank the Government of India for facilitating this work.

I am extremely thankful to Kluwer Law International for facilitating the preparation of the book in this form, which would not have been possible without the professional expertise of its highly experienced team.

As always, I acknowledge the unwavering and unconditional support and understanding of my wife, Asha and my kids Pranjal, Prakriti and Anukriti, who helped me through some difficult times and supported my intellectual pursuit. For this, I remain eternally grateful.

CHAPTER 1
Introduction: The Politics of Taxation

Abstract

This chapter introduces states' conflicting concerns for tax allocation and identifies the existing debate on the source rule, the consequent leakages of incomes sourced in various nations and the measures to plug those leakages, especially the issues of financial transparency, removal of bank secrecy rules, the automatic reporting scheme and the automatic exchange of information. This chapter also gives a broad overview of some major international tax disputes, both within and outside India, which have taken the territoriality debate to the centre stage.

1.1 BACKGROUND: COMPETING CONCERNS AND POLITICS

In his sweeping account of international legal history, *The Shield of Achilles*,[1] Philip Bobbitt has dubbed international law as 'a site for contesting international power according to competing ideologies formed by a particular view of law, and what law ought to be, and how it ought to be enforced. Every leadership of every state has such a view - self-interested, culturally idiosyncratic, haunted by historical threats, excited by historic visions - that is its own view of international law.'[2] The proposition applies to international tax law[3] in equal measure, if not more, - with the result that the tax allocation remains essentially a politico-economic question.

International taxation has taken centre stage in the ongoing political and economic crisis today, where states are struggling to make ends meet. Tax revenue is badly needed from any source today, and states are, therefore, devising new initiatives to improve their tax collection. The conclusion of 'tax information exchange agreements'

1. PC Bobbit, *The Shield of Achilles: War, Peace and the Course of History* (Penguin 2003).
2. *Ibid.*, 356.
3. The term 'international tax law' is about how tax systems of sovereign states mutually interact with each other and how they reconcile it bilaterally. In this sense, the term 'international tax law' is a misnomer, since there is no overriding international law of taxation. *See generally*, S Basu, *Global Perspectives on E-Commerce Taxation Law* (Ashgate 2007) 47.

(TIEAs) and the initiative of states to create a system for the automatic exchange of information about taxpayers are steps in that direction.[4] The actions of states are, however, not confined to the augmentation of their tax collection only. States are also endeavouring to address the issue of aggressive tax planning of multinational companies.

1.1.1 G20 and OECD Efforts

On the international stage, defects of the international tax rules have come to share G20 agenda and communiqué space with other great international coordination challenges of the day, such as climate change.[5] With the G20 support, the Organisation for Economic Co-operation and Development (OECD) has been making attempts to address the phenomenon of 'Base Erosion and Profit Shifting' (BEPS).[6] Michael C. Durst, in his just-published book,[7] has explored the 'base erosion and profit shrinking' tax planning structures of multinational companies of the developed nations to reduce their tax liabilities in the countries where they conduct business, including world's low-income developing countries.[8]

1.1.2 Base Erosion and Profit Shifting

In 2013, the OECD came up with a report entitled *Addressing Base Erosion and Profit Shifting*, which described studies and reports showing the impact of profit shifting of multinational corporations.[9] The report considered several empirical studies, which demonstrated how multinationals had indulged in large-scale shifting of profits to low-tax countries. A 2011 study conducted by Reuven S. Avi-Yonah and Yaron Lahave, for example, was referred to. This detailed study found that the effective tax rates of multinationals in the European Union (EU) tend to be higher than the effective tax rates of multinationals in the United States (US) despite the corporate tax rate in the US, being about 10% higher than the average statutory corporate tax rate in the EU.[10] The

4. C Peters, *On the Legitimacy of International Tax Law* (IBFD 2014) 1.
5. G20 Leaders' Communiqué, Brisbane Summit, 15-16 November 2014, http://www.g20.utoronto.ca/2014/2014-1116-communique.html accessed 12 November 2018.
6. BEPS refers to corporate tax planning strategies used by multinationals to 'shift' profits from higher-tax jurisdictions to lower-tax jurisdictions, thus 'eroding' the 'tax-base' of the higher-tax jurisdictions.
7. MC Durst, *Taxing Multinational Business in Lower Income Countries: A Problem of Economics, Politics and Ethical Norms* (Institute of Dev Stud, ICTD 2018).
8. MC Durst, 'Poverty, Tax Competition, and Base Erosion' (2018) vol. 89(12) Tax Notes Intl 1189.
9. OECD, *Addressing Base Erosion and Profit Shifting* (OECD Pub 2013) 14 (hereafter 'OECD (2013)').
10. The study compared the effective tax rate of the largest 100 multinationals in the US with the effective tax rates of the 100 largest multinationals in the EU from 2001 to 2010. *See* RS Avi-Yonah & Y Lahave, 'The Effective Tax Rate of the Largest US and EU Multinationals', University of Michigan Law School, Program in Law and Economics, WPN 41 (2011); *also see* OECD (2013) (n. 9) 25-31.

BEPS Report finally concluded that 'a number of indicators show that the tax practices of some multinational companies have become more aggressive over time, raising serious compliance and fairness issues'.[11] Furthermore, the report acknowledged that 'current international tax standards may not have kept pace with changes in global business practices'.[12] According to the OECD, BEPS have put the integrity of corporate income tax at stake, and a lack of response would further undermine competition, as some businesses, such as those which operate cross-border and have access to sophisticated tax expertise, may profit from BEPS opportunities and therefore have unintended competitive advantages compared with enterprises that operate mostly at the domestic level.[13] The OECD apprehended that profit shifting will lead to an inefficient allocation of resources and distort investment decisions if the international community cannot find a solution to the problem.[14] Thus, to address the problem of profit shifting and base erosion, the OECD suggests in its BEPS Report a comprehensive action plan with the focus on various 'pressure areas'[15] and the purpose to 'provide concrete solutions to realign international standards with the current global business environment'.[16]

Based on the findings in the BEPS Report, the OECD launched an 'Action Plan on BEPS' in which the OECD identified fifteen actions to address the problem of BEPS.[17] This Action Plan makes suggestions to prevent tax strategies 'that artificially segregate taxable income from the activities that generate it'.[18] An analysis of these proposals shows that the criteria to determine the country of residence and the country of source play an important part in this Action Plan on BEPS. In fact, some of these proposals counter BEPS by modifying the definition of the country of residence to prevent the abuse of treaty benefits. Other suggestions intend to alter the permanent establishment (PE) concept[19] and therefore focus on the country of

11. OECD (2013) (n. 9) 6.
12. *Ibid.*, 7.
13. *Ibid.*, 8.
14. *Ibid.*
15. The OECD describes six 'pressure areas': (1) international mismatches in entity and instrument characterisation including hybrid mismatch arrangements and arbitrage, (2) application of treaty concepts to profits derived from the delivery of digital goods and services, (3) the tax treatment of related party debt-financing, captive insurance and other inter-group financial transactions, (4) transfer pricing, (5) the effectiveness of anti-avoidance measures, such as CFC regimes, thin capitalisation rules and rules to prevent tax treaty abuse and (6) the availability of harmful preferential tax regimes. *See* OECD (2013) (n. 9) 47.
16. OECD (2013) (n. 9) 51.
17. Action 1 addresses the digital economy tax challenges; Action 2 intends to neutralise the effects of hybrid mismatch arrangements; Action 3 strengthens the CFC rules; Action 4 wants to limit base erosion via interest deductions, etc.; Action 5 counters harmful tax practices by account transparency and substance; Action 6 prevents treaty abuse and Action 7 the artificial avoidance of PE status; Actions 8-10 focus on TP; Action 11 establishes methodologies to collect and analyse data on BEPS; Action 12 requires disclosure of aggressive tax planning arrangements; Action 13 re-examines TP documentation; Action 14 makes DRM more effective; and Action 15 develops an MLI to implement BEPS measures. *See* OECD (2013) (n. 9) 14-24.
18. OECD (2013) (n. 9) 13.
19. The concept of permanent establishment was developed in the middle of nineteenth century in the German states to prevent double taxation among the Prussian municipalities; *see also* AA Skaar, *Permanent Establishment: Erosion of a Tax Treaty Principle* Series on International

source.[20] In a competing fashion, several important developing countries have initiated their own pact to develop cooperative strategies on these issues outside the framework of the OECD and the United Nations (UN).[21]

Treaty abuse was one of the key BEPS concerns,[22] and to effectively address this concern, the MLI (Multilateral Convention to Implement Tax Treaty Related Measures) contained several provisions including minimum standards such as modification of the preamble of the existing tax treaties[23] and incorporation of the principal purpose test[24] that all MLI signatories, including India, were expected to accept. To comply with BEPS minimum standard, India has agreed to modify the title and preamble of its tax treaties to specifically declare that the intention of the tax treaties is not only to eliminate double taxation but also to prevent non-taxation or reduced taxation through tax evasion or avoidance. Further, the MLI contemplates an optional provision to specify that the treaty is also for development of economic relationship and cooperation in tax matters. Though India has not adopted this optional provision, such non-inclusion is of no consequence as this provision merely seeks to codify an underlying treaty objective. Even before the MLI, some of the treaties that India had signed such as those with Russia and Mauritius were also done to promote economic ties with the countries. The principal purpose test seeks to deny benefit under the treaty if it is reasonably possible to conclude that in the facts of the case, one of the principal purposes of an arrangement or a transaction is to obtain a tax benefit, directly or indirectly. However, the provision clarifies that despite the desire of obtaining tax benefit(s) under the treaty, the treaty benefit cannot be denied so long as the grant of the benefit is in accordance with the objective and purpose of the relevant provisions of the treaty. In general, the principal purpose test has two tests (requirements), i.e., a subjective test and an objective test.[25] The subjective element needs to be demonstrated by the tax administration, i.e., 'if it is reasonable to conclude, having regard to all relevant facts and circumstances that obtaining the benefit was one of the principal purposes of any arrangement or transaction that resulted directly or indirectly in that benefit'. The onus of objective element is on the taxpayer, i.e., 'if it is established that granting that benefit in these circumstances would be in accordance to the object and purpose of the relevant provisions of the Covered Tax Agreement'.[26] Unlike the definition of tax or allocation of taxing rights, the principal purpose test is regarded by developed and

Taxation (Kluwer Law and Taxation 1991) 72. In tax treaties, permanent establishment is defined as a place of business in the host country, and the definition includes several examples of permanent establishments. *See* M Kobetsky, *International Taxation of Permanent Establishments: Principles and Policy* (CUP 2011) 110-111.

20. LU Cavelti, C Jaag and TF Rohner, 'Why Corporate Taxation Should Mean Source Taxation: A Response to the OECD's Actions Against Base Erosion and Profit Shifting' (2017) vol. 9(3) WTJ (IBFD) 352.
21. B Well and CH Lowel, 'Income Tax Treaty Policy in the Twenty First Century: Residence vs. Source' (2013) vol. 5(1) Colum J Tax L 1.
22. Action 6 of BEPS.
23. MLI, Art. 6.
24. *Ibid.*, Art. 7.
25. IJ Valderrama, 'BEPS Principal Purpose Test and Customary International Law' (2020) vol. 33 Leiden J Int'l L 745, 758.
26. *Ibid.*

developing countries as one of the most important and desirable solutions to tackle treaty abuse by multinationals.[27] The MLI also contemplates an optional inclusion of simplified limitation of benefits rule which provides for objective parameters such as listing, ownership, activity and specified entities which a person needs to fulfil in order to be regarded as a qualified person entitled to treaty benefit.

1.1.3 The US Concerns: Financial Transparency Issues

The need for fundamental tax reform has been a front-page material in the major newspapers, with US multinationals being portrayed as public enemy. The US, on its part, has persistently tried to curb tax base erosion for almost the entire post-World War I era, and yet the problems remain. In 2014, the US Congress became somewhat obsessed with the problem of corporate inversion transactions, in which companies historically headquartered in the US attempt to shed that geographical link because of potential tax savings. Since residence taxation can easily be avoided by channelling international investments through tax havens, the developed countries are extremely cautious. Bank confidentiality and other secrecy provisions in these havens make it difficult for the residence country to obtain information about its residents' foreign-source income. Residents can channel their income from the source country, through a country with an appropriate tax treaty, and then park them in a convenient haven, which may not be tax evasion but only avoidance. Countries with developed tax administrations also find it difficult to combat these arrangements, let alone the poorer countries, for which the task is virtually impossible.

1.1.4 The Financial Transparency Endeavours: The FATCA Agreements

With a view to strictly plugging the leakage of incomes sourced in the US, the Obama Administration introduced Foreign Account Tax Compliance Act (FATCA),[28] which was widely characterised as a watershed in the fight for increased financial transparency. FATCA was adopted by Congress in March 2010, requiring foreign banks to automatically report the account data of their US clients to the Internal Revenue Service (IRS), while imposing a punitive 30% withholding tax on US-source payments going to incompliant financial institutions. The sanctions threat has compelled all countries hosting internationally active banks to enter into bilateral FATCA agreements to remove legal barriers to the requested automatic reporting of account information. For traditional secrecy jurisdictions, this meant the removal of banking secrecy provisions that had previously prevented such transfers of data. Accordingly, they could also no longer turn down requests from third countries for additional information simply by referring to the domestic legal situation. By weakening the bargaining position of

27. *Ibid.*, 12.
28. LN Gerston, *Reviving Citizen Engagement: Policies to Renew National Community* (CRC Press 2015) 79.

traditional secrecy jurisdictions, FATCA, thus, enabled the emergence of the multilateral automatic exchange of information (AEOI) regime sponsored by the OECD. The US Government, however, itself has neither signed the multilateral AEOI agreement nor has reciprocated automatic information reporting under its bilateral FATCA treaties.[29] As a result, secretive US states like Delaware or South Dakota enjoy a competitive advantage vis-à-vis other secrecy jurisdictions in the attraction of hidden capital. Some scholars call it the US' ability to redistribute financial wealth internationally through the enforcement of organised hypocrisy.[30]

1.1.5 The European Commission's Response

On 30 August 2016, the European Commission sent shockwaves throughout the entire investment community when it imposed a massive USD 14.5 billion in penalties on Apple, Inc., USA, for receiving illegal tax subsidies from the Irish Government.[31] In the past few years, the European Commission, in fact, ordered nine multinational corporations[32] to repay a heavy amount of back taxes to many European Governments for receiving illegal tax subsidies.[33] The question concerning the source of income is one of the major aspects of disputes between these multinational corporations and the Commission.

1.1.6 Automatic Exchange of Information (AEOI)

Like developed countries, developing countries, too, need to deal with the challenge of BEPS. Taxpayers, resident in these countries, assiduously endeavour to arrange their affairs so that they are completely concealed from the Revenue authority. The Automatic Exchange of Information (AEOI) project seeks to address this issue. The main difference between developed and developing countries is the extent to which they are aware of it and the extent to which they have the capability to act on that awareness. India's initial reluctance to sign the historic multilateral convention on global automatic exchange of information,[34] which was already signed by fifty-one countries, stunned many in the tax world. Arun Jaitley, the then Finance Minister, in

29. L Hakelberg and M Schaub, 'The Redistributive Impact of Hypocrisy in International Taxation' (2018) vol. 12(3) Regulation & Governance 353.
30. *Ibid.*
31. JGS Yang and VNA Metallo, 'The Emerging International Taxation Problems' (2018) vol. 6(1) Int J Fin Stud 6, 7.
32. These corporations are: Apple: EUR 13 billion to Ireland; McDonald's: EUR 1 billion to Luxembourg; Amazon: EUR 400 million to Luxembourg; Starbucks: EUR 30 million to the Netherlands; Google: GBP 130 million to the UK; Gap: GBP 130 million to the UK; Microsoft: EUR 497 million to various European Governments; Ikea: EUR 1 billion to the Netherlands; and Fiat: EUR 30 million to Luxembourg.
33. Yang and Metallo (n. 31) 8.
34. The Multilateral Competent Authority Agreement (the MCAA) is a multilateral framework agreement that provides a standardised and efficient mechanism to facilitate the automatic exchange of information in accordance with the Standard for Automatic Exchange of Financial Information in Tax Matters (called the 'Common Reporting Standard'). It avoids the need for several bilateral agreements to be concluded. Since the Berlin signing ceremony on 29 October

his blog, sought to pin India's non-participation on the issues regarding the constitutionality of 'confidentiality' clauses in India's double tax avoidance agreements (DTAAs), opining that in a choice between unauthorised disclosure and disclosure as per treaties, the latter is both a fair and beneficial proposition. Jaitley also called for a reconsideration of the strict view taken by the Supreme Court in favour of disclosure.[35]

The Indian Government had repeatedly been highlighting its predicament to the Indian Supreme Court in disclosure of information and repeatedly sought modifications of the order dated 4 July 2011 pronounced by a Bench comprising BS Reddy and SS Nijjar JJ.[36] A review petition was also filed against this order. Strangely, at that time, the parties in opposition doubted the bona fides of the then Government in seeking such modification/review, without fully realising the predicament of India in its commitment to various countries in obtaining information and parting with information by way of a mutual cooperation process, while maintaining confidentiality at the same time. India finally overcame its inhibitions and joined the global convention on 3 June 2015, in Paris, along with Australia, Canada, Costa Rica, Indonesia and New Zealand.[37]

1.1.7 Cross-Border Transactions and Increasing Stakes

The competing concerns of developed and developing countries have assumed greater significance today with a prodigious increase in cross-border transactions and dramatic changes in the level of foreign investment in emerging economies. Economic forces unleashed by freer trade and the enhanced mobility of many of the factors of production have led to intense tax competition among developed and developing economies alike. Emerging market economies are particularly susceptible to the sirens of tax competition due to their even greater need for the benefits provided by foreign business enterprises.[38] Starting from a baseline of less than USD 1 billion in 1990, a recent United Nations Conference on Trade and Development (UNCTAD) survey projected India as the second most important foreign direct investment (FDI) destination (after China) for transnational corporations during 2010-2012.[39] According to Ernst and Young, FDI in India in 2010 was USD 44.8 billion, and in 2011 experienced

2014, around 100 jurisdictions have signed the CRS Multilateral Competent Authority Agreement based on Art. 6 of the Multilateral Convention.

35. India's Non-signing of Automatic Info Exchange agreement, 'Confidentiality' vs 'Disclosure' Crossfire, http://www.taxsutra.com/content/indias-non-signing-automatic-info-exchange-agreement-%E2%80%98confidentiality%E2%80%99-vs-disclosure accessed 6 October 2018.
36. *Ram Jethmalani v Union of India* (2011) 8 SCC 1.
37. 'India joins the Multilateral Competent Authority Agreement (MCAA) on Automatic Exchange of Information (AEOI)', PTI News, http://pib.nic.in/newsite/PrintRelease.aspx?relid=122256, accessed 17 November 2018.
38. WB Barker, 'An International Tax System for Emerging Economies, Tax Sparing, and Development: It Is All About Source' (2007) 29(2) U Pa J Intl L 349, 350.
39. *See* TNN: '*India Pips China, US to Emerge as Favourite Foreign Investment Destination*', TOI, http://timesofindia.indiatimes.com/articleshow/49160838.cms?utm_source=contentofinterest&utm_medium=text&utm_campaign=cppst, accessed 27 September 2018.

an increase of 25% to USD 50.8 billion.[40] According to the Financial Times, in 2015, India overtook China and the US as the top destination for the FDI. In first half of the 2015, India attracted investment of USD 31 billion compared to USD 28 billion and USD 27 billion of China and the US, respectively.[41]

As a result, sustained political pressures are increasingly being mounted by the developed economies on the developing ones to reconsider and restrict their existing source rule regime of non-resident taxation on the strict principle of territorial nexus.[42] While on the one hand, the efforts of cross-border operators to insist upon a strict territorial presence in the taxing state and to exploit the statutory weaknesses in the present regime, with judicial imprimatur having been accorded by the municipal courts in some cases,[43] have raised serious revenue concerns for these economies, the respective governments' persistent endeavour to plug the statutory lacunae by suitable legislative amendments, on the other hand, has provoked sharp reactions from the international tax scholars and the stakeholders of transnational trade and investment.

Agencies such as the Tax Justice Network (TJN), Oxfam and Christian Aid are raising the concerns of voices that were not sufficiently heard in the past. In this climate, there is a continuing host of articles about tax havens, letterbox companies, the 'exploitation' of developing countries, bank secrecies and 'tricks' of multinational companies and wealthy individuals in the international newspapers. It should, therefore, be clear that it is a mistake to put the described initiatives of states in the context of their budgets only. There can be no doubt that states are also responding to this vivid and intense debate in society about the 'fairness' of our taxing systems.[44]

1.2 THE INDIAN EXPERIENCE

In the Indian context, the doctrine of territorial nexus appears to have been read into the source rule owing to the use of the expression 'any business connection' in the Indian Statute,[45] which came to be explained by a three-judge Bench of the Indian Supreme Court in *RD Aggarwal* 'as a relation between the non-resident's business and

40. JV Parekh, *'Foreign Direct Investment in Indian Retail Sector'*, http://www.fnbnews.com/FB-Specials/Foreign-Direct-Investment-in-Indian-retail-sector, accessed 27 September 2018.
41. *See* C Fingar, 'India Grabs Investment League Pole Position', FT Report 29 September 2015, https://www.ft.com/content/fdd0e3c2-65fc-11e5-97d0-1456a776a4f5#axzz3n8D9cCEN, accessed 27 September 2018.
42. Income resulting from international activities may be taxed where the income is earned (the source country), or where the person who receives it is normally based (residence country). Residence taxation of income is based on the principle that people and firms should contribute towards the public services provided by their residence state, on all their income wherever it comes from. Source taxation is justified by the view that the country which provides the opportunity to generate income has the right to tax it. The doctrine of territorial nexus means that the person, event or an activity sought to be taxed must have territorial nexus with the nation seeking to tax.
43. *See, e.g., Ishikawajima-Harima Heavy Industries Ltd v DIT* [2007] 288 ITR 408 (SC); *see also Jindal Thermal Power Co Ltd v DCIT* [2010] 321 ITR 31 (Kar) and *Vodafone International Holding BV v Union of India* [2012] 341 ITR 1 (SC).
44. Peters (n. 4) 2.
45. Income Tax Act 1961 s. 9(1)(i).

the activity in the taxable territories, which facilitates or assists the carrying on of that business'. In *RD Aggarwal*, the question which came up for consideration was whether the relationship of the taxpayer with the non-residents for whom he was canvassing orders in taxing territories without authority to accept orders, amounted to business connection. Rejecting the Revenue's contention and upholding the territoriality principle, the Court held that since the acceptance of orders, the payment of price and the delivery of goods were made by the non-residents outside the taxing territories and none of the operations such as procuring of raw materials or manufacture of finished goods took place within the taxing territories, there was no business connection with India so as to confer tax jurisdiction on Indian tax authorities in respect thereof.[46]

1.2.1 *Carborandum Co*

The territorial nexus test,[47] however, came to create difficulties in the context of taxation of fees for technical services, received by a non-resident, and a curious situation arose in *Carborandum Co,*[48] where the taxability of technical fees received by Carborandum, a US company, for providing certain services from abroad, by post, to an Indian company, fell for consideration. The Revenue sought to tax this income on the ground of the services being utilised in India, which, they argued, established a nexus. Rejecting the Revenue's contention, the Supreme Court held that a territorial nexus in the context of services would require rendering of services in the taxable territories and not its mere utilisation.[49]

Though decided in 1977, this was a case under the 1922 Act.[50] Concerned with this strict territoriality argument in *Carborandum Co,*[51] India came up with an amendment in 1976,[52] which refined and expanded the concept of territorial nexus in section 9(1).

1.2.2 The 1976 Amendment

This amendment inserted clauses (v), (vi) and (vii) in section 9[53] which provides that certain types of income, such as interest, royalty, fees from technical services and so on shall be taxable in India on the basis of residence of payer, location of debt, right or property concerned and the place of utilisation of services rendered, irrespective of the place of its rendition. If the payer is the Indian Government or an Indian resident, these incomes shall be *ipso facto* charged to tax in India, except where in the case of a resident payer, the corresponding debt, right, property or services are located or used outside India. If the payer is a non-resident, the aforesaid income shall be charged to

46. *CIT v RD Aggarwal* [1965] 56 ITR 20 (SC).
47. At (n. 42).
48. *Carborandum Co v CIT* (1977) 108 ITR 335 (SC).
49. *Ibid.*
50. The Indian Income Tax Act 1922.
51. *Carborandum Co* (n. 48).
52. The Finance Act 1976 s. 4.
53. *Ibid.*

tax in India, where the corresponding debt, right, property or services are located or used in India.[54] These amendments, thus, diluted the requirement of a 'strict territorial presence' as judicially construed in *Carborandum Co*, and the mere residence of the payer of interest being in India or location of debt, right or property and utilisation of services in India was sufficient to trigger India's taxing rights.

1.2.3 *Ishikawajima* and the 2007 Amendments

This legal position held the field until 2007, when the Indian Supreme Court in *Ishikawajima*[55] severely limited the scope of 1976 amendment by holding that despite the deeming fiction in section 9, for any such income to be taxable in India, there must be sufficient territorial nexus between such income and the territory of India and for establishing such territorial nexus, the services have to be rendered as well as utilised in India. In this case, Ishikawajima, a non-resident company incorporated in Japan, provided services to persons resident in India. It formed a consortium along with five other enterprises. The consortium was awarded by Petronet, a turnkey project for setting up a liquefied natural gas (LNG) receiving, storage and re-gasification facility in Gujarat. Ishikawajima was to develop, design, engineer, procure equipment, materials and supplies, to erect and construct storage tank including marine facility (jetty and

---

54. Clauses (v), (vi) and (vii) of section 9(1), inserted through the 1976 Amendment, read as follows:

> 9(1). The following income shall be deemed to accrue or arise in India:
>
> ...
>
> (v) income by way of interest payable by--
> (a) the Government; or
> (b) a person who is a resident, except where the interest is payable in respect of any debt incurred, or moneys borrowed and used, for the purposes of a business or profession carried on by such person outside India or for the purposes of making or earning any income from any source outside India; or
> (c) a person who is a non-resident, where the interest is payable in respect of any debt incurred, or moneys borrowed and used, for the purposes of a business or profession carried on by such person in India;
>
> (vi) income by way of royalty payable by--
> (a) the Government; or
> (b) a person who is a resident, except where the royalty is payable in respect of any right, property or information used or services utilised for the purposes of a business or profession carried on by such person outside India or for the purposes of making or earning any income from any source outside India; or
> (c) a person who is a non-resident, where the royalty is payable in respect of any right, property or information used or services utilised for the purposes of a business or profession carried on by such person in India, or for the purposes of making or earning any income from any source in India:
>
> (vii) income by way of fees for technical services payable by--
> (a) the Government; or
> (b) a person who is a resident, except where the fees are payable in respect of services utilised in a business or profession carried on by such person outside India or for the purposes of making or earning any income from any source outside India; or
> (c) a person who is a non-resident, where the fees are payable in respect of services utilised in a business or profession carried on by such person in India or for the purposes of making or earning any income from any source in India.

55. *Ishikawajima* (n. 43).

island breakwater) for transmission and supply of LNG to purchasers, to test and commission the facilities, etc. Referring to the provisions of section 5(2) of the Act,[56] the Indian Supreme Court held that the provisions of section 9(1)(vii) of the Act, relating to fees for technical services, must be read with section 5, which takes within its purview the territorial nexus, i.e., (a) resident and (b) receipt or accrual of income.[57]

Thus, the Court held that a sum paid by a resident to a non-resident by way of fees for technical services would not always come within the purview of section 9(1)(vii) of the Act unless it had sufficient territorial nexus with India. The services of a non-resident to a resident utilised in India may not have much relevance in determining whether the income of the non-resident accrues or arises in India. The Supreme Court, accordingly, theorised that for section 9(1)(vii) to be applicable, it was necessary that the services not only be utilised within India but also be rendered in India or have such a 'live link' with India.[58]

The Indian Government viewed this interpretation as being in conflict with the express legislative intent.[59] The Government, therefore, inserted an *Explanation in section 9*, by the Finance Act 2007,[60] clarifying that where income of a non-resident is deemed to accrue or arise in India under clauses (v), (vi) and (vii) of section 9(1), such income shall be chargeable to tax, regardless of whether the non-resident has a residence or place of business or business connection in India. The amendment had a retrospective effect from 1 June 1976.

1.2.4 *Jindal Thermal* and the 2010 Amendments

However, the effect of this amendment was short-lived. The Karnataka High Court in *Jindal Thermal Power Co*[61] reiterated the territorial nexus test by holding that the 2007 Explanation, in its then form, did not do away with the requirement of rendering of services in India under section 9 as laid down in *Ishikawajima*.[62] In this case, the question arose whether fee for technical services paid by *Jindal Thermal* to an American company for commissioning of a power plant in India under a contract was taxable in India so as to attract liability to deduct tax at source. The company contested the liability to deduct tax on the ground that the technical services were not rendered in India, although the services were utilised in India. Upholding the taxpayer's plea, the High Court explained the existing law in the following terms:

> The *Explanation* incorporated in section 9(2) declares that 'where the income is deemed to accrue or arise in India under clauses (*v*), (*vi*), (*vii*) of sub-section (1), such income shall be included in the total income of the non-resident; whether or not the resident has a residence or place of business or business connection in India.' The plain reading of the said provision suggests that criterion of residence,

---

56. At (n. 45).
57. *Ishikawajima* (n. 43).
58. *Ibid.*
59. The Finance Bill 2007, Explanatory Memo (hereafter called 'the ExMemo').
60. The Finance Act 2007 s. 5.
61. *Jindal Thermal Power Company Ltd v DCIT* [2010] 321 ITR 31 (Kar) (hereafter '*Jindal*').
62. *Ishikawajima* (n. 43).

> place of business or business connection of a non-resident in India has been done away with for fastening the tax liability. However, the criteria of rendering service in India and the utilisation of the service in India laid down by the Supreme Court in *Ishikawajima Harima Heavy Industries Ltd.'s* case (*supra*) to attract tax liability under section 9(1)(*vii*) remains untouched and unaffected by the *Explanation* to section 9(2).[63]

The Indian Government, therefore, sought to reiterate the aforesaid rule, *vide* the Finance Act 2010,[64] by substituting the 2007 Explanation with a new Explanation,[65] specifically stating that the income of a non-resident shall be deemed to accrue or arise in India under clauses (v), (vi) and (vii) of section 9(1) and shall be included in his total income, irrespective of whether the non-resident has a residence or place of business or business connection in India or of services being rendered in India. This amendment, too, takes effect retrospectively from 1 June 1976. The much-hyped Direct Tax Code (DTC), which could not see the light of the day, retained the same feature.[66] These amendments, however, stirred up a hornet's nest and have, specifically, been assailed on the twin grounds of the principle of territorial nexus and the constitutional doctrine of extraterritoriality.

1.2.5 *Vodafone* and the 2012 Amendments

The same territoriality debate, once again, arose in *Vodafone v Union of India*,[67] which entailed the offshore acquisition by Vodafone (a company resident in the Netherlands) of the entire share capital of CGP Investments (a company resident in the Cayman Islands), which, in turn, held 67% controlling interest in Hutchison Essar (a company resident in India). The Indian tax jurisdiction was invoked to levy capital gains tax on this apparent offshore transaction on the ground that there was a transfer of underlying assets (i.e., 67% controlling interest in Hutchison Essar), which was situated in India. Negating the Revenue's claim, the Supreme Court gave a serious setback to the Indian source rule jurisprudence by holding that section 9(1)(i) of the Act cannot, by a process of interpretation, be extended to such indirect transfer of controlling interests in Hutchison, which had occurred in consequence of the transfer of the CGP share outside India. According to the Indian Supreme Court, the words 'underlying assets' do not find

---

63. *Jindal* (n. 61).
64. The Finance Act 2010 s. 4.
65. The Explanation reads as follows: For the removal of doubts, it is hereby declared that for the purposes of this section, the income of a non-resident shall be deemed to accrue or arise in India under clause (v) or clause (vi) or clause (vii) of subsection (1) of section 9 and shall be included in his total income of non-resident, whether or not:
    (a) the non-resident has a residence or place of business or business connection in India; or
    (b) the non-resident has rendered services in India.
66. The Direct Tax Code s. 5, https://www.incometaxindia.gov.in/Documents/direct-taxes-code-2013-31032014.pdf, accessed 2 October 2018.
67. *Vodafone International Holding BV v Union of India* [2012] 341 ITR 1 (SC) (hereafter '*Vodafone*').

place in section 9(1) so as to bring within its purview the controlling interest in the Indian Company.[68]

In a swift move, the Indian Government inserted three clarificatory amendments[69] *vide* the Finance Act 2012, with retrospective effect, to bring Vodafone-like transactions within the ambit of the Indian source rule:

(1) An Explanation was added to section 2(14) to define capital asset as including 'any rights in or in relation to an Indian company, including rights of management or control or any other rights whatsoever'.
(2) Another Explanation was added to section 2(47) in order to clarify the definition of 'transfer' as inclusive of 'disposing of or parting with an asset or any interest therein, or creating any interest in any asset in any manner whatsoever, directly or indirectly, absolutely or conditionally, voluntarily or involuntarily, by way of an agreement (whether entered into in India or outside India) or otherwise, notwithstanding that such transfer of rights are characterised as being effected or dependent upon or flowing from the transfer of a share or shares of a company registered or incorporated outside India.
(3) The expression 'through' in section 9(1) was intended to clarify to 'mean' and include 'by means of', 'in consequence of' or 'by reason of'.

These amendments generated a lot of heat among foreign investors The Indian Government was accused of creating a negative sentiment for FDI. John Preston of the PwC Global Tax Policy Network dubbed it as 'extraterritorial tax grab'.[70] Leading the foreign pressure against the amendments was George Osborne, the United Kingdom (UK) Chancellor of Exchequer, who complained to the Indian Finance Minister about the 'arbitrary and punitive treatment to the UK telecom major'.[71]

The British telecom major, on its part, launched an international arbitration under the Bilateral Investment Treaty (BIT), an agreement between India and the Netherlands.[72] The Indian Government, however, persisted that the investment treaty did not cover taxation. Later, as a non-binding reconciliation proposal, approved by the

68. *Ibid.*
69. The Finance Act 2012 ss 3 and 4.
70. J Preston, 'Shaping the Tax System', http://www.pwc.com/en_GX/gx/tax/publications/assets/pwc-global-tax-policy-trends.pdf, accessed 9 October 2018; *see also* S Rajadhyaksha, G Reghuvaran and B Chatterjee, 'The Curious Case of Extraterritorial Taxation in India', The Hindu (New Delhi, 2 April 2012), https://www.lexology.com/library/detail.aspx?g=9f54a7b2-0e08-4e3f-a1fa-6b66fc91b786, accessed 9 October 2018.
71. 'Osborne Raises Vodafone Tax Issues with Pranab', The Hindu (New Delhi, 2 April 2012), https://www.thehindu.com/business/osborne-raises-vodafone-tax-issue-with-pranab/article3273229.ece, accessed 22 December 2018.
72. V Ram, 'Vodafone Serves Arbitration Notice on Indian Govt Over New Tax Plan', The Hindu Business Line (London, 17 April 2012), https://www.thehindubusinessline.com/info-tech/vodafone-serves-arbitration-notice-on-indian-govt-over-new-tax-plan/article20422749.ece1, accessed 22 December 2018.

Government, came a cropper;[73] it finally prepared itself for a long period of international arbitration on the matter. An International Arbitration Tribunal, headed by Sir Franklin Berman, commenced hearing in February 2019 in Vodafone's challenge to India using a retrospective legislation and the Indian Government objection to tax matters being covered under the Netherlands-India BIT. On 25 September 2020, the Tribunal finally announced the arbitral award, holding that India had violated the 'fair and equitable treatment' guaranteed to Vodafone under the 1995 Bilateral Investment Promotion and Protection Agreement (BIPA) between the Republic of India and the Kingdom of Netherlands (the Netherlands-India BIT). Although this award does not mark the end of the dispute as India is all set to challenge this award before the municipal courts in Singapore, it may have significant implications for the pending arbitration proceedings as it may operate as a persuasive precedent for other pending tax claims against India. While the concept of 'binding' precedent does not exist in the realm of BIT arbitrations, it is not uncommon for tribunals to afford weight to earlier decisions on comparable issues by other BIT tribunals, of course, subject to 'compelling contrary grounds', in order to fulfil their obligation to contribute to the harmonious development of investment law so as to foster predictability. Another substantial question of law, which the Vodafone award raises, is whether an arbitral tribunal has the power to virtually and substantially declare a parliamentary legislation of a competent Parliament of a sovereign nation to be non-est and unenforceable. This was articulated by India's Solicitor General, Tushar Mehta, in his opinion to the Indian Government in the following words:[74]

> The question of law — the power of an arbitral tribunal to virtually and substantially declare a parliamentary legislation of a competent Parliament of a sovereign nation to be non-est and unenforceable — itself is an issue which needs to be challenged. I therefore, opine that the Union of India must challenge the said award and must file all available proceedings to challenge the award and/or to protect the interest of Union of India.

A more detailed exposition of this case and the related aspects is made in the subsequent chapters.

1.2.6 *Nokia*

The Nokia tax controversy took the territorial nexus debate to a more absurd level. Here, the question arose whether royalty paid by Nokia India (Indian subsidiary) to Nokia Finland (Foreign Parent) for software downloaded into handsets made in India

73. *Cabinet Approves Non-binding Conciliation to Resolve Vodafone Tax Issue*, India Today (New Delhi, 4 June 2013), https://www.indiatoday.in/business/corporate/story/vodafone-tax-dispute-british-telecom-major-vodafone-tax-issue-hutchison-essar-finance-minister-p-chidambaram-cabinet-165589-2013-06-04, accessed 9 October 2018.
74. 'Solicitor General Tushar Mehta Recommends Indian Government to Challenge PCA Award in Vodafone Tax Case', Bar and Bench (27 October 2020), https://www.barandbench.com/news/sg-tushar-mehta-urges-centre-challenge-award-vodafone-tax-case, accessed 1 November 2020.

was taxable in India, thereby requiring the Indian subsidiary to deduct a 10% tax on such payments under section 115A of the Indian Statute.[75]

The Nokia contested the action of the Indian Tax authorities on the basis of an argument that since the transfer of technology took place outside India, there was no territorial nexus for invoking India's tax jurisdiction. This argument did not find favour with the Indian tax officials, as Nokia downloaded the software in the Indian made handsets, thereby making its products marketable and enhancing its profits. Deriving sustenance from the UN Model, which swears by the source rule of taxation, India persisted that the source of the MNC's income was clearly in India. According to a recent report in *The Economic Times*, India and Finland have reportedly reached an agreement on this high profile tax case under the Mutual Agreement Procedure (MAP) by paying its EUR 202 million (INR 1,629 crore) dues to the Government.[76] The present debate, therefore, has serious revenue implications.[77]

1.2.7 *Cairn*

The *Cairn*, too, witnessed a somewhat-Vodafone-type conundrum as it also involved an offshore entity. Here the Indian assets of Cairn UK Holdings (CUH) were held by Cairn India Holdings Ltd (CIHL), a Channel Islands-based[78] subsidiary of CUH, that, in turn, was fully owned by Cairn Energy PLC. Cairn Energy wanted to exit its stake in the Indian exploration operations by listing its Indian assets. To enable that, the Indian assets held by CIH had to be transferred to a company registered in India. This was achieved by creating Cairn India Ltd (CIL), a group company registered in India. By way of a subscription and share purchase agreement and a share purchase deed, shares constituting the entire issued share capital of CIHL were transferred to CIL, the consideration for which was partly in cash and partly in the form of shares of CIL. CIL then divested 30.5% of its shareholding by way of an Initial Public Offering (IPO). As a result of divesting of its stake in the subsidiaries and part of IPO proceeds, CUH received approximately INR 6,101 crore (approximately USD 931 million).

The 2012 amendment clarified that a company located outside India would be deemed to be situated in India if it derived its value from assets located in India. It followed that if shares of the company (situated outside India) were transferred to another entity, whether Indian or not, the Indian tax authorities could claim capital gains tax on the profit from the transaction. The tax authorities immediately noticed the arrangement and found how Cairn Energy has made a profit from the share transfer. As the oil fields in Rajasthan had not been developed in 2006, the tax authorities estimated the cost incurred in those fields at just INR 2,178 crore when the share transfer took

75. IT Act (n. 45) s. 115A.
76. *Nokia Says It Paid 202 Million Euro To Settle Tax Row With India*, The Economic Times (New Delhi, 27 April 2018), https://economictimes.indiatimes.com/tech/hardware/nokia-paid-202-million-euro-to-settle-tax-row-with-india/articleshow/63942891.cms, accessed 2 October 2018.
77. *Tax from Vodafone-Like Deals May Fetch Government Rs 40,000 Crore*, The Economic Times (New Delhi, 25 April 2012), http://articles.economictimes.indiatimes.com/2012-04-25/news/31399045_1_tax-havens-income-tax-amendment, accessed 14 May 2013.
78. A tax haven country.

place. But the value of shares transferred to CUH was INR 26,682 crore. Thus, a capital gains tax of INR 10,248 crore was slapped on Cairn Energy PLC on the profits from the above transfer.

Cairn, too, spurned the one-time window of interest waiver by the Indian Government and instead elected to take the arbitration route under the UK-India BIT. In a major setback to India, the international arbitration tribunal, in its verdict on 22 December 2020, asked India to pay INR 8,000 crore as damages to Cairn. On the lines of *Vodafone*, the tribunal reportedly concluded that the Cairn tax issue does not amount to 'tax dispute' but a 'tax-related investment' dispute, which is why it falls under its jurisdiction and that India's tax demand from Cairn amounts to a breach of fair treatment under the bilateral investment protection pact.[79] Meanwhile, the Income Tax Appellate Tribunal (ITAT) has upheld the capital gains tax levy against Cairn,[80] and the latter has moved the Delhi High Court against that order. The tax authorities have already started the recovery proceedings by selling part of Cairn's Energy shares in Vedanta to recover its tax dues.[81] Thus, territoriality debate has been a topic of heated polemics in India.

1.2.8 The Object of This Study

The research, undertaken in this book, seeks to evaluate the territoriality principle both in terms of its theoretical foundation and its operational dynamics in the context of the source rule. This research assumes significance as the existing literature on the subject, although in abundance, is extremely monothematic in as much as it restricts itself to a mere comparison of the principles of the source-based and residence-based taxation systems[82] or, sometimes, to the applied aspects of the source rule such as intangible

79. India loses tax arbitration case against Cairn; told to pay Rs 8,000 cr (BusinessToday.in, December 23, 2020), https://www.businesstoday.in/current/corporate/breaking-india-loses-tax-arbitration-case-against-cairn-told-to-pay-rs-8000-cr/story/425747.html, accessed 23 December 2020.
80. *Cairn UK Holdings Ltd v DCIT* [2017] 79 taxmann.com 128 (ITAT-Del).
81. *IT Department Sells Part of Cairn's Energy Shares in Vedanta to Recover Its Dues,* The Hindu Business Line (New Delhi, 9 July 2018), https://www.thehindubusinessline.com/companies/cairn-says-tax-office-in-india-sold-216-mn-of-vedanta-shares/article24370200.ece, accessed 12 November 2018.
82. IFA, *Source and Residence: New Configuration of Their Principles* (vol 90a, IFA: Cahiers de Droit Fiscal International 2005); RSJ Martha, *The Jurisdiction to Tax in International Law: Theory and Practice of Legislative Fiscal Jurisdiction* (Springer 1989); K Andersson, 'An Economist's View on Source Vs Residence Taxation: The Lisbon Objectives and Taxation in European Union' (2006) vol. 60(10) BIFT 395; K Vogel, 'Worldwide vs Source Taxation of Income: A Review and Revaluation of Arguments (Part I)' (1988) vol. 8(9) Intertax 216 (hereafter 'Vogel Part I'); K Vogel, 'Worldwide vs Source Taxation of Income: A Review and Revaluation of Arguments (Part II)' (1988) vol. 10 Intertax 310 (hereafter 'Vogel Part II'); K Vogel, 'Worldwide vs Source Taxation of Income: A Review and Revaluation of Arguments (Part III)' (1988) vol. 11 Intertax 393 (hereafter 'Vogel Part III'); D Pinto, 'Exclusive Source or Residence Based Taxation: Is a New and Simpler World Tax Order Possible?' (2007) July BFIT 277; M Lang et al. (eds), *Source Versus Residence* (Kluwer 2008).

property[83] or e-commerce.[84] Research has also been conducted on more generic concepts like the worldwide taxation versus source taxation,[85] or to the general relevance of the residence and the source rule,[86] or to a general argument advancing the preference of one rule over the other,[87] or to various aspects of mitigating difficulties of the source rule through treaty relief, etc.[88] There is a whole body of research on jurisprudential and fairness issues in international taxation as well.[89] But a nuanced critique of the concept of territorial nexus itself as a principle of tax apportionment has not at all been attempted so far in any of the earlier studies. The reason for making this intervention in the literature is to address this gap in international tax scholarship on the shifting paradigm of the territoriality doctrine in the source rule. This book, therefore, aims at a very close assaying of the concept and contours of territorial nexus doctrine as it has emerged in the international tax jurisprudence since its inception and to refine it as a viable and mutually accepted basis of international tax allocation so that the international tax regime does not transform itself as a tool of economic and political coercion. The Indian source rule regime from the standpoints of its normative underpinnings of economic efficiency and fairness will serve as a principal reference point.

1.3 EMERGING CHALLENGES: NEED TO REVISIT THE SOURCE RULE

As argued in the early part of this chapter, globalisation and e-commerce have intensified the jurisdictional crisis. A sharp decrease in transaction costs has increased inter-nation interdependence among businesses. Further, trans-border business transactions can be effected without a product even physically crossing a national border. The businesses of multinational companies rely heavily upon exchanges of valuable intangible properties, patents, trademarks, licences and other information goods and services to earn income in different jurisdictions. Moreover, the Internet has sparked the rise of new industries and businesses, such as the rapidly growing online advertising sector. In contrast to the dynamic nature of e-commerce, the jurisdictional tax rules and concepts governing the taxation of global business profits have changed relatively little since the 1960s. The 1996 report of the US Treasury reflects this

83. EL Guruli, 'International Taxation: Application of Source Rule to Income from Intangible Property' (2005) vol. 5 HBTLJ 205.
84. D Pinto, *E-Commerce and Source-Based Taxation*, vol. 6 Doctoral Series (IBFD 2002).
85. *See generally*, Vogel, Part I II III (n. 82).
86. R Yu, 'E-Commerce: Relevance of Source and Residence Rules' (2001), http://raymondyu.net/pub/papers/ecom_sr.pdf, accessed 22 December 2018.
87. Barker (n. 38).
88. MS Schadewald and TA Kaye, 'Source of Income Rules and Treaty Relief from Double Taxation Within the NAFTA Trading Bloc' (2001) vol. 61(2) La L Rev 353.
89. NH Kaufman, 'Fairness and the Taxation of International Income' (1998) vol. 29(2) L & Pol Int Bus 145; *see also* PB Musgrave, 'Sovereignty, Entitlement, and Cooperation in International Taxation' (2001) vol. 26(4) Brooklyn J Intl L 1335 and MJ Graetz, 'Taxing International Income: Inadequate Principles, Outdated Concepts, and Unsatisfactory Policies' (2001) vol. 54(3) Tax L Rev 261.

concern.[90] There is an emerging consensus among international tax scholars regarding the need to revisit and modify the current characterisation and sourcing regimes to correct the tax distortions caused by the collapse of jurisdictional frontiers.[91]

1.3.1 Physical Presence Paradigm

This strict paradigm of physicality in the territorial nexus doctrine in the tax apportionment is now being increasingly questioned, underscoring an urgent imperative to reformulate these theorisations, which, at present, have hitherto been largely moulded to cater to the needs and aspirations of the developed countries. Historical experience shows that efforts to deal with the problems of international double taxation were driven by economic and political interests of the various countries. While the developed countries would focus and emphasise on residence-based taxation – allocating more tax revenue to the country of residence, which in case of the developed countries also happens to be the country, where the capital, know-how and expertise is located – such allocation of taxing rights makes sense, when the economic activity takes place between two equally developed countries, because the fiscal effect should be mostly neutral on both countries. However, when the economic activities take place between unequally developed countries, the fiscal effects of the residence rules will lead to situations, when the developing country has to give up its taxing rights in favour of the other country. However due to the differences, it is likely not to benefit from a similar reciprocal measure by the other country, because the developed country is less likely to be in the position of country of source in respect of the developing country.[92]

The votaries of a strict physical nexus also tend to derive support from the constitutional doctrine of extraterritoriality. In fact, one of the fiercest critiques of the 2010 amendment of the Indian statute[93] rests on its perceived extraterritorial operation without any territorial nexus.[94] Yet another legal onslaught mounted by the territorial nexus theorists on the legislations, which tend to deviate from the strict physical presence path, is on the ground of its breach of international customary law.[95] Both these premises are apparently questionable as revealed in this book.

90. *See generally* the US Department of Treasury Report (1996), *Selected Tax Policy Implications of Global Electronic Commerce*, https://www.treasury.gov/resource-center/tax-policy/Documents/Report-Global-Electronic-Commerce-1996.pdf, accessed 14 October 2018.
91. Guruli (n. 83) 240.
92. Committee of Experts on International Cooperation in Tax Matters, 'Revision of the Manual for the Negotiation of Bilateral Tax Treaties' (Seventh session Geneva, 24-28 October 2011), Item 5(h) of the provisional agenda, http://unpan1.un.org/intradoc/groups/public/documents/un/unpan008579.pdf, accessed 6 September 2014.
93. The Finance Act (n. 52) s. 4.
94. NM Desai, 'Budget 2010-11: Non-resident Services Outside India: Taxed Retroactively', http://www.nishithdesai.com/fileadmin/user_upload/pdfs/Budget_2010-11-_Non-resident_services_outside_India-_Taxed_retroactively.pdf, accessed 7 October 2018.
95. *Ibid.*

1.4 CONCLUSION

This book is written according to the following outline. In addition to the introductory chapter, it comprises five more chapters. The introductory chapter gives a brief presentation on the topic and surveys the mutually conflicting concerns of nations for tax allocation. It identifies the existing debate on the source rule in terms of base erosion, the consequent leakages of incomes sourced in various nations and the measures to plug those leakages, especially the issues of financial transparency, removal of bank secrecy rules, the automatic reporting scheme and the automatic exchange of information. This chapter also gives a broad overview of some major international tax disputes, both within and outside India, which have brought to the fore the territoriality debate.

Chapter 2 traces the historical evolution of the source rule as a distinctive concept of international tax law discourse and also critiques its normative underpinnings. This chapter examines the historical process of evolution of the alternate basis of taxation based on 'situs' or 'source' in order to investigate whether a strict territorial nexus as a normative principle is ingrained into the source rule jurisprudence. Apart from the introduction, this chapter consists of a two-part examination. Part 1 discussed at section 2.2 delineates the emergence of the source rule from its early non-legislative phase to its legislative form and its further refinement with the monumental efforts of the League of Nations, the Organization for European Economic Co-operation (OEEC)[96] and its later version, the Organisation for Economic Cooperation and Development (OECD),[97] the UN and other international organisations in the twentieth century, more particularly after World War I. It is also argued in the section 2.2 how the US experience was a major influence in the shaping of these rules. An overview of the emerging treaty framework in the process and the consequent development of the twin jurisdictional precepts of taxation, i.e., source and residence, have also been given, along with an analysis of the issues of jurisdictional overlap. Part 2 discussed at section 2.3 presents a detailed exposition of the theoretical precepts of the source rule, viz., *benefit theory*, *neutrality theory* and *inter-state equity theory*, in order to probe the linkages of the source rule with the territorial nexus doctrine. An analysis has also been made of these theoretical precepts and their relationship with the doctrine of economic allegiance identified and emphasised by the four economists in their Report.[98] The concluding section 2.4, then, recapitulates the finding that the source taxation rules and its normative precepts, right from its inception, have been grounded in the economic nexus of an income with the source state as illustrated in the League's reports. The requirement of a physical presence has never been a paramount attribute of this linkage.

96. It was formed in 1948 to administer American and Canadian aid in the framework of the Marshall Plan for the reconstruction of Europe after World War II. In 1961, the OEEC was superseded by the OECD.
97. In 1961, the OECD consisted the European founder countries of the OEEC plus the US and Canada.
98. GWJ Bruins, Luigi Einaudi, ERA Seligman and Sir Josiah Stamp, *Report on Double Taxation* (League of Nations 1923-1928) (hereafter 'the Four Economists' Report).

Chapter 3 studies the similarities and differences of the two Model Tax Conventions (the OECD and the UN Models) and juxtaposes their distinguishing features with the domestic tax laws of India in the context of rights to tax four categories of incomes: *income from immovable property, business profits, investment income* (including dividends, interests and royalties) and *capital gains*. This comparative analysis aims at investigating whether rights to tax these incomes in an international context necessarily posits the proposition of a strict territorial presence. Taking Chapter 2 as the point of departure, where this book focuses on how the concept of economic allegiance between the source state and the income has been narrowed to mean a strict territorial presence by the vociferous votaries of residence taxation, this chapter presents a comparative critique of the two model treaties, i.e., the OECD Model and the UN Model, to explain how economic connection as the ultimate jurisprudential justification for taxing rights permeates through the provisions of the two treaty structures. This chapter, in addition to the introductory section, consists of five sections. The four sections, sections 3.2-3.5, follow the pattern of comparing and analysing the treaty schemes of the Models in the context of immovable property income, business profits, investment income and capital gains respectively, and then, set out the model schemes against the respective provisions of Indian domestic laws and also against some of the internationally emerging trends, in order to investigate whether rights to tax these incomes in an international context necessarily presuppose a strict territorial presence, contrary to the economic allegiance formulations of the four economists.[99] Section 3.6 concludes the findings of this comparative investigation.

Chapter 4 investigates the proposition whether the territorial nexus, in the sense it was understood by the Indian Supreme Court in *Ishikawajima*,[100] is an internationally accepted principle of tax jurisdiction, and if yes, what is the law regarding application of this principle vis-à-vis the municipal law in India? Apart from the *introductory section*, this chapter comprises five sections. While section 4.2 focuses on the thematic divergence between the concept of territorial jurisdictional nexus in public international law and the concept of territorial nexus in tax law, section 4.3 examines and analyses the municipal courts' decisions to see how judicial reasoning has been influenced by the territoriality principle of international law, while the concept of connecting factors for tax nexus has been recognised only much later by the courts. Section 4.4 evaluates the hypothesis whether customary international law supports the requirements of a territorial presence in a state for its tax claims. Section 4.5 addresses the purely legal question of hierarchy of international custom vis-à-vis the municipal laws of states. Section 4.6 concludes the chapter by analysing some of the latest policy developments in the context of the new digital economy by analysing their economic rationale which forms the underlying justification for the source rule in international taxation.

Chapter 5 focuses on the constitutional debate relating to the extraterritorial operation of law and examines whether the economic-nexus-based tax jurisdiction and absence of a physical presence breaches the constitutional doctrine of extraterritoriality

99. 'The Four Economists' Report (n. 98).
100. *Ishikawajima* (n. 43).

or due process. This chapter consists of five sections. Section 5.1 presents an introductory setting to this extraterritoriality-based constitutional challenge, which is being mounted on the economic nexus principle of tax allocation, where there is no physical presence of the entity or the tax object in a state's territory. Section 5.2 presents a historical background of the extraterritoriality doctrine and, in the process, examines the linkages among the concepts of sovereignty, territoriality and comity which offers a continuing rationale for the extraterritorial operation of law. Section 5.3 deals with the question whether the extraterritorial operation of law is circumscribed by constitutional imperatives and this question is studied by critiquing the existing legal and constitutional framework in different parts of the world, more particularly the UK, the US, Canada, Australia and India. Section 5.4 evaluates some recent judicial trends in India in order to assess the extraterritorial operation of law on the anvil of the constitutional principles. Section 5.5 concludes the chapter by analysing and summarising the broad and expansive concepts of 'nexus' appearing in Article 245(1) of the Indian Constitution and by underscoring the tenuous reasoning, employed in *Ishikawajima*[101] and *Vodafone*[102] to restrict the contours of this constitutional concept.

Chapter 6 concludes the research by holding that the territorial nexus debate, based on a strict physical presence, is essentially a contrived debate initiated by the theorists of residence taxation and some interested tax lawyers. Retrospective legislative changes introduced by India in 2012, to tax capital gains arising on indirect transfer of Indian assets through tortuous structural arrangements by non-residents, have been dubbed as unfair and discriminatory. India losing the *Vodafone* and *Cairn* arbitration cases has again sparked a heated debate recently. This chapter assesses international principles and practices in this regard, and evaluates the argument whether retrospective legislative amendment by India resulted in an unfair and discriminatory treatment to Vodafone and Cairn.

101. *Ibid.*
102. *Vodafone* (n. 67).

CHAPTER 2

Historical Evolution of the Source Rule and Its Theoretical Underpinnings

Abstract

This chapter traces the historical evolution of source taxation to examine whether a strict territorial nexus as a normative principle is ingrained into the source rule jurisprudence. This examination comprises a two-part analysis. Part 1 discussed in section 2.2 delineates shaping of the source rule from its early non-legislative phase to its legislative form. Part 2 discussed in section 2.3 presents a detailed exposition of the theoretical precepts of the source rule, viz., benefit theory, neutrality theory and inter-state equity theory in order to probe the linkages of the source rule with the territorial nexus doctrine.

2.1 INTRODUCTION

Historically, the genesis of the source rule as a conceptual basis of tax rights allocation lies in the opening of the economies all over the world. Where economies are closed, there need be little concern for a proper jurisdictional basis for the imposition of income tax. It is only where the economic activities that give rise to the taxable base have foreign components or the persons or entities involved have foreign allegiance that nations must grapple with the question of the appropriate basis for taxation.[103]

This chapter examines the historical process of evolution of the alternate basis of taxation based on 'situs' or 'source' in order to investigate whether a strict territorial nexus as a normative principle is ingrained into the source rule jurisprudence. This examination consists of two parts. Part 1 discussed in section 2.2 delineates the emergence of the source rule from its early non-legislative phase to its legislative form and its further refinement with the monumental efforts of the League of Nations, the

103. WB Barker, 'Optimal International Taxation and Tax Competition: Overcoming the Contradictions' (2002) vol. 22(2) Nw J Intl L and Bus 161, 180.

OEEC[104] and its later version, the OECD,[105] the UN and other international organisations in the twentieth century, more particularly after World War I.

Section 2.3 discussing about Part 2 presents a detailed exposition of the theoretical precincts of the source rule in order to address the research question formulated in the first chapter of this book and to probe the linkages of the source rule with the territorial nexus doctrine.

2.2 PART 1: THE HISTORICAL EVOLUTION

2.2.1 The Early Phase

In an inchoate and non-legislative form, taxation on the alternate basis of 'inhabiting' or 'situs' of property dates back to at least the fourteenth century.[106] Harris points out that although the traditional tax[107] charged on the vill was, in principle, charged on the inhabitants of the vill, in practice, there were exceptions to this rule particularly in the case of localities imposing tax on the basis of land, where the occupier was inevitably charged.[108] This embryonic distinction between taxation on the basis of residence and on the basis of source or situs came to be further developed in the early poll taxes and subsidies.[109]

2.2.2 Source Rule in Its Legislative Form

Legislatively, the 1489 Law of the UK can be said to be the first express tax on land on the basis of situs and on movables on the basis of residence.[110] The direct tax law of 1515, however, is the first that clearly and expressly taxed movables of persons resident in England and movables situated in England of those not resident.[111] The first truly comprehensive income tax system was that of the UK, which began in 1799.[112] The UK Income Tax Act of 1803 extended the jurisdictional reach compared to its predecessor. It adhered to the basic principles of residence and source familiar to contemporary tax systems; UK residents were taxed on their worldwide income and

104. The Organization for European Economic Co-operation: It was formed in 1948 to administer American and Canadian aid in the framework of the Marshall Plan for the reconstruction of Europe after World War II. In 1961, the OEEC was superseded by OECD.
105. The Organisation for Economic Co-operation and Development: In 1961, the OECD consisted the European founder countries of the OEEC plus the United States and Canada.
106. P Harris, *Income Tax in Common Law Jurisdictions: From the Origins to 1820* vol. 1 (Cambridge 2006) 44, 55, 58-59.
107. The fifteenth and the tenth.
108. Harris (n. 106) 44, citing R Schofield, *Taxation under the Early Tudors, 1485-1547* (Blackwell 2004) 42-43.
109. *Ibid.*
110. *Ibid.*, 55, 413-418. This provision came during the reign of the Tudors, particularly during the reign of Henry VIII, which provided for assessment with respect to goods and chattels 'only in every such place where he is most conversant, inhabited and commorant'.
111. *Ibid.*, 57-58.
112. *Ibid.*, 413-418; also *see* WB Barker, 'A Comparative Approach to Income Tax Law in the United Kingdom and the United States' (1996) vol. 46(1) Cath UL Rev 7, 12.

non-residents were taxed on their income originating from the UK.[113] First income tax laws of Prussia, Austria and the Netherlands were also grounded on the principles of residence and source, with Italy being an exception, in levying only the source-based income tax.[114]

2.2.3 The Twentieth Century Developments and Recent Trends

2.2.3.1 The Early Twentieth Century Phase

The subject of international taxation, however, did not attract much attention until the twentieth century as comprehensive taxation of income was still a relatively new form of taxation.[115] Only two nations, the UK and the US, had developed comprehensive income taxation, both foreign and domestic, in the nineteenth century.[116] Further, apart from the three internationally and commercially oriented powers viz., the Netherlands, the UK, and the US, the other economies were relatively closed,[117] and most countries had currency control legislation in place. Thus, most taxation was strictly territorial in nature.[118]

2.2.3.2 The Post-World War I Phase

The source rule jurisprudence began taking a distinctive shape only after World War I. The economic consequences of the War left nations scurrying for more and more revenue, with an over-expansion of source jurisdiction becoming a norm. Nations proceeded to assume that the easy fix to their revenue needs was to be found in the taxation of foreigners.[119] Thus, some trading nations unilaterally elected to facilitate free trade, by sacrificing their domiciliary taxation,[120] which very often resulted in deleterious double taxation, which attracted the attention of many international organisations. Tax rates during and just after World War I were high enough to turn double taxation from a nuisance into a serious issue.[121]

113. PA Harris, *Corporate-Shareholder Income Taxation and Allocating Taxing Rights Between Countries: A Comparison of Imputation Systems* (IBFD 1996) 287.
114. *Ibid.*, 288-293.
115. Harris (n. 106); also *see* Barker (n. 103) 182.
116. *Ibid.*
117. V Tanzi, *Taxation in an Integrating World* (Brookings Institution 1995) 15.
118. RJ Jeffery, *The Impact of State Sovereignty on Global Trade and International Taxation* (Kluwer 1999) 43-44.
119. MB Carroll, *Prevention of International Double Taxation and Fiscal Evasion: Two Decades of Progress under the League of Nations* (League of Nations 1939) 7-8.
120. *Ibid.*, 8.
121. DM Ring, 'International Tax Relations: Theory and Implications' (2007) vol. 60 Tax L Rev 83, 89.

2.2.3.3 *The Role of the International Chamber of Commerce*

The International Chamber of Commerce (ICC), which was formed in 1920, directed early attention to double taxation.[122] The ICC was formed in Paris in 1919 to promote trade and investment, open markets for goods and services, and facilitate the free flow of capital.[123] One of the foundational objects of the ICC was the elimination of double taxation as indicated in the following early resolution:

> RESOLVED, That the International Chamber of Commerce, in meeting duly assembled, composed of representatives of commercial and industrial organizations of the allied countries [victors of World War I], urge prompt agreement between the Governments of the allied countries in order to avoid that individuals or companies of any one country may be liable to more than one tax on the same income, taking into consideration that the country to which ... such company belongs has right to claim the difference between the tax paid and the home tax.[124]

In 1920, the ICC adopted a resolution seeking 'prompt agreement between the Governments of the Allied countries in order to prevent individuals or companies from being compelled to pay a tax on the same income in more than one country'.[125] The ICC presented resolutions regarding double taxation at its 1923 Rome Conference.[126] The resolutions included features that remain till today (classification of income by category for taxation and allocation of business income among the source nations to which it corresponds).[127] Ultimately, the resolutions were not adopted, largely due to British opposition derived from a strong preference for residence-based taxation and their view that the resolutions granted too much taxation to the source countries.[128] For a capital exporter, the British position was not surprising.

2.2.3.4 *The League of Nations' Contributions*

The double taxation debate provided a simultaneous trigger for the League of Nations (hereafter 'the League') to deal with the problem of international double taxation in 1921.[129] Two very important reports contributed to the success of the League's work:

122. ERA Seligman, *Double Taxation and International Fiscal Cooperation* (Macmillan 1928) 114.
123. A group of industrialists, financiers and traders determined to bring economic prosperity to a world that was still reeling from the devastation of World War I, founded the International Chamber of Commerce and called themselves 'the merchants of peace'. The world had few working international structures in the immediate aftermath of the first of the twentieth century's global conflicts. There was no world system of rules to govern trade, investment, finance or commercial relations. The private sector started filling the gap without waiting for governments. It was an idea that took hold, https://iccwbo.org/about-us/who-we-are/history/, accessed 24 December 2018.
124. International Chamber of Commerce, Congress of London 1921, brochure 11, 3 (Brochures 1-16, ICC Paris Archives); *see generally* MJ Graetz and MM O'Hear, 'The "Original Intent" of US International Taxation' (1997) vol. 46 Duke LJ 1021, 1066-1074.
125. Graetz and O'Hear (n. 124) 1066 (quoting the ICC); also *see* Seligman (n. 122) 114.
126. *Ibid.*, 1069.
127. *Ibid.*, 1069-1070.
128. *Ibid.*, 1071-1072.
129. Barker (n. 103) 183.

the first being a theoretical study of double taxation by the four economists[130] and the second a study conducted by a group of technical experts, entrusted with the study of double taxation and evasion from the perspective of administration and practicality.[131]

2.2.3.4.1 The Economists' Report: The Economic Allegiance Principle

The economists were required to determine general principles as the basis of an international tax framework capable of preventing double taxation. They identified the concept of economic allegiance as a basis to design such international tax framework. Economic allegiance was perceived as a measure of the existence and extent of the economic relationships between a particular state and the income or person to be taxed.[132] The economists selected four factors comprising economic allegiance, viz.:

(1) origin of wealth or income;
(2) situs of wealth or income;
(3) enforcement of the rights to wealth or income; and
(4) place of residence or domicile of the person entitled to dispose of the wealth or income.[133]

Among those factors, the economists concluded that, in general, the greatest weight should be given to:

(1) the origin of the wealth, i.e., source; and
(2) the residence or domicile of the owner who consumes the wealth.[134]

The origin of wealth was defined for these purposes as 'all stages involved in the creation of wealth', viz.:

(1) the original physical appearance of the wealth;
(2) its subsequent physical adaptations;
(3) its transport;
(4) its direction; and
(5) its sale.[135]

Thus, the economists argued that tax jurisdiction should generally be allocated between the state of source and the state of residence depending on the nature of the

130. *See generally* the Four Economists' Report.
131. Technical Experts, *Double Taxation and Tax Evasion Report and Resolutions Submitted by the Technical Experts to the Financial Committee* Document F 212 vol. 4 sec 1 (League of Nations 1925) (hereafter called 'the 1925 Technical Report').
132. OECD (2014), 'Fundamental Principles of Taxation' in *Addressing the Tax Challenges of the Digital Economy* (OECD Pub 2014) 36 (hereafter 'OECD (2014)').
133. The Four Economists' Report (n. 130) 4025.
134. *Ibid.*, 4029-4030.
135. *Ibid.*

income in question. In this framework, in simple situations where all or a majority of factors of economic allegiance coincide, jurisdiction to tax would go exclusively with the state where the relevant elements of economic allegiance have been characterised. In more complex situations in which conflicts between the relevant factors of economic allegiance arise, jurisdiction to tax would be shared between the different states on the basis of the relative economic ties the taxpayer and his income have with each of them.[136]

On the aforesaid premise, the economists deliberated taxing rights allocation for the various types of wealth or income. In their final conclusion, the economists opined that the place of production of income was 'of preponderant weight' and 'in an ideal division a preponderant share should be assigned to the place of origin'. In other words, in allocating jurisdiction to tax on business profits, greatest importance was attached to the nexus between business income and the various physical places contributing to the production of the income.[137] The economists ultimately recommended that the country of source should exempt all non-resident income, thus abolishing source taxation and establishing resident taxation as the only appropriate jurisdiction to tax. Their economic theory ceded very little income tax jurisdiction to source countries.[138] However, the League's final proposals were based largely on the technical experts' recommendations, which advocated source over residence.[139]

2.2.3.4.2 The Technical Experts' Report

While recognising the economic justification of the economic advisors,[140] the technical group refrained from adopting 'any one single solution'.[141] The group rather favoured an approach that would establish source as supreme but would provide the basis for a modification of this hierarchy in favour of residence through treaties between nations. In its final form, the League adopted three model conventions that set forth different ways of eliminating double taxation keeping in view the fiscal peculiarities and objectives of the nations, signatory to the convention, that is, choices that would depend on their level of trade and whether they were debtor or creditor nations.[142]

2.2.3.4.3 Adoption of 1928 Model Conventions

These deliberations led to the adoption of model conventions in 1928,[143] which was a landmark moment in the developmental process of international tax jurisprudence. This basic structure for international taxation of income announced nearly nine decades ago in the 1928 League of Nation's Model Treaty forms the common basis for

136. OECD (2014) (n. 132) 37.
137. *Ibid.*
138. Carroll (n. 119) 41-42.
139. The 1925 Technical Report (n. 131) 4075.
140. *Ibid.*, 4073-4074.
141. *Ibid.*, 4080.
142. Carroll (n. 119) 21, 22.
143. *Ibid.*, 20.

more than 1,200 bilateral tax treaties now in force throughout the world.[144] Even though, many of the Report's conclusions proved to be controversial and were not entirely followed in double tax treaties,[145] nevertheless, the theoretical principles enunciated in the 1923 Report is still considered as the 'intellectual base' from which the various League of Nations models[146] and, consequently, virtually all modern bilateral tax treaties developed.[147]

2.2.3.5 The US Contribution

The final resolution of the League was shaped by some valuable insights from the US, which had descended quite late on the scene.[148] Although in its original 1913 Tax Act, the US had adopted the deduction from income method for foreign taxes to eliminate double taxation,[149] in 1918, the US adopted, to the surprise of even its proponents, the foreign tax credit (FTC) with little opposition or even notice.[150] The purpose of this change was to provide equity to individual taxpayers by eliminating double taxation.[151] Faced with the economic and political conditions of the time, the US had to adopt a realistic and practical policy and to go against the common view that capital-exporting nations might grow tired of subsidising the tax revenues of foreign governments.

After World War I, the export of American goods depended considerably on the export of capital.[152] Further, as a practical matter, most nations were limited to source taxation. Thus, the tax system reflected the US' objectives to encourage the export of capital and to favour other nations' tax systems for practical reasons, which may not have reflected the tax philosophy of the US. Thus, the US, otherwise committed to comprehensive income taxation, allied with the debtor nations to establish the primacy of source.

Thus, drawing upon the valuable insights of the economists and the technical group, the League of Nations Tax Committees built upon the practical experience of government treaty experts to deal with the menace of double taxation. Double taxation avoidance, therefore, was not addressed by any alternative model such as 'formulary

---

144. Graetz and O'Hear (n. 124) 1023, citing RS Avi-Yonah, 'The Structure of International Taxation: A Proposal for Simplification' (1996) vol. 74(6) Tex L Rev 1301, 1303.
145. In particular, the economists' preference for a general exemption in the source state for all 'income going abroad' as a practical method of avoiding double taxation was explicitly rejected by the League of Nations, who chose as the basic structure for its 1928 Model the 'classification and assignment of sources' method – i.e., attach full or limited source taxation to certain classes of income and assign the right to tax other income exclusively to the state of residence. *See* OECD (2014) (n. 132) 37.
146. HJ Ault, 'Corporate Integration, Tax Treaties and the Division of the International Tax Base: Principles and Practice' (1992) vol. 47 Tax L Rev 565, 567.
147. RS Avi-Yonah, 'The Structure of International Taxation: A Proposal for Simplification' (1996) vol 74 Tex L Rev 1301.
148. The US joined the deliberations in 1927. *See* Carrol (n. 119) 11.
149. Revenue Act of 1913 ch 16 s. 2 38 Stat 114.
150. Revenue Act of 1918 ch 18, ss 222(a)(1), 238(a), 240(c). 40 Stat 1057, 1073, 1080-1082
151. Graetz and O'Hear (n. 124) 1049-1050.
152. *Ibid.*

apportionment',[153] or another system based on the principles identified by the economists. The resulting allocation of income was described as one in which 'neither the country of origin nor the country of residence makes a complete sacrifice in favour of the other'.[154]

2.2.3.6 The OEEC-OECD Efforts

The next major contribution to this project came from the OEEC, established in 1948 as part of the US-Canadian aid distribution under the Marshall Plan.[155] From 1958 to 1961, the OEEC Fiscal Committee undertook the task of developing a model treaty[156] because of the 'increasing importance of the uncertainty in existing treaties as an impediment to international commercial transactions'.[157] The OEEC released four reports between 1958 and 1961, including draft treaty provisions and commentary.[158] In 1961, the OECD superseded the OEEC and took over its Fiscal Committee and the treaty project.[159] In 1963, the OECD issued its Model Tax Convention and Commentary, which restricted the source country's ability to collect tax on investment income.[160] Subsequently revised Model Treaties were released in 1977, 2000 and 2010 (with updates in the interim and thereafter).[161] The last update occurred in 2017. The updated 2017 OECD Model Tax Convention[162] comprises the treaty-based recommendations developed through the BEPS project, and a few other changes that were not developed as part of the work on BEPS (e.g., changes to the international shipping provision and changes to the Commentary on Article 5 on PEs). The 2017 update also

153. Under formulary apportionment, a unitary business is defined based on whether the parent corporation exercises legal and economic control over its subsidiaries. That unitary business is treated as a single taxpayer and its income is calculated by subtracting worldwide expenses from worldwide income, based on a global accounting system, without regard to legal distinctions among units. The resulting net income is apportioned among taxing jurisdictions based on a formula that takes into account various factor Each jurisdiction then applies its tax rate to the income apportioned to it by the formula and collects the amount of tax resulting from this calculation; *see* KA Clausing and RS Avi-Yonah, 'Reforming Corporate Taxation in a Global Economy: A Proposal to Adopt Formulary Apportionment' (2007) The Hamilton Project, Brookings Institution 12.
154. MB Carroll, *Double Taxation Relief: Discussion of Conventions Drafted at International Conference of Experts, 1927, and Other Measures* (Washington: US GPO 1928) 17.
155. OECD, History, http://www.oecd.org/about/history/, accessed 11 November 2018.
156. UN, *United Nations Model Double Taxation Convention Between Developed and Developing Countries* (UN Pub, 2001) xviii.
157. AA Kragen, *Double Income Taxation Treaties: The OECD Draft* (1964) vol. 52(2) Calif L Rev 306, 307.
158. OEEC, *The Elimination of Double Taxation: Report of The Fiscal Committee of the OEEC* (OEEC 1961), Annexures A-E, reprinted in Legislative History, 4619, 4643-4651.
159. OECD History (n. 155).
160. OECD, *Draft Double Taxation Convention on Income and Capital* (OECD Pub 1963).
161. OECD, *Model Double Taxation Convention on Income and on Capital* (OECD Pub 1977); OECD, *Model Tax Convention on Income and on Capital* (OECD Pub 2000); OECD, *Model Tax Convention on Income and on Capital* (OECD Pub 2005); OECD, *Model Tax Convention on Income and on Capital* (OECD Pub 2010).
162. OECD, *Model Tax Convention on Income and on Capital* (Condensed version, OECD Pub 2017) (hereafter 'OECD MTC (2017)').

includes the changes and additions made to the observations and reservations of OECD member countries and the positions of non-OECD economies.

2.2.3.7 *The UN Role*

Developing countries dissatisfied[163] with the pro-residence orientation of the OECD Model Treaty prompted the UN (which had replaced the League in 1945)[164] to make a serious foray into the business of model tax treaty drafting. The UN's Ad Hoc Group of Experts on Tax Treaties between Developed and Developing Countries tackled the problem of drafting a model treaty to promote investment into the developing countries and protect tax revenue. The Ad Hoc Group produced its first report in 1969, which reflected the OECD Model Treaty as its starting point. In 1980, the first model treaty was released. Although it favoured source jurisdiction more than the OECD Model Treaty, it still reflected a compromise in that it granted neither source nor residence countries exclusive jurisdiction to tax.[165] The Model Convention was revised in 2001 and again in 2011. In 2004, the Group of Experts became the Committee of Experts on International Cooperation in Tax Matters. The Committee maintains detailed Commentaries on the United Nations Model Convention and is also responsible for the publication of several useful manuals on tax issues important for developing countries, such as transfer pricing and the administration of tax treaties.[166] A more recent draft model treaty was released in 2013, the latest being its 2017 update.

2.2.3.8 *The US Model Convention*

The last major player to enter the drafting universe (although it produced a draft before the UN) was the US with its 1976 Model Treaty.[167] Subsequent models appeared in 1977, 1981, 1996, and 2006.[168] Differences exist between the US and OECD Model Treaties, reflecting special concerns of the US, such as the treatment of citizens and the prevention of treaty shopping. Yet, once again, the similarity between treaty models is striking, revealing common perceptions on the nature of the problem and the structure and content of its solution.

163. Generally, developing countries are capital importers, and thus are more frequently the source country in a transaction than the residence country.
164. History of the United Nations, http://www.un.org/en/sections/history/history-united-nations/, accessed 11 November 2018.
165. *See* Chapter 3 of this book for a more detailed analysis.
166. BJ Arnold, 'An Introduction to Tax Treaties', p. 5, https://www.un.org/esa/ffd//////wp-content/uploads/2015/10/TT_Introduction_Eng.pdf, accessed 7 March 2018.
167. US Treasury Dept, 'United States Model Convention on Income and Capital' (1976) (reprinted in WH Diamond and DB Diamond, *International Tax Treaties of All Nations*) 10 volumes (Dobbs Ferry: Oceana Publications Inc., 1975–1976) 417.
168. Treasury Dept, *Model Income Tax Treaty of May 17, 1977*, reprinted in 1 Tax Treaties (CCH) 212; Treasury Dept, *Model Income Tax Treaty of June 16, 1981*, reprinted in 1 Tax Treaties (CCH) 211; *United States Model Income Tax Convention of Sept. 20, 1996*, reprinted in 1 Tax Treaties (CCH) 210; *United States Model Income Tax Convention of Nov. 15, 2006*, reprinted in 1 Tax Treaties (CCH) 209.

2.2.4 The Economic Allegiance and the Shaping of 'Nexus'

These historical developments bring out the fact that the economic allegiance principle, identified by the four economists,[169] constitutes the compelling justification for the tax rights of source states. This concept of economic allegiance or nexus has its roots in the doctrine of sovereignty, recognised in public international law. Sovereignty demarcates the state's tax jurisdiction to regulate tax matters and to enforce ensuing tax claims. Since jurisdiction derives from sovereignty, jurisdiction can extend as far as sovereignty exists.[170]

Therefore, the outer limits of a sovereign state's taxing powers, viewed in relation to other states, are set by public international law. Within these limits, every state is free to set rules that regulate its tax jurisdiction over natural and juristic persons and one of the most important limitations of state tax jurisdiction is the requirement for a sufficient legal connection between a sovereign state and a targeted subject, giving rise to the state's right to tax.[171] Hellerstein explains that 'in fiscal terms, there are no questions more fundamental than whether, and the circumstances under which, a national or subnational state may require a person to contribute to the public treasury'.[172] Notion of economic allegiance, as famously explained by Schanz, pertains to economic ties that the taxpayer has with a particular country.[173] It can be of varying intensity, from the mere consumption in a country to different forms of investment and business activities undertaken within the state territory.[174] Harris and Oliver explicate the issue as follows:

> [E]ach community is only one member of a larger community, the community of nations. As members of various communities are mobile and may receive services from governments other than their own, the issue arises as to who are the persons from which a particular government may appropriately extract taxes. In other words, on whom does the obligation to fund a particular government fall? This issue is traditionally analysed according to the doctrine of economic allegiance.[175]

Schindel and Atchabahian[176] use the term 'jurisdictional connection' by referring to the factors signalling sufficient legal connection. The jurisdictional connection is

169. GWJ Bruins, Luigi Einaudi, ERA Seligman and Sir Josiah Stamp, who authored the League of Nations Report on Double Taxation.
170. JJ Ramon, *The Impact of Sovereignty on Global Trade and International Taxation* (Kluwer 1999) 26.
171. RSJ Martha, *The Jurisdiction to Tax in International Law: Theory and Practice of Legislative Fiscal Jurisdiction* (Springer 1989) 46; *see also* K Vogel, 'Double Tax Treaties and Their Interpretation' (1986) vol 4(1) Berk J Intl L 7 and W Schön, 'Persons and Territories: On the International Allocation of Taxing Rights' (2010) vol. 6 BTR 554.
172. W Hellerstein, 'Jurisdiction to Tax in the New Economy: International, National, and Subnational Perspectives' (2003) vol. 38(1) Ga L Rev 1.
173. G Von Schanz, 'Zur Frage Der Steuerpflicht' (1892) vol. 9(II) FinanzArchiv 1, 4.
174. K Vogel, '*Worldwide vs. Source Taxation of Income: A Review and Re-Evaluation of Arguments*' in *Influence of Tax Differentials on International Competitiveness: Proceedings of the Munich Symposium on International Taxation* (Kluwer Law and Taxation 1990) 122.
175. P Harris and D Oliver, *International Commercial Tax* (CUP 2010) 43.
176. A Schindel and A Atchabahian, 'General Report', in *Source and Residence: A New Configuration of Their Principles* (vol 90a, IFA Cahiers de droit fiscal international 2005) 21.

defined as 'the criteria connecting the material element of the taxable event with the scope of a state's taxing power'.[177] Knechtle calls it 'fiscal attachment' and makes a distinction between 'personal' fiscal attachment and 'economic' fiscal attachment, i.e., this specific legal relationship can be based either on the factors pertaining to the personality of the taxable subject or on the factors pertaining to his economic interests.[178] In a similar vein, Kemmeren, analysing the legal relationship between the state and the taxable subject, asserts that 'a relationship can, therefore, reveal itself through a political and/or economic connection with the state concerned'.[179] Pires similarly makes a difference between factors of a personal nature (e.g., nationality and residence) and factors of a real nature (e.g., PE location).[180]

Martha classifies this nexus under two rubrics:[181] *first,* the nationality criterion, which signifies the only connecting factor that subjugates the taxable subject to the sphere of the state's personal sovereignty; *second,* the other criteria (viz., fiscal residence and the source of income) that subjugate the subject to the sphere of the state's territorial sovereignty. Fiscal residence may be described as a special, intimate relationship formed between a taxpayer and a state on the basis of the taxpayer's personal attributes (e.g., the domicile of a natural person). Conversely, the source of income stands for a connection that is based on the location of the taxpayer's economic interests (e.g., economic activity giving rise to income) in the state territory. The existence of this legitimising connection is often labelled in the literature as tax nexus.[182] 'Nexus describes whether a taxpayer, property, or activity has sufficient connection with a state to be subject to that state's tax jurisdiction.'[183]

However, the term 'nexus' is generally used only in respect of source taxation.[184] Even the IBFD Tax Glossary describes the term 'nexus' as a 'term generally used in the context of a state's jurisdiction to tax foreign or non-resident persons'.[185] This is

177. *Ibid.*
178. AA Knechtle, *Basic Problems in International Fiscal Law* (Kluwer 1979) 35-36.
179. E Kemmeren, *Principles of Origins in Tax Conventions: A Rethinking of Models* (PijnenburgVormgevers/Uitgevers 2001) 20.
180. M Pires, *International Juridical Double Taxation of Income* (Kluwer 1989) 109.
181. Martha (n. 171).
182. *See, e.g.*, BJ Arnold and MJ McIntyre, *International Tax Primer* (Kluwer 2002) 15; RL Doernberg and L Hinnekens, *Electronic Commerce and International Taxation* (Kluwer 1999); L Cerioni and PM Herrera, 'The Nexus for Taxpayers: Domestic, Community and International Law' in M Lang, P Melz and L Kristoffersson (eds), *Value Added Tax and Direct Taxation: Similarities and Differences* (IBFD 2009) 571.
183. P Mines, 'Nexus' in JJ Cordes, RD Ebel and J Gravelle (eds), *The Encyclopedia of Taxation and Tax Policy* (The Urban Institute 2005) 269.
184. J Li, *International Taxation in the Age of Electronic Commerce: A Comparative Study* (CTF 2003) 88. Arnold's describes it in same vein: '[N]exus rules are used to determine whether a non-resident's connections with a country justify taxation by that country'; BJ Arnold, 'Threshold Requirements for Taxing Business Profits Under Tax Treaties', in BJ Arnold, J Sasseville and EM Zolt (eds), *The Taxation of Business Profits Under Tax Treaties* (CTF 2003) 62.
185. 'Nexus' in International Tax Glossary (IBFD) reads as follows:

> As such it refers to whether the relevant factors connecting that person to the jurisdiction in question are such as to justify the exercise of such jurisdiction. Factors that may be considered relevant – which may vary according to the facts and

probably because fiscal residence as a connecting factor that justifies taxation by the residence state of the taxpayer is quite obvious and unambiguous. However, one cannot ignore the fundamental point that fiscal facts not related to the source of income, such as nationality or fiscal residence of the taxpayer, also represent connecting factors from which income tax nexus emanates. It is for this reason that some scholars find the nexus requirement as a question prior to the endless 'source versus residence' debates.[186]

That is why the four economists[187] had to grapple with this nexus question, right at the outset. They came up with the concept of 'economic allegiance' as the basis for tax allocation and outlined four questions to serve as the determinants of economic allegiance:[188]

(1) Where is the yield physically or economically produced?
(2) Where are the final results of the process as a complete production of wealth actually to be found?
(3) Where can the rights to the handing-over of these results be enforced?
(4) Where is the wealth spent or consumed or otherwise disposed of?

The economists came to theorise that the economic allegiance doctrine, in its purest form, would allocate tax revenue to each state that rightfully claims economic allegiance with a person. Nevertheless, they conceded that 'income is such a composite product and such a complex conception that even theoretically it is not easy to assign in a quantitative sense proportions of allegiance of the different countries interested'.[189] They concluded that economic allegiance should be determined by reference to the first and the fourth questions, which essentially correspond to the concepts of source and residence.

The economists, however, clarified that the economic allegiance doctrine does not require physical presence in a state to sanction taxation. Production of wealth focuses upon 'the community the economic life of which makes possible the yield'.[190] The production of yield may have one physical location and another economic location. Moreover, the latter overrides the former:

> Physical situs is one thing; origin or economic location is quite another thing; they do not necessarily coincide. Physical situs is of importance in economic allegiance only to the extent that it reinforces economic location.[191]

---

circumstances or the tax in question within one jurisdiction, or as between jurisdictions – include physical presence or economic activity or a combination of both.

186. RM Bird and JS Wilkie, 'Source- vs. Residence-Based Taxation in the European Union: The Wrong Question?', in S Cnossen (ed.), *Taxing Capital Income in the European Union* (OUP 2000) 94-96.
187. Bruins et al. (n. 169).
188. The Four Economists' Report (n. 130).
189. *Ibid.*, 4031.
190. *Ibid.*, 4027.
191. *Ibid.*, 4028-4029.

On this basis, the place of consumption, the market or the place of demand, can be an essential part of wealth production, and thus give rise to economic allegiance even if there is no physical presence:

> The oranges upon the trees in California are not acquired wealth until they are picked, and not even at that stage until they are packed, and not even at that stage until they are transported to the place where demand exists and until they are put where the consumer can use them.[192]

The non-resident may owe significant economic allegiance to the residence state, but this does not justify, in principle, exclusion of source taxation. The question is not about valid fiscal assertions, but rather, about revenue allocation between states which are entitled to assert. Thus, it is not the territorial nexus, but the economic nexus, which is determinative of the taxing rights.

2.3 PART 2: THEORETICAL PREMISE

The economic nexus doctrine, having so evolved historically, obtained a robust theoretical underpinning in the three principal theories, set out by the scholars, forming the bedrock of source-based tax jurisprudence, viz., *benefit theory, neutrality theory* and *inter-nation equity*.

2.3.1 Benefit Theory

The first theoretical foundation of the source rule is the benefit theory of taxation, which has much older antecedents than the source rule itself. In 1651, Thomas Hobbes defined the philosophical basis for paying taxes as an obligation in exchange for security under the state, in proportion to what they consumed in society.[193] In 1692, Sir William Petty said, 'it is generally allowed by all that men should contribute to the public charge but according to the share and interest they have in the public peace; that is, according to their estates and riches'.[194] At the time, the benefit theory was applied explicitly to support taxation in the early American colonies, such as New England as explained by Harris, thus:

> [The] duty of every inhabitant to contribute towards the support of the colony was based upon the theory of benefit received by reason of the existence of the government. The amount of the contribution was determined by the ability of the inhabitant to pay, and his ability, by the amount of land and property he

192. *Ibid.*, 4027.
193. Thomas Hobbes put it thus: '[T]he benefit that everyone receiveth ... is the enjoyment of life, which is equally dear to poor, and rich ... when the Impositions, are layd upon those things which men consume, every man payeth Equally for what he useth'; *see* T Hobbes, *Leviathan* (first published 1651, London Pelican Classics 1968).
194. W Petty, 'A Treatise of Taxes and Contributions' in CH Hull (ed) *The Economic Writings of Sir William Petty* (CUP 1899) Ch. XV: Excize.

> possessed, while every able-bodied freeman was required to pay a specified sum as a poll tax.[195]

A later American recognition of the benefits of government and hence of taxation is in the famous saying, 'taxes are what we pay for civilized society'.[196]

Klaus Vogel, however, was the first jurist to adopt the benefit doctrine as an epistemological rationale for source taxation under which a jurisdiction's right to tax rests on the totality of benefits and services provided to the taxpayers that interact with a country.[197] It is argued that the country where income originates should be compensated for the cost of providing public services. Since a large part of the governmental cost is traceable to the necessity of maintaining a suitable business environment,[198] the non-resident beneficiary of the governmental resources ought to make good of that cost. Economic production results not just out of the actions of isolated individuals, but also as a result of interaction between these individuals and the state; and the state, therefore, may tax all property, goods, labour, services and the like, which have become identified with the economic structure of the state.[199] The provision of education, police, fire and defence protection are among the more obvious examples. But the state can also provide conducive and operational legal structures for the proper functioning of business, for example, in the form of a stable legal and regulatory environment, the protection of intellectual property and the knowledge-based capital of the firm, the enforcement of consumer protection laws, or well-developed transportation, telecommunication, utilities and other infrastructures.[200] Skaar puts it thus:

> [A] Permanent Establishment is merely a piece of evidence of economic allegiance and not a reason for source-based taxation. The circumstances that short term business operations may accumulate substantial profits from domestic sources indicate on the contrary that the taxpayer benefits substantially from the infrastructure of the host country, even though no permanent establishment exists [sic]. It seems that an enterprise which does not need to invest in immovable facilities, or other fixed places of business, may still derive considerable advantages from the communities in which its income sources are located.[201]

195. Harris (n. 106) 176, citing FR Jones, 'History of Taxation in Connecticut: 1636-1776' in *Johns Hopkins University Studies in Historical and Political Science* 14th Series (No. 8) 15.
196. *Compañía General de Tabaco de Filipinas v Collector of Internal Rev,* (1927) 275 US 87, 100; President Roosevelt later described taxes as 'dues that we pay for the privileges of membership in an organized society'; *see* B Randolph, *Public Papers and Addresses of Franklin D Roosevelt,* SI Rosenman (ed.) (Address in Worcester, Massachusetts, 21 October 1936) vol. 5 (Random House 1938) 522-523.
197. D Pinto, *E-Commerce and Source-Based Taxation,* vol. 6 Doctoral Series (IBFD 2002) 17.
198. TE Geu, 'Professor TS Adams (1873-1933) on Federal Taxation: Déjà vu All Over Again' (1993) vol. 10 Akron T J 29,32, citing TS Adams, *The Taxation of Business,* (1917) vol. 11 Nat'l Tax Ass'n PROC. 185, 187.
199. D Pinto, 'Exclusive Source or Residence Based Taxation: Is a New and Simpler World Tax Order Possible?' (2007) BIT 287, citing AL Harding, *Double Taxation of Property and Income, A study in the Judicial Determination of the Conflicting Claims of Taxing Jurisdictions Advanced by the American States* (Harvard 1933).
200. *Ibid.,* 288.
201. AA Skaar, *Permanent Establishment: Erosion of a Tax Treaty Principle* (Kluwer Law and Taxation 1991) 559, 560.

Apart from the direct benefits suggested by Skaar, the non-resident entities, even in the absence of a physical presence or a PE, benefit from the source country's legal system to enforce payment for transactions, to maintain a pro-competitive and conducive business environment and to uphold intellectual property rights in the context of digitised services and intangible products.[202] The value of goods and services is not only created by their supply. It is also created by the demand of these goods and services in the source state. Customer base creates demand and without demand, there will not be any value.[203] Supply and demand together constitute an economic transaction. Vogel sums it up as follows:

> [I]t cannot convincingly be denied that providing a market contributes to the sales income at least to some extent as providing the good [sic] does. There is no valid objection, therefore, against a claim of the sales state to tax part of the sales income.[204]

2.3.1.1 *Benefit Theory and Physical Nexus*

The aforesaid survey of various aspects of benefit theory clearly suggests that benefits derived are to be seen and evaluated in an economic context and as long as an enterprise or a person derives economic benefit from a state, whether by physical presence within the state or without, the source state shall have the right to be compensated in lieu of the benefits conferred. Thus, to insist on a territorial presence in the source state, cannot be justified in terms of the very principle, which forms the jurisprudential foundation of source taxation.

2.3.1.2 *Critique and Assaying the Counter-Arguments*

The territorial nexus theorists, however, have subjected the benefit principle to severe criticism, drawing upon the ideas of liberal political thinkers of the nineteenth century, including J.S. Mill and others. Seligman[205] considered that the idea that taxes should vary according to the benefits that persons receive from government was 'a principle based on "a false political philosophy" from which follows "a false political economy"'.[206] Henry Simons called it 'a significant element in a reactionary social philosophy, constructed from the gratuitous implications of *laissez-faire* economics'.[207]

This liberal critique, however, largely emanated from the fact that the primary focus of the liberals was on the individual and his freedom from state interference, which was in sharp contrast with the communal view of the taxpayer-government relationship canvassed by the benefit theorists of Germany. The overarching liberal

202. Pinto (n. 197) 289.
203. GOI, *High Power Committee Report* (Ministry of Fin 2001) [2001] 251 ITR 118.
204. AJ Cockfield, 'Reforming the Permanent Establishment Principle Through a Quantitative Economic Presence Test' (2003) vol. 38 CBLJ 400, citing Vogel Part III 393, 400.
205. ERA Seligman, *Progressive Taxation in Theory and Practice* (2nd edn, Princeton 1908).
206. DG Duff, 'Benefit Taxes and User Fees in Theory and Practice' (2004) vol. 54(4) UTLJ 391.
207. HC Simons, *Personal Income Taxation* (1st edn, Chicago 1938).

narrative of limiting government, as shaped by political philosophers such as Mill and Bentham, addressed the changing role of government and taxation from a point of view of freedom and happiness of the individual. In contrast, the Germanic concept of *Finanzwissenschaft*[208] tended to treat the state as representative of the people as a whole, not as individuals. The liberal critique, therefore, is quite tenuous in the context of modern democracies and the concept of welfare state in developing nations.

The second and the principal ground on which the benefit theory has been questioned is the unquantifiability of benefits received from government. Bastable puts it thus: 'The theory that taxation is the price of the State's services, and finds its measure for each citizen in the amount of benefit received, is, as regards the latter part, quite unsupported by history.'[209]

This unquantifiability argument weighed so heavily on the minds of the four economists that in their report on double taxation,[210] they went on to infer that the benefit theory had been on decline and was supplanted by the 'ability-to-pay' principle, which is the underlying theme of residence taxation. However, as rightly explicated by Vogel,[211] immeasurability of state benefits is only relevant for ascertaining tax liability, but for the purpose of allocating tax jurisdiction, the benefit arguments still remain valid, germane and compelling. Further, a source taxation regime only reaches income earned within the source country. Consequently, such a regime usually does not take the taxpayer's full income into account, and therefore, it cannot be grounded on an ability-to-pay principle.[212] It is, therefore, rationalised as a benefit-based charge imposed by the source country.[213]

The third ground on which the benefit principle has been assailed pertains to the question of discrimination. It is contended that the benefit theory operates discriminatorily qua the non-residents, which is in derogation to the widespread commitment under international tax treaties that there should be non-discrimination between non-residents taxed on a source basis and residents taxed on a residence basis. The contention, however, does not appear convincing for the simple reason that if the residents are not taxed under a set of rules grounded in a benefits rationale (they are not), then matching the tax treatment of non-residents to that of residents will naturally push outcomes away from what a pure benefits rationale would demand.[214]

Fourth, it is argued that source-based tax claims run counter to modern notions of progressive income taxation, thereby reflecting an ability-to-pay principle rather

208. It is a German term for 'public finance'.
209. CF Bastable, *Public Finance* (first published 1892, 3rd edn, Macmillan 1932) Book III Ch III 298-299.
210. The Four Economists' Report (n. 130) 4022.
211. OECD (2014) (n. 132) 38, citing Vogel Part III (n. 204).
212. JC Fleming et al., 'Fairness in International Taxation: The Ability-to-Pay Case for Taxing Worldwide Income' (2001) vol. 5(4) Fla Tax Rev 299, 307.
213. American Law Institute, *Proposals on United States Taxation of Foreign Persons and of the Foreign Income of United States Persons* (ALI 1987) 18-19, 29, 34, 37-38.
214. MA Kane, 'A Defense of Source Rules in International Taxation' (2015) vol. 32(2) Yale J on Reg 315.

than a benefits principle.[215] Here, ability to pay conceives a determination of paying ability on the basis of taxpayer's comprehensive income, not on portions of his income that have been subdivided into different jurisdictional pots based on source.[216] But this argument, like the unquantifiability argument referred *supra*,[217] is only relevant for the determination of tax liability, but it has no bearing on the allocation of tax rights among nations, which must ultimately rest on some sort of benefits rationale, if only because there is no plausible alternative justifying the widely accepted source-based rules.[218] Moreover, if income tax were to be conceived as justified in terms of payment for benefits provided by a jurisdiction to a taxpayer, then allocating a taxpayer's income to different tax jurisdictions would be quite appropriate.

Finally, some analysts suggest that source-based tax should be limited to the value of source-country government benefits provided to non-residents.[219] Based on this reasoning, imposition of a significantly lower tax than that paid by residents on similar amounts of income is argued because the value of government benefits conferred on non-residents is significantly less than the value of such benefits provided to residents. This is, however, too constricted a view of the benefits conferred on the foreign investors and of their valuation. Government benefits received by non-residents who invest or do business in source country are not limited to basic services such as roads, police and fire protection. A non-resident who invests in or carries on a business in source-country profits from government activities that create and foster general public safety, national security, a fair legal system, a transparent and safe financial infrastructure, a healthy and educated workforce, transportation and communication infrastructure, legal protection of intellectual property licensed or sold in source country by the non-resident, and redistributive assistance to the poor that contributes to a stable social order.[220] In other words, the benefits bestowed on non-resident earners by source country are quite similar to benefits received by residents, thus justifying a substantial source tax.

Graetz gives an apt illustration in this regard. Take the case of a non-resident who extracts minerals from the source country. The non-resident exploits the source country's resource endowment and, in this circumstance, there is broad international acceptance of the source country's right to levy a substantial source tax.[221] This analysis also offers a strong justification for imposing a comparable taxing regime on a foreign person who carries on a non-extractive business in source country. The

215. *See, e.g.*, RA Green, 'The Future of Source-Based Taxation of the Income of Multinational Enterprises' (1993) vol. 79 Cornell L Rev 18, 29, citing JA Pechman, 'The Future of the Income Tax' (1990) vol. 80(1) Am Ec Rev 6 (1990).
216. Kane (n. 214) 315.
217. Vogel Part III 393, 400.
218. Kane (n. 214) 315.
219. Harris (n. 113) 455-458; also *see* CE McLure Jr, 'Source-Based Taxation and Alternatives to the Concept of Permanent Establishment', *Report of the Proceedings of the World Tax Conference: Taxation Without Borders* (CTF 2000).
220. RS Avi-Yonah, 'International Taxation of Electronic Commerce' (1997) vol. 52(3) Tax L Rev 507, 520-521.
221. MJ Graetz, 'Taxing International Income: Inadequate Principles, Outdated Concepts, and Unsatisfactory Policies' (2001) vol. 54(3) Tax L Rev 261, 298; also *see* McLure (n. 219).

physical, legal, and economic infrastructure of source country (i.e., its market) on which the non-resident depends is largely the result of source-country government activities mentioned above. Stated differently, the benefits provided by the source-country government to non-resident earners are quite similar to government benefits received by its residents, thus justifying a substantial source tax.[222] If the non-resident mineral exploiter can be taxed for accessing and exploiting a natural resource deposit of source country, there is no rationale to exclude taxation of non-resident for accessing and exploiting the source-country market. This is, however, subject to administrative and jurisdictional considerations of source country.[223]

Thus, the benefit doctrine is a valid normative basis for source taxation, and it takes into account all sorts of nexus with the source state which have resulted into economic benefits to an enterprise.

2.3.2 Neutrality Theory

The theory of neutrality is the second normative precept, which provides the jurisprudential underpinnings of international income tax law. The neutrality theory means that economic processes should not be affected by external influences such as taxation. There are two principal dimensions of this neutrality as suggested by Richard Musgrave: *Capital Export Neutrality (CEN)* and *Capital Import Neutrality (CIN)*.

2.3.2.1 Capital Export Neutrality (CEN)

CEN means that the tax system does not distort decisions about the location of economic activity. It requires residents of any given nation to face the same tax burden no matter where they choose to invest. Investors, thus, can choose the location of their investments based on purely business considerations, i.e., where they can get the highest pre-tax return. For example, a British investor considering investments in France, the US, China, or at home, should choose the location that brings the highest pre-tax returns.[224] CEN, thus, supports residence-based tax jurisdiction for reason of tax parity as imposing the same tax rate regardless of location ensures this. The economic literature often suggests that if either national or worldwide economic efficiency is the goal, source countries should forgo any tax on foreign businesses operating within their borders.[225] But countries universally impose source-based taxes

222. SE Shay, JC Fleming Jr and RJ Peroni, 'What's Source Got to Do with It: Source Rules and U.S. International Taxation' (2002) vol. 56 Tax L Rev 81, 90-91.
223. Harris (n. 113) 456-457.
224. DA Weisbach, 'The Use of Neutralities in International Tax Policy' (2014) University of Chicago, Coase-Sandor Inst for Law and Econ Research Paper 697/2014, 3, https://ssrn.com/abstract=2482624, accessed 26 December 2018.
225. Several scholars have opined that zero is the optimal tax rate on inward investment. *See, e.g.*, RH Gordon, 'Taxation of Investment and Savings in a World Economy' (1986) vol. 76(5) Am Econ Rev 1086; also *see* J Slemrod, 'Effect of Taxation with International Capital Mobility' in HJ Aaron, H Galper and JA Pechman (eds), *Uneasy Compromise: Problems of a Hybrid Income-Consumption Tax* (Brookings Institution 1988) 115.

whenever there is a substantial business activity by both foreign and domestic companies.

Thus, CEN, in practice, has come to mean that if the source country imposes tax, the residence country should grant a credit for the foreign tax. To illustrate,[226] if the US imposes a 40% income tax and that the EU imposes a 30% income tax, the US investors must pay a 40% tax on income earned in the EU in order to satisfy CEN. That requires the US to tax its residents on their worldwide income and to provide a FTC for the full amount of tax paid to the EU. Under such a tax system, the US investors in the EU will pay tax to the EU on their income at a rate of 30%. They also will be taxed at a 40% rate in the US on that income and receive a credit for the 30% tax paid to the EU. Thus, they will have to pay 10% of their EU earnings to the US in taxes, which leaves them with a total tax payment equal to 40% of their income.

The analysis is similar with one difference for EU-based investors investing in the US. The US will collect 40% of the EU investors' income in the US. But since the US tax liability exceeds the EU tax liability by 10%, the EU does not collect additional tax. That, however, is not the end of the story. In order to satisfy CEN, the EU must provide a tax rebate to its investors of 10% of their US income. Without a rebate, the EU investor would not pay tax at the same rate on their US income as on their EU income (30%).[227] The rebate brings a high foreign tax rate down to the lower domestic tax rate, thereby achieving CEN for EU taxpayers.[228]

Typically, economists regard CEN as essential for worldwide economic efficiency, because the location of investments would be unaffected by capital income taxes.[229] CEN is not only neutral about where such investments are made but also is indifferent about which country collects the tax revenue when capital originating in one country produces income in another.

2.3.2.2 *Capital Import Neutrality (CIN)*

CIN, on the other hand, implies that all investors in a jurisdiction (residents and non-residents) face the same effective rate of tax. It requires that all investments in a given country pay the same marginal rate of tax regardless of the residence of the investor. In other words, all business activity within a country is subject to the same overall level of taxation.[230] If CIN holds, all investors receive the same after-tax return,

226. This illustration is quite standard, and it can be found in one form or another in many articles and books, with many more citing the result.
227. Such a provision often is referred to as an unlimited FTC because the credit is not limited to the residence country's tax on that income.
228. MS Knoll, 'Reconsidering International Tax Neutrality' (2011) vol. 64 Tax L Rev 99, 101-102.
229. For a review of the economic literature, *see* the US Treasury Dept, *The Deferral of Income Earned Through U.S. Controlled Foreign Corporations: A Policy Study* (Office of Tax Policy Department of the Treasury 2000) 23-54 (hereafter 'the Treasury Study').
230. *See* the Treasury Study (n. 229).

regardless of their residence. They, therefore, face the same prices for future versus present consumption and the allocation of savings is efficient.[231]

In terms of the illustration referred above, CIN requires that the US investors pay tax at the same rate as EU investors in every market. Both EU and US investors in the EU pay tax at 30%. Because all investors in the EU, whether EU residents or US residents, pay 30% tax to the EU, it follows that if the US does not tax the EU income of US investors, then both groups of investors will pay tax at the same rate. Similarly, EU investors in the US would pay tax to the US at a rate of 40%. If the EU neither taxes nor provides a rebate to its investors investing abroad, the EU investors will pay the same tax in the US as their US competitors.[232] CIN, thus, tends to support taxation by the source country with the residence country exempting foreign-source income.

2.3.2.3 A Look at CEN Versus CIN Debate

Thus, the international income tax policy debate is dominated today by a simple matrix, where CEN and CIN form the normative universe, which require respectively worldwide taxation with a FTC or 'territorial' taxation with foreign earnings exempt from tax. In theory, CEN gives the prime claim to tax international income to the country of residence and CIN awards that right to the country of source.

Therefore, it goes without saying that it is impossible to achieve CEN and CIN simultaneously in the absence of either a worldwide government or identical income tax bases and rates in all nations.[233] A choice, therefore, must be made between these conflicting norms or since both residence and source countries exercise their rights to tax income, some 'compromise' may be worked out between them. CEN enjoys the greatest normative support in both government analyses and the academy.[234] This is because distortions in the location of investments are thought to be costlier than distortions in the allocation of savings.

---

231. Joint Committee on Taxation, *Study of Present-Law Taxpayer Confidentiality and Disclosure Provisions as Required by Section 3802 of the Internal Revenue Service Restructuring and Reform Act of 1998* (US Govt Printing Office 2000) vol. II: Study of Disclosure Provisions Relating to Tax-Exempt Organizations, http://www.jct.gov/s-1-00vol2.pdf, accessed 6 November 2018; also *see* Joint Committee on Taxation, *Factors Affecting the International Competitiveness of the United States* (US Govt Printing Office 1991) (hereafter 'the JCT 1991 Report'), https://www.jct.gov/publications.html?func=startdown&id=3006; also DF Bradford and US Treasury Dept, *Blueprints for Basic Tax Reform* (2nd edn, US Department of Treasury 1984), https://www.treasury.gov/resource-center/tax-policy/Documents/Report-Blueprints-1977.pdf, accessed 6 November 2018; *The President's Tax Proposals to the Congress for Fairness, Growth, and Simplicity* 383 (May 1985) 383, https://www.treasury.gov/resource-center/tax-policy/documents/report-reform-proposal-1985.pdf, accessed 6 November 2018; *see also* M Keen, 'The Welfare Economics of Tax Coordination in the European Community: A Survey' (Institute of Fiscal Studies 1993).
232. Knoll (n. 228) 102.
233. *Ibid.*, 103.
234. RJ Peroni, 'Back to the Future: A Path to Progressive Reform of the U.S. International Income Tax Rules' (1997) vol. 51(4) U Miami L Rev 975.

CEN, however, has not been viewed favourably by legal scholars and multinational business groups for the increasing concern for business 'competitiveness'.[235] It is argued that, in the absence of perfect competition, deviations from CIN may enable high marginal cost producers to co-exist with, or even drive out low-cost producers.[236]

Further, any additional tax at home will be ultimately passed on to consumers in the foreign market in the form of higher prices, and this will go on to increases their cost of capital vis-à-vis that of foreign competitors, with the result that beneficial foreign projects will be forgone and undertaken by foreign-based companies. It is in the context of business competition and expansion opportunities that Musgrave discusses CIN. She explains that the idea embodied in CIN is that if all investors in a jurisdiction are taxed at the same rate, regardless of their residence, then taxation should not affect competition in that jurisdiction.[237]

Scholars like Vogel consider CIN to be far superior to CEN as it does not give any special incentive for business to relocate towards low-tax jurisdictions, thereby reducing distortions in cross-border capital flows.[238] Capital importing nations also get their due share of taxes. CEN is also criticised, among other reasons, as failing to consider the reasons for foreign direct investment, such as economies of scale or scope that allow successful businesses to exploit opportunities worldwide rather than just domestically.[239] CEN is also based on the flawed assumption that foreign firms do not respond to changes induced by home-country taxation.[240]

Further, CEN, with its focus on worldwide efficiency, seeks to improve worldwide rather than national well-being. Graetz[241] rightly considers it problematic in as much as in our democratic society, we the people have organised a national government to protect our safety and security, to maintain our liberty, and to promote the well-being of our citizens and residents. By assigning the task of improving the lot of the nation's citizens, including those who are the least advantaged, to our government, we have made both economic growth and redistribution of income or wealth a matter of national, rather than worldwide concern.[242] Although we take quite seriously our obligations to foreigners and show respect for their rights, we must consider our obligation for the well-being of our fellow citizens as more pressing than for people in need elsewhere in the world.[243]

Moreover, CEN presents a narrow view of economic efficiency.[244] If economic efficiency were the sole goal of tax policy, we would see only per capita taxes or head

235. Competitiveness is defined as the ability of a firm, headquartered in the home state with production facilities abroad, to compete with resident companies in the host country and multinational firms based elsewhere; *see* the Treasury Study (n. 229) 55.
236. Keen (n. 231).
237. PB Musgrave, *United States Taxation of Foreign Investment Income* (Harvard 1969) 119-121.
238. *See* K Vogel, 'The Search for Compatible Tax Systems' in H Stein (ed), *Tax Policy in the 21st Century* (Wiley 1988).
239. Graetz (n. 221) 287.
240. MA Desai and J Hines, 'Evaluating International Tax Reform' (2003) vol. 56(3) Natl Tax J 487, 493.
241. Graetz (n. 221).
242. *Ibid.*, 277.
243. *See generally* J Rawls, *The Law of Peoples* (Harvard 1999).
244. Graetz (n. 221) 282.

taxes. The economic efficiency question, therefore, must entail, from a national perspective, what international income tax rules will enhance people's standard of living, now and in future generations, for example, by promoting economic growth.[245] Second, there are other important values and singular focus on economic efficiency as the guiding light is not apposite. Our domestic income tax policy debate or any substantial change therein is, generally, guided by a coherent set of multiple principles, even if contentious.[246] There is great dispute over the meaning of these norms and about the priority to be accorded to each, but since Adam Smith, it has been commonplace to say that a tax system should be fair, economically efficient, and reasonably easy to administer and comply with.[247] For these and several other factors such as the relative stability in the price of goods and services, there seems to be a greater acceptance of CIN.

2.3.2.4 Neutrality Theory: Whether It Supports a Strict Territorial Nexus?

As illustrated in the foregoing discussion, CIN supports source taxation on the premise that all investments in a state must attract the same rate of tax. Thus, it is investment, and not physical presence of the enterprise in the territory of the source state, that justify the taxing rights of the source state. It is based on this reasoning that domestic laws[248] of countries subject all investment income to its tax jurisdiction, differences in the degree of their taxes notwithstanding.[249] Indian treaty practices also betray an identical leaning. This aspect has been further expounded in Chapter 3.

2.3.3 Inter-Nation Equity

The third theoretical premise is the doctrine of inter-nation equity, which has been an important consideration in the debate on the division of taxing rights between source and residence countries. Peggy Musgrave adopted the expression 'inter-nation equity' in her work[250] published in the 1960s. She explained that 'international revenue sharing, as an aspect of the taxation of foreign investment, is a matter of inter-nation equity', and that 'although this problem is of little interest to the private investor, it is a major concern of the countries involved'.[251]

Over the years, inter-nation equity has been variously described by Peggy Musgrave and Richard Musgrave, encompassing different but related concepts. They have called it an 'equitable division of the tax revenue between countries',[252] which

245. Graetz (n. 221).
246. *Ibid.*, 294.
247. A Smith, *An Inquiry in to the Nature and Causes of the Wealth of Nations* (first published 1776, Regnery Publishing 1998) 945-947.
248. IT Act 1961 s. 9(1), clauses (iv), (v), (vi).
249. These differences have been examined in the next chapter.
250. PB Musgrave, *Taxation of Foreign Investment Income – An Economic Analysis* (John Hopkins Press 1963) 49, and RA Musgrave, *Fiscal Systems* (Yale 1969).
251. PB Musgrave (n. 250) 130, 133.
252. PB Musgrave (n. 250) 49; also, RA Musgrave (n. 250) 238.

underscores the concept of fairness. They have also called it 'the problem of tax shares in international business',[253] which brings into focus the competing concerns of the nations for revenue collections. They have also explained it in terms of equitable 'allocation of national gain and loss',[254] as it involves the allocation of national gains and losses from foreign investment between home and host states. When residents of home state invest abroad, the income generated by foreign investment is a national gain to the home state. If host state taxes this income, the gain to home state is reduced.

The concept of 'inter-nation equity' differs from the notion of 'inter-individual equity', which is based on the ability-to-pay principle. Inter-individual equity is concerned with the sharing of the tax burden among taxpayers in a country. This may also be called 'intra-nation equity'. Inter-nation equity, on the other hand, is an international problem and is concerned with the sharing of the tax base between nations. Inter-nation equity is also distinguished from international neutrality. International tax neutrality towards investment is defined 'as a situation in which the pattern of taxation does not interfere with or affect the taxpayer's choice between investing at home and investing in foreign countries'.[255]

2.3.3.1 The Source-Residence Dialectics in Terms of Inter-Nation Equity

While there is no denying the fact that that for equity reasons, an income tax should apply to a taxpayer's entire income, wherever earned or derived, but it is difficult to accept the other proposition that taxpayer's entire income necessarily needs to be taxed by a single country – the residence country.[256] Two arguments are generally advanced in favour of the residence countries: *first*, since the income tax seeks to tax the taxpayer's entire welfare as measured today by the income tax base and this income tax base is conceptualised as an attribute of the taxpayer,[257] a country has prescriptive jurisdiction over the persons of its nationals, wherever they may be, under customary international law;[258] *second*, the income tax is a tax on consumption and savings, and

253. PB Musgrave, 'International Tax Base Division and the Multinational Corporation' (1972) vol. 27(4) Public Fin 394; *see also* PB Musgrave, 'Interjurisdictional Equity in Company Taxation: Principles and Applications to the European Union', in S Cnossen (ed), *Taxing Capital Income in the European Union: Issues and Options for Reform* (OUP 2000) 46-77; PB Musgrave, 'Sovereignty, Entitlement, and Cooperation in International Taxation' (2001) vol 26(4) Brooklyn J Intl L 1335 and PB Musgrave, 'Combining Fiscal Sovereignty and Coordination: National Taxation in a Globalizing World' in I Kaul and P Conceicao (eds), *The New Public Finance Responding to Global Challenges* (OUP 2006) 167.
254. PB Musgrave and RA Musgrave, 'Inter-Nation Equity' in RM Bird and JG Head (eds), *Modern Fiscal Issues* (Toronto 1972) 63, 68; PB Musgrave and RA Musgrave, 'Fiscal Coordination and Competition in an International Setting' in L Eden (ed), *Retrospectives on Public Finance* (Duke 1991) 61, 65-66.
255. Musgrave (n. 237) 109.
256. NH Kaufman, 'Equity Considerations in International Taxation' (2001) vol. 26(4) Brooklyn J Intl L 1466, 1466.
257. RA Musgrave and PB Musgrave, *Public Finance in Theory and Practice* (5th edn, McGraw-Hill 1989) 223.
258. *Ibid.*, 215.

these, being attributes of persons not places, are not susceptible to source. The income tax base is, accordingly, not susceptible to source.[259]

But these arguments do not stand a close scrutiny for several reasons: *first*, because even the broadest income tax base is neither a realistic measure of a person or his well-being nor does it even measure consumption and savings. The comprehensive income tax base is the sum of what can be measured – the results of transactions and thus, the classification of the income tax as a personal tax really would hardly have any significance under international law.[260]

Second, it is sometimes argued that basing income tax on considerations of equity and value judgments is an idea antithetical to the rise of positivism in international law, which eschews value judgments.[261] Even the argument that the comprehensive income tax base is not susceptible to source is also not entirely correct as new wealth does, in fact, derive from specific geographic sources.[262]

Third, historical experience also does not bear testimony to the assumption that equity requires the taxation of worldwide income by a single sovereign. As Graetz and O'Hear point out, the US international tax system may not have sprung from a perceived necessity for equity reasons to tax a resident's worldwide income.[263] TS Adams was apparently influenced by the unflinching belief that double taxation is inherently unfair, and source-based taxation should be primary, but he did emphasise a need for residence-based taxation to serve as a backstop in a world relatively devoid of international tax cooperation.[264] However, meaningful international tax cooperation would definitely ensure that each country, with which a taxpayer had ties, is able to impose its tax on the portion of the taxpayer's income arising within that country. In that event, the taxpayer's entire comprehensive income tax base would be subject to tax, different parts of it by different countries. A worldwide system of source taxation would thus achieve the same tax goal, i.e., income tax should apply to a taxpayer's entire income, wherever earned or derived. Other means might be employed to achieve the same result.[265]

Thus, source taxation, too, has strong roots in inter-state equity considerations. George Kopits explains:

> [T]ax policy toward the multinational firm may be dictated by intercountry equity considerations. These involve allocation of the firm's tax base among the countries

259. HJ Ault and DF Bradford, 'Taxing International Income: An Analysis of the U.S. System and Its Economic Premises' in A Razin and J Slemrod (eds), *Taxation in the Global Economy* 11, 31 (Chicago 1990).
260. Kaufman (n. 256) 1467.
261. NH Kaufman, 'Fairness and the Taxation of International Income' (1998) vol. 29(2) L & Pol Int Bus 145, 147-148.
262. *Ibid.*, 156-158.
263. *See generally*, Graetz and O'Hear (n. 124).
264. *Ibid.*, 1054-1059.
265. *See, e.g.*, Vogel Part I, 216, 219, citing Georg Von Schanz, *Zur Frage Der Steuerpflicht* (On the Question of Tax Burden) (1882) vol. 9 (II) Finanzarchiv 1, 4.

where it operates on the basis of value judgments as to each country's fair revenue share.[266]

Similarly, Diane Ring notes that 'The question of inter-nation equity incorporates both political and moral judgment',[267] and this presents us with the knotty questions of working out the precise design of a source tax formulation that might be imposed – whether it should be construed in terms of a true benefits tax or a tax on pure economic rents? How would it align with the existing tax regime in other countries? Since designing a tax to achieve either of these two ends is not easy, some sort of an income and/or withholding tax may serve as a reasonable proxy.[268]

At the time of the Ottawa work on the taxation of electronic commerce, the concern for inter-nation equity was recognised by stating that 'any adaptation of the existing international taxation principles should be structured to maintain fiscal sovereignty of countries, to achieve a fair sharing of the tax base from electronic commerce between countries'.[269]

It must be emphasised here that these tax rules have been driven not by the concerns for taxpayers as much as by the states' fiscal demands. Under inter-nation equity, therefore, each country should receive an equitable share of tax revenue from cross-border transactions.[270] If that being so, source rules are just like legal instruments that capture a factual predicate relevant to an underlying normative jurisdictional theory. As Kane points out, the source rules, rather, are mere assertions of the right to tax, irrespective of any underlying theoretical precepts justifying such right.[271] The state asserts the right to tax the income simply because it has the raw power to do so, not because such right is legitimised under some legal determination, the source rule, for instance.[272]

This argument receives considerable traction as the tax difficulties for developing countries are long-standing and increasingly well known. They not only have much lower per capita national incomes than developed countries, but also convert a much smaller percentage of that income into government revenue.[273] This means that taxation raised from multinational companies and wealthy individuals is more precious to them than it is to developed countries, hence the focus of so much attention from development campaigners in recent years on the avoidance and evasion of such taxes. It is in this context that the normative contours of the source rule would have to be conceived.

266. GF Kopits, 'Taxation and Multinational Firm Behavior: A Critical Survey' (1976) vol. 23(3) IMF Staff Papers 624, 662-663.
267. Ring (n. 121).
268. K Brooks, 'Inter-Nation Equity: The Development of an Important but Underappreciated International Tax Value' in R Krever and JG Head (eds), *Tax Reform in the Twenty First Century* (Kluwer 2008) 23.
269. OECD, *Taxation and Electronic Commerce-Implementing the Ottawa Framework Conditions* (OECD Pub 2001) 228.
270. Kaufman (n. 261) 145.
271. Kane (n. 214) 317-318.
272. Kane (n. 214).
273. *See generally*, M Hearson, 'The Challenges for Developing Countries in International Tax Justice' (2018) vol. 54(10) J Dev Stud 1932.

This is not to suggest that the source country's right to tax is without any limitation. It is severely limited by practical constraints. Capital importing countries find it difficult to tax highly mobile income where the geographical source can easily be moved. Any attempt to tax such income may result in capital flight, i.e., the capital may move to another country that does not tax that type of income. The residence country, therefore, may be better situated to tax highly mobile income, as historically persons have not been as mobile as income. Globalisation, however, has increased the mobility of persons and income and countries are increasingly relying on stable factors such as land and employees. High wage / high tax countries have even found that their employee tax base can disappear offshore with devastating local effects.[274]

2.3.3.2 Equity Considerations and the Territorial Nexus Debate

It is clearly discernible from the aforesaid discussion that the concept of inter-nation equity renders the territoriality argument altogether irrelevant as any strict test for territorial presence militates against the concept of equity and fairness, which has been accepted as a valid normative concept by international tax law scholarship and also in the OECD literature.[275]

There is considerable public outrage today over an international tax system that seems increasingly to be allowing multinational corporations (MNCs) to take the benefits from societies in which they operate, but then escape paying their fair share of tax contribution towards those benefits. Tax rules are also commonly shaped by lobbying from big business. In addition, the network of tax treaties tends to favour the residence countries of multinationals over the source countries where they invest, which include most developing countries. The result of all these problems is that developing countries collect much less tax than they otherwise could, preventing them from paying for public services and the fight against poverty. Foreign direct investment stock in low-income countries has more than doubled since the 1990s as a share of Gross Domestic Product (GDP) but tax revenues have not kept up. The UNCTAD has estimated that the amount of tax avoided in developing countries may be equal to nearly half of the amount of corporate income tax revenue collected.[276] A 2009 Report prepared for the UK Department for International Development analysed existing literature on the tax gap suffered by developing countries due to tax avoidance and tax evasion.[277] The Report noted that the provision of public services and infrastructure is a key factor for economic development and growth. Many developing countries fail to raise the tax revenue required to finance their public sectors. In 2005, the average tax

274. Harris and Oliver (n. 175) 104.
275. OECD (2001) (n. 269) 228.
276. UNCTAD, *World Investment Report 2015: Reforming International Investment Governance* (UN Pub 2015) 200.
277. C Fuest and N Riedel, 'Tax Evasion and Tax Avoidance in Developing Countries: The Role of International Profit Shifting' (2010) Oxford University Centre for Business Taxation WPN 1012/2010, https://assets.publishing.service.gov.uk/media/57a08b3de5274a31e0000a66/60670_TaxEvasionReportDFIDFINAL1906.pdf, accessed 24 December 2018.

revenue to GDP ratio in the developed world was approximately 35%. In the developing countries, it was equal to 15%, and in the poorest of these countries, the group of low-income countries, tax revenue was just 12% of GDP.[278]

Against this backdrop, raising the bar of territorial nexus, in contradistinction to economic nexus, will aggravate the situation and further erode the tax base of developing countries, as reflected in the BEPS Report.[279]

2.4 CONCLUSION

Thus, it is quite evident from the historical evolution of the tax jurisdictional rules that the source taxation precept, right from its inception, has been grounded in the economic nexus of an income with the source state as illustrated in the League's Reports. The requirement of a physical presence has never been a paramount attribute of this linkage. The preceding analysis of the theoretical premise of source taxation also throws light on how the three normative bases of the source rule, viz. benefit, neutrality and equity, do not necessarily mandate a strict territorial presence. The very definition of 'economic allegiance' is clearly based on a benefit theory of taxation, which is used to justify both what we would regard as source-based taxation ('production of wealth') and what we would regard as residence-based taxation ('possession of wealth' and 'disposition of wealth').[280] The concept of neutrality is also an economic concept that is related to the decision-making of economic actors,[281] which makes the physical location of investment irrelevant. The principle of inter-nation equity requires that taxation is based on the principle of economic allegiance,[282] so that the state contributing to the earning of income are not denied a fair deal in tax allocation.

278. *Ibid.*, 1.
279. OECD, *Addressing Base Erosion and Profit Shifting* (OECD Pub 2013) 13, 67.
280. RS Avi-Yonah, 'All of a Piece Throughout: The Four Ages of U.S. International Taxation' (2005) vol. 25(2) Va Tax Rev 313, 320.
281. A Auerbach, 'The Theory of Excess Burden and Optimal Taxation' in A Auerbach and M Feldstein (eds), *Handbook of Public Economics* (vol 1 ch 2, Elsevier 1985) 61.
282. A Schäfer and C Spengel, 'ICT and International Corporate Taxation: Tax Attributes and Scope of Taxation' (2002) Centre for European Economic Research (ZEW) and University of Mannheim DPN 02-81, 32, http://ftp.zew.de/pub/zew-docs/dp/dp0281.pdf, accessed 26 January 2019.

CHAPTER 3

The Nexus Debate in Treaty Structures: A Comparative Critique of the OECD and UN Models

Abstract

This chapter entails a comparative critique of the two model treaties, and juxtaposes their distinguishing features with the domestic tax laws of India in the context of rights to tax four categories of incomes: *income from immovable property, business profits, investment income* (including dividends, interests and royalties) and *capital gains*. These analyses aim at investigating whether rights to tax these incomes in an international context necessarily posits the proposition of a strict territorial presence. This chapter comprises five sections, apart from the introduction, which follow the pattern of comparing and analysing the provisions of the Models with regard to these incomes and then, set out the model schemes against the respective provisions of Indian domestic law and also against some of the internationally emerging trends, in order to investigate the premise of territoriality.

3.1 INTRODUCTION

Tax treaties are formal bilateral agreements between two countries. Tax treaties are also referred to as tax conventions or double tax agreements (DTA) or DTAA. Income and capital tax treaties are also commonly referred to as 'comprehensive tax treaty', due to the fact that they include provisions for all or most types of income, e.g., business income, passive income and employment income.[283] They prevent double taxation and fiscal evasion, and foster cooperation between the contracting parties by enforcing their respective tax laws. In this regard, they protect foreign investors from

283. R Rohatgi, *On International Taxation, Volume 1: Principles* (IBFD 2018) 45.

discriminatory tax treatment and offer (potential) support for the resolution of cross-border tax disputes through MAP.[284]

India has signed double tax avoidance treaties with more than eighty-eight countries around the world, but presently around eighty-five treaties are in force, most recent treaties being with Iran[285] and Hong Kong.[286] As one of the largest developing counties with a huge FDI inflow, it appears quite reasonable for India to follow the UN Model, which generally prefers the source principle as compared to the OECD Model. Indian tax treaties, however, evince a great deal of flexibility and combine features from both the OECD and UN Model Conventions with a higher emphasis on source state taxation. It is for this reason that the OECD Commentaries carry significant weight in the interpretive process in the Indian treaty contexts, wherever the wordings of the OECD Model are followed in drafting a certain provision as in such a case it would be reasonable to assume that the contracting states intended such a provision to have the same meaning as it has in the OECD Model. If the wording of a provision deviates from the OECD Model, two alternatives have to be considered in such an event: Either the difference in wording may also entail a difference in meaning or the meaning may still be similar to the OECD Model, despite the difference in wording. This problem cannot be solved in general but only through interpretation in each individual case.[287]

The courts in India have also been referring to the OECD Commentaries in resolving the tax disputes arising in international transactions.[288] However, as stated above, where there is a difference in the terms of the treaties vis-à-vis the OECD Model Convention, the Indian courts have held the Commentaries wholly inapplicable and unreasonable and have pointed to 'futility in seeking to apply the same as a guide for interpretation and construction of the articles in the agreement'.[289] The OECD Commentaries are, however, not meant to be binding, and they are just to be treated as a guide for construction. The OECD Commentaries clarify this aspect by stating that, although they are not designed to be annexed in any manner to tax treaties, which, unlike the Model Convention, are legally binding instruments, they can be of great assistance in the application and interpretation of tax treaties and in the settlement of disputes.[290]

This chapter studies the similarities and differences of the two principal Model Conventions and juxtaposes their distinguishing features with the domestic tax laws of India in the context of rights to tax four categories of incomes: *income from immovable property*, *business profits*, *investment income* (including dividends, interests and

284. *Ibid.*, 51.
285. Signed on 17 February 2018.
286. Signed on 19 March 2018.
287. M Lang and F Brugger, 'The Role of the OECD Commentary in Tax Treaty Interpretation' (2008) 23 ATF 95, 100.
288. *CIT v Visakhapatnam Port Trust* (1983) 144 ITR 146 (AP); *see also Union of India v Azadi Bachao Andolan* (2003) 263 ITR 706 (SC); *CIT v Davy Ashmore Ind Ltd* (1991) 190 ITR 626 (Cal); *CIT v RM Muthaiah* (1993) 202 ITR 508 (Kar); *DDIT v Balaji Shipping (UK) Ltd* (2008) 117 TTJ 865 (Mum).
289. *CIT v SRM Firms* (1994) 208 ITR 400 (Mad).
290. OECD MTC (2017), Introduction para. 29.

royalties) and *capital gains*. The object in this comparative analysis is to investigate whether rights to tax these incomes in an international context necessarily posits the requirement of a strict territorial presence. In the preceding chapter, this book argues how the concept of economic allegiance between the source state and the income has been narrowed to mean a strict test of territorial presence by the vociferous votaries of residence taxation. This chapter takes this debate to the tax treaty laws and focuses on a comparative critique of the two model treaties, i.e., the OECD Model and the UN Model, to explain how economic connection as the ultimate jurisprudential justification for taxing rights permeates through the provisions of the two treaty structures and how the barriers of physical nexus are gradually being overcome. By elucidating the underlying principles through this comparison, this chapter throws considerable light on the policies, which countries, like India, may pursue, while signing new tax agreements in order to obviate any unintended results emanating therefrom.

3.2 RIGHT TO TAX INCOME FROM IMMOVABLE PROPERTY

A look at Article 6 of both the OECD[291] and the UN[292] Models reveals that income derived by a resident of a contracting state from immovable property (including income from agriculture or forestry) situated in the other contracting state may be taxed in that other state. The income from immovable property also includes property accessory to immovable property, livestock and equipment used in agriculture and forestry, rights to which the general law relating to landed property apply, usufruct of immovable property and rights to variable or fixed payments as consideration for the working of, or the right to work, mineral deposits, sources and other natural resources.[293] This income shall include income derived from the direct use, letting, or use in any other form of immovable property.[294] Income from immovable property of an enterprise is also included within the scope of these provisions.[295] Thus, income derived from immovable property through a business enterprise shall be taxed in accordance with Article 6 and not in accordance with Article 7. Article 6 of the UN Model Convention, in fact, reproduces Article 6 of the OECD Model Convention with the exception of the phrase 'income from immovable property used for the performance of independent personal services' which appears at the end of paragraph 4 of the UN Model Convention. This phrase is included in the UN Model Convention as a result of the retention of Article 14 dealing with Independent Personal Services.

Thus, the provisions of both the Models are identical, giving the source state the primary right to tax income from immovable property of an enterprise, with the residence state also having the residual right to tax the same after grating relief for the tax paid in the source state. Income from immovable property which is attributable to

291. OECD MTC (2017) (n. 290) Art. 6 paras 1-4.
292. United Nations Model Double Taxation Convention between Developed and Developing Countries (UN Pub 2017) Art. 6 paras 1-4 (hereafter 'UN MTC 2017').
293. OECD MTC (2017) (n. 290) Art. 6 para. 2; UN MTC (2017) Art. 6 para. 2.
294. OECD MTC (2017) (n. 290) Art. 6 para. 3; UN MTC (2017) Art. 6 para. 3.
295. OECD MTC (2017) (n. 290) Art. 6 para. 4; UN MTC (2017) Art. 6 para. 4.

a PE shall be deemed as business profits, which are subject to different rules. The US Model Convention[296] also being identical, we see a great deal of convergence of views on this issue.

This convergence is owing to the fact that the treaty models recognise the very close economic connection between the source of this income[297] and the source state, as the income-generating source is situated in that state and it is that state, which is the protector and facilitator of that property under its law, enabling it to generate income and providing the economic linkage for triggering tax rights. The economic linkage has to be understood in this context of benefits and facilities extended by the source state,[298] and the physical location of the property, i.e., *lex situs,* per se, cannot and should not be taken to read into the provisions a rigid requirement of a physical presence in the source state territory. Even the definition of the concept of immovable property has been conceived in terms of the law of the contracting state, where the property is situated.[299] This is specifically intended to obviate 'difficulties of interpretation over the question whether an asset or a right is to be regarded as immovable property or not'.[300] Giving primacy to the state where income-generating activities take place is quite in alignment with the principle of economic allegiance, enunciated by the four economists.[301]

3.2.1 Indian Domestic Laws and Treaty Practices

India follows these rules without any reservation as reflected in its domestic law[302] as well as its tax treaties.[303] As per section 9(1)(i) of the Indian Tax Law, all income accruing or arising, whether directly or indirectly through or from any property in India is deemed to accrue or arise in India. The provisions of Indian tax treaties in this regard are identically worded with certain country-specific variations here and there.

The Indian treaties broadly incorporate the OECD and UN provisions in this regard. A controversy, however, was raised by the tax authorities in *Kulandagan Chettiar*[304] with regard to interpretation of the expression 'may be taxed' in Article 6 of the India-Malaysia Treaty, where a question arose whether income arising from a property situated in Malaysia was taxable in India as well. The tax authorities sought to tax it in India, arguing that the expression 'may be taxed' in the treaty does not preclude it to be taxed by the other contracting party, i.e., India in this case. This view

296. United States Model Income Tax Convention (hereafter 'US MTC') Art. 6.
297. OECD MTC (2017) (n. 290) Commentary on Art. 6 para. 1.
298. D Pinto, 'Exclusive Source or Residence Based Taxation: Is a New and Simpler World Tax Order Possible?' (2007) BFIT 287, citing AL Harding, *Double Taxation of Property and Income, A study in the Judicial Determination of the Conflicting Claims of Taxing Jurisdictions Advanced by the American States* (Harvard 1933).
299. OECD MTC (2017) (n. 290) Art. 6(2).
300. OECD MTC (2017) (n. 290) Commentary Art. 6 para. 2.
301. *See* the Four Economists' Report.
302. Indian Income Tax Act 1961 s. 9(1) (i).
303. *See, e.g.,* India-Singapore DTAA Art. 6.
304. *CIT v PVAL Kulandagan Chettiar* (2004) 267 ITR 654 (SC); also *see DCIT v Torqouise Investment & Finance* [2008] 300 ITR 1 (SC), *Pooja Bhatt v DCIT* (2009) 123 TTJ 404 (Mum).

of the Revenue authorities was in consonance with the existing international practices. Rejecting the Revenue's contention, the Indian Supreme Court, however, answered, thus:

> Wherever the parties intended that income is to be taxed in both the countries, they have specifically provided in clear terms. Consequently, it cannot be said that the expression 'may be taxed' used by the contracting parties gave option to the other Contracting States to tax such income. In our view, the contextual meaning has to be given to such expression. If the contention of the Revenue is to be accepted then the specific provisions permitting both the Contracting States to levy the tax would become meaningless.[305]

The explanation of the phrase 'may be taxed' in Article 6 of the Indian treaty by the Indian Supreme Court in *Kulandagan Chettiar*, however, created difficulties in bringing to tax the income of an Indian resident whose immovable property or other source of income was situated outside India and which was otherwise includible in the taxable income of the taxpayer under the Indian law. Accordingly, based on an expert committee recommendation, the Indian Government issued Notification No. 91/2008 dated 28 August 2008, providing that where any income of a resident of India 'may be taxed' in the other country, such income shall be included in his total income chargeable to tax in India in accordance with the provisions of the Indian Tax Law and relief shall be granted in accordance with the method for elimination or avoidance of double taxation provided in such agreement.[306] This legislative intervention had the effect of overruling the *Kulandagan Chettiar* law. Relying on this notification in *Shah Rukh Khan*,[307] the Mumbai Bench of the ITAT rejected the plea of the taxpayer to exclude its income from Dubai Villa in view of India-United Arab Emirates (UAE) treaty in the following words:

> 13.4 We have carefully considered the rival submissions. On this aspect, at the outset, we may say that the action of the lower authorities deserves to be upheld in view of the Notification Nos. 90 & 91/2008 dated 28/08/2008. In fact, the entire controversy is arising from the understanding of the expression 'may be taxed in that other State' as mentioned in Para-1 of Article-6 of the Double Taxation Avoidance Agreement between India and UAE. The meaning of the said expression has been explained by our Co-ordinate Bench in the case of *Essar Oil Ltd.* v *Addl. CIT* [2014] 42 taxmann.com 21 (Mum - Trib) in the following words:
>
> '(*i*)The ratio of all the judgments rendered by the Hon'ble High Courts, as discussed herein above and confirmed by the Hon'ble Supreme Court specifically in the case of Turquoise Investment, on the interpretation of the expression 'may be taxed', that once the tax is payable or Bank of Baroda 23 paid in the country of source, then country of residence is denied of the right to levy tax on such income or the said income cannot be included in return of income filed in India, would no longer apply after the insertion of

305. *Kulandagan Chettiar* (n. 304).
306. *See* Notification No. 91/2008 dated 28 August 2008, https://incometaxindia.gov.in/Communications/Notification/9201100000000000754.htm, accessed 30 December 2020.
307. *Shah Rukh Khan v ACIT* [2017] 79 taxmann.com 227 (Mum).

> provision of sub-section (3) of section 90 w.e.f. 1st April, 2004, i.e. assessment Year 2004-05. The said provision as conferred upon the Central Government a power to issue notification, assigning meaning to the terms used in the DTAA, which has neither been defined under the Act nor in the agreement provided that such a meaning should not be inconsistent with the provisions of the Act or agreement. In pursuance of such a statutory empowerment, Central Govt. has issued a notification on 28th August, 2008, clearly specifying that where the DTAA entered into by the Central Govt. with the Govt. of any other country provides that any income of a resident of India 'may be taxed' in the other country, such income shall be included in his total income chargeable to tax in India in accordance with the provisions of the Income Tax Act, 1961 and relief shall be granted in accordance with the method for elimination or avoidance of double taxation provided in such agreement. This meaning assigned to the term 'may be taxed' has changed its complexion; ii) The notification dated 28th August 2008, reflects a particular intent and objective of the Government of India, as understood during the course of negotiations leading to formalization of treaty. Therefore, such a notification has to be reckoned as clarificatory in nature and hence interpretation given by govt. of India through this notification will be effective from 1st April 2004, i.e., from the date when provision of section 90(3) was brought in the statute, giving a Legal frame work for clarifying the intent of one of the negotiating parties; iii) The phrase 'may be taxed' is not appearing in the statute, but it is appearing in the agreement and therefore, the interpretation as understood and intended by the negotiating parties should be adopted. Here one of the parties i.e., Government of India has clearly specified the intent and the object of this phrase. If phrase is used in a statute, then 'any interpretation given by the High Court or the Supreme Court is binding on all the subordinate Courts and has to be reckoned as law of the land. However, the meaning assigned by Government of India for a phrase or term used in the agreement through notification will prevail at least from the assessment year 2004-05. Because, while interpreting the treaty, the intention of the parties to the agreement has to be Bank of Baroda 24 given primacy and has to be understood in that manner only. Therefore, the notification is not contrary to the provisions of the Act. Consequently, the earlier judgments rendered in assessee's case prior to assessment year 2004-05, will not have binding precedence in this year or subsequent year;'
>
> 13.5 In view of the aforesaid precedent, it has to be held that income from the Dubai Villa is liable to be taxed in India inasmuch as the same is includible in the return of income and whatever taxes that may have been levied in the other contracting State, the credit thereof is required to be allowed as per law.

The legal development was noticed by another Bench of the Tribunal in a recent decision in *Technimont (P) Ltd,*[308] where an Indian company sought to exclude its profits from the branch offices in UAE and Qatar, invoking the treaty partner jurisdiction. The Bench rejected the taxpayer's arguments and explained the legal development, thus:

308. *Technimont (P) Ltd v ACIT* [2020] 116 taxmann.com 996 (Mum).

10. It may be recalled that, with effect from 1st April 2004, a new sub-section 3 was inserted in Section 90, and this new sub-section provided that '(*a*)ny term used but not defined in this Act or in the agreement referred to in sub-section (1) shall, unless the context otherwise requires, and is not inconsistent with the provisions of this Act or the agreement, have the same meaning as assigned to it in the notification issued by the Central Government in the Official Gazette in this behalf.' In exercise of the powers so vested in the Central Government, *vide* notification no. 91 of 2008 dated 28th August 2008, it was notified as follows:

> In exercise of the powers conferred by sub-section (3) of section 90 of the Income-tax Act, 1961 (43 of 1961), the Central Government hereby notifies that where an agreement entered into by the Central Government with the Government of any country outside India for granting relief of tax, or as the case may be, avoidance of double taxation, provides that any income of a resident of India 'may be taxed' in the other country, such income shall be included in his total income chargeable to tax in India in accordance with the provisions of the Income-tax Act, 1961 (43 of 1961), and relief shall be granted in accordance with the method for elimination or avoidance of double taxation provided in such agreement.

11. The effect of Hon'ble Supreme Court's judgment in *Kulandagan Chettiar's* case (*supra*) thus was clearly overruled by the legislative developments. It was specifically legislated that the mere fact of taxability in the treaty partner jurisdiction will not take it out of the ambit of taxable income of an assessee in India and that 'such income shall be included in his total income chargeable to tax in India in accordance with the provisions of the Income-tax Act, 1961 (43 of 1961), and relief shall be granted in accordance with the method for elimination or avoidance of double taxation provided in such agreement.' A coordinate bench of this Tribunal, in the case of *Essar Oil Ltd* (*supra*) also proceeded to hold that this notification was retrospective in effect inasmuch as it applied with effect from 1st April 2004 *i.e.*, the date on which sub-section 3 was introduced in Section 90.

The Tribunal, thus, rightly noted that this legislative change was specifically brought about to affirm that the mere fact of taxability in the treaty partner jurisdiction will not take an income out of the ambit of Indian Tax Law as this has an effect of eroding the tax base of India, despite a strong economic linkage of the income with the resident taxpayer. The application of tax law in such cases, however, will be subject to double taxation avoidance relief provided in the relevant treaty as stipulated in the notification.

The *Kulandagan Chettiar* judgment, however, is important not so much for its interpretation of the phrase 'may be taxed' in Article 6 of the treaty, but for underlying the concept of 'economic relation or nexus' which forms the underlying rationale of source taxation. Rajendra Babu CJ, speaking for the Court, explained it, thus:

13. We need not to enter into an exercise in semantics as to whether the expression 'may be' will mean allocation of power to tax or is only one of the options and it only grants power to tax in that State and unless tax is imposed and paid no relief can be sought. Reading the Treaty in question as a whole when it is intended that even though it is possible for a resident in India to be taxed in terms of sections 4 and 5, if he is deemed to be a resident of a Contracting State where his personal and economic relations are closer, then his residence in India will become irrelevant. The Treaty will have to be interpreted as such and prevails over sections 4 and 5

> of the Act. Therefore, we are of the view that the High Court is justified in reaching its conclusion, though for different reasons from those stated by the High Court.[309]

This judicial view is in consonance with paragraph 1 of the OECD Commentary on Article 6, which also tends to justify this allocation to the source state due to the fact that there is always a very close economic connection between the source of this income and the source state.[310]

This increasing focus on the economic linkages of the source of income is being judicially recognised all over the world. In *Royal Bank of Canada*,[311] the UK First-Tier Tribunal upheld the taxing rights of the HMRC in respect of income indirectly derived by the non-resident from immovable property situated in the UK. In this case, Canadian bank loaned funds to a Canadian oil & gas company, for the exploration and extraction of oil in the UK sector of the North Sea. At the time, licences for this activity were only issued to UK resident companies and non-resident companies had to generally enter into an 'Illustrative Agreement' with a UK licence holder. Under this agreement, the development and exploitation costs were to be incurred by the Canadian company in return for the licence holder's share of the oil won from licensed area. Due to financial difficulties, the Canadian company, later, sold its interest in the oilfield to the BP group. The consideration for the sale included an entitlement to royalty payments contingent on production from the oil field linked to the excess of the market price of the oil above an agreed level. The Canadian company subsequently went into receivership, by which time, the oil price had risen, and some payments were made pursuant to the sale agreement. Even after the sale of the remainder of its assets, the Canadian company still owed the bank a substantial sum and its rights to all future payments were assigned to the bank with the approval of the Canadian courts. BP group subsequently transferred its interest in the oil field to another company, and the bank became entitled to the royalty payments pursuant to a novation agreement between all three parties. The bank accounted for the payments for Canadian tax as receipts of its banking business in Canada and as a partial recovery of the bad debt it had previously recognised in respect of its loan to the Canadian company. There was no dispute that the bank had a PE in the UK and the payments in question were not attributable to that PE. UK taxing rights depended on qualification of the payments as income from immovable property within Article 6. Article 6(2) of the UK-Canada Treaty, which is based on the OECD Model, generally requires immovable property to be defined in accordance with the law of the contracting state in which the property is situated. However, it includes in any event 'rights to variable or fixed payments as consideration for the working of, or the right to work, mineral deposits, sources and other natural resources'. Both parties agreed that this specific inclusion in the definition determined the issue. The taxpayer argued that this expression is concerned with a grant, not a transfer, of a right to work and that the payments must be made in consideration of the grant of the right to work to be income from immovable property. The Tribunal concluded that the definition in Article 6(2) should not be confined to payments made

309. *Kulandagan Chettiar* (n. 304).
310. OECD MTC 2017 (n. 290) Commentary on Art. 6 para. 1.
311. *Royal Bank of Canada v HMRC* [2020] UKFTT 267 (TC).

directly to the owner of the rights in exchange for the grant of a right to exploit them. The judge's reasoning is quite instructive on the issue:[312]

> I see no reason for limiting the scope of Art 6(2) to cover only payments which are made directly to the owner of the rights in exchange for the grant of a right to exploit them. The apparent purpose of granting taxing rights on profits from natural resources to the state where the resources are situated would otherwise potentially be capable of avoidance by simply granting a licence to work those resources at a price equal to the cost of the works, then the grantee assigning that right to a third party in exchange for payment of substantial royalties. The focus must be on the ultimate source of the profit and it would be irrational and inconsistent with the apparent purpose of the provision if it were possible to avoid local taxation on that profit simply by interposing an assignment of the royalty rights (possibly even to an associated company resident in a low tax jurisdiction) after they had been granted.

The Tribunal supported its conclusion with the OECD Commentary which refers to income that is 'indirectly derived from immovable property'. The Tribunal specifically stressed the point that the *lex situs* principle may be misused by creating legal structures and the focus, therefore, must be on the ultimate source of the profit. The Tribunal further held that if it were possible to avoid local taxation on that profit simply by interposing an assignment of the royalty rights after they had been granted, it would be irrational and inconsistent with the object of the provision.

3.3 RIGHTS TO TAX BUSINESS PROFITS: THE BASIC PRINCIPLES

The limitation imposed by the source state and the balance of fiscal interests of the source and the residence states are the keys to deal with rights to tax business profits. Logically, three basic principles can be identified in the two model conventions in this regard:

(1) The *PE principle* for identifying the source of business profits and delimiting the jurisdictional boundary of the source state.
(2) The *profits attribution principle* for attributing the profits to the PE.
(3) The *independent enterprise principle* and the *arm's length principle*, limiting the source state tax jurisdiction.

3.3.1 The PE Principle

The PE-related regulations are not new and they can be traced back to the late eighteenth century in the tax treaty between Austria-Hungary and Prussia.[313] However, it was only due to a prodigal growth in cross-border activities after World War I that the

312. *Royal Bank of Canada* (n. 311).
313. M. Kobetsky, 'History of Tax Treaties and the Permanent Establishment Concept', in *International Taxation of Permanent Establishments: Principles and Policy* 106-151 (CUP 2011).

peril of double taxation, which could arise from situations in which countries wanted to tax such transactions and severely hamper international trade development, engaged the attention of international tax scholars and led the League of Nations to develop the PE concept in the late 1920s. The work performed at the time was mainly based on the fact that countries had an interest in avoiding impediments to their trading relationships.[314] In many treaties, it was also recognised that each state could claim a share of the taxes generated by international trading practices.[315] Rules continued to evolve over the years, which finally resulted in framing of Article 5 of the 2014 version of the OECD Model Tax Convention.[316] The UN Model uses the OECD Model as a basis to define the status of PEs, albeit it introduces some amendments to the OECD texts.

The OECD Model and the UN Model both clearly give taxing rights in respect of business profits of an enterprise of a contracting state to that state unless the enterprise carries on business in the other contracting state through a PE situated therein. If the enterprise carries on business as aforesaid, the profits that are attributable to the PE may be taxed in that other state. This is called the PE principle.

3.3.1.1 The PE Concept: Fixed Place of Business PE

The definition of the term 'PE' envisages a fixed place of business in the OECD Model,[317] which seems to suggest the notion of a physical presence, which primarily has three requirements:

(1) there must be a place of business;
(2) the place of business must be fixed i.e., established at distinct place, with a certain degree of permanence; and
(3) the business of the enterprise must be, wholly or partly, carried on through that place of business.

The UN Model is based on the OECD Model and embodies similar rules in the context of the fixed place of business PE,[318] even though it introduces certain new

314. L Friedlander and S Wilkie, 'Policy Forum – The History of Tax Treaty Provisions and Why It is Important to Know About It' (2006) 54 Canadian Tax J 4.
315. J-F Dutriez, 'Attribution of Profits to a Permanent Establishment of a Company Engaged Online Sales of Goods through a Local Warehouse' (2018) vol. 25(3) Int'l TP Journal 185, 185.
316. The OECD Model Tax Convention (the version before 2010) reads as follows: 'The profits of an enterprise of a Contracting State shall be taxable only in that State unless the enterprise carries on business in the other Contracting State through a permanent establishment situated therein. If the enterprise carries on business as aforesaid, the profits of the enterprise may be taxed in the other State but only so much of them as is attributable to that permanent establishment.' *See* OECD, *Model Tax Convention on Income and on Capital* (Condensed version, OECD Pub 2008), Art. 7 para. 1 (hereafter 'OECD MTC (2008)').
317. OECD MTC (2017) (n. 290) Art. 5 para. 1.
318. UN MTC (2017) (n. 292) Art. 5 para. 1.

parameters in the PE concept with a view to lowering the minimum threshold for source state taxation of business profits.[319]

It is, however, noteworthy here that even the OECD Commentary proceeds to clarify that there is no requirement of existence of any premises and a certain amount of space at its disposal will also fulfil the requirement of a PE.[320] A place of business may thus be constituted by a pitch in a market place, or by a certain permanently used area in a customs depot (e.g., for the storage of dutiable goods).[321] Even a place of business, situated in the business facilities of another enterprise, will also constitute a PE, for instance, in a case where the foreign enterprise has at its constant disposal certain premises or a part thereof owned by the other enterprise.[322] An illustration of this is the Belgian case,[323] where the Brussels Court of Appeal held that a German resident engaged in the transportation of vehicles had a PE in Belgium as he had a space of 3 m by 6 m at his disposal on the premises of his principal supplier in Belgium, together with telephone and telex, where he and four of his staff members worked. Also, there is no requirement of a formal legal right to use the place and a PE can exist, for instance, in a case where an enterprise illegally occupies a certain location where it carries on its business.[324]

3.3.1.2 Concept of 'Fixed'

The OECD further considers that in order to be 'fixed', there must exist a link between business place and a specific geographical point situated in the territory of a state.[325] For example, a satellite cannot create a PE, as under the extant rules of international law, its location cannot be considered to be at a specific geographical point in the territory of a state.[326] Further, the area where the satellite signals are received cannot be said to be at the disposal of the satellite operator so as to constitute a fixed place PE.[327] This does not, however, mean that the equipment constituting the place of business has to be actually fixed to the soil on which it stands.[328] It is enough that the equipment remains on a particular site.[329] The notion of permanence is intended to exclude places of business which are 'purely temporary in nature.'[330]

319. *See, for more information,* UN Committee of Experts on International Cooperation in Tax Matters, E/C.18/2017/CRP.7 *Proposed Base Erosion and Profit Shifting Related Changes to the UN Model Double Tax Convention Between Developed and Developing Countries*, 3-37, https://www.un.org/development/desa/financing/document/proposed-base-erosion-and-profit-shifting-related-changes-united-nations-model-double accessed 3 January 2021.
320. OECD MTC (2017) (n. 290) Commentary para. 1 of Art. 5(1) para. 10.
321. *Ibid.*
322. *Ibid.*
323. *Cour de Cassation* of 15 February 1980 (1980) J1. De Droit Fiscal 321.
324. OECD MTC (2017) (n. 290) Commentary para. 1 of Art. 5(1) para. 11.
325. *Ibid.*, para. 21.
326. *Ibid.*, para. 27.
327. *Ibid.*, para. 27.
328. *Ibid.*, para. 21.
329. *Ibid.*
330. *Ibid.*, para. 28.

3.3.1.3 PE for Short Period

This rule, however, does not require a rigid construction and the Commentary clarifies that a place of business may constitute a PE, even though it exists for a very short period of time, looking to the nature of business which is such that it will only be carried on for that short period of time.[331] For example, assume that an individual, resident in state A, decides to buy a stock of customised clothes to sell at a fair taking place in state B. This fair only lasts for a period of four months. Because of the nature of the business (selling of a stock of clothes at a fair), the activity has short duration, but it is fully carried on in state B. Therefore, the fair stall could constitute a PE.[332] In a Canadian case, a stand at a trade fair, occupied regularly for three weeks a year, through which the enterprise obtained contracts for a significant part of its annual sales, has also been held to constitute a PE.[333] In the Hotel Manager case of Germany,[334] the *Bundesfinanzhof* held that a UK hotel management company had a PE in Germany when it entered into a twenty-year contract to supply a general manager to a firm, running a hotel. According to the Court, the general manager's office constituted a PE (and not the entire hotel) as the UK company had a secured right to use this office for the purposes of the agreement.

3.3.1.4 Intermittent or Incidental Use of Home Office

Further, the revised commentary also spells out that an intermittent or incidental use of the home office of an employee for carrying out the enterprise's business cannot constitute a fixed place PE, but if it is used on a continuous basis for carrying out the enterprise's business in the circumstances, where the nature of employment required an office, it will form a fixed place PE.[335]

3.3.1.5 Slackening of Physical Presence Barriers

It may, thus, be noted that a certain degree of physical presence associated with the definition of PE in the OECD Model constitutes the common refrain of the OECD treaty structure which has the support of the theorists of residence taxation. However, the Commentaries, over the years, have modified the rigours of these rules as any rigid construction lacks a general consensus in this regard to the extent that even the OECD countries have underplayed this physical presence paradigm many a times and there has been an increasing focus on the economic linkages in the determination of PE, based on the core functions performed in the source state. In *Toronto Blue Jays Baseball Club and Another v Ontario (Minister of Finance)*,[336] for example, an Ontario Court

331. *Ibid.*, para. 18.
332. Rohatgi (n. 283) 139.
333. *Joseph Fowler v MNR* (1990) 90 DTC 1834 (Tax Court of Canada).
334. Bundesfinanzhof, 3 February 1993, IR 80-81/91, IStR, p. 226 (1993) BStBl., II, 462.
335. OECD MTC (2017) (n. 290) Commentary para. 1 of Art. 5(1), para. 18.
336. (15 February 2005) Docket: C41861, Ontario Court of Appeal (2005) 7 ITLR 591.

rejected the contention to treat lockers as a PE, which were used by the sportsmen in 'away' games, played outside Ontario, as none of the vital functions of sports businesses, i.e., the making of contracts, the selling of tickets, the licensing of concessions, the negotiation of sponsorships and advertising or the sale of media rights, were carried on there. This core function test enunciated by the Ontario Court was a manifestation of a growing emphasis on the economic allegiance in the context of taxing rights of the states.

A similar trend was noticed in *Universal Furniture Ind AB,*[337] where a Swedish company employed a Norwegian salesman, who operated one day per week from his home and spent the rest of the week on the road soliciting orders. The company had no ownership rights over the salesman's home and neither did it pay him any expenses for use of his home as an office. The salesman used his home office for planning his itinerary of customer visits, making telephone calls and making business issues with his employer. These activities were held to constitute core activities of the taxpayer company and the home office was held to be a PE of the taxpayer company, with the result that profits arising from the contracts made as a result of the salesman's activities were taxable in Sweden.

However, in *Dudney,*[338] the Court of Appeal strangely did not consider the existence of a fixed place of business PE, where the US resident was contracted to provide services of staff training and installation of new systems to the Canadian clients and he carried out this work at the client's premises using the client's equipment. He was given access to the office accommodation during the client's normal business hours. The Court unfortunately got carried away by the use of client's office accommodation by the US resident and it did not consider the explanation given in the OECD Commentary that there is no requirement of a formal legal right to use that place and a PE can exist, for instance, in a case where an enterprise even illegally occupies a certain location where it carries on its business.[339] Even the factum of core activities, in respect of rendition of services, having been performed at the client's premise, was not considered by the Court of Appeal.

The *Dudney* approach was, therefore, rightly jettisoned by the South African Tax Court, on an identical set of facts, in a case[340] dealing with the South Africa-US treaty which is modelled on the OECD version. In this case, the US company was a consulting group with offices in ten countries, rendering advisory services to, *inter alia*, the airline industry. It signed a contract in South Africa to perform services for a local airline. It commenced its contract in February 2007 and the final phase ended in May 2008, a success fee being paid in 2009. The company was allocated space at the client's premises where it was provided exclusive use of the boardroom. The taxpayer's employees had access to these premises on week days and during working hours only. These employees did not spend all of their time in the boardroom but were required to

337. *Universal Furniture Ind AB v Government of Norway,* Case No. 99-00421A Stavanger Country Court 19 November 1999.
338. *R v Dudney* (20 January 2000) Docket: A-707-98, Court of Appeal, Canada (2000) 2 ITLR 627.
339. OECD MTC (2017) (n. 290) Commentary para. 1 of Art. 5(1), para. 11.
340. *AB LLC and BD Holdings LLC* v *SARS* (13276) [2015] ZATC 2 (15 May 2015).

work in other areas, for example, meeting with employees in other divisions. However, all of this work took place within the same geographical premises. The aggregate fees paid amounted to the equivalent of approximately USD 8.5 million. The South African Revenue Service (SARS) raised assessments for the fees earned in 2007, 2008 and 2009, to which the company unsuccessfully lodged objection. The company argued that it was not liable for tax in South Africa, as it did not carry on business through a PE in South Africa. In this regard it relied on Article 5 of the South Africa-US Income Tax Treaty (1997). The company also sought to rely on the *Dudney*. Rejecting the arguments, the Tax Court held that such a PE did, indeed, exist in the present circumstances, observing that the company had a presence in the client's boardroom throughout its stay in South Africa and that it had exclusive use of the space for the entire duration of the contract. Vally J put it, thus:

> To put it differently, it had at its disposal constant access to the boardroom during working hours. Access during nonworking hours was neither necessary nor requested. This flows directly from the fact that compliance with its obligations in terms of the contract required regular intensive interaction with employees of [the South African customer], which, it goes without saying, was most suitable during normal working hours.[341]

In *McDermott Industries (Aust) Pty Ltd*,[342] the Full Federal Court ruled that there was a deemed PE in Australia because the Singapore company used the barge equipment in Australia, even though there were no employees of the Singapore company in Australia.

In a South Korean case,[343] a Philippines tax resident company (i.e., junket operator) was engaged by a South Korea casino operator to bring in overseas high rollers to play at the casino. Some employees of the Philippines company provided guidance to the high rollers and exchanged casino tokens in an office forming part of the casino. The Korean tax authorities took the view that the activities performed by the Philippines company at the casino would create a PE, and imposed corporate income tax and value-added tax (VAT) on the basis that all income should be attributable to the PE. The Supreme Court held that the activities performed by the Philippines company in an office forming part of the casino constituted a PE in South Korea. However, the Court also clarified the number of profits attributable to the PE should be assessed under a functional analysis.

3.3.1.6 Indian Law and Treaty Practices

The concept of PE in India has been historically evaluated in the context of the business connection principle enshrined in Indian domestic law which is generally used to interpret the provisions of tax treaties to assert the existence of a PE.[344] Section 9 of the

341. *Ibid.*, para. 42.
342. *McDermott Industries (Aust) Pty Ltd v CTC of Australia* [2005] FCAFC 67.
343. Judgment dated 25 June 2020 in Case 2017Du72935 (Supreme Court of South Korea).
344. L Oats, A Miller and E Mulligan, *Principles of International Taxation* (6th edn, Bloomsbury 2017) 286.

Income Tax Act 1961 provides that income from any business connections in India is deemed to arise in India. This is so irrespective of whether income actually arises in India. Where profits arise partly in India and partly abroad, Indian tax jurisdiction will be limited to an amount that is 'reasonably attributable' to the business operations carried out in India.[345] Thus, a concept of a fixed place of business has never been an essential element in the existence of a PE under the Indian legislation and this aspect of law was re-asserted vide an amendment introduced by the Finance Act 2002 which inserted clause (iiia) in section 92F of the Act, clarifying that PE includes a fixed place of business. Thus, a fixed place of business is one of the components of PE, but the concept of existence of business connection goes beyond that.

The emerging international trends in the context of determination of a PE are visible in Indian treaty practices as well, which are often more influenced by the UN Model and the principles of domestic law relating to business connection which is often 'used to interpret the provisions of treaties so as to assert the existence of a PE'.[346]

In *Rolls Royce Plc,*[347] Rolls Royce, a UK resident company had a subsidiary tax resident company in India. The Indian company was paid for supplying marketing and support services, including organisation of conferences and air shows, media relations, market research, press monitoring, identifying market opportunities for the UK company, arranging discussions between it and current and potential customers and suppliers and various types of administrative and technical support. The UK company argued that these services were merely preparatory or auxiliary and thus did not constitute a PE. The Delhi Bench of ITAT, however, noted that its major customer, Indian Air Force was told to send request for quotation to Indian company which screened it and forwarded it to the UK company. The correspondence of the company also showed that the Indian company took an active role in soliciting the orders and liaising with the customers. The Tribunal, accordingly, held that under Indian domestic law, there was a 'business connection.'[348] Regarding the question as to whether the taxpayer had a PE in India within the meaning of Article 5(1), 5(2)(f) and 5(4) of the Indo-UK DTAA, it was noted that the Indian subsidiary had an office in India at DLF Centre, New Delhi and all the cost incurred by it in the provision of the support services, including salaries and expenses of employees, the cost of operating office premises and any payment to sub-contractors, was reimbursed by the UK company and the Indian company was to receive service fees at a determined percentage of the reimbursed expenses. The employees of the UK Company visited India frequently and the DLF premises were being occupied and used during such visits. In view of these facts, the UK Company was held to have a fixed place PE in India. The following observations of the Tribunal are noteworthy:

> 20 The term 'place of business' covers any premises, facilities or installations used for carrying on the business of the enterprise whether or not they are

345. There is no statutory definition of 'reasonably attributable'. Profits of a PE are determined by reference to the branch accounts. These must be kept as if the PE were an Indian company.
346. Oats, Miller and Mulligan (n. 344) 286.
347. *Rolls Royce Plc v DDIT* [2008] 19 SOT 42 (Delhi).
348. *Ibid.*, para. 19.

used exclusively for that purpose. A place of business may also exist where no premises are available or required for carrying on the business of the enterprise and it simply has a certain amount of space at its disposal. It is immaterial whether the premises, facilities or installations are owned or rented by or are otherwise at the disposal of the enterprise. A place of business may thus be constituted by a pitch in a market place. Again, the place of business may be situated in the business facilities of another enterprise. This may be the case for instance where the foreign enterprise has at its constant disposal certain premises or a part thereon owned by the other enterprise.

21 As noted above, the mere fact that an enterprise has a certain amount of space at its disposal which is used for business activities is sufficient to constitute a place of business. No formal legal right to use that place is, therefore, required. Thus, for instance, a permanent establishment could exist where an enterprise illegally occupied a certain location where it carried on its business. Article 5(1) does not refer that the premises should belong to the assessee but if it is able to use the same, it is an identified and distinct location and on which he exercises the control, it will be considered as a PE within the meaning of Article 5(1) of the treaty. In the present case, we have found that the premises though in the name of RRIL are being occupied for the business operation in India. The cost of maintenance of such premises are [sic] being paid for by the appellant. The premises are also available to all the employees of appellant in respect of any business operations in India. Accordingly, it can be said that the appellant has a PE in India within the meaning of Article 5(1) of the treaty.

3.3.1.6.1 Virtual Projection Test

The Indian Supreme Court in a recent judgment in Formula One Championship Ltd,[349] had an occasion to deal with the concept of a fixed place PE. In this case, the taxpayer, Formula One World Championship Limited (FOWC), a UK tax resident, acquired commercial rights in the F1 Championships held all across the world for a period of one-hundred years. In India, FOWC entered into a race promotion contract with Jaypee Sports International Limited (Jaypee), which gave Jaypee the right to host, stage and promote the Formula One Grand Prix racing event in India for a payment to FOWC. The basic issue before the Court was whether FOWC had a PE under the India-UK Double Taxation Avoidance Agreements (DTAA) so as to render the amounts received by FOWC from Jaypee taxable in India. The Court while referring to the definition of PE provided under Article 5 of the DTAA, held that FOWC had a fixed place PE in India for two main reasons: *First*, FOWC was the exclusive commercial rights holder in relation to F1 Championships and was exploiting such commercial rights in India, which resulted in the presence of its business in India. These rights, among others, included the right to host, stage and promote F1 Championship events, as well as exclusive media rights.[350] *Second*, Jaypee's capacity to act was extremely restricted during the event and it was FOWC which played a dominant role in conducting the F1 Championship racing event in India. Accordingly, FOWC had the right to use and control over,

349. *Formula One Championship Ltd v CIT* [2017] 80 taxmann.com 347 (SC).
350. *Ibid.*, para. 73.

the Buddh International Circuit.[351] Relying on the virtual projection test laid down by the Andhra Pradesh High Court in *Visakhapatnam Port Trust,*[352] the Court held that not only the Buddh International Circuit was a fixed place where the commercial/economic activity of conducting F-1 Championship was carried out, 'one could clearly discern that it was a virtual projection of the foreign enterprise, namely, Formula-1 (i.e. FOWC) on the soil of this country.'[353] The Court also observed that the time period was not a significant consideration, given the kind of business activity involved in the instant case – i.e. racing and the exploitation of all the rights FOWC had as commercial rights holder.[354] However, the presence of FOWC was 'fixed' under Article 5(1) of the DTAA, as it had exclusive access to the event for the whole period of the event (including time preceding and succeeding the event). Also, the five-year contract with Jaypee indicated repetition.[355] Accordingly, it was held that FOWC had control over the circuit which constituted its fixed place of business.

In *E-Funds IT Solutions Inc,*[356] however, the Indian Supreme Court contradicted itself by holding that e-Fund India was a separate entity, entitled to provide services to the US parent company and it would not become location PE under Article 5(1) merely because there was interaction or cross transactions between the Indian subsidiary and the foreign Principal under Article 5(1). The Court further held that even if the foreign entities had saved and reduced their expenditure by transferring business or back office operations to the Indian subsidiary, it would not by itself create a fixed place or location PE. This reasoning is clearly in teeth of the virtual projection test reiterated by the Apex Court in *Formula One.*[357] In this case, the Indian subsidiary was clearly a virtual projection of its parent inasmuch as the US companies were rendering different types of management and support services to customers located outside India and the Indian subsidiary was rendering support services which, in turn, enabled the US parent to render services to their clients abroad. Further, the Court moved on the erroneous assumption in this case that the concept of PE is not included in the Indian statute. This judgment, therefore, does not lay down correct law and is clearly distinguishable from *Morgan Stanley & Co,*[358] where the Indian subsidiary was merely providing back office support for its US parent. In this case, however, it was not transfer of mere back office operations as the US parent was essentially doing marketing work only and its contracts of marketing work with its clients were assigned, or sub-contracted to its subsidiary eFunds India as mentioned in its Transfer Pricing (TP) report. The TP report of the taxpayer also stated that the President of the US parent managed the operations of eFunds India and other entities of the group in the UK and Australia. The employees of these entities reported to the President and the President's overall reporting was to

351. *Ibid.*, para. 74.
352. *CIT v Visakhapatnam Port Trust* (1983) 144 ITR 146 (AP).
353. *Formula One* (n. 349), para. 76.
354. *Ibid.*, para. 70.
355. *Ibid.*
356. *ADIT v E-Funds IT Solutions Inc* [2017] 86 taxmann.com 240 (SC).
357. At (n. 349).
358. *DIT v Morgan Stanley & Co* [2007] 292 ITR 416 (SC).

the US parent. Thus, eFunds India was hit by the virtual projection test explained in *Formula One*.[359]

Similarly, in *Samsung Heavy Industries Co Ltd*,[360] the Supreme Court did not consider the Mumbai project office of the South Korean Company (Samsung) as PE, even though it was specifically opened after the approval of the Reserve Bank of India (RBI) for coordination and execution of Vasai East Development Project for Oil and Natural Gas Corporation Ltd (ONGC). The Supreme Court held that this project office was established merely to coordinate and execute delivery of documents in connection with construction of offshore platform modification of existing facility of ONGC. However, in this case, the Court seems to have misread the board's resolution of the company, paragraph 2 of which clearly stated that it was the appointment of the general manager, which was for two purposes: *first*, establishing a project office and *second*, coordinating and executing delivery of documents in connection with construction of offshore platform modification of existing facilities. Thus, it was the office of the general manager, and not the project office, which was established to coordinate and execute delivery documents in connection with construction of offshore platform modification of existing facilities. The opening of project office was essentially meant for coordinating and executing the entire ONGC contract for carrying out the 'work', *inter alia*, of surveys, design, engineering, procurement, fabrication, installation and modification at existing facilities, and start-up and commissioning of entire facilities covered under the 'Vasai East Development Project' and this was not noticed by the Court which clearly established the fact of the taxpayer's business being carried through a fixed place in India. Thus, the Mumbai project office was a virtual projection of Samsung through which it carried out its business of installation and modification, start-up and commissioning of entire facilities covered under the 'Vasai East Development Project' in India. The judgment, therefore, was based on erroneous assumption that the project office was merely meant to coordinate and execute delivery documents in connection with construction of offshore platform modification of existing facilities.

In *Nokia Networks OY*,[361] where a Finland company, Nokia Networks OY (Nokia) sold global system for mobile communications (GSM) equipment manufactured by it to Indian telecom operators. Apart from supply of the equipment, there were also installation contracts and for this purpose of installation activity and other connected activities, Nokia had established a Liaison Office (LO) in 1994. Two such agreements were signed in 1995 between Nokia (through the LO) and Indian Cellular Operators *viz*., Modi Telstra India Ltd and Skycell Communication Ltd. These contracts were signed by Nokia during the period when there was a LO of Nokia in India. Later on, a wholly owned subsidiary, Nokia India Private Limited (NIPL) was incorporated on 23 May 1995 and all the contracts for installation were either assigned or separately entered by the NIPL with the customers. Marketing Support Agreement was also entered in the year 1996 and 1997 between Nokia and NIPL for providing marketing services to it for which NIPL was compensated with cost plus mark-up. The Indian

359. *Formula One* (n. 349).
360. *DIT v Samsung Heavy Industries Co Ltd* [2020] 117 taxmann.com 870 (SC).
361. *Nokia Networks OY v JCIT* [2018] 94 taxmann.com 111 (Del-Trib) (SB).

subsidiary also entered into technical support agreement with customers. The question arose whether the Indian subsidiary constituted a PE of Nokia so as to attribute an additional profit from the GSM equipment to it. The majority view decided against the existence of PE and held that the provision of telephone facts and conveyance services provided by the Indian subsidiary to the employees of Nokia did not make the offices of Indian subsidiary at the disposal of the former. The correctness of the majority decision is suspect and the minority view appears to be more aligned with the virtual projection principle, affirmed in *Formula One*.[362] Thus, when a subsidiary company survive for carrying on its business activities of its parent or is entirely connected with and dependent on the business of its parents, then the subsidiary would become merely an alter-ego or a virtual projection of its parent and consequently it must be treated as a PE of the non-resident parent, as rightly pointed out in the dissenting opinion. The following observations of Pramod Kumar, the dissenting Tribunal Member, are quite illuminating:[363]

> 39. 'The Law & Practice of Tax Treaties - An Indian Perspective' by Nilesh Modi (Second Edition, 2014; ISBN-13: 978-81-8473-531-4; at page 447), refers to, what it considers to be, 'true test for constitution of a PE' by the subsidiary, in respect of a foreign company, as 'whether:
> - The business of the foreign enterprise is carried out by its local affiliate; or
> - The local affiliate is the *alter ego* of the foreign enterprise or, speaks his masters voice only or, is a mere façade; or
> - The foreign enterprise carries on a business in State S, using the premises or personnel, of its local subsidiary.'
>
> 39A. The reference to '*alter ego*' of the foreign enterprise, as is used in Nilesh Modi's book, is more of a colloquial and factual expression rather than a legal term. This term is now also increasingly used in the tax literature worldwide.
>
> 39B. The expression '*alter ego* companies' seems to be rather appropriate expression for dealing with a particular type of subsidiaries which constitute PEs of the parent foreign enterprise, and that is how I intend to use it in this analysis. It does refer to the situations in which a subsidiary should be treated as a permanent establishment of its non-resident parent company for the reason that the way and manner in which carries out its business activities, it is nothing but an avatar of, a virtual projection of, or an extension of, its non-resident parent company in the country in which the subsidiary is domiciled.

Thus, the core business activities argument or the existence of income-generating activities in the state, which is the underlying logic of the virtual projection test, has become the mainstay of PE determination in the context of non-resident taxation in international tax law, which is a reassertion of the economic allegiance principle of the source rule jurisprudence.

In *FRS Hotel Group*,[364] an Indian Company (BAHDL) developed and owned a five Star deluxe hotel known as Swissotel Kolkata. It engaged a Luxembourg Company, *FRS Hotel Group (Lux) S.a.r.l. (FRS)*, to provide certain services in different phases of hotel

362. *Formula One* (n. 349).
363. *Nokia Networks OY* (n. 361).
364. *FRS Hotel Group (Lux) S.a.r.l., in re* [2018] 94 taxmann.com 23 (AAR - New Delhi).

development and operation so that the hotel property i.e., Swissotel Kolkata, can be developed and operated as per international standards similar to other Swissotel properties across the globe. For this purpose, various agreements were signed between BAHDL and FRS to provide services in connection with hotel management, such as establishing hotel standards and policies, sales and marketing centralised reservations etc. FRS sought advance ruling on the issue as to whether payments received by FRS from the BAHDL for provision of global reservation services ('GRS') would be chargeable to tax in India as 'Fees for Technical Services' or 'Royalty' under section 9(1)(vi)/9(1)(vii), read with provisions of Article 12 of India-Luxembourg treaty. The Authority for Advance Ruling of India (AAR) held that the Kolkata hotel constituted a fixed place PE, as the terms of the various agreements proved that the hotel was completely at the disposal of FRS. As per the agreements, FRS, at the very stage of inception, i.e., the construction of the hotel, was called upon to oversee the design and construction of the property to ensure that it is compliant with its brand standards and the Indian company was required to submit progress reports of construction to FRS, which was to then mark out the deficiencies as it deemed fit. Such deficiencies are to be rectified by the Indian Company in the designated period of three months. Once the hotel was constructed, its operation and management rested with FRS and the Indian Company had undertaken that it would not interfere in FRS' exercise of the exclusive authority over such operation and management. Right from the employment of the hotel staff (including the managerial personnel) to taking decisions over capital improvements, every possible operational right stood vested in FRS. The Indian Company was barred from even contacting directly any of the hotel staff. Some of the core functions of the operation of the hotel such as sales and marketing, reservation etc. have also been outsourced to FRS. FRS was also authorised to designate a suitable vendor who would supply goods and services for the operation and management of the hotel. With regard to these services as well, FRS was given complete autonomy with no interference from the owner. Thus, FRS, which was admittedly engaged in the business of operation and management of the hotels, had taken over all the important functions in relation to the operation and management of the Indian hotel. The AAR, accordingly, held that all the three requirements of a fixed Place PE, viz., existence of a fixed place, the fixed place being at the disposal of the non-resident and the non-resident carrying on its business (wholly or partly) through such fixed place, stood satisfied.

In *ULO Systems LLC,*[365] the taxpayer's equipment as well as personnel stationed on the vessel of main contractor for carrying out grouting, coupled with the fact that food and accommodation was made available to the personnel free of cost was, held to be a fixed place PE of the taxpayer.

The virtual projection principle, enunciated by the Indian Supreme Court, is not an abstract legal construct. It is firmly grounded in the developing tax policy landscape, which increasingly exhibits greater acceptance for the economic nexus rule for tax allocation. Article 5(7) of the OECD Model[366] instructs us that although a subsidiary company by itself will not constitute a PE of the parent company, the Commentary was

365. *ULO Systems LLC v DCIT* [2019] 105 taxmann.com 259 (Del-Trib).
366. OECD MTC 2017 (n. 290) Art. 5 para. 7.

updated in 2005 to clarify that if the parent company has space or premises belonging to the subsidiary at its disposal and carries on business through it, then the parent will have a PE.[367] The key question is: whose trade is being carried on at the subsidiary's premises? Is it solely the trade of the subsidiary of is the parent company also using them for its core activities?[368] In 2002, the Italian Supreme Court went to the extent of holding that the activities of a single subsidiary company could constitute as a PE for several non-resident fellow subsidiaries.[369] The OECD thinktank reacted sharply to this ruling and introduced a clarification in 2005 in the Commentary to the effect that the determination of existence of a PE must be done separately for each company of the group and not for the group as whole.[370]

This emerging nexus doctrine, which tends to undermine physical presence and focus more on economic connection, becomes far more pronounced in the other stipulations laid down in the UN Model, which display a considerable divergence in what constitutes a PE. *Assembly activities, duration of projects, furnishing of services, insurance business* and *agent sales* are among the most contentious issues. The OECD Model has generally stricter rules for their recognition as a PE as illustrated in the discussion following hereafter.

3.3.1.7 Building Sites: Construction PE

The general definition of PE in connection with building and construction activities, as envisaged in the 1963 draft[371] was made more certain by incorporating a special rule to cover this type of activity in the OECD Model in 1977,[372] which continues to hold the field since then. This rule provides that a building site or construction or installation project constitutes a PE only if it lasts more than twelve months. However, there is no specific definition of their term 'building site or construction or installation project' in the Model. The question of definition is, however, partially addressed by the Commentary, which explains that the term 'building site or construction project' includes the construction or renovation of buildings, roads, bridges or canals, the laying of pipelines, and excavating and dredging.[373] The only limitation imposed is that such activities must involve more than mere maintenance or redecoration.[374] On the other hand, the term 'installation project' should not necessarily be restricted to mean an installation related to construction project, as it also includes the installation of new

367. The 2005 Update to the Model Tax Convention: Public Discussion Draft dated 15 March 2004, https://www.oecd.org/ctp/treaties/34576874.pdf, accessed 3 January 2021.
368. Oats, Miller and Mulligan (n. 344) 258.
369. Supreme Court judgments 3367, 3368, and 3369 of 7 March 2002; 431926 of 26 March 2002; 7682 and 7689 of 25 May 2002; 10925 of 22 September 2002; and 17373 of 6 December 2002.
370. OECD, *Model Tax Convention on Income and on Capital* (Condensed version, OECD Pub 2005) Commentary on Art. 5 paras 41.1-42 (hereafter 'OECD MTC (2005)'). This is retained in OECD MTC (2017) (n. 290) para. 117.
371. OECD Model Draft (1963) Art. 5(2)(g).
372. OECD, Model Double Tax Convention on Income and on Capital (OECD Pub 1977) Art. 5(3) (hereafter 'OECD MTC (1977)').
373. OECD MTC (2017) (n. 290) Commentary Art. 5(3) para. 50.
374. *Ibid.*

equipment in existing buildings or even outdoors (i.e., unconnected to any building).[375]

The UN Model makes two significant departures: *first*, it includes, unlike the OECD Model, supervisory services in its definition of a construction PE.[376] *Second*, it lays down a six-month duration test[377] for building sites (as compared to twelve months in the OECD Model.[378] The reason for including supervisory services is that they are unequivocally covered by the construction PE provisions, rather than by the general 'fixed place of business' provisions. A subcontractor, therefore, supplying supervisory services to a construction or installation site would not need a fixed place of business to have a PE but would need to be present in the other contracting state for the minimum specified period of six months. A PE may arise even if an enterprise has no physical presence in the state where the construction or installation takes place.

The UN position was noted by the OECD later and the revised OECD Commentary added that on-site planning and supervisory activities of the erection of a building are also covered.[379] However, it was left to the states to include them specifically in their bilateral treaties. This is the result of a substantial change introduced in 2003 in the Commentary on Article 5 of the OECD Model. The previous version provided that planning and supervision of the erection of a building are covered by this term, if carried out by the building contractor and not by another enterprise whose activities in connection with the construction concerned are restricted to planning and supervising the work.[380]

The temporal test of twelve and six months provided in the OECD and the UN Models respectively underlines the fact that a PE may still arise even if an enterprise has no physical presence in the state where construction or installation takes place. Generally, these tests apply to each individual site or project separately.[381] The time previously spent by the same contractor on other sites or projects which are totally unconnected with the present site or project cannot, however, be included.[382] Further, a site or project should be regarded as a single unit even where it is based on several contracts, even concluded with different persons, provided it forms a coherent whole, both commercially and geographically.[383] A building site would, thus, form a single unit even if the orders are placed by several persons, if it forms a coherent whole in terms of the proviso, a row of houses, for instance.[384] Likewise, if the contractor's activity has to be relocated as the project progresses, because of its intrinsic nature, for instance, roads or canals being constructed, waterways dredged, or pipelines laid, the activities performed at each place are parts of the same single project and must be

375. *Ibid.*
376. UN MTC (2017) (n. 292) Art. 5(3)(a).
377. *Ibid.*
378. OECD MTC (2017) (n. 290) Art. 5(3).
379. OECD MTC (2017) (n. 290) Commentary Art. 5(3) para. 50.
380. OECD, *Model Tax Convention on Income and on Capital* (Condensed version, OECD Pub 2000) Commentary Art. 5 para. 17 (hereafter 'OECD MTC (2000)').
381. OECD MTC (2017) (n. 290) Commentary Art. 5(3) para. 51.
382. *Ibid.*
383. *Ibid.*
384. *Ibid.*

regarded as a PE if, as a whole, it lasts more than twelve months.[385] Similarly, where parts of a substantial structure, for example an offshore platform, are assembled at various locations within a country and moved to another location within the country for final assembly, this is part of a single project.[386] A site does not cease to exist when the work is temporarily discontinued. Seasonal or other temporary interruptions should be included in determining the life of a site/project.[387]

A main contractor might subcontract the whole of a project to another enterprise and have no employees or on-site presence of its own. The period spent by a subcontractor working on the building site must be considered as time spent by the main contractor on that project. Thus, if the project exists beyond the time threshold stipulated in the treaty, the main contractor enterprise could find itself liable to taxation on the source principle on the net profits arising to it from the contract.[388]

Though the OECD has generally moved to shorter duration presence for PE purposes in its Commentary,[389] the approach has not been extended to building sites, where twelve-month presence is still required. This divergence in the time threshold appears to be a result of the residence taxation approach of the developed countries, which insists on a certain degree of physical presence for invoking the source jurisdiction. The source taxation theorists, however, view it differently because as long as the generation of income from an economic activity is sourced in a territory, the economic linkage for triggering taxation is established and it is unjustified to insist on a time threshold in the context of ensuring a physical presence. The bottom line, however, is that both the OECD and UN Models seek to aggregate 'connected projects' or 'commercially and geographically coherent projects' in measuring the breach of temporal threshold.

3.3.1.7.1 *Gradual Trend: The OECD 2002, 2011 Reports and BEPS Developments*

It may, thus, be noted here that there has been a gradual trend towards reducing the time threshold and diluting the physical presence barrier and focusing on the concept of economic allegiance. Miller and Oats seem to rightly argue that if the underlying rationale for seeking to tax part of the profits of a non-resident firm carrying out construction, assembly or installation services in a state is that the breaching of a time limit signifies that a debt of economic allegiance has arisen, then there seems little justification for applying such a time limit on a project-by-project basis.[390] A foreign enterprise carrying out a series of small projects within the source state, in respect of which the number of days that activities are carried out in the source state breaches the time limit, would also appear to owe a debt of economic allegiance.[391] The rationale for

385. *Ibid.*, para. 57.
386. *Ibid.*
387. *Ibid.*, para. 55.
388. *Ibid.*, para. 54.
389. *Ibid.*, Commentary on Art. 4, para. 6.
390. A Miller & L Oats, *Principles of International Taxation* (3rd edn, Bloomsbury 2012) 235.
391. *Ibid.*

applying the temporal threshold to the duration of a single construction project was, thus, unclear.

Some developing countries has been opposing the temporal thresholds altogether.[392] They base their opposition on three principal grounds: *first*, they maintain that construction, assembly and similar activities could, as a result of modern technology, be of very short duration and still result in a substantial profit for the enterprise; *second*, it is argued that a time limit could be used by foreign enterprises to set up artificial arrangements to avoid taxation in their territory; and *third*, and more fundamentally, they simply believe that the period during which foreign personnel remain in the source country is irrelevant to their right to tax the income (as it is in the case of artistes and sportspersons).

3.3.1.7.2 Judicial Approach to Measuring Time Limit

The same trend was visible in the court decisions as well. In *Gurtler, Herbert & Co Inc,*[393] for instance, the Court explained the legal position to the effect that the duration of various projects could be aggregated if the said projects were interconnected i.e., they were performed for the same customer in the same geographic area and that performing work in the same geographic area for unrelated customers will disentitle aggregation. In *Air Drilling,*[394] a French company carried on the activities of drilling holes in the seabed for oil and gas projects in different jurisdiction (including Spain) and each single project lasted for less than twelve months. The French Court held that the projects were 'commercially and geographically' a coherent whole and that the durations of projects can be aggregated for measuring the time limit. In *Turnkey Contracts,*[395] where a Swiss company performed several turnkey contracts in Germany, the German Federal Tax Court upheld the 'aggregate approach' and held that from a commercial point of view, the projects in Germany involved similar functions, were chronologically connected and, from a geographical point of view, were performed at the same site. In a Letter Ruling by the US IRS, drilling activities at various sites in the US were held to be commercially interconnected because the activities were under the same contract and there was a pre-determined contract price for all the drilling activities under that contract.[396] It was also held that the said drilling activities were also geographically interconnected because several units of a construction project were executed at different locations with relative proximity.

These issues have found considerable traction and influenced the treaty negotiations even by the countries following the OECD Model. Canada, for instance, agreed to the OECD-prescribed period only in seven of the treaties with middle-income countries.

392. UN MTC 2017, Commentary on Art. 5(3) (n. 292) 157 para. 10.
393. *Gurtler, Herbert & Co Inc v Municipality of Stavanger* Case No. 00-260A dated 18 September 1980 (Stanvanger byrett (Stavanger County Court)).
394. Conseil d'Etat (French Supreme Administrative Court) Case No. 16,905 dated 29 June 1981, *Droit Fiscal*, 33, 1, 111.
395. Germany, Bundesfinanzhof (Federal Fiscal Court), I R 99/97, 21 April 1999, *Bundessteuerblatt*, 1999, II, 694.
396. A Mehta, *Permanent Establishment in International Taxation* (Taxmann 2012) 226-227.

This time period was reduced for the other twelve treaties with middle-income countries. In case of treaties with low-income countries, the periods of fourteen treaties were reduced, ranging from a required three to nine months.[397] Canada, thus, tends to grant shorter periods in this part of the PE article if the country is a middle- or low-income country, thereby deviating from the OECD-suggested period of time for high-income countries.[398]

3.3.1.7.3 OECD Deliberations and Reports

These trends led to worrisome uncertainty in international tax jurisprudence. A concerned OECD deliberated these issues and came up with its 2002 Report related to the OECD Model Convention,[399] which was the first significant move in this direction. The report declared that it is the project as a whole that must be considered in the context of construction and installation. Thus, constructing, for example, an oil platform at different locations within a state and then installing one at a further location within that state would constitute a single project within that state for determining the temporal threshold. The OECD 2011 Report[400] bolstered this trend further, recommending that the Commentary should make it clear that an enterprise which subcontracts an entire construction or installation project would have a construction PE in the same way as if the construction services had been supplied by its own staff. It would, thus, be possible for an enterprise to have a construction PE without any of its own staff having been physically present in the host state, provided that the activities of the subcontractor were such that a PE arose according to the usual tests of fixed space of business and minimum time period. If the subcontractor firm itself is resident outside the state where the construction site is located, then the subcontractor firm could also have a PE in the construction site state.

3.3.1.7.4 BEPS Action 7 and Multilateral Instruments

The BEPS Action 7 Discussion Draft[401] comprehensively addressed the issue of artificial splitting of contracts in order to avoid having a construction site for more than twelve months. A non-resident construction enterprise might divide up the construction projects between separate group companies and contend that it had two separate projects in a state, each existing for less than twelve months and so there was no PE.

397. K Brooks, 'Canada's Evolving Tax Treaty Policy Toward Low-Income Countries' in AJ Cockfield (ed.), *Globalization and The Impact of Tax on International Investments* (Toronto 2009) 7.

398. *Ibid.*

399. OECD, 'Issues in International Taxation' in *2002 Reports Related to the OECD Model Tax Convention* No. 8 (OECD Pub 2003) 92 paras 59, 60.

400. OECD Centre For Tax Policy and Administration, 'Interpretation and Application of Article 5 (Permanent Establishment) of the OECD Model Tax Convention' (OECD Pub 2011) 21, para. 48.

401. OECD's New Discussion Draft on Action 7: Prevent the Artificial Avoidance of PE Status (OECD Pub 2015) 34 para. 47.

The Final Report on Action 7[402] laid down 'the principal purposes test', which barred any benefit under the Convention in respect of any income or capital, if the obtaining of that benefit was one of the principal purposes of any arrangement or transaction. The benefit, however, shall still be available, if the granting of the benefit itself is found to be in accordance with the object and purposes of the Convention. This is set out in Article 7 of the Multilateral Instrument.[403] Article 14 of the MLI offers another option, which the countries may include in their treaties for the purpose of aggregation of period of different contracts. According to this option, the aggregation will be permissible if two conditions are satisfied:

(1) The enterprise must carry on its relevant activities in source country for a period exceeding thirty days in aggregate but less than the prescribed days in the applicable DTA.
(2) Connected activities are carried on at different times by one or more of closely related enterprises at the same project site or any other place identified in that Comprehensive Tax Agreement (CTA) for a period exceeding thirty days.

The OECD Model was also accordingly revised to incorporate a specific rule to deal this kind of tax planning, according to which if two enterprises are 'closely related' and carry on connected activities at the same building/construction/installation site during different periods of time, each lasting between thirty days and twelve months, then the various time periods will be taken together to decide the breach of temporal threshold.[404] However, the OECD rule still fell short of including connected activities at different places for the purpose of aggregation. The expression commercial and geographical coherence, on the other hand, has a much wider connotation. Gelineck explains that geographical coherence means that operations must take place within either a single place or a limited area if the business is of a mobile nature. There is no specific requirement with regard to the size of this area and, therefore, it should be determined on a case-by-case basis.[405] Commercial coherence takes into consideration the customers of the business. If many different customers are served in a small geographical area, the commercial test may not be met. On the other hand, if a business has one customer in many different geographical areas in the same state, the commercial coherence test might be met, but not the geographical test.[406] 'Connected activities', viz., whether contracts are with the same persons or related persons; whether the additional contracts with a person is a logical consequence of a previous contract concluded with that person or related persons; whether a single contract could cover all

402. OECD, *Preventing the Artificial Avoidance of Permanent Establishment Status, Action 7 — 2015 Final Report, OECD/G20 Base Erosion and Profit Shifting Project* (OECD Pub 2015) 42 section C para. 17 (hereafter 'BEPS Action 7 Final Report 2015').
403. Multilateral Convention to Implement Tax Treaty Related Measures to Prevent Base Erosion and Profit Shifting (hereafter 'the MLI') Art. 7.
404. OECD MTC (2017) (n. 290) Art. 5 para. 4.1.
405. MS Gelineck, 'Permanent Establishments and the Offshore Oil and Gas Industry – Part 1' (2016) vol. 70(4) BIT 206, 210.
406. *Ibid.*

the activities in the absence of tax planning; whether the nature of work shows same or similar activities; or whether the same employees are working on the different contracts.[407]

3.3.1.7.5 Indian Domestic Law and Treaty Practices

India, being one of the largest developing countries invariably opts for a shorter period in its treaties, ranging from ninety-one days to six months,[408] for a building site, a construction, assembly or installation project or supervisory activities in connection therewith to be recognised as a PE. As noted in the OECD Commentary, India has reserved the right to replace the phrase 'construction or installation project' with the phrase 'construction, installation or assembly project or supervisory activities' in connection therewith and also the right to negotiate the temporal threshold.[409] In doing so, India has aligned itself with the UN Model, which describes a construction PE as a 'building site, a construction, assembly or installation project or supervisory activities in connection therewith … .'

3.3.1.7.6 Implication of 'In Connection Therewith'

It may however be noted here that while interpreting the phrase 'building site, a construction, assembly or installation project or supervisory activities in connection therewith' in the context of India-USA Treaty,[410] the Delhi Bench of the ITAT, in *Aspect Software Inc v DCIT*,[411] came to hold that the term 'in connection therewith' appearing in the treaty would apply to the entire preceding words *viz.*, a 'building site or construction, installation or assembly project or supervisory activities' and that the term installation project cannot be read *dehors* the words accompanying it. Thus, according to the Tribunal, the installation project should be in connection with the building site or construction in order to constitute a PE. This interpretation, however, does not appear to be correct for the simple reason that both OECD and the UN Commentaries bar such a construction. The OECD Commentary clearly lays down that the term 'installation project' should not necessarily be restricted to mean an installation related to construction project, as it also includes the installation of new equipment in existing building or even outdoors (i.e., unconnected to any building).[412] The UN Commentaries also incorporate this rule in paragraph 15.[413] Thus, it is clear that an 'installation project' does not need to be in connection with building site or construction. It may be noted that the OECD Model does not consider the supervisory activities

407. OECD MTC (2017) (n. 290) Commentary on Art. 5(3) para. 53.
408. Except India-Russian Treaty, where a twelve-month period is stipulated. *See* India-Russia Treaty, Art. 5(2)(j).
409. OECD MTC (2017) (n. 290) Position on Art. 5 (Permanent Establishment) and its Commentary, para. 11.1.
410. India-USA Treaty, Art. 5(2)(k).
411. [2020] 117 taxmann.com 610 (Del-Trib).
412. *Ibid.*
413. UN MTC (2017) (n. 292) Commentaries to Art. 5 para. 15.

for the purposes of construction PE, which were included in the UN Model and the phrase 'in connection therewith' has been incorporated to specifically clarify that the supervisory activities in question must necessarily be in connection with a 'building site or construction, installation or assembly project. *Aspect Software Inc*, therefore, was not correctly decided.

In respect of services,[414] furnished within a contracting state by an enterprise through employees or other personnel, India generally prefers a much lower PE threshold in its treaties, i.e. the continuance of these activities within the state for a period or periods aggregating more than ninety days within any twelve-month period or the performance of the services within that state for a related enterprise (associated enterprise).[415] Even the recent changes in the some of the treaties are on the same lines.[416]

Further, it is not necessary that the project site must belong to the provider of supervisory services. In *Steel Authority of India Ltd*,[417] the Indian company entered into a contract of technical supervision services with a German company, for erection of certain machinery in India. The Delhi Bench of ITAT repelled the contention that since the project site did not belong to the German company, the supervisory services cannot be taxed in India in terms of Article 5(2)(i) of the India-Germany treaty. It was, accordingly, held that since the duration of supervision services exceeded six months, the German company had a PE in India and it was not necessary that the provider of services must have control and dominion over the project site.

The construction PE clauses in some of the Indian treaties specifically provide that for determining the existence of a construction PE, the work carried out in India by a foreign enterprise for various projects had to be viewed on aggregate basis without double counting of the days when the work was done on more than one project on the same day.[418] However in the cases where the treaty does not specifically mentions aggregation, a view has been taken in some of the judicial decisions that the aggregation of contracts cannot be resorted to in measuring the time limit.[419] This view does not take into consideration the emerging jurisprudence which focuses on the concept of connected activities and commercial and geographical coherence. The subsequent decisions of the Indian courts, however, have kept abreast of the emerging principles of aggregation based on projects being connected or forming a coherent whole, geographically and commercially. Thus, in *Tiong Woon Project and Contracting Pte Ltd, In re*,[420] where various projects were carried out for different principles, and for

414. Services other than royalties and fee for technical services, which are governed by a separate article in the treaties.
415. India-UK Treaty, Art. 5(2)(k); also *see*, India-USA Treaty, Art. 5(2)(l) and India-Singapore Treaty, Art. 5(6).
416. India-Mauritius Treaty, Art. 5(2) sub-para. (j), providing for a ninety-day time limit with effect from 1 April 2017.
417. *Steel Authority of India Ltd v ACIT* [2007] 105 ITD 679 (Del-Trib).
418. *See, e.g.*, India's tax treaties with Austria, Australia, Belgium, Bulgaria, Canada, Denmark and the USA.
419. *ADIT v J Ray Mc Dermott Eastern Hemisphere Ltd* [2016] 69 taxmann.com 429 (Mum); *see also Sumitomo Corporation v DDIT* [2019] 108 taxmann.com 528 (Del-Trib).
420. *ADIT v Valentine Maritime (Mauritius) Ltd* [2011] 14 taxmann.com 129 (AAR - New Delhi).

different work, the AAR held it to be independent projects, having no interconnection and interdependence and did not approve aggregation of time period of various projects to measure the breach of time threshold under Article 5.3 of the India-Singapore Treaty.

However, in *Valentine Maritime (Mauritius) Ltd,*[421] which was a case under India-Mauritius treaty, the Tribunal in the absence of the specific provision did not approve the aggregation approach on the ground that the three projects were not inextricably interconnected and interdependent, even though the projects were for the same customer in the same geographic area. The similar projects for the same customer in the same geographical area definitely meet the requirement of commercial and geographical coherence in terms of existing international law. Geographical diversification does not necessarily create two (or more) sites or projects. As long as two or more building lots in one country form a coherent whole, that is, are operated at one place or for one and the same ordering party, for related parties, or for parties who act jointly and in coordination, these places should be aggregated and treated as one single unit for the determination of the minimum period.[422] The OECD Commentary acknowledges one building site for a row of houses, even if the orders have been placed by several persons.

3.3.1.8 *Services PE*

The UN Model addresses the notion of 'services permanent establishments' in a way that forms a clear line of demarcation between the UN and OECD paradigms.[423] The OECD Model has no special provisions for services, and the OECD commentary has reiterated time and again that services provision must be treated in the same way as provision of goods.[424] In other words, the same sort of presence in the territory is required to justify source country taxation, a presence having a certain degree of fixed physical presence in that country over a certain period of time. The UN Model perspective is that rendering of services has certain special features and aspects, and the normal 'bricks and mortar' presence does not constitute the right minimum economic footprint for taxation of services by the host country and militates against the concept of inter-nation equity and fairness vis-à-vis source states.

421. [2011] 45 SOT 34 (Mum).
422. K Vogel, Klaus Vogel on *Double Taxation Conventions* (4th edn, Kluwer Law International 2015) 371.
423. UN MTC (2017) (n. 292) Art. 5(3)(b) which reads as follows:

> The term 'permanent establishment' also encompasses:
>
> (b) The furnishing of services, including consultancy services, by an enterprise through employees or other personnel engaged by the enterprise for such purpose, but only if activities of that nature continue (for the same or a connected project) within a Contracting State for a period or periods aggregating more than six months within any twelve-month period.

424. OECD MTC (2017) (n. 290) Commentary on Art. 5(3) 154, para. 132.

International tax scholarship[425] has often used the General Agreements on Trade in Services (GATS) framework[426] to bring out the special features of services, which may be used to develop policies on taxing profits from trade in services. This framework succinctly brings out the four principal modes of delivery of services, which can be tabulated as follows:

	Means of Delivery	*Presence Status*
Mode 1:	**Cross-border Supply:** Services cross the border but not supplier	Thus, supplier not present in the state, for example, telecoms, services supplied by post
Mode 2:	**Consumption Abroad:** Consumer crosses the border to the supplier's state	Thus, supplier once again not present in the state, for example, tourism, repair of machinery
Mode 3:	**Commercial Presence:** Service delivered within the state, through the commercial presence of the supplier	Thus, supplier present within the state, for example, a foreign subsidiary or branch
Mode 4:	**Movement of Natural Persons:** Either employees or persons in business on own account	Thus, supplier present within the state, but not through a commercial presence, for example, short-term consultancy, involving experts' visit

From the above illustration, it is evident that in the GATS context, physical presence of the supplier is not a distinguishing feature in terms of whether services have been provided from one country to another. Services are different to goods in this respect, where trade involves the export of goods from one country into another. The OECD Model does not adequately address this distinction between the provision of goods and services. While the OECD Model gives taxing rights to the residence state of the supplier in respect of first two modes of delivery, in the case of the third mode, taxability of services is subject to the PE threshold rules. It is, however, the fourth mode, which poses the greatest challenge in terms of taxing rights allocation.

A number of OECD countries are, therefore, unwilling to adopt the principle of exclusive residence taxation of services that are not attributable to a PE situated in their territory but are performed in that territory. More so, after the deletion of Article 14 of the OECD Model in 2000, which dealt with income from independent personal services,[427] states do not always find this approach acceptable and intend to tax services performed in their territories, even if no fixed place of business or agent is

425. Oats, Miller and Mulligan (n. 344) 295; *see also* M Lennard, 'The UN Model Tax Convention as Compared with the OECD Model Tax Convention – Current Points of Difference and Recent Developments', 2009 vol. 15(1) Asia-Pacific Tax Bull 4, 5.
426. General Agreement on Trade in Services Art. I(2).
427. *See* OECD, *Model Tax Convention on Income and on Capital* (Condensed version, OECD Pub 1998) Art. 14.

required for their performance. This dissonance finds expression in the OECD Commentary.[428] India, too, has rejected the proposition and the OECD Commentary takes note of it.[429]

Having noted the relevance of the aforesaid arguments, the Commentary proposes an optional provision to determine a service PE. Under this provision, activities carried on by a foreign enterprise providing services in the source state are deemed to be carried on through a PE in two situations:

(1) where the services are performed through an individual who is present in that state for a period or periods exceeding in the aggregate 183 days in any twelve-month period and more than 50% of the gross revenues attributable to the enterprise during this period or periods are derived from such services; or
(2) the services are performed for a period or periods exceeding in the aggregation 183 days in any twelve-month period, and these services are performed for the same project or for connected projects through one or more individuals who are present and perform such services in that state.[430]

Thus, in either scenario, a minimum level of physical presence in the source state is required in the OECD proposal. However, while in the first scenario the presence of the individual through whom an enterprise derives most of its revenues constitutes the connecting factor, the second scenario focuses on the duration of the activities carried on by the individuals through whom the services are performed.[431]

Even this alternative provision of the OECD raises several important questions for developing countries, both at the level of the underlying policy as well as its administrability. For instance, an important question is whether a developing country is at a disadvantage as compared to developed countries and their resident taxpayers by not being able to ascertain the gross revenues of such a person (effectively worldwide) during a particular period, so as to determine the gross revenues threshold of 50% attributable to active business activities of the enterprise during this period or periods.[432]

In its latest paper, the UN Tax Committee's subcommittee on the definition of PEs,[433] takes note of the OECD approach as one of the possibilities but, it is not the general approach supported in the paper. The current UN services provision is the most favoured approach today.

428. OECD MTC (2017) (n. 290) Commentary on Art. 5 paras 136-138.
429. *Ibid.*, para. 36.
430. *Ibid.*, para. 144.
431. *Ibid.*, para. 154.
432. Lennard (n. 425) 6.
433. UN Economic and Social Council Committee of Experts on International Cooperation in Tax Matters, 'Proposal for Amendments of the United Nations Model Double Taxation Convention between Developed and Developing Countries: Further Issues Relating to Permanent Establishment', 4th session Geneva, 20-24 October 2008, https://www.un.org/esa/ffd/wp-content/uploads/2014/10/4STM_EC18_2008_CRP3.pdf, accessed 7 January 2021.

3.3.1.8.1 *Indian Domestic Law and Treaty Practices*

The domestic law in India on the taxability of services is far too broad and as long as the services are utilised in India, they would be taxed in India, irrespective of whether the non-resident has a residence or place of business or business connection in India or has rendered services in India or not.[434] Thus, a US enterprise performing consultancy services in China on behalf of an Indian enterprise would technically be liable to tax in India. The collection of this tax, however, may pose some constraints for two reasons: *first*, India has to know about the arrangements. *Second*, if the payment is not being made from India, it can hardly do anything to physically collect the tax. If the payment is, however, made from India, e.g., by the Indian firm, India can, subject to the rules contained in the India-USA treaty, collect tax by levying a withholding tax on the payment made to the US enterprise.

As for its treaties, India, being one of the largest developing countries, prefers to lean towards the UN Model and invariably opts for a shorter period in its treaties. Thus, in respect of services,[435] furnished within a contracting state by an enterprise through employees or other personnel, India generally prefers a much lower PE threshold in its treaties as follows:

(1) If services are rendered to an unrelated party, the activities within the state must continue for a period or periods aggregating more than ninety days within any twelve-month period.
(2) If services are rendered to a related party, they must be performed within that state for a period or periods aggregating more than thirty days within any twelve-month period.[436]

---

434. At (n. 302), s. 9(1)(vii)(c), which reads as follows:

> (vii) income by way of fees for technical services payable by—
> (c) a person who is a non-resident, where the fees are payable in respect of services utilised in a business or profession carried on by such person in India or for the purposes of making or earning any income from any source in India:
>
> [Explanation. —For the removal of doubts, it is hereby declared that for the purposes of this section, income of a non-resident shall be deemed to accrue or arise in India under clause (v) or clause (vi) or clause (vii) of sub-section (1) and shall be included in the total income of the non-resident, whether or not, —
> (i) the non-resident has a residence or place of business or business connection in India; or
> (ii) the non-resident has rendered services in India.]

435. Services other than royalties and fee for technical services are governed by a separate article in the treaties.

436. India-UK Treaty, Art. 5(2)(k); India-USA Treaty, Art. 5(2)(l) and India-Singapore Treaty, Art. 5(6).

In a few treaties, the expression 'twelve-month period' has been replaced by the term 'fiscal year.'[437] Further in some treaties, the services within that state to a related enterprise by themselves constitute a service PE, without meeting any temporal threshold.[438]

The phrase 'the continuance of these activities within the state' employed in the treaty provisions here unequivocally indicate that it altogether eliminates the physical presence imperative in the determination of a service PE. Thus, if the activities continue for a period exceeding the duration specified in the treaty, it would *ipso facto* result in the creation of a service PE. This aspect of law came to be illustrated by the ITAT in a recent case,[439] where an UAE LLC (ABB FZ) was engaged in the business of providing regional services to a related party in India. The employees of ABB FZ were present in India for twenty-five days, during which services were provided. However, the employees continued to provide services on a regular basis from the UAE through emails, video conferencing, and other electronic modes for more than nine months within a twelve-month period.[440] The Tribunal determined that ABB FZ had a Service PE in the facts presented and held that the presence of employees is not required in the source country for a Service PE to exist. The Tribunal explained that it is not the presence of the employees, but the furnishing of services for more than the specified period of time (regardless of the place of performance) that determines whether the non-resident employer has a Service PE in India. Explaining the inherent rationale for such construction, the Tribunal held that in the present age of technology, where the services, information, consultancy, management, etc. can be provided through various virtual modes (e.g., email, internet, video conference, remote monitoring, remote access to desktop), the physical presence of the foreign taxpayer's employees is not relevant for determining the existence of a Service PE in the source state.

3.3.1.8.2 *Services Rendered Through 'Other Personnel'*

Another aspect of the service PE rules in India is that such services must be rendered through its 'employees and other personnel', an expression appearing in the Indian treaties as well as the UN Model. The use of the words 'other personnel' here clearly indicates that services rendered through even non-employees of the foreign enterprise, who are entrusted by the non-resident with task of providing services, will meet the requirement of the provision. In *Cummins Inc,*[441] however, where the non-resident taxpayer granted the right to KPIT-GBS, an Indian company, to provide business process outsourcing (BPO) services to the group companies of the taxpayer, the ITAT came to hold that no service PE was created in the case as KPIT-GBS was not the employees of the taxpayer. The reasoning of the Tribunal runs thus:

437. India-Singapore Treaty, Art. 5(6).
438. India-USA Treaty, Art. 5(2)(l).
439. *ABB FZ-LLC v DCIT* [2017] 83 taxmann.com 86 (Beng).
440. Article 5(2)(i) of the India-UAE tax treaty provides that a non-resident has a service PE in the source country if it furnishes services through its employees in the source country, and such services continue for a period of more than nine months in a twelve-month period.
441. *Cummins Inc v DDIT* [2019] 111 taxmann.com 161 (Pune).

> We have noted above that the MSA BPO and the Addendum are the umbrella Agreements providing for the rendition of BPO services by KPIT-GBS to Cummins (which expression includes not only the assessee but all the worldwide Cummins group entities). Thus, reference to employees of Cummins in clause X of the Addendum, as actually relating to employees of the concerned Cummins entity, came to be misunderstood by the DRP as relating to the employees of the assessee alone, which led to the confusion. No material has been placed before us to demonstrate that the employees of the assessee were involved in the rendition of the BPO services to various Cummins entities in UK, India or China.

This reasoning is inherently flawed as the Tribunal seems to have completely missed the import of the phrase 'other personnel' appearing in the provision, which entails within its ambit even the personnel of other enterprises authorised by the non-resident. Rawal[442] explains it thus:

> The term 'personnel' may be interpreted on the basis of use of this term in the Commentary. Note the following observation in the OECD Commentary:
>
> > 'The business of an enterprise is carried on mainly by the entrepreneur or persons who are in a paid-employment relationship with the enterprise (personnel). This personnel includes employees and other persons receiving instructions from the enterprise (e.g., dependent agents).'[443]
> >
> > ...
>
> To furnish services within the host country an enterprise may send its own employees or may engage(subcontract) a company to provide such services ... If such services otherwise meet the rationale of Service PE, then considering such service as resulting in Service PE may be justified.

Thus, 'personnel' must not necessarily be an individual, even a non-individual, say, a company or a partnership firm may be included within the meaning of the term.[444] In *e-Funds IT Solutions,*[445] the Delhi High Court interpreted the term 'other personnel' to mean persons (other than employees) engaged or appointed by a foreign company. In *Lucent Technologies International Inc,*[446] the Tribunal considered the employees of even the affiliates of the non-resident as 'other personnel'. In *Teradata Operations Inc,*[447] the Tribunal concluded that even the seconded employees rendering services on behalf of the non-resident in India will fulfil the requirement of a service PE. Thus, services rendered through any human intervention, on behalf of the taxpayer, is capable of creating a debt of economic allegiance so as to warrant allocation of taxing rights to the source state. Any contrary construction will render the words 'other personnel' otiose and encourage artificial arrangements for profit shifting, a loathsome phenomenon in the post-BEPS scenario.

442. R Rawal, *The Taxation of Permanent Establishments: An International Perspective* (Spiramus 2006) 372.
443. OECD, *Model Tax Convention on Income and on Capital* (Condensed version, OECD Pub 2010) Commentary on Art. 5 para. 10 (hereafter 'OECD MTC (2010)').
444. Rawal (n. 442).
445. *DIT v e-Funds IT Solutions* [2014] 42 taxmann.com 50 (Delhi).
446. *Lucent Technologies International Inc v DCIT* [2009] 28 SOT 98 (Del-Trib).
447. *Teradata Operations Inc v DCIT* [2020] 116 taxmann.com 404 (Del-Trib); also *see Huawei Technologies Co Ltd v ADIT* [2020] 122 taxmann.com 130 (Del-Trib).

3.3.1.8.3 'Any Twelve-Month Period' Versus Fiscal Year

It may also be noted here that the expression 'any twelve-month period', appearing in the treaty for calculating the threshold must be interpreted to mean the entire period for which services have been furnished in a source state although such period may span across several fiscal years and it should not be restricted to the duration of one fiscal year or previous year alone. The Indian law recognises this dichotomy and wherever there is an intention to restrict this twelve-month period to connote a fiscal year or the previous year, the treaty provisions include the phrase 'in any fiscal year' in lieu of the words 'in any twelve-month period.'[448]

However, the Indian Tribunal took a contrarian view in a recent decision,[449] holding that in terms of Article 5(2)(k)(i) of India-UK treaty, the expression 'any twelve-month period' would mean the relevant previous year or the financial year. This view of the Tribunal does not appear to be correct, *first*, being contrary to the express wordings of the treaty; and *second*, it incentivises artificial arrangements of spreading the services across different fiscal years.

The phraseological distinction of the two concepts, viz. 'in any twelve-month period' and 'in a fiscal year', is recognised internationally. While some countries, Argentina, for example, chose to limit the twelve-month period to the span of a fiscal year,[450] many countries, like Albania, Armenia, Azerbaijan, Lithuania, Serbia, South Africa, Thailand, Vietnam, Hong Kong and China reserved the right to consider any twelve-month period to measure the breach of threshold.[451] Under Canada-US treaty, the expression 'any twelve-month period' is interpreted as a rolling twelve-month period and not the fiscal year.[452]

Phraseological predilection in treaty drafting betrays the unquestionable intention of the treaty partners in this regard and courts must construe them accordingly. This issue fell for consideration in a 2013 case[453] before the Supreme Administrative Court of Austria, which upheld the view that the threshold has to be calculated on the basis of the 'entire period' of services rendered even though it may span across various years. The votaries of a contrarian view, sometimes, rely on Madras High Court decision in *Bangkok Glass Industry Co*,[454] to espouse the contention that the threshold period has to be determined on the relevant fiscal year the source state. However, in *Bangkok Glass Industry Co*,[455] this issue did not specifically arise for consideration and

448. *See, e.g.*, India-Singapore Treaty, Art. 5(6)(a) and 5(6)(b).
449. *Linklaters LLP v DCIT* [2019] 111 taxmann.com 198 (Mum).
450. OECD, *Model Tax Convention on Income and on Capital* (Condensed version, OECD Pub 2014) Positions on Art. 5 (Permanent Establishment) and Its Commentary para. 12 (hereafter 'OECD MTC (2014)').
451. *Ibid.*, para. 14.
452. G Thornton, 'International Tax CRA Relief on International Tax Issues Caused by COVID-19 Extended', 20 July 2020, https://www.grantthornton.ca/insights/coronavirus-covid-19/cra-relief-on-international-tax-issues-caused-by-covid-19-extended/, accessed 9 January 2021.
453. IBFD Case No. 95/13/0137 (Supreme Administrative Court of Austria).
454. *Bangkok Glass Industry Co Ltd v ACIT* [2013] 34 taxmann.com 77 (Mad).
455. *Ibid.*

the Court merely assumed that since the threshold period was not met in the relevant financial year, the income was not taxable.

3.3.1.8.4 Delivery PE

Another difference lies in the exclusionary paragraph 4 of Article 5 of the OECD and UN Models, which conceives of certain activities to be excluded from the definition of a PE, being preparatory and auxiliary. The word 'delivery' has been omitted from the paragraph 4(a) and 4(b) lists of preparatory and auxiliary activities in the UN Model. In other words, the use of facilities, per se, solely for the purposes of delivery of goods or merchandise belonging to the enterprise is an activity that can constitute sufficient economic nexus to the host country to trigger source country taxation under the UN Model, but not under the OECD Model. This difference is clearly based on the reasoning that the presence of a stock of goods for prompt delivery facilitates sales of the product and earning of profit in the host country and represents a continuing economic connection with the source country, and as such may constitute a PE and be subject to source country taxation. Thus, a 'warehouse' used for any purpose is (subject to the other conditions being fulfilled) will constitute a PE under the general principles of the UN Model.[456]

The OECD, too, seems to have realised during the BEPS action plan phase that delivery does form an economic nexus with the source state, albeit in a restricted manner and its total exclusion as PE is not efficacious. Paragraph 22 of the revised Commentary[457] states that where a non-resident enterprise maintains a very large warehouse in which a significant number of employees work for the main purpose of storing and delivering its goods that the enterprise sells online to customers in that state, the warehouse will constitute an essential part of the enterprise's sale/distribution business and cannot be excluded under paragraph 4 of Article 5.

A recent change to these exclusion rules has been introduced as a result of the BEPS Action 7, known as the 'anti-fragmentation' rule.[458] Historically, many businesses have used the ancillary activities exception to 'fragment' their business into separate entities, in order to claim that the business is 'solely' ancillary. This new rule provides that, even though activities might appear preparatory or auxiliary, when viewed in isolation, this is not enough. If the activities 'constitute complementary functions that are part of a cohesive business operation', that is not solely ancillary, the exception cannot be used. Thus, even the exclusion of delivery under the OECD stipulations will have to be tested on the anvil of the new anti-fragmentation provisions.

456. UN MTC (2017) (n. 292) Commentary on Art. 5 para. 4.
457. Renumbered as para. 62 of the Commentary on Art. 5 in OECD MTC (2017).
458. OECD MTC (2017) (n. 290) Art. 5(4) and 5(4.1).

3.3.1.8.5 Indian Domestic Law and Treaty Practices

In the domestic law of India, delivery is not included in the exclusions listed[459] in the 'business connection' concept under section 9 of the Income Tax Act 1961. Rather, Explanation 2(b) of section 9(1)(i) treats a person habitually maintaining a sock of goods and merchandise and regularly delivering the same therefrom on behalf of a non-resident constitutes a business connection.

In the Indian tax treaties as well, there is a general preference towards the UN Model,[460] even though exceptions have been made with some countries.[461] In some tax treaties, 'occasional' delivery of goods has been excluded from the ambit of PE.[462]

In practical terms, the real effect of this difference may not be significant, as a need would then arise to determine the amount of income attributable to the PE (i.e., to the delivery business alone), which may not be of much consequence in terms of its taxability. The Commentary to the UN Model recognises that only a small amount of income would normally be allocated to a PE whose only activity is delivery.[463] Under either model, the inclusion of delivery where there is otherwise a PE would allow source country taxation of the income of the PE as a whole, including from delivery, so the real difference is where delivery is all that happens domestically.[464]

3.3.1.9 Dependent Agent PE: Maintenance of Stocks

Apart from omission of the word 'delivery', under the UN Model, in contrast to the OECD Model, there is a dependent agent PE rule under Article 5(5) of both the models, which presents certain striking dissimilarities. Under the OECD prescription, a person, acting on behalf of a non-resident enterprise, constitutes a dependent agent PE of a non-resident enterprise in a source state, if three conditions are satisfied:

(1) He habitually concludes contracts or habitually play the principal role leading to the conclusion of contracts routinely concluded, without material modifications, by that enterprise; and
(2) The contracts, so signed, are:
    (a) in the name of the enterprise; or
    (b) for the transfer of ownership of or for granting the right to use property owned by the enterprise or that the enterprise has right to use; or
    (c) for the provision of services by the enterprise.
(3) His activities are not limited to preparatory or auxiliary activities spelt out in Article 5(4).[465]

459. At (n. 302), s. 9(1)(i) Expl 1(b), 1(c) and 1(d).
460. *See, e.g.*, India's tax treaties with UK, Japan, Russia, Australia, Spain and Nepal.
461. *See, e.g.*, India-China tax treaty.
462. *See, e.g.*, India-US Treaty, India-Canada Treaty, India-Singapore Treaty and India-Turkey Treaty.
463. UN MTC (2017) (n. 292) Commentary on Art. 5 para. 21.
464. Lennard (n. 425) 7.
465. OECD MTC (2017) (n. 290) Art. 5 para. 5.

Further, where an independent agent, acting for the enterprise in the ordinary course of that business, acts exclusively or almost exclusively on behalf of one or more enterprises to which it is closely related, that person shall constitute a dependent agent PE with respect to any such enterprise.[466]

The UN Model, however, introduces a still broader version of dependent agent PE and includes a situation where a person does not habitually conclude contracts, or plays the principal role leading to the conclusion of the contracts, but does habitually maintain in the source state a stock of goods or merchandise from which he regularly delivers goods or merchandise to customers on behalf of the non-resident enterprise.[467] The concept is based on a view that the presence of stock, and its delivery by the agent, forms an adequate economic nexus with the source country so as to justify source taxation by the country concerned.

3.3.1.9.1 Indian Law and Treaty Practices

The UN variant of dependent agent PE has also been incorporated in the Indian Income Tax Act to bring, within the definition of PE, a person, who habitually maintains a sock of goods and merchandise and regularly delivers the same therefrom on behalf of a non-resident.[468] Indian tax treaties are also aligned with these provisions.[469]

3.3.1.9.2 Refining the Nexus Rule: Some Recent Trends – BEPS and Multilateral Instruments (MLIs)

The OECD activity exemption rule,[470] in general, came in for consideration in the BEPS project.[471] BEPS Action 7 recognised that in view of the dynamic business environment, an activity cannot be earmarked as being 'preparatory and auxiliary' in nature and that determination of whether an activity is preparatory and auxiliary in nature is

466. OECD MTC (2017) (n. 290) Art. 5 para. 6.
467. UN MTC (2017) (n. 292) Art. 5 para. 5(b).
468. At (n. 302), s. 9(1)(i) Expl 2(b).
469. *See, e.g.*, India-Australia Treaty, Art. 5(5)(b) which reads as follows:

> A person acting in one of the Contracting States on behalf of an enterprise of the other Contracting State - other than an agent of an independent status to whom paragraph (6) applies - shall be deemed to be a permanent establishment of that enterprise in the first-mentioned State if: (b) the person has no such authority, but habitually maintains in that State a stock of goods or merchandise from which the person regularly delivers goods or merchandise on behalf of the enterprise.

470. OECD MTC (2017) (n. 290) Art. 5 para. 4.
471. The OECD/G20 BEPS Project creates new or reinforced international standards as well as concrete measures to help countries tackle BEPS. It represents the results of a major and unparalleled effort by OECD and G20 countries working together on an equal footing with the participation of an increasing number of developing countries. Its 15 action plans aim at equipping governments with domestic and international instruments to address tax avoidance, ensuring that profits are taxed where economic activities generating the profits are performed and where value is created. *See* OECD, *Explanatory Statement: OECD/G20 Base Erosion and Profit Shifting Project* (OECD Pub 2015) 4.

a fact-specific exercise and can vary, depending on the nature of the business activities of a foreign company. Action 7 noted that the issues involved were two-fold: *First*, whether an activity undertaken by a foreign company in another country is preparatory and auxiliary in nature, based on the nature of its business? *Second*, whether activities of the enterprise have been fragmented between different places of business or entities in order to constitute preparatory and auxiliary activities?

On the first issue, Action 7 suggested that exclusions in the definition of PE in the Model Convention should be made subject to a 'preparatory and auxiliary' condition, i.e., exclusion would only be available if such activities are preparatory or auxiliary in nature, as against earmarked activities defined in existing tax treaties.[472] This stipulation, thus, insisted on an evidence-based determination of activities being preparatory or auxiliary in nature. On the second issue, it proposed anti-fragmentation rules, which restrict a foreign company and its group companies from fragmenting a cohesive business operation into several small operations in order to demonstrate that each of these is only engaged in a preparatory or auxiliary activity.[473] Accordingly, the OECD adopted a revised Article 5(4) in its updated 2017 Model Convention, incorporating the above changes.[474]

The Multilateral Convention to Implement Tax Treaty Related Measures to Prevent BEPS (Multilateral Instrument or MLI), effective from 1 July 2018, provides options for amending the 'preparatory and auxiliary' clause in bilateral tax treaties. One of the options comprises the BEPS Action 7 mandates mentioned above.[475] Anti-fragmentation rules have also been included in the MLI, wherein exemption for specific activities will not be available, on the lines of Article 5.4.1 of the 2017 OECD Model Convention. The MLI, thus, provides that the PE exemption paragraph of the OECD Model Convention would not apply if the same or a closely related enterprise carried on business activities from a place in the same country and that place constituted a PE or the combination of activities of both the enterprises would not be of a preparatory or auxiliary character, if those activities constituted complementary functions of a cohesive business operation.[476]

BEPS project looked at the definition relating to Agency PE contained in Article 5(5) and 5(6) as well. Action 7 called for a review of that definition to prevent certain common tax avoidance strategies to circumvent the existing PE definition, such as replacing subsidiaries that traditionally acted as distributors by *commissionaire* arrangement,[477] or by not formally concluding contracts in a state and arranging its

472. BEPS Action 7 Final Report 2015 (n. 402) 28.
473. *Ibid.*, 39.
474. OECD MTC (2017) (n. 290) Art. 5(4), 5(4.1).
475. MLI (n. 403) Art. 13(2), 13(3).
476. *Ibid.*, Art. 13(4).
477. A *commissionaire* arrangement is an arrangement through which a person sells products in a state in its own name but on behalf of a foreign enterprise that is the owner of these products. Through such an arrangement, a foreign enterprise is able to sell its products in a state without technically having a permanent establishment to which such sales may be attributed for tax purposes and without, therefore, being taxable in that state on the profits derived from such sales.

formal finalisation and authorisation outside, even though the contracts were substantially negotiated in that state, or by creating an Artificial structure of an 'independent agent' where the person habitually exercises an authority to conclude contracts, so that it falls within exception of Article 5(6), even though it is closely related to the foreign enterprise on behalf of which it is acting.[478]

The BEPS Action Plan 7 Report came with the suggestion to analyse the 'in substance' functions of an agent in a country on behalf of a foreign company in order to determine whether an Agency PE has been constituted instead of the existing condition of formal conclusion of a contract mandated in the OECD Model Convention. The following amendments were, thus, proposed:[479]

(1) The clause 'authority to conclude contracts' to create a PE should be deleted. Instead, a clause should be included that an Agency PE should be constituted if an agent 'habitually plays the principal role leading to the conclusion of contracts that are routinely concluded without material modification by the enterprise'.
(2) An Agency PE is constituted when the activities of a dependent agent (given above) relate to transfer of ownership and rights relating to property owned by a foreign company or provision of services by it.
(3) The definition of an independent agent should be restricted. An agent should not be considered an independent agent if it acts exclusively on behalf of one or more foreign companies with which it is closely associated.

The revised Article 5(5) and 5(6) of the updated 2017 OECD Model Convention stand adapted accordingly on the above lines.[480] The MLI, too, has adopted the recommendations of BEPS Action 7.[481] These provisions are not minimum standard provisions and there is an option available to countries under the MLI to reserve the right not to apply this article in its entirety. Any modification of a treaty depends on adoption and notification of this provision by the other contracting state.

These recent trends and modifications of the treaty structures clearly suggest that the focus of international taxation rules is on the economic connection of income earned. International tax law scholars have increasingly realised that the taxing rights of the source state cannot be permitted to be curtailed or constricted by creating legal structures and artificial arrangements to shift away the profit of a substantial economic activity taking place in the source state. The extended dependent agency PE (DAPE) rule which covers a person who habitually plays the role of the principal leading to the conclusion of contracts, stricter independent agent exclusion rule which denies exclusion to the agents who work exclusively for an enterprise and its closely related enterprises permitting specific activity exemption only if such activities qualified to be preparatory or auxiliary, preventing artificial disintegration of cohesive business

478. BEPS Action 7 Final Report 2015 (n. 402) 15, paras 5-8.
479. *Ibid.*, 16-17.
480. OECD MTC (2017) (n. 290) 32.
481. MLI (n. 403) Art. 12.

activities for the purpose of specific activity exemption under a preparatory or auxiliary category and preventing artificial splitting of contracts between related parties such that each contract does not exceed the relevant time thresh hold under the treaty for triggering a construction PE are all steps to reinforce the economic connection of income earned for the assumption of taxing rights of the source state.

3.3.1.9.3 India's Stance on These Developments

While India has accepted all the above changes to PE definition provided in the MLI, there is no reciprocal acceptance of it by a number of India's treaty partners. Canada, Sweden, Switzerland and the UAE, for instance, have placed reservations with respect to all PE provisions of the MLI. Accordingly, in keeping with the matching principle, the PE definition in such Indian treaties shall remain unchanged. Further, some countries have opted for only specific PE provisions of the MLI and have discarded the other provisions. Thus, it does not appear likely that the extended DAPE rule would be incorporated in most of India's tax treaties pursuant to the MLI. But the DAPE definition in many Indian treaties is already broader, as compared to the OECD patterned treaties, even before the MLI was rolled out. Indian treaties with Japan, Russia, Singapore, Australia and the UK, for instance, entail within its ambit persons who habitually secure orders, which is in convergence with the MLI regime. The MLI rules related to preparatory or auxiliary exemption, anti-fragmentation and anti-splitting of contracts are currently not incorporated in any of the existing Indian treaties. These rules will be assessed while finalising PE provisions, subject to India's treaty partner adopting these provisions. Some of India's tax treaties which would be affected as result of one or more of these changes include the treaties with Australia, Ireland, Japan, the Netherlands, Russia and the UK.

The developed and developing economies, by and large, have joined the BEPS initiative to adapt to the changing international taxing paradigm and updated their tax laws to assiduously guard their tax bases. Significant changes are being made to the domestic laws as well, especially those related to digital economy. India's significant economic presence test[482] rule is a step in that direction, which is inspired by BEPS Action 1. The Explanatory Memorandum to the amending Bill[483] declares that the restrictive physical nexus regime in Indian law is being replaced within an economic presence test based on the relevant transaction fulfilling the prescribed economic threshold. The Explanatory Memorandum also observes that the inclusion of the significant economic presence concept in the domestic law will enable India to negotiate for the incorporation of this economic nexus in the tax treaties. In this regard, India has already reserved the right to 'include a provision in Article 5 to the effect that that an enterprise having a significant economic presence in a contracting state, based

482. At (n. 302), s. 9(1)(i) Expl 2A.
483. The Indian Finance Bill 2020.

on criteria identified in chapter VII of the final report on Action 1 of the OECD/G20 BEPS project would be deemed to have a PE in that state.'[484]

3.3.1.10 Insurance Services PE

The concept of economic link, as against a physical territorial link, as a fundamental jurisdictional basis of taxing rights becomes more evident when we look at the special PE provision incorporated in the UN Model in respect of insurance activities, which is yet another major distinguishing feature between the two models.[485] The ease, with which a non-resident insurance company can create a huge client base in the source state through the activities of persons representing the foreign insurer on a part-time basis, forms the compelling rationale for including this provision.

This special feature of the insurance sector was of concern to some countries, not only developing countries, when the UN Model was developed. The UN Model Commentary takes note of this and records that if an insurance agent was independent, the profits would not be taxable to the enterprise in accordance with the provisions suggested in Article 5(7), while if the agent was dependent, no tax could be imposed because insurance agents normally had no authority to conclude contracts as would be required under Article 5(5)(a).[486] Therefore, a special provision was added for the existence of a deemed PE where an insurance enterprise collects premiums in the territory of that other state or insures risks situated therein through a person other than an agent of an independent status to whom Article 5(7) applies. The special provision does not apply to reinsurance, where the risk has been transferred from one insurance company to another one. In the case of reinsurance probably, the link was perceived as too economically remote to the source country.

While the OECD Model does not contain any specific provision for insurance services, the OECD Commentary acknowledges the potential problem with insurance business, thus: '[I]t is conceivable that these companies do large-scale business in a state without being taxed in that state on their profits arising from such business'.[487]

The OECD Commentary goes on to suggest that a provision along the lines of that in the UN Model could be adopted depending on the factual and legal situation prevailing in the contracting states.[488] As a result, even the OECD member countries began to include a deeming provision which stipulates that insurance companies of a state are deemed to have a PE in the other state on the basis of premiums collected or

484. OECD MTC (2017) (n. 290) para. 14.7.
485. UN MTC (2017) (n. 292) Art. 5 para. 6, which reads as follows: 'Notwithstanding the preceding provisions of this article, an insurance enterprise of a Contracting State shall, except in regard to re-insurance, be deemed to have a permanent establishment in the other Contracting State if it collects premiums in the territory of that other State or insures risks situated therein through a person other than an agent of an independent status to whom paragraph 7 applies.'
486. *Ibid.*, Commentary on Art. 5(6) paras 27-28.
487. OECD MTC (2017) (n. 290) Commentary on Art. 5(6) para. 114.
488. *Ibid.*

risks insured in that other state through an agent established there - other than an agent, already constituting a PE by virtue of Article 5(5).[489]

The reasoning expressed in the UN Commentary on this point was vindicated in light of some major cases arising later, which related to US insurance enterprises, providing insurance to Canadian customers.[490] In one case,[491] although the Court rejected the suggestion that the absence of a specific provision of insurance business along the lines of that in the UN Model mean that the US and Canada must have been content with the fact that large-scale insurance business could be conducted in the other state without a PE arising, the judge stated that the only way for one state to tax the profits of insurance business conducted in that state by an enterprise of the other state via independent agents was by way of appropriate amendments to the treaty.[492]

While the BEPS proposals no longer single out the insurance sector for specific measures, the general changes proposed to the PE threshold and the specific shift from a legally binding test to a substance-based evaluation would have its bearing, particularly, on those insurance groups that have mobile sales personnel, agents and representative offices across various jurisdictions. Broadly, a strict agency PE rules to include contracts where the intermediary 'habitually concludes contracts, or habitually plays the principal role leading to the conclusion of contracts that are routinely concluded without material modification by the enterprise' (clearly extending beyond the place of signing a contract) and a strict requirement for an agent to be considered 'independent', such that an agent will not be considered independent where the agent acts exclusively or almost exclusively for one or more enterprises to which it is closely related,[493] will also generally impact the insurance sector as many insurance entities operate across jurisdictions on a freedom of services basis without a taxable presence. Thus, under the new provisions, the fact that the mobile sales force negotiates the key terms of contracts is critical and could result in this team creating a PE of the Insurer in a country if the 'negotiates material elements' test is met. The commentary in paragraph 32.5 and 32.6 offers some insight in this regard, explaining that the threshold is 'aimed at situations where contracts that are essentially being negotiated ... are subject to formal conclusion, possibly with further approval or review, outside that State', and broadens the scope to cover standardised contracts as well.[494]

489. *Ibid.*
490. *American Income Life Insurance Company v Canada* (2008) TCC 306; *see also Knights of Columbus v R* 2008 Tax Court of Canada 307.
491. *Ibid.*
492. *Ibid.*, 79.
493. The expression 'closely related' replaces the word 'connected' from the previous discussion draft and is broadly defined on the basis of the vote and value of a company's shares (directly or indirectly more than 50%).
494. S Ma'ilei and J Brown, 'PE Issues in Global Insurance Distribution', International Tax Review, 3 August 2015, https://www.internationaltaxreview.com/article/b1f9jp8z6l4rpz/pe-issues-in-global-insurance-distribution, accessed 9 January 2021.

3.3.1.10.1 Indian Law and Treaty Practices

In its domestic legislation, India has sought to align itself with the post-BEPS changes, even though there are no specific provisions in respect of insurance industry per se. The newly inserted Explanation 2(a) to section 9(1)(i) of the Income Tax Act 1961,[495] declares that 'business connection' shall include any business activity carried out through a person who, acting on behalf of the non-resident, has and habitually exercises in India, an authority to conclude contracts on behalf of the non-resident or habitually concludes contracts or habitually plays the principal role leading to conclusion of contracts by that non-resident and the contracts are in the name of the non-resident or for the transfer of the ownership of or for the granting of the right to use, property owned by that non-resident or that non-resident has the right to use or for the provision of services by the non-resident. Thus, if the non-resident insurer carries out his business through a person who, acting on behalf of the non-resident, has and habitually exercises in India, an authority to conclude contracts on behalf of the non-resident or habitually concludes contracts or habitually plays the principal role leading to conclusion of contracts by that non-resident and the contracts are in the name of the non-resident etc., it will trigger taxability in terms of Indian domestic law.

India, in its early tax treaties,[496] has not specifically incorporated this special provision relating to insurance business, but in its recent treaties, India has veered towards the UN position and there is a visible trend towards inclusion of this provision.[497]

3.3.2 The Profit Attribution Principle

The second principle is the principle of attribution of profits to the PE. As per the PE principle, the state of source would tax the profits to the extent that they are attributable to a PE and the profits that are not attributable to the PE shall be taxable only in the state of residence. But there is a significant divergence on the criteria of the attribution of profits to a PE. The OECD Model stresses the nexus of business profits with the PE's activities, which follows that the state of source may only tax business profits arising from a PE's activities.[498]

495. *Inserted vide* the Indian Finance Act, 2018, with effect from 1 April 2019.

496. *See, e.g.*, India's tax treaties with the UK, The US, Canada, China, Japan, France, Germany, Denmark, Australia, Belgium, Bangladesh, Brazil, Bulgaria, and South Africa.

497. *See, e.g.*, India-Austria's Treaty, Art. 5, para. 7, which reads as follows: 'Notwithstanding the preceding provisions of this article, an insurance enterprise of a Contracting State shall, except in regard to re-insurance, be deemed to have a permanent establishment in the other Contracting State if it collects premiums in the territory of that other State or insures risks situated therein through a person other than an agent of an independent status to whom paragraph 6 applies.' *See also* Art. 5 para. 6 of tax treaties with Albania, Armenia, Bhutan, Botswana and Cyprus, Art. 5 para. 7 of treaty with Croatia and Art. 5 para. 8 of treaty with Belarus – to name a few.

498. The OECD Model reads as follows: 'Profits of an enterprise of a Contracting State shall be taxable only in that State unless the enterprise carries on business in the other Contracting State through a permanent establishment situated therein. If the enterprise carries on business as

The UN Model, on the other hand, suggests a modification that more closely aligns with the calculation of the PE's taxable income, based on the economic linkages of the income-generating activities. It proposes a 'force of attraction' principle – under which once an enterprise has a PE in a jurisdiction, all income derived by the enterprise in the jurisdiction should be subject to tax there. Thus, under the UN Model, in addition to profits of the PE that are calculated as per the OECD Model, the profits of the PE will include profits that are attributable to:

(i) sales of goods or merchandise of the same or similar kind as those sold through the PE; and
(ii) other business activities carried on of the same or similar kind as those carried on through that PE.[499]

These two additional clauses in the UN Model widen the corresponding article in the OECD Model by including a limited force of attraction rule.[500] This enables the country, in which the PE is situated, to tax not only the PE profits, but other profits of the enterprise as well, which are derived in that country to the extent allowed under the article.[501] Under the UN Model, if a non-resident enterprise carries on the 'same or similar activities of its PE by circumventing it, the profits thus gained shall also be attributable to the PE and be subject to tax accordingly. The 'same or similar' activity of a PE under the 'same or similar conditions' is the restriction placed on the force of attraction principle. If, for example, the activities of the enterprise are different from those of the PE, the profits should not be attributable to the PE.

In practice, tax treaties of countries mostly adopt this OECD concept of PE-activity nexus on the grounds of administrative convenience and economic efficiency. Some tax treaties, concerned with their rights to tax source income, try to counter tax avoidance by a force of attraction principle with stringent restrictions. For example, under Germany-Philippines tax treaty, if it can be proved that the enterprise is engaging

---

aforesaid, the profits that are attributable to the permanent establishment in accordance with the provisions of paragraph 2 may be taxed in that other State.' *See* OECD MTC (2017) (n. 290) Art. 7, para. 1.

499. The UN Model reads as follows:

> Profits of an enterprise of a Contracting State shall be taxable only in that Contracting State unless the enterprise carries on business in the other Contracting State through a permanent establishment situated therein. If the enterprise carries on business as aforesaid, the profits that are attributable to the permanent establishment in accordance with the provisions of paragraph 2 of this Article may be taxed in that other Contracting State, *see* UN MTC (2017) (n. 292) Art. 7 para. 1.

500. It is contrasted with a full force of attraction principle, which seeks to tax other unconnected income derived by the enterprise in the state the permanent establishment is situated; *see* L Olivier and M Honibal, *International Tax, A South African Perspective* (5th edn, Siber Ink CC 2011) 348, citing *International Tax Glossary* (IBFD 2001) 151; *see also* R Rohatgi, *Basic International Taxation* (2nd edn, Richmond Law & Tax 2005) 106.

501. The UN Model commentary notes that the force of attraction rule is limited to business profits covered by Art. 7 and does not extend to income from capital (dividends, interest, and royalties) covered by other treaty provisions; *see* UN MTC (2017) (n. 292) Commentary on Art. 7(1) 215, para. 6.

in the same or similar activities as the PE solely for the purpose of avoiding taxes of the state of source, then the profits arising directly from those activities shall be taxed by the state of source. The onus to prove that the same or similar activities by the PE is designed 'solely for the purpose of avoiding taxes of the state of source', makes the application of the force of attraction principle quite difficult in practice. There are similar provisions in the bilateral tax treaties between Germany and Indonesia, India, Pakistan, Turkey, Papua New Guinea and Mexico.

3.3.2.1 Indian Law and Treaty Practices

In Indian domestic statute,[502] taxability of income attributable to a PE falls within the scope of expression 'income accruing or arising, whether directly or indirectly, through or from any business connection in India' in terms of section 9(1)(i) of the Income Tax Act.[503] However, there is no specific clause comparable with the force of attraction principle contained in Article 7 of the tax treaties. It is, therefore, sometimes argued by the tax professionals in India that the Indian Tax Law does not contain 'force of attraction principle'[504] and its incorporation in the treaties, therefore, becomes meaningless in the absence of its provision in the charging section, as 'a tax treaty, by itself, cannot fasten a tax liability where the liability is not imposed by a local Act'.[505] This aspect of international tax law is well settled that unless a state has the right to tax a non-resident under its domestic law, it cannot tax that non-resident by virtue of any treaty. Thus, before there can be any taxation of a non-resident's business profits, that non-resident must have a taxable business presence in the host state under the host state's domestic law.[506] The Indian Supreme Court in *Kulandagan Chettiar*,[507] put the law, thus:

> Where tax liability is imposed by the Act, the treaty may be resorted to for reducing or altogether avoiding the tax liability. In case of any conflict between the treaty provisions and the Act, the provisions of the treaty would prevail over the provisions of the Act.

The question, therefore, arises, whether the force of attraction principle has no legal mandate under the Indian Tax Law. A close look at the municipal law of India does not support this contention. By section 5(2) of the Act, the income of a non-resident from whatever source derived is includible in the total income:

(i) if it is received or deemed to be received in India; or
(ii) if it accrues or arises or is deemed to accrue or arise to him in India during the year.

502. At (n. 302).
503. *Ibid.*
504. Rawal (n. 442) 54.
505. *Kulandagan Chettiar* (n. 304).
506. Oats, Miller and Mulligan (n. 344) 260.
507. *Kulandagan Chettiar* (n. 304).

Under section 9(1)(i) of the Act,[508] all income shall be deemed to accrue or arise in India, if it accrues or arises, whether directly or indirectly:

(a) through or from business connection in India; or
(b) through or from any property in India; or
(c) through or from any asset or source of income in India; or
(d) through the transfer of a capital asset situated in India.

Explanation 1, appended to sub-clause 9(1)(i), further clarifies that in the case of a business of which all the operations are not carried out in India, the income of the business deemed under this clause to accrue or arise in India shall be only such part of the income as is reasonably attributable to the operations carried out in India. Explanation 2 to section 9(1)(i),[509] as amended vide the Finance Act 2018[510] provides an inclusive definition of 'business connection', as per which, any business activity, if carried out through a person, acting on behalf of a non-resident, shall constitute a business connection, if two conditions are satisfied:

(1) if that person:
  (i) has and habitually exercises in India, an authority to conclude contracts on behalf of the non-resident; or
  (ii) habitually concludes contracts; or
  (iii) habitually plays the principal role leading to the conclusion of contracts by the non-residents; and
(2) if the contracts are:
  (i) in the name of the non-resident; or
  (ii) for the transfer of ownership or right to use of property which the non-resident owns or has the right to use; or
  (iii) for the provision of services by the non-resident.[511]

The provision, further, provides that a business connection shall also be formed if, the person, acting on behalf of the non-resident:

508. At (n. 302), s. 9(1)(i), which reads as follows:

> 9. (1) The following incomes shall be deemed to accrue or arise in India: —
> (i) all income accruing or arising, whether directly or indirectly, through or from any business connection in India, or through or from any property in India, or through or from any asset or source of income in India, [* * *] or through the transfer of a capital asset situate in India.
> [Explanation 1]. —For the purposes of this clause—
> (a) in the case of a business of which all the operations are not carried out in India, the income of the business deemed under this clause to accrue or arise in India shall be only such part of the income as is reasonably attributable to the operations carried out in India.

509. Inserted by the Finance Bill 2003, with effect from 1 April 2004.
510. With effect from 1 April 2019.
511. At (n. 302), Expl 2(a).

(1) has no such authority but the following two conditions are met:
  (a) if the person habitually maintains in India a stock of goods or merchandise; and
  (b) he regularly delivers goods or merchandise therefrom on behalf of the non-resident;[512] or
(2) habitually secures orders in India, mainly or wholly for the non-resident or the group controlled by the non-resident.[513]

The 'business connection' will, however, not include cases where the business activity is carried out through a broker, general commission agent or any other agent having an independent status, if such person is acting in the ordinary course of his business,[514] except where such broker, general commission agent or any other agent works mainly or wholly on behalf of a non-resident or on behalf of that non-resident and other non-residents controlled by him.[515]

From a conjoint reading of the above provisions of the Indian law, it emerges that the term 'business connection', which is the Indian equivalent of a PE concept, is much wider in connotation than PE and the expression, 'whether directly or indirectly through or from business connection in India', is capable of entailing, within its ambit, the limited force of attraction principle, referred to in the tax treaties.[516] The expression 'indirectly attributable' came to be explained by the Mumbai Bench of the ITAT in *Linklaters LLP*[517] in the following words:

> 145. Learned CIT(A) has apparently taken note of the profits in respect of the work performed in the PE itself but he has not taken note of the position that it is only in respect of the profits directly attributable to work done in the PE but it is in respect of profits 'directly' or even 'indirectly' attributable to the permanent establishment. The import of 'directly or indirectly attributable to PE' has been clearly ignored. The inclusion of 'profits indirectly attributable to the PE' clearly incorporates a force of attraction principle in the India-UK tax treaty, but the CIT(A) has simply not taken note of that aspect of the matter. In the impugned order, the CIT(A) has, *inter alia*, observed that, 'I also agree with the learned A.R.'s arguments that as per Article 7, only that portion of income, which is attributable to the permanent establishment in India, can be taxed in India', and that, 'only that portion of income relating to rendering of such services in India can be attributed to the services of PE the appellant in India'. This approach of the CIT(A) is clearly incompatible [sic] the force of attraction rule embedded in Article 7(2) of India-UK tax treaty. In this view of the matter, we cannot, and do not, approve the action of the CIT(A) in this respect.

Thus, it is manifest that the expression 'indirectly attributable' alludes to a force of attraction rule in the Indian tax legislation. The Indian Supreme Court in *RD*

512. *Ibid.*, Expl 2(b).
513. *Ibid.*, Expl 2(c).
514. *Ibid.*, first proviso to Expl 2.
515. *Ibid.*, second proviso to Expl 2.
516. VJ Shah, S Sheth and K Mehta, 'India' in E Reimer, S Schmid and M Orell (eds), *Permanent Establishments: A Domestic Taxation, Bilateral Tax Treaty and OECD Perspective* (6th edn, Wolters Kluwer 2018) s. 10.2.
517. *Linklaters LLP v ITO* [2011] 9 ITR (T) 217 (Mum).

Aggarwal,[518] recognised the wide expanse of the expression 'business connection' in the following terms:

> [A] business connection may take several forms: it may include carrying on a part of the main business or activity incidental to the main business of the non-resident through an agent, or it may merely be a relation between the business of the non-resident and the activity in India, which facilitates or assists the carrying on of that business.

A strict territorial presence, therefore, is not a *sine qua non* for a business connection.

Coming to the treaty practices in India, Article 7(1) of Indian tax treaties is, generally, in line with the UN Model. Around thirty of the Indian treaties incorporate force of attraction principle. Many Indian treaties adopt Article 7(1) as per the UN Model Convention i.e. a limited force of attraction approach, as reflected in the phrase 'directly or indirectly attributable to that PE'.[519] Some treaties adopt only part of Article 7(1) of the UN Model (sale of similar goods).[520] Some treaties adopt the OECD Model with a variation with the use of expression 'directly or indirectly attributable to that PE'.[521] Some treaties adopt the provisions of the UN Model with a 'right to prove otherwise clause', where an enterprise can prove that profit from sale of same or similar goods/activities are not attributable to PE.[522]

This restricted force of attraction principle has received judicial recognition in several cases. In *Roxon OY*, the Mumbai Bench of the ITAT has held as follows:[523]

> 11. It does not, however, mean that 'force of attraction rule' is now completely abandoned in the tax treaties. It is alive but in a somewhat subdued and different form altogether. The rule, underlying the modern treaties is an improvised and highly restricted 'force of attraction rule'. This 'restricted force of attraction' rule, in essence, additionally expands source State taxation by permitting States where non-residents maintain traditional PEs to tax other income that is attracted to PE, even though that income is not directly related to the PE. In UN Model Convention (1979 draft), this newer version of the force of attraction rule, finds place. It is implicit in the following provision in Article 7(1) of the UN Model Convention:
>
>> 'The profits of an enterprise of a Contracting State shall be taxable only in that State unless the enterprise carries on business in the other Contracting State through a PE situated therein. If the enterprise carries on business as aforesaid, the profits of the enterprise may be taxed in the other State but only so much of them as is attributable to (a) that PE, (b) sales in that other State of goods or merchandise of the same or similar kind as those sold through that PE; or (c) other business activities carried on in that other State of the same or similar kind as those effected through that PE.'

518. *CIT v RD Aggarwal* (1965) 56 ITR 20 (SC).
519. *See, e.g.*, Indian Treaties with Canada, Belgium, Denmark, Italy and USA.
520. *See, e.g.*, India-New Zealand or India-Indonesia Treaty.
521. *See, e.g.*, treaties with Japan, Singapore, United Kingdom, Malta and Oman, for instance.
522. *See* India-Germany Treaty and India-Cyprus Treaty.
523. *DCIT v Roxon OY* (2007) 106 ITD 489 (Mum).

In *WNS North America Inc*,[524] the Tribunal once again upheld in principle the force of attraction rule and excluded the marketing and management services from the ambit of taxability. The Tribunal explained the contours of the restrictive application of the force of attraction rule in India in the following words:

> 8 There is no scope of any ambiguity as the [sic] Article 7(1) gives a clear understanding that the force of attraction Rule applied only in respect of the business carried on by an enterprise of Contracting State in the other Contracting State through PE as well as without involvement of PE. Therefore, the two essential conditions emerge for applying the force of attraction rule are (i) the business activity carried on should be in the other State where the PE is situated (ii) the business activity carried on must be of the same or similar kind as those effected through PE. In the case in hand the condition of business activity carried on in the other State where the PE is situated is not satisfied because the marketing and management services in question are provided by the assessee outside India.

In *Varian India*,[525] the Tribunal illustrated the principle in the following terms:

> 38. The basic condition for application of 'Force of Attraction Rule' is that, it has to be established that the foreign enterprise has a P.E. in India and then only it can be said to be brought within the fiscal jurisdiction of another country to such a degree that such another country can tax the profits which the enterprise derived from that country. To fall within the realm of 'Force of Attraction Rule' two basic requirements which would satisfy [sic] is that (i) the foreign enterprise has a P.E. in the other State for the purpose of selling goods and merchandise and (ii) the direct sale by the foreign enterprise is the same or similar kind of goods or merchandise as sold by the P.E. in India [sic] In this case, we have already held that the assessee do not [sic] constitute a P.E. of various VGCs, therefore, 'Force of Attraction Rule', will not be applicable in this case. Thus, this issue becomes purely academic in this case.

However, in some of the Indian treaties, the expression 'indirectly attributable' has already been defined and, therefore, the application of the force of attraction rule in these cases shall have to be restricted within the ambit of the definition. A Special Bench of the ITAT in *Clifford Chance*,[526] for example, excluded the operation of the force of attraction principle in the context of India-UK treaty as the expression 'profits indirectly attributable to' was defined in Article 7(3)[527] of the treaty in express terms. The following observations of the Special Bench are instructive in this regard:

---

524. *ADIT v WNS North America Inc* [2013] taxmann.com 321 (Mum).
525. *Varian India(P) Ltd v ADIT* [2013] 33 taxmann.com 249 (Mum).
526. *ADIT v Clifford Chance* [2013] 143 ITD 1 (Mum).
527. India-UK Treaty, Art. 7 para. 3, which reads as follows:

> Where a permanent establishment takes an active part in negotiating, concluding or fulfilling contracts entered into by the enterprise, then, notwithstanding that other parts of the enterprise have also participated in those transactions, that proportion of profits of the enterprise arising out of those contracts which the contribution of the permanent establishment to those transactions bears to that of' the enterprise as a whole shall be treated for the purposes of paragraph 1 of this Article as being the profits indirectly attributable to that permanent establishment.

> 35. In our opinion, when the connotations of 'profits indirectly attributable to permanent establishment' are defined specifically in Article 7(1) of the India-UK DTAA which clearly explains the scope and ambit of the profits indirectly attributable to the PE and the provisions of said article being unambiguous and capable of giving a definite meaning, there is really no need to refer to the provisions of Article 7(1) of UN Model Convention which are materially different from the provisions of Article 7(1) of the India-UK DTAA read with Article 7(3) thereof. The reliance of the Division Bench of this Tribunal on the provisions of Article 7(1)(b) and Article 7(1)(c) of the UN Model Convention as well as on the UN Model Convention Commentary to come to a conclusion in the case of Linklaters LLP (supra) that the connotations of 'profits indirectly attributable to permanent establishment' used in Article 7(1) of the Indo-UK treaty incorporates a force of attraction rule thereby bringing an enterprise having a PE in another country within the fiscal jurisdiction of that another country to such a degree that such another country can properly tax all profits that the enterprise derives from that country - whether the transactions are routed and performed through their PE or not - is clearly misplaced and we are unable to subscribe to this proposition.

Even though India recently amended its tax treaty with Norway and Sri Lanka, wherein the force of attraction rule has been removed and a new protocol, signed with Australia, also seeks to do away with the force of attraction rule, the force of attraction rule still has the support of many states which vigorously support source-based taxation. They argue that such a rule has various potential administrative benefits, as it is not necessary, then, for the source state to absolutely determine whether particular activities are related to the PE or the income involved is attributable to it. The states favouring such a rule often prefer it not because they seek particularly broad taxing rights in this area, but because they want to ensure that difficulties of attribution do not prevent them from in practice exercising what may be well accepted and relatively conservative taxing rights.[528]

But as indicated in the preceding para, the rule must have its foundation in the domestic law in the absence of which it cannot be implemented through treaty provisions alone.[529] In a recent Canada Revenue Agency (CRA) audit of a company resident in India (NRCO) that carried on a service business in Canada through a PE, the interpretation and interaction of Article 7 of the Canada-India Tax Treaty and the relevant taxing provisions of the Canada Income Tax Act fell for consideration. The CRA proposed to assess NRCO on all profits earned on its Canadian customer service contracts, regardless of whether the services were performed inside Canada (onshore services) or outside Canada (offshore services). CRA's rationale was based on its interpretation of Article 7 of the Canada-India Treaty and on the principle that a tax treaty overrides the Income Tax Act (ITA). More particularly, the scope of the Business Profits article of the Canada-India Treaty (i.e., Article 7) is extended to include certain profits of an enterprise even though the activities are not directly carried on through the PE. This force of attraction rule in Article 7 of the Canada-India Treaty even goes further than the force of attraction rule in the UN Model and allows Canada or India, as the case may be, to tax similar business activities carried on outside its country. After lengthy

528. Lennard (n. 425) 17.
529. *Kulandagan Chettiar* (n. 304).

internal deliberations, CRA did finally agree to it that in the absence of a domestic law, it could not tax NRCO for the profits attributable to offshore services.[530]

3.3.3 The Independent Enterprise and the Arm's Length Principles: Limits on Source Taxation

A PE is not an independent legal entity as its business activities as well as business profits are controlled by the enterprise. But in order to give effect to the PE principle and delimit the tax jurisdiction of source state, the OECD Model, until 2008, provided that profits attributable to a PE were the profits which the PE might be expected to make as if:

(1) it were a distinct and separate enterprise (i.e., the independent enterprise principle); and
(2) it were engaged in the same or similar activities acting under the same or similar conditions and dealing wholly independently with the enterprise of which it was a PE.[531] This is known as the arm's length principle.

Similar rules continue to exist even today in the UN Model.[532]

However, a new functional separate entity approach (FSEA) and the principles for attribution of profits to a PE were set forth in the OECD's Attribution reports in 2008 and 2010 with the intent of achieving a uniform rule in this regard, which is known as the Authorised OECD Approach (AOA). Under the AOA, the profits that have to be attributed to a PE are 'the profits the PE would have earned at arm's length, particularly in its relations with related parties, as if it were a separate and independent legal entity engaged in the same or similar activities under the same or similar conditions, taking into account the functions performed, assets used and risks assumed by the enterprise through the PE and through the other parts of the enterprise'.[533]

This change was apparently necessitated because conflicting views among the states with regard to the implementation of the existing attribution rule, which led to a great deal of uncertainty in this regard. One view preferred to look at the profits of the company as a whole and decide how much of them were to be attributed to the PE. The other view argued that the PE should be treated as a functionally separate enterprise and its profits calculated without reference to the profits of the company as a whole. This uncertainty is revealed through various consultations, drafts reports, updates and reports issued by the OECD from time to time.[534] A Discussion Draft released by the

530. J Wilson and DC Hill, 'Relationship Between Tax Treaties and Domestic Tax law: Scenario Involving the Canada-India Tax Treaty', https://www.lexology.com/library/detail.aspx?g=fab88c7f-8b54-43f7-8eb0-d7e0bbe27afd, accessed 1 December 2018.
531. OECD MTC (2008) (n. 316) Art. 7 para. 2.
532. UN MTC (2017) (n. 292) Art. 7 para. 2.
533. OECD MTC (2017) (n. 290) Art. 7.
534. *See, e.g.*, the OECD 1993 Report, *Attribution of profits to Permanent Establishments*, OECD Model Tax Convention (OECD Pub 1993) full version vol II R (13)-1.

OECD in 2001[535] went to some lengths to set out a 'working hypothesis' for the attribution of profits to a PE to the effect that the PE is a 'distinct and separate enterprise' rather than any approach which merely attempts to apportion the total profits of the form. Thus, the approach to the attribution of profits to a PE placed heavy reliance on the content of the OECD's transfer pricing principles.

The July 2008 Report of the OECD was the culmination of series of discussion documents and draft reports produced from 2001 onwards. In its Final Report in 2008, the OECD sought a complete overhaul of the approach to the interpretation of Article 7 of the Model,[536] and set out how profits of an enterprise are to be attributed to a PE and taxed by the source state. The OECD insisted that the question of attributing profits to PEs was to be determined without being constrained by either the original intent or any historical interpretation of Article 7.[537] It recommended application of the arm's length principle as the fairest way to allocate taxing rights on the lines of Article 9. This Report was subsequently updated in the OECD 2010 Report, which provided background to the 2010 changes to the OECD Model and Commentary on Article 7. Pursuant to this Report, the AOA came to be incorporated in the 2010 OECD Model Convention,[538] thereby making the transfer pricing principles, relating to associated enterprise, applicable to PEs by treating the latter as functionally separate entity. The OECD had already published landmark guidance on transfer pricing in 1995,[539] which were also meant to be applied for the calculation of profits to be attributed to a PE.

It may be noted here that these transfer pricing principles are aimed at transactions between companies in the same corporate group. Even though the OECD recognised that dealings between different parts of the same company (e.g., head office (HO) and branch) are not the same as transactions between companies in the same corporate group, it still insisted that the transfer pricing principles would apply by analogy.

Under the AOA, the profit attribution to PEs is divided into a two-step procedure:[540]

Functional and Factual Analysis

(1) The first step comprises a functional and factual analysis to determine the role of PE in relation to the enterprise as a whole. The Commentary on Article 7 gives some guidance on the factors needed to form a view of the PE as a distinct and separate entity. It states that a functional and factual analysis,

535. OECD, *Discussion Draft on the Attribution of Profits to Permanent Establishments* (OECD Pub 2001).
536. OECD, *Report on the Attribution of Profits to Permanent Establishments* (OECD, 2008).
537. *See, e.g.*, OECD MTC (2008) (n. 316) Commentary on Art. 7 para. 6.
538. OECD, *Model Tax Convention on Income and on Capital* (Condensed version, OECD Pub 2010 (hereafter 'OECD MTC (2010)').
539. OECD, Transfer Pricing Guidelines for Multinational Enterprises and Tax Administrations (OECD July 1995) (hereafter 'the OECD 1995 TP Guidelines').
540. OECD, *2010 Report on The Attribution of Profits to Permanent Establishments* (OECD 2010) 14-20 (hereafter 'the OECD Attribution Report 2010').

along the lines set out in the OECD's transfer-pricing guidelines,[541] should be carried out to establish the economically significant activities and responsibilities undertaken by the PE. This would, broadly, entail establishing the rights and obligations arising out of transactions between the PE and separate enterprises,[542] identifying the significant 'people functions' (SPF) relevant to the attribution of economic ownership of assets and the attribution of economic ownership of assets to the PE,[543] identifying the SPF relevant to the assumption of risks and the attribution of risks to the PE.[544]

Allocating Profits to the PE

(2) In the second step, the fictitious dealings between the PE and the parent company are determined in order to evaluate, whether prices in intra-company-transactions have been set in accordance with the arm's length principle. Thus, dealings between a PE and its HO should be compared with transactions between independent enterprises, based on the comparability factors detailed in the TP Guidelines. This two-step analysis may result in two possible situations:

(1) If the first step determines that a PE is engaged in routine dealings with its HO and it does not undertake any SPF, it is entitled to routine remuneration for its services, since all its SPF-related decisions are taken

541. OECD, *Transfer Pricing Guidelines for Multinational Enterprises and Tax Administrations* (OECD 2017) (hereafter 'the OECD 2017 TP Guidelines').

542. For example, if a PE takes the form of manufacturing and sales operation, the sales revenue from independent customers arising from the factory's output might properly be attributed to the PE rather than the head office. Similarly, the obligation to pay for the raw materials used by the factory might properly be attributed to the factory.

543. Thus, if a head office in a state procures fixed assets, keeps the fixed asset register or implements a maintenance schedule, then this will not affect the attribution of the assets to the PE in which the assets are actually being used. The treatment of intangibles, on the other hand, will be different. Intangibles are to be attributed to the business location where the work of developing, acquiring and its management take place. The provision of identifying 'people functions' is taken from the OECD's work on transfer pricing dealing with arm's length terms between connected enterprises, rather than parts of the same enterprise. Economic ownership of intangibles rests with the location in which the related risks are borne. If an enterprise owns, for example, a patent for a particular drug which is sold by a distributor in many states, the economic ownership will belong to that part of the enterprise which carries out the research to develop the drug and it will bear the losses if the medical trials are unsuccessful or of the manufacturing licences are not obtained.

544. This is necessary in a case, where one part of an enterprise has economic ownership of an asset, but a different part of the enterprise may bear the risks associated with the use of that asset. To illustrate, road building equipment may be economically owned by a PE in a state, but the head office, located in another state, may have the power to determine on which road building projects the equipment will be used. The risk associated with profits or losses, arising from the equipment, thus, lie with head office. Likewise, a PE in one state may be relying on the successful development of a new drug for its future profits. If another part of the enterprise is developing that drug, then not only the developer of the drug but also the PE which hoped to market it would be adversely affected if the trials fail. If the PE takes an active part in managing the development of the drug (possibly due to its effect on the profits of the PE) then both bear risk in connection with the development of the drug.

by the HO and it neither assumes any significant risk nor owns any assets of note. In the second step, the cost and arm's length mark-up are determined accordingly for such a PE.

(2) However, if it is identified at the first step that the PE is undertaking certain SPF, owns assets and assumes risks, a detailed comparability analysis at the second step is required to determine the arms' length consideration of such dealings. Attribution, based on the Profit Split Method, Revenue Split, etc., may also be applied, depending on the facts and circumstances of the case.[545]

3.3.3.1 The AOA: Mounting Criticism

The AOA has been viewed with scepticism by both OECD members and non-members. It has been criticised on several grounds. *First,* the AOA involves a longwinded process of consultation and development in contrast to much simpler procedure existing until 2008. Lynne Oats and others rightly consider this procedure as 'difficult to apply'.[546] They also point to a lack of detailed guidance on how to apply it except for companies in the financial services sector.[547] Further, despite the existence of specific guidelines,[548] the AOA can assume an even higher level of difficulty due to the varying international regulation in the case of banks. Minimum capital requirements and a more detailed evaluation of the risks assumed and creditworthiness are some of the trickier areas.

Second, the starting point for any attribution of profits to a PE is the branch accounts. However, this approach restricts, in many cases, the source state's right to amend the profits shown in the branch accounts in accordance with the general principle for attribution of profits set out in the relevant treaty and in line with its domestic law. The AOA, thus, entails the risk of erosion of tax base in the source state, with no practical benefits. Some scholars have, therefore, rightly argued that in certain circumstances, the AOA may transfer profits from the PE state to the residence state of the enterprise. This is a product of the unlimited recognition of 'deductible' notional expenses in case in which the domestic law of the PE state would otherwise disallow such deductions.[549] The 2010 OECD Commentary also includes a number of clauses that highlight the requirement of an 'effective connection' between the PE and the

545. The OECD Attribution Report 2010 (n. 540) 14-20.
546. Oats, Miller and Mulligan (n. 344) 264.
547. *Ibid.*
548. For the financial sector the OECD dedicated two sections of the 'Report on the attribution of profit to permanent establishments' to banks (Part II) and to 'enterprises carrying on global trading of financial instruments' (Part III). Although the guidelines in these sectors are more detailed, they did not end up the doubts and perplexity still exists about its application.
549. L. Nouel, 'The New Article 7 of the OECD Model Tax Convention: The End of the Road?' (2011) vol. 65(1) BFIT 5.

holdings, liabilities, intangible assets and capital assets.[550] The respective assets will only be considered part of the business assets of the PE if such an effective connection exists. This strict 'effective connection test', in the absence of clear guidelines, severely limits the taxing rights of the source state.[551] Kofler and Thiel also note in their illuminating article that when economic ownership of an asset (e.g., a machine or inventory) is transferred to the HO or another PE, the AOA, in essence, does not restrict a domestic law provision regarding an immediate realisation of hidden reserves upon a cross-border transfer of assets within an enterprise. Likewise, it does not restrict the realisation of arm's length profits on other cross-border internal 'dealings' (e.g., internal services), where no real transaction takes place and there is no corresponding cash flow. This may be seen as discriminatory if no similar charge is levied upon a purely domestic transfer of assets or other internal dealings.[552]

Third, although it is feasible in theory to treat the PE as a functionally separate entity, this is expected to be difficult in practice. Due to the fact that the AOA is based on fictitious dealings that have to be assumed between the parties, difficulties in determining the taxable intra-group transactions might arise. Schoueri explains that a PE is more of an integrated entity than a separate one due to the control that the HO has on it and therefore the arm's length price (ALP), based on fiction, cannot reflect economic reality, as multinational enterprises (MNEs) do not treat each subsidiary as a separate entity but rather as integrated entities, whose prices can be controlled by an MNE, considering the respective tax implications.[553] The PE, for instance, has no sources of finance separate from the enterprise and it is difficult to determine the level of return on finance (e.g., interest payable) which ought to be deducted from the taxable profits of the PE. Kobetsky reflects a similar perception:

> [A] permanent establishment is one part of a whole enterprise with a unitary profit motive and common control. For highly integrated international enterprises, such as bank, the use of the separate entity fiction is inappropriate from both a normative and practical perspective.[554]

The problem is further compounded by the supporting documentation available to evidence the pricing policies between PE and HO/other parts of the enterprise, which will be less formal in practice than that needed for transactions between separate legal entities (e.g., fellow subsidiaries).[555] Also, the OECD's position itself is not very clear on the approach. While it recommends the FSEA principle, the traces of the single entity approach are still followed and included in the guidelines.

550. OECD MTC (2017) (n. 290) Commentary on Art. 10 (dividends), paras 32.1, 32.2; Commentary on Art. 11 (interest) paras 25.1, 25.2; Commentary on Art. 12 (royalties) paras 21.1, 21.2; Commentary on Art. 13 (capital gains) paras 27.1, 27.2 and Commentary on Art. 21 (other income) paras 5.1, 5.2.
551. G Kofler and S van Thiel, 'The "Authorised OECD Approach" and EU Tax Law' (2011) vol. 51(8) Euro Tax 327, 328.
552. *Ibid.*, 329-330.
553. LE Schoueri, 'Arm's Length: Beyond the Guidelines of the OECD' (2015) vol. 69(12) BFIT 690.
554. M Kobetsky, 'Article 7 of the OECD Model: Defining the Personality of Permanent Establishments' (2006) vol. 60(10) BFIT 411.
555. Oats, Miller and Mulligan (n. 344) 268.

Fourth, Article 7 includes the distributive rule regarding business profits. Since the states have different accounting systems, profits and losses cannot be determined without clear accounting standards. Usually, such standards are established by domestic laws of the contracting states, and they may deviate from one another.[556]

Fifth, a functions, assets and risks (FAR) based attribution ignores the contribution to business profits made by demand-side factors such as access to marketplace etc. India has taken the position that business profits are contributed by both demand and supply of the goods. Accordingly, a jurisdiction contributes towards demand in two significant ways: *first,* by facilitating the economy and the ability of their resident to pay; and *second,* by maintenance of markets that enables the sales. Further, the state that facilitates the production or supply of goods also contributes towards the business profits. Where the economies of both the treaty partners contribute to the business profits, there exists sufficient economic justification for profits to be allocated among them in a manner that avoids double taxation.[557] Baker argues that the argument regarding demand-side factors, albeit interesting, may not prove ultimately persuasive because in his opinion, the taxation of a PE is the taxation of profits and not of sales or value added.[558] Baker's argument, however, negates the very normative justification for source taxation, proposed by the source taxation theorists, which takes into consideration the demand-side or the market factors in the generation of business profits.[559]

Finally, under new Article 7(2) of the OECD Model, after the attribution of profits to a PE, such income is taxable and the extent to which it is taxable is to be determined under the source state's domestic law, provided there is conformity between Article 7(2) and other provisions of the treaty, such as Article 24(3) on non-discrimination.[560] However, if the domestic law does not recognise dealings recognised under Article 7(2) or prevents a PE from deductibility of expenses not exclusively incurred for the purposes of the PE, there will be a conflict, which may result in difference between the taxable income of a PE in the source and residence states. The Commentary interprets Article 7(2) as having a non-discrimination role which prevails over the domestic law of the source state.[561] This interpretation, however, runs afoul of the language of Article 7 and its history because the provision is not drafted as a non-discrimination provision and Article 24(3) expressly deals with non-discrimination of the PE. Vann rightly argues that new Article 7 does not prevail over a domestic law provision that

556. E Reimer, M Orell and S Schmid, *Permanent Establishment: A Domestic Taxation, Bilateral Tax Treaty and the OECD Perspective* (3rd edn, Wolters Kluwer 2014) 143.
557. CBDT, 'Report on Profit Attribution to Permanent Establishments' dated 18 April 2019, https://www.incometaxindia.gov.in/Lists/Press%20Releases/Attachments/757/CBDT_stakeholder_comments_Permanent_Establishment_18_4_19.pdf, accessed 14 January 2021.
558. P Baker QC, 'CBDT Draft Report on PE Profit Attribution – Treading the Unbeaten Path?', https://www.taxsutra.com/content/cbdt-draft-report-pe-profit-attribution-treading-unbeaten-path, accessed 14 January 2021.
559. *See, for more information,* RS Avi-Yonah, 'International Taxation of Electronic Commerce' (1997) vol. 52(3) Tax L Rev 507, 520-521; *see also* AJ Cockfield, 'Reforming the Permanent Establishment Principle Through a Quantitative Economic Presence Test' (2003) vol. 38 CBLJ 400, citing Vogel Part III 393, 400.
560. OECD Model (2010) (n. 538) Commentary on Art. 7(2) 139, para. 30.
561. *Ibid.*, 139 para. 33.

prevents deduction of expenses of non-resident and resident enterprises, if the expenses are paid overseas.[562] Vann, therefore, suggests that the old Article 7(3) should have been included in the 2010 Commentary as an option for some countries, with a specific statement that it deals with a non-discrimination problem not addressed by Article 24, i.e., to provide a deduction for expenses incurred overseas if such expenses are proscribed by the domestic law of the source state.[563]

In view of the above considerations, the AOA, right from its inception, has not been received, with much enthusiasm, by countries, both developed and developing. Six out of the thirty-one OECD Member countries that approved the 2010 OECD Model made a reservation indicating that they intend to use the previous version of Article 7(Chile, Greece, Mexico, New Zealand, Portugal and Turkey).[564]

Furthermore, the UN Committee of Experts on International Cooperation in Tax Matters also agreed not to include the AOA in the future version of the UN Model Tax Convention.[565] The UN Committee saw the OECD approach as having the potential to change the balance between source and resident taxation, contrary to the interests of many developing countries.[566] It also ran counter to paragraph 3 of Article 7 of the UN Model, which generally disallowed deductions for amounts 'paid' (other than towards reimbursement of actual expenses) by a PE to its HO. That rule was seen as continuing to be appropriate in the context of the UN Model Convention, whatever changes were made to the OECD Model Tax Convention and commentaries.[567] The Committee finally resolved not to adopt the approach to Article 7 outlined in the OECD 2008 report as relevant to the UN Model Convention. In updating its Model Convention, even the US has declined to follow the 'Authorized OECD Approach' to the attribution of profits reflected in the OECD 2010 Model. The UK, too, has had mixed success in getting the new OECD Article 7 into its recent treaties.[568] Australia treaties and domestic law[569] also do not align with the AOA with respect to the attribution of profits.[570]

562. RJ Vann, 'Do We Need 7(3)? History and Purpose of the Business Profits Deduction Rules in Tax Treaties' Paper presented at the Tax History Conference, Cambridge 2010.
563. *Ibid.*
564. UN Committee of Experts on International Cooperation in Tax Matters, *Report on the Fifth Session'* Economic and Social Council Official Records (hereafter 'the UN Experts' Report 2009') 2009 Supp 25 (UN Pub 2010) 9, paras 31, 34.
565. *Ibid.*
566. The UN Experts' Report 2009 (n. 564) 9, para. 31.
567. *Ibid.*, para. 34.
568. J Schwarz, 'Model Treaty 2016: What Does it Say about the US and BEPS?' 21 February 2016, http://kluwertaxblog.com/2016/02/21/us-model-treaty-2016-what-does-it-say-about-the-us-and-beps/?_ga=2.103386121.846281485.1544359381-449772679.1544359381, accessed 11 December 2018.
569. The Income Tax Assessment Act 1997(UK), subdivision 815-C.
570. N Houseman & G Condoleon, *Attribution of Profit to Permanent Establishments: Asia Overview* (PWC 2014) 5, https://www.pwc.com/jp/en/tax-focus-on/assets/attribution-of-profit-to-permanent-establishments-asia-overview.pdf, accessed 11 December 2020.

3.3.3.2 *BEPS Debates on Profit Attribution*

The profit attribution polemics dominated all through the BEPS deliberations as well. Action 7 focused on whether the existing rules of Article 7 of the OECD Model would be appropriate for determining the profits that would be allocated to PEs resulting from the changes to the definition of PEs.[571] The conclusion was that these changes do not require substantive modifications to the existing guidance concerning the attribution of profits to PEs under Article 7 of the OECD Model, but that there is a need for additional guidance on the application of Article 7 due to these changes, in particular for PEs outside the financial sector.[572] Accordingly, the OECD released its additional guidance on 22 March 2018,[573] setting out general principles of the attribution of profits to PEs in light of aforesaid changes to Article 5. The Report explains that after it has been established that a PE exists in terms of Article 5(4) of the OECD Model that are not preparatory or auxiliary in nature, the attribution of profits to the PE should be determined under an analysis of the amounts of revenue and expense that the PE would have recognised if it were a separate and independent enterprise.[574] The above principle applies regardless of whether a tax administration has adopted the AOA.[575]

This additional analysis, however, still leaves the most important questions unanswered. For instance, it is still unclear how the 2018 guidance fits into the overall framework of the current OECD guidance relating to the attribution of profits to a PE, and therefore the degree to which member jurisdictions are committed to following the guidance. The executive summary states that the 2018 guidance is designed to provide high-level general principles, but does not specify whether the new guidance is designed to supplement the current AOA rules or act as commentary to them. The guidance also does not address the lack of a common set of jargons and concepts between the AOA, which is applicable to Article 7 cases, and an analysis under Article 9. In the absence of such harmonisation of the two approaches, the result in any particular case may differ depending on which analysis is performed first - the Article 7 or the Article 9 analysis. The revised examples, though providing more details on how the AOA would apply, do not provide any additional clarity on this crucial issue.

Being conscious of the apprehensions relating to the AOA, the Report clarifies that this principle applies regardless of whether a tax administration adopts the AOA contained in Article 7 in the 2010 version of the OECD Model, or any other approach used to attribute profits under a previous version of Article 7 of the model. The Report also makes it clear that the guidance does not intend to extend the application of the AOA to countries that have not adopted that approach in their treaties or domestic legislation.[576]

571. OECD MTC (2017) (n. 290) Art. 5.
572. BEPS Action 7 Final Report 2015 (n. 402) 45.
573. OECD, *Additional Guidance on the Attribution of Profits to Permanent Establishments*, BEPS Action 7 (OECD Pub 2018) (hereafter 'OECD Additional Guidance (2018)').
574. *Ibid.*, 10, para. 6.
575. *Ibid.*
576. OECD Additional Guidance (2018) (n. 573) 10, para. 6.

3.3.3.3 *Indian Domestic Tax Law and Treaty Practices: Reactions to the AOA*

Not convinced with the appropriateness of the OECD approach to attribution of profits to PE, India has reserved its right to use the updated version of Article 7 of the Model Tax Convention in 2010 (and the Commentary), as well as any subsequent changes made to it. India, in fact, is the only country among all the 'observer' nations, to expressly state that it does not agree with the OECD approach.

The domestic law of India contains basic framework for attribution of profits to a 'business connection' or 'Permanent Establishment'. Section 9(1)(i) of the Act provides the legal framework to the effect that income from a 'business connection' in India shall be taxable in India but only to the extent as is reasonably attributable to operations carried out in India.[577] Rule 10 of the Income Tax Rules, 1962 provides that if the tax authority is of the opinion that income arising to a non-resident cannot be properly ascertained, the amount of such income may be calculated at:

(i) a percentage of turnover, as may be considered appropriate; or
(ii) an amount which bears the same proportion to the total profits of business of such person as the receipts accruing or arising bear to the total receipts of business; or
(iii) in any other manner deemed suitable by the Revenue authorities.

Thus, the rules for attribution of profits to a business connection or a PE, contained in Rule 10, grant the tax authorities wide powers to determine profit attribution and this has led to a considerable degree of adhocism in profit attribution in terms of Rule 10. Applying a global profit rate on India specific turnover would result in estimation of total profits from Indian turnover, though the entire activities giving rise to such profits, e.g., research and development, manufacturing, marketing and selling may not have been carried out in India. For example, in some cases, certain marketing activities as well as negotiation and conclusion of sale contracts may have been carried out in India, but all other activities, e.g., research and development, manufacturing, technical services etc. may have been carried out outside India. In such cases, the Indian courts have, in the past, used an ad hoc basis for estimating the profits attributable to India specific activities, based on facts of each case. In *Anglo-French Textile Company,*[578] for instance, the Supreme Court of India returned a finding that in the facts of the case, 10% of profits were to be attributed to operations carried out in India. In *Hukum Chand Mills,*[579] the Supreme Court found that attribution of 15% of profits was reasonable in the facts of that case. More recently, in *Motorola Inc,*[580] a Special Bench of the ITAT held that attribution of 20% of profits was sufficient for role played by the PE in negotiation and conclusion of contracts and supply of equipment

577. At (n. 302), s. 9(1)(i) Expl (a).
578. *Anglo-French textile Ltd v CIT* (1954) 25 ITR 27 SC).
579. *Hukum Chand Mills Ltd v CIT* (1976) 103 ITR 548 (SC).
580. *Motorola Inc. v DCIT (2005)* 95 ITD 269 (Del-Trib) (SB).

in India by the PE of the taxpayer. Similarly, in *Galileo International Inc*,[581] 15% of total revenues were considered to be attributable to the Indian PE on the basis that the PE played a role in negotiating contracts. In *Nipro Asia Pte Ltd*,[582] the Delhi Bench of the ITAT held that Rule 10 of the Income tax Rules, 1962 can be invoked if the tax authority is of the opinion that amount of income accruing to non-resident companies on account of business connection in India is not ascertainable.

Indian tax treaties show a similar trend. In some of the treaties, in fact, the provisions on the lines of the domestic law rules have been incorporated. In India-Mauritius Treaty, for instance, Article 7(2) provides for estimation of profits attributable to PE on a reasonable basis in a case where determination of profits attributable to it presents exceptional difficulties. A similar provision is also found in treaties with many other countries such as Bangladesh, Canada, Bhutan, Denmark, Italy etc. Thus, unless the domestic law of India and its tax treaties are modified to specifically incorporate the AOA, the transfer pricing principles cannot be made applicable for the purpose of attribution of profits to PEs.

Some tax lawyers, however, have begun canvassing the view that the Indian judiciary has accorded sanction to the general application of principles of transfer pricing to attribution of profits to PEs,[583] basing their arguments on the holdings of the Indian Supreme Court in *Morgan Stanley*.[584] However, a close scrutiny of holdings in *Morgan Stanley*[585] does not bear that out. In *Morgan Stanley*, the case related to an associated enterprise, which was also held to constitute a service PE and since remuneration paid to the associated enterprise was already at arm's length and justified by a transfer pricing analysis, the Court upheld the reasoning of the AAR that there was no further need for attribution of profits to it. This judgment is, thus, rendered on the peculiar facts of the case and does not lay down any general rule of universal application that for attribution of profits to PEs, transfer pricing regulations will *ipso facto* come in to play.

It may also be noted that in *Morgan Stanley*, the AAR, in its decision had mixed up the concepts of arm's length analysis and attribution of profits and proceeded to equate an arm's length analysis with the attribution of profits itself and it is this assumption of the AAR that the Indian Supreme Court erroneously upheld, without going into the questions of whether these were two different notions and whether the attribution of profits necessarily presupposes a transfer pricing analysis. Kapadia J put it thus:

> Under the impugned ruling delivered by the AAR, remuneration to MSAS was justified by a transfer pricing analysis and, therefore, no further income could be attributed to the PE (MSAS). In other words, the said ruling equates an arm's length analysis (ALA) with attribution of profits. It holds that once a transfer pricing analysis is undertaken; there is no further need to attribute profits to a PE. The impugned ruling is correct in principle insofar as an associated enterprise, that

581. *DIT v Galileo International Inc* [2009] 180 Taxman 357 (Delhi).
582. *DDIT v Nipro Asia Pte Ltd* (2017) 79 taxmann.com 154 (ITAT-Del).
583. Houseman & Condoleon (n. 570) 9.
584. *Morgan Stanley* (n. 358).
585. *Ibid.*

> also constitutes a PE, has been remunerated on an arm's length basis taking into account all the risk-taking functions of the enterprise. In such cases nothing further would be left to be attributed to the PE. The situation would be different if transfer pricing analysis does not adequately reflect the functions performed and the risks assumed by the enterprise. In such a situation, there would be a need to attribute profits to the PE for those functions/risks that have not been considered. Therefore, in each case the data placed by the taxpayer has to be examined as to whether the transfer pricing analysis placed by the taxpayer is exhaustive of attribution of profits and that would depend on the functional and factual analysis to be undertaken in each case.[586]

It may further be noted here that transfer pricing provisions,[587] which were introduced in India in 2001,[588] only apply to international transactions[589] carried out between associated enterprises. Certain specified domestic transactions were brought within its ambit much later.[590] The expression 'international transaction' itself has been defined to mean a transaction between two or more associated enterprises and includes purchase, sale or lease of tangible or intangible property, provision of services, or lending or borrowing money, or any other transaction that has a bearing on the profits, income, losses or assets of the enterprise.[591] 'Associated enterprise', for the purpose, means, in relation to another enterprise, an enterprise that participates, directly or indirectly, in the management, control or capital of the other enterprise.[592] The provisions also set out a certain shareholding participation threshold under which two or more enterprises are deemed to be associated with each other.[593] A PE, thus, is not an associated enterprise as defined in the domestic law. The domestic transfer pricing rules, therefore, do not apply to PEs as such. In *Morgan Stanley*,[594] however, it was assumed by the Supreme Court that the transfer pricing provisions apply to the PEs as well. The observation of Kapadia J brings this out:

> The object behind enactment of transfer pricing regulations is to prevent shifting of profits outside India. Under Article 7(2) not all profits of MSCo would be taxable in India but only those which have economic nexus with PE in India. A foreign enterprise is liable to be taxed in India on so much of its business profit as is attributable to the PE in India. The quantum of taxable income is to be determined in accordance with the provisions of IT Act. All provisions of IT Act are applicable, including provisions relating to depreciation, investment losses, deductible expenses, carry-forward and set-off losses etc.[595]

In *Morgan Stanley*, the Court also erroneously proceeded to assume that the UN Model Convention also makes the principles of transfer pricing applicable to attribution

586. *Morgan Stanley* (n. 358) para. 32.
587. At (n. 302), Chapter X: Special Provisions Relating to Avoidance of Tax.
588. By Finance Act 2001 with effect from 1 April 2001.
589. At (n. 302), s. 92.
590. Finance Act 2012 with effect from 1 April 2013.
591. At (n. 302), s. 92B.
592. At (n. 302), s. 92A.
593. *Ibid.*
594. *Morgan Stanley* (n. 358).
595. *Ibid.*, para. 32.

of profits to PEs. The assumption is clearly brought out in the following words of Kapadia J:

> Article 7 of the UN Model Convention, inter alia, provides that only that portion of business profits is taxable in the source country which is attributable to the PE. It specifies how such business profits should be ascertained. Under the said article, a PE is treated as if it is an independent enterprise (profit centre) dehors the head office and which deals with the head office at arm's length. Therefore, its profits are determined on the basis as if it is an independent enterprise. The profits of the PE are determined on the basis of what an independent enterprise under similar circumstances might be expected to derive on its own. Article 7(2) of the U.N. Model Convention advocates the arm's length approach for attribution of profits to a PE.[596]

In so assuming, the Court failed to consider the historical development of this contentious issue of interpretation of Article 7 and principle of profits attribution to the PE. The UN Committee of Experts on International Cooperation in Tax Matters saw the OECD approach as having the potential to change the balance between source and resident taxation, contrary to the interests of many developing countries.[597] The Committee also felt that it ran counter to paragraph 3 of Article 7 of the UN Model, which generally disallowed deductions for amounts 'paid' (other than towards reimbursement of actual expenses) by a PE to its HO. That rule was seen as continuing to be appropriate in the context of the UN Model Convention, whatever changes were made to the OECD Model Tax Convention and commentaries.[598] The Committee, therefore, resolved not to adopt the approach to Article 7 outlined in the OECD 2008 report as relevant to the UN Model Convention. *Morgan Stanley*, thus, was decided under the mistaken impression that the application of transfer pricing rules to the attribution of profits to a PE has been ratified by the UN Model Tax Convention.

Further, a bare reading of Circular No. 23 of 1969[599] and Circular No. 5 of 2005,[600] which have been referred to by the Court in *Morgan Stanley*, makes it plain that these circulars do not make the transfer pricing regulations generally applicable to the attribution of profits to the PE. While the 1969 Circular, which already stands withdrawn by the Central Board of Direct Taxes (CBDT) by Circular No. 7 of 2009,[601] merely explained the scope of 'business connection' in terms of section 9(1), Circular No. 5 of 2004 lies within a far narrower compass and applies only to taxation of IT enabled business process outsourcing units in India.[602] It is very incongruous to imagine that on one hand, India would issue circulars to make transfer pricing regulations applicable to profit attributions to PEs and on the other hand, it would go

596. *Ibid.*, para. 31.
597. The UN Experts' Report 2009 (n. 564) 9, para. 31.
598. *Ibid.*, para. 34.
599. CBDT Circular No. 23/1969 dated 23 July 1969.
600. CBDT Circular No. 5/2004 dated 28 September, 2005.
601. CBDT Circular No. 7/2009 dated 22 October 2009.
602. *See* Circular No. 5 (n. 600).

on to vociferously oppose the new Article 7 of the OECD Model Convention at various international fora. *Morgan Stanley*,[603] therefore, was not correctly decided.

The subsequent cases, for example, *Rolls Royce*,[604] *Set Satellite*,[605] *Galileo International Inc*,[606] and *BBC Worldwide Ltd*[607] merely follow *Morgan Stanley* and do not add to the strength of the precedent. Thus, there is apparently no warrant for the proposition that profit attribution to PEs at arm's length, necessarily entail the mechanics of transfer pricing, spelt out by the OECD.[608]

In view of India's stated objections to the OECD approach and also with a view to bringing greater clarity and predictability, a committee was formed by the CBDT[609] to examine the existing scheme of profit attribution to a PE and to recommend changes to Rule 10. The committee in its report[610] stated that profit attribution by apportionment under Rule 10 should be in accordance with India's position and views. The committee broadly focused on the formulary apportionment method and the fractional apportionment method as options to attribute profits to a PE. The committee rejected the formulary apportionment method as it required an apportionment of consolidated profits of the enterprise earned from different jurisdictions and it may not be feasible and practical to obtain details related to operations in other jurisdictions. The committee, however, found the option of fractional apportionment more feasible and practical since it would largely be based on information related to Indian operations. This was in line with Indian tax treaties and Rule 10. The committee prescribed a three-factor method based on equal weight accorded to sales, representing demand, and manpower and assets, which represent supply including marketing activities.[611] On profit attribution in the case of a digital economy business, the committee unanimously decided that

603. *Morgan Stanley* (n. 358).
604. *Rolls Royce Singapore Pvt Ltd v ADIT* (2011) 202 Taxman 45 (Del).
605. *Set Satellite Singapore v DDIT* (2008) 307 ITR 205 (Bom).
606. *Galileo International Inc v* DCIT [2008] 19 SOT 257 (Delhi).
607. *DIT v BBC Worldwide Ltd*, (2011) 203 Taxman 554 (Del).
608. The OECD 2017 TP Guidelines (n. 541).
609. Central Board Direct Taxation, India's apex body on direct tax administration.
610. Report on Profit Attribution to PEs submitted by the Committee to Examine the Issues related to Profit Attribution to Permanent Establishment (PE) in India and Amendment of Rule 10 of Income-tax Rules 1962 (hereafter 'the CBDT Committee Report on Profit Attribution'), http://incometaxindia.gov.in/News/Public_consultation_Notice_18_4_19.pdf#search=cbdt%20draft%20report%20on%20profit%20attribution, accessed 21 January 2021.
611. The formula gives equal weightage to the three factors: sales, employees (headcount and wages) and assets as under:
Profits attributable to operations in India = Profits derived from India x [SI/3xST + (NI/6xNT) + (WI/6xWT) + (AI/3xAT)] where,

SI = sales revenue derived by Indian operations from sales in India
ST = total sales revenue derived by Indian operations from sales in India and outside India
NI = number of employees employed with respect to Indian operations and located in India
NT = total number of employees employed with respect to Indian operations and located in India and outside India
WI = wages paid to employees employed with respect to Indian operations and located in India
WT = total wages paid to employees employed with respect to Indian operations and located in India and outside India
AI = assets deployed for Indian operations and located in India
AT = total assets deployed for Indian operations and located in India and outside India

the user contribution can be a substitute for either assets or employees, and supplement their role in contributing to the profits of the enterprise. The committee, however, noted that different weights are to be assigned to different categories of digital businesses, basis the level of user intensity. Recognising the need to avoid double taxation of profits, the committee recommended that the profits derived from Indian operations that have already been subject to tax in India in the hands of a subsidiary should be deducted from the apportioned profits. The committee also favoured the view that in a case where no sales take place in India, and the profits that can be apportioned to the supply activities are already taxed in the hands of an Indian subsidiary, there may be no further taxes payable by the enterprise.

3.3.3.4 Restrictions on the Deductibility of PE Expenses

Indian domestic law[612] incorporates certain restrictions on the deductibility of PE expenses that are not incurred in India. Section 44C was introduced in the Act for this purpose. The CBDT issued a circular in 1976[613] wherein it explained the intent behind the provision. The circular stated that it is extremely difficult to scrutinise and verify claims in respect of HO expenses, particularly in the absence of account books of the HO which are kept outside India. It added that foreign companies operating through branches in India sometimes try to reduce the incidence of tax in India by inflating their claims in respect of HO expenses. Section 44C defines HO expenses and lays down limit to which such expenses can be claimed as deduction from PE profits. It covers all executive and general administration expenses including rent, rates, taxes, insurance, salary, travelling etc. incurred by the non-resident outside India.

The limit of deduction is restricted to 5% of adjusted total income[614] or an amount of so much of HO expenditure, which is attributable to the business or profession of the taxpayer in India, whichever is less.[615] In *Emirates Commercial Bank*, the Bombay High Court clarified that section 44C cover only those expenses which are common for various locations and require apportionment and do not affect the expenses exclusively incurred for Indian PE.[616]

In its tax treaties, India, generally, provides for deduction of expenses which are incurred for the purposes of the business of the PE, whether incurred in India or elsewhere.[617] However, these are attribution rule only and once the expenses are

---

Profits derived from Indian operations = amount higher of the following amounts:

a. The amount arrived at by multiplying the revenue derived from India x Global operational profit margin, or
b. 2% of the revenue derived from India

Profits derived from India = Revenue derived from India x Global operational profit margin as referred in paragraph

612. At (n. 302), s. 44C.
613. CBDT Circular No. 202/1976 dated 5 July 1976.
614. At (n. 302), s. 44C(a).
615. *ibid.*, s. 44C(c).
616. *CIT v Emirates Commercial Bank Ltd* (2003) 62 ITR 55 (Bom).
617. *See, e.g.*, India-Mauritius Tax Treaty, Art. 7.

attributed, whether these expenses are deductible will have to be determined on the basis of Indian domestic law. In some treaties, India has expressly provided that these deductions shall be 'in accordance with the provisions of and subject to the limitations of the taxation laws of that State'.[618]

In *State Bank of Mauritius*,[619] however, the Mumbai Bench of the Tribunal, in the context of India-Mauritius treaty came to the conclusion that Article 7(3) of the India-Mauritius DTAA, unlike the India-US treaty is not subject to the domestic law and thus a disallowance by the revenue under section 43B of the domestic law was held to be impermissible. However, this view of the Tribunal is clearly erroneous. The India-Mauritius Treaty follows the wordings of old Article 7(3) of the OECD Model and the OECD Commentary on this article makes it clear that these rules are mere rule of attribution only and once the expenses are attributed, whether these expenses are deductible will have to be determined on the basis of domestic law of the contracting states. The following observations in the Commentary[620] are illuminating in this regard:

> Paragraph 3 only determines which expenses should be attributed to the permanent establishment for purposes of determining the profits attributable to that permanent establishment. It does not deal with the issue of whether those expenses, once attributed, are deductible when computing the taxable income of the permanent establishment since the conditions for the deductibility of expenses are a matter to be determined by domestic law, subject to the rule of Article 24 on non-discrimination (in particular, para 3 and 4 of that Article).

Since the provisions of the OECD Model and Indo-Mauritius Treaty are *pari materia*, it is the domestic law of India that will determine the extent of deductibility of the expenses in question in view of the OECD Commentaries.[621] *State Bank of Mauritius*, therefore, was not correctly decided.

Thus, all these international debates and discussions, coupled with the judicial holdings of the municipal courts, infallibly point to the incessant easing of physical presence barriers to the attribution of business profits and its taxability by the source state.

3.3.3.5 International Transportation: An Exception to the PE Rule

An enterprise, engaged in international shipping and air transportation, may have branches in different countries and its business activity, therefore, usually involve many countries. Therefore, the PE principle may require that the business profits be taxed in many countries. However, it is not only difficult to determine the apportionment of profits to the involved countries (thus the PEs), but the total taxes thus incurred may be too heavy a burden for the enterprise to bear, which in some cases may even outrun its accounting profits. Since it is common knowledge that the

618. India-USA Treaty, Art. 7; also, India-UK Treaty, Art. 7.
619. *State Bank of Mauritius Limited v DDIT* (2012)149 TTJ 708 (Mum).
620. OECD MTC (2010) (n. 538) Commentary on Art. 7(3) 163 para. 30.
621. *Kulandagan Chettiar* (n. 304); *see also* Lang and Brugger (n. 287) 100.

international transportation industry earns a relatively low profit, it was considered reasonable to tackle its international taxes, which under the PE principle would be overwhelmingly heavy, in a different way for its better development.[622]

Until 2017, the OECD Model provided that profits from the operation of ships or aircraft in international traffic would be taxable only in the contracting state in which the place of effective management of the enterprise is situated. If the place of effective management of a shipping enterprise or of an inland waterways transport enterprise is aboard a ship or a boat, then it shall be deemed to be situated in the contracting state in which the home harbour of the ship or boat is situated, or, if there is no such home harbour, in the contracting state of which the operator of the ship or boat is a resident.[623]

A review of the OECD treaty practices and some non-OECD practices, however, reveals that the most of these states favoured the idea of assigning taxing rights to the state of the enterprise.[624] Article 8 was, accordingly, revised in 2017 Model Convention, giving taxing rights of profits from operation of ships or aircrafts in international traffic to the state of residence of the enterprise and such profits shall also include profits from the participation in a pool, a joint business or an international operating agency.[625] As per Article 3, the term international traffic means any transport by ship or aircraft, except a purely domestic traffic when the ship or aircraft is operated solely between places in the contracting states.[626] Even if part of the voyage or transport takes place outside the state, it will not make a domestic traffic international in terms of Article 8, unless there is a stop in another state, which is not limited to mere refuelling or maintenance.[627]

The OECD Commentary further points out that shipping and airline enterprises, apart from the actual operation of their ship or aircraft to ply passengers and cargo, also carry out other activities which are not directly connected with such operation, but which do make minor contribution to these operations. These activities shall also be considered to be ancillary to the operation of ships and aircraft in international traffic.[628] These ancillary activities could typically include, for example:

(1) Leasing a ship or aircraft on charter fully equipped, crewed and supplied must be treated like the profits from the carriage of passengers or cargo, including leasing a ship or aircraft on a bare boat charter basis when it is an ancillary

622. UN MTC (2017) (n. 292) Commentary on Art. 8, 239, para. 2.
623. OECD MTC (2010) (n. 538) Art. 8.
624. OECD MTC (2017) (n. 290) Commentary on Art. 8 para. 2.
625. *Ibid.*, Art. 8, which reads as follows:

> Article 8: International Shipping and Air Transport
> 1. Profits of an enterprise of a Contracting State from the operation of ships or aircraft in international traffic shall be taxable only in that State.
> 2. The provisions of paragraph 1 shall also apply to profits from the participation in a pool, a joint business or an international operating agency.

626. *Ibid.*, Art. 3 para. 1(e).
627. *Ibid.*, Commentary on Art. 3 para. 6.2.
628. *Ibid.*, Commentary on Art. 8 para. 4.2.

activity of an enterprise engaged in the international operation of ships or aircraft. A regular of a ship or aircraft on a bare boat charter basis will be subjected to Article 7.[629]

(2) Lease of containers by an enterprise engaged in international shipping or air transport.[630]
(3) Operation of ship or aircraft by other enterprises under a code sharing or slot-chartering arrangement.[631]
(4) Operation of a bus service by an airline company, connecting a town with its airport primarily to provide access to and from that airport to the passengers of its international flights.[632]
(5) Provision of goods or services to another enterprise engaged in international traffic operation with reference to sales or advertising activities.[633]
(6) Provision of goods or services to another enterprise engaged in international traffic operation under a pooling arrangement, viz., provision of spare parts or maintenance or ground handling services etc.[634]

Even investment income will fall under Article 8, if underlying investment forms an integral part of the business operating the ships or aircrafts in international traffic so that the investment may be considered to be directly connected with such operation.[635] Profits from ship building yards, however, shall stand excluded.[636]

This article is a special rule and is meant to take precedence over the general rule relating to business profits and the PE principle is not applied to profits falling within its scope of application.[637] Thus, where the enterprise does not exclusively engage in international shipping or air transport activities, Article 8 will only apply to the portion of profits arising from those activities and rest of the profits will subjected to Article 7.[638]

The UN Model, on the other hand, offers two alternatives, namely Article 8 (alternative A) and Article 8 (alternative B).[639] Alternative A is the same as the pre-2017 OECD Model. Alternative B, however, provides for limited source country taxation of international shipping, in the cases where the shipping activities arising from such operation in the other contracting state are '*more than casual*'.[640] If such activities are more than casual, such profits may be taxed in that other state. The Commentary to the UN Model explains that the phrase 'more than casual' means a scheduled or planned

629. *Ibid.*, Commentary on Art. 8 para. 5.
630. *Ibid.*, para. 9.
631. *Ibid.*, para. 6.
632. *Ibid.*
633. *Ibid.*, paras 8-8.1.
634. *Ibid.*, paras 10-10.1.
635. *Ibid.*, para. 14.
636. *Ibid.*, para. 12.
637. P Baker QC, *Double Tax Conventions: A Manual on the OECD Model Tax Convention* para. 8B.06.
638. OECD MTC (2017) (n. 290) Commentary on Art. 8 para. 21.
639. UN MTC (2017) (n. 292) Art. 8.
640. *Ibid.*, Art. 8, alternative B, para. 2.

visit of a ship to a particular country to pick up freight or passengers.[641] The profits to be taxed in that other state shall be determined on the basis of an appropriate allocation of the overall net profits derived by the enterprise from its shipping operations. The tax computed in accordance with such allocation shall then be reduced by a certain percent, which shall be established through bilateral negotiations.[642] This alternative provision had to be incorporated due to resistance from many developing countries, which lacked strong domestic shipping lines, and did not wish to forego this revenue where the link to the economy was 'more than casual'.[643] Thus, it is the concept of economic connection, which forms the basis of taxing rights under the UN Model.

3.3.3.5.1 *Indian Domestic Law and Treaty Practices*

Even though India has opted for the OECD version of Article 8 in its tax treaties with various countries, its domestic law incorporates specific provisions for a deemed basis of taxation for non-residents' profits from operation of ships and aircraft in international traffic, based on an economic connection.[644] Thus, under the domestic provisions, a non-resident, engaged in the business of operation of ships or aircraft, a sum equal to 7.5 %[645] and 5 %[646] respectively of the aggregate of the specified amounts shall be deemed to be the profits and gains of such business chargeable to tax under the head 'Profits and gains of business or profession'. The specified amount for the purposes of this section is:

(1) The amount paid or payable (whether in or out of India) to the taxpayer or to any person on his behalf on account of the carriage of passengers, livestock, mail or goods shipped at any port or place in India.
(2) The amount received or deemed to be received in India by or on behalf of the taxpayer on account of the carriage of passengers, livestock, mail or goods shipped at any port or place outside India.

In the case of operation of ships, the specified amount shall also include any demurrage charges or handling charges or any other amount of similar nature.[647]

Indian treaties, broadly modelled on the OECD version, mostly grant exclusive rights to the residence state of an enterprise to tax profits derived from the operation of aircraft or ships in international traffic.[648] Some of the treaties, however, use the

641. *Ibid.*, Commentary on Art. 8, 167, para. 13.
642. *Ibid.*, Art. 8, alternative B, para. 2.
643. *Ibid.*, Commentary on Art. 8, 239, 3.
644. At (n. 302), ss 44B, 44BBA.
645. In the case of operation of ship, *see* (n. 302) s. 44B.
646. In the case of operation of aircraft, *see* (n. 302) s. 44BBA.
647. At (n. 302) s. 44B expl.
648. *See, e.g.*, treaties with Australia, UK, Singapore and USA.

expression 'may be taxed' in the residence state of the enterprise.[649] The expression 'may be taxed in the other contracting state' in terms of the Indian Government's Notification No. 91/2008 dated 28 August 2008, would mean that such income shall be included in his total income chargeable to tax in India in accordance with the provisions of the Indian Tax Law and relief shall be granted in accordance with the method for elimination or avoidance of double taxation provided in such agreement.[650] Some treaties also accord taxing rights to the state, where place of effective management of the enterprise is situated.[651]

But the interpretation of these provisions is not free from difficulties. None of the model conventions and some of Indian treaties (the India-Germany Treaty, for instance) define the term 'operation of ships or aircrafts in international traffic'. Further, in some of the treaties (for instance, the US, Singapore, Malaysia, the UAE), although the term has been defined, the definitions are variedly worded. Given these differences, the meaning and scope of the term has been a matter of significant debate in India, mostly in the context of the activities, which are claimed to be ancillary to international shipping and transport operations.

In *Balaji Shipping*,[652] where the taxpayer, apart from hiring chartered ships, had taken container slot space under an agreement with the carrier for his use on 'as and when required' basis, the question arose whether freight income of the taxpayer on account of transportation of cargo in international traffic through slot charter arrangement by the ships operated by other enterprises can be said to be profits from operation of ship under Article 9 of Indo-UK Treaty. Answering in affirmative and relying on the contemporaneous exposition rule in the treaty interpretation laid down by the Indian Supreme Court,[653] the Tribunal held that the words or expressions used in the treaty, if not defined in the treaty itself, should be understood in the sense in which the contracting states understood them at the time of execution of the treaty, which can be gathered from the provisions of domestic laws of the contracting states and in the absence thereof from the various commentaries available at the time of such agreement. In the absence of any definition in the Indo-UK treaty or any guidance from the domestic laws of the contracting states, the Tribunal examined the OECD Commentary on Article 8 and noted that two kinds of profits were covered by it: *First*, the profits which are directly obtained by the enterprise from the transportation of cargo or passengers in the international traffic by the ships whether owned or leased or at the disposal of such enterprise or profits from activities directly connected with such operation; and *second*, the profits from the activities, which are ancillary to such operation. As per the Commentary, ancillary activity is that activity which makes a minor contribution relative to the activity of operation of ship and such activity must be so closely related that it should not be regarded as separate business or source of

649. *See, e.g.*, India-Bangladesh Treaty, Art. 9 in the context of shipping operations; also India-Greece Treaty, Art. 6; India-Philippines Treaty, Art. 9; and India-Sri Lanka Treaty, Art. 8 para. 2.
650. CBDT Notification No. 91/2008 dated 28 August 2008.
651. *See, e.g.*, India-Bhutan Treaty, Art. 8 para. 1.
652. *DDIT v Balaji Shipping UK Ltd* (2008) 117 TTJ 865 (Mum).
653. *Kulandagan Chettiar* (n. 304); also, *UOI v Azadi Bachao Andolan* (2003) 263 ITR 706 (SC).

income. Since Article 8 of OECD Model Convention and Article 9 of Indo-UK Treaty are similarly worded, paragraph 6 of OECD Commentary discussed above would apply in defining the scope of Article 9(1) of Indo-UK Treaty as per the rule of contemporaneous exposition.[654] These findings were approved by the Bombay High Court.[655]

In *KLM Royal Dutch Airlines,*[656] a Netherlands company had obtained a licence to use certain premises situated in Bombay (presently Mumbai) from the Airport Authority of India. It had also entered into an agreement with a company named 'C' for handling the cargo in India on its behalf. Under the said agreement, it was liable to pay to 'C' for management, supervision, document handling, physical handling and tracking and tracing export and import cargo at Bombay. During the relevant assessment years, it made payment to 'C' after adjustment of the licence fee/rent payable by it to the Airport Authority of India. The Revenue treated the amount so adjusted as the taxpayer's income chargeable to tax in India under Article 6 of the Netherlands-India Treaty. The Delhi High Court held that the recovery of the charges payable by the taxpayer to 'C' towards licence fee/rent did not arise from any activity outside the activity of cargo handling in international traffic and the same, therefore, was an ancillary activity in the context of Article 8 of the treaty.

In *Safmarine Container Lines NV,*[657] a non-resident company registered in Belgium, was in business of operation of ships. Its business was to collect cargo from station of exporter, i.e., from Ludhiana, and then to bring it to Mumbai port from where its vessels carried it to destination station out of India, i.e., Nairobi. It received certain amount as inland haulage charges (IHC), i.e., charges towards transporting goods from exporter's place to port, which it claimed as non-taxable in terms of Article 8 of India-Belgium Treaty. The Revenue rejected the claim. Rejecting the Revenue's contention, the Tribunal held that since inland transportation, i.e., activity of transporting goods from Ludhiana to Mumbai, was incidental to activity directly connected with international traffic, i.e., transportation of goods from Mumbai to Nairobi, the case of the taxpayer would squarely fall under Article 8(2)(b)(ii) of the treaty and could not be subjected to tax in India. The same view was upheld in *AP Moller Maersk A/S.*[658]

In *MISC Berhad,*[659] the question arose whether the benefit of Article 8 of Indo-Malaysian treaty was admissible in respect of the freight income, attributable to voyage performed on feeder vessels which were operated by third party. This was also a case where the expression 'profits from the operation of ships or aircraft in international traffic' was already defined in India-Malaysia Treaty.[660] The taxpayer, in this case, transported cargo in two stages: *first*, from Indian port to hub port through feeder vessels of other enterprise and second, from the hub port to the final destination through the ship, owned by the taxpayer. The Revenue rejected the claim on the ground that chartering of some space (i.e., slot chartering) in the feeder vessels cannot

654. *Balaji Shipping* (n. 652).
655. *DIT v Balaji Shipping UK Ltd* (2012) 253 CTR 460 (Bom).
656. *DIT v KLM Royal Dutch Airlines* [2009] 178 Taxman 291 (Delhi).
657. *DDIT v Safmarine Container Lines NV* [2009] 120 ITD 71 (Mum).
658. *DDIT v AP Moller Maersk A/S* [2018] 90 taxmann.com 326 (Mum.).
659. *MISC Berhad v ADIT* (2014) 150 ITD 213 (Mum).
660. India-Malaysia Treaty, Art. 8, para. 2.

be equated with chartering of complete ship so as to fall within the ambit of Article 8 of the treaty.[661] Rejecting the Revenue's argument and relying on the Bombay High Court decision in *Balaji Shipping,*[662] the Tribunal held that the term 'charter' or 'charterer' means hiring of vessels or a ship or a part of its space under an agreement for a voyage. Thus, even a part of a space or a slot charter or a voyage charter of a part of a ship for a particular journey is also considered as charter of ship. But the Tribunal clarified that in the case of transportation of cargo by feeder vessels belonging to other enterprise, if it is only a part of main voyage by the mother ship i.e., owned or leased by the taxpayer's enterprise, then it has to be taken as a part and parcel of the operation, which is inextricably linked with the completion of the entire voyage. The linkage between the transportation by feeder vessels and mother vessels of the ship owned by the taxpayer has to be established.[663]

In *Delta Airlines,*[664] the taxpayer had a code sharing agreements with a third party carrier, whereby it had only booked the tickets and the actual transportation was done by third party aircrafts. The question, therefore, arose whether receipts attributable thereto would be eligible for treaty benefits in the context of Article 8 of the India-US treaty,[665] which, too, defined the expression 'profits from the operation of ships or aircraft in international traffic. In other words, the basic question which fell for consideration was whether the code sharing arrangement with third party, in which the taxpayer was merely booking tickets for its customers, can be said to be slot/space charter arrangement so as to make it eligible for benefit under Article 8 of the Indo-US treaty. Rejecting the taxpayer's claim, Indian Tribunal held that there is nothing on record to suggest that the taxpayer had entered into agreement with the third party in the nature of slot charter/space charter. The right to book flights under code sharing agreements is not exclusive unlike the charter agreement as there are no fixed space/slot or seats for which the booking rights are exclusively with the taxpayer only. The role of the taxpayer in respect of bookings so made under code sharing agreement is essentially in the nature of booking agent and not as a charterer. Article 8(1) is the substantive provisions. Hence the first and crucial test for eligibility under Article 8(1) is that such profit should be derived from operation of aircraft in international traffic by the ship or aircraft owned/leased/chartered by the taxpayer. The receipts for activities under Article 8(2)(a), (b) and (c) are only for enlarging the scope of profits from other related activities but the qualifying condition of such transportation through ship or aircraft owned/leased or chartered by the taxpayer have to be still independently fulfilled under Article 8(1) & (2) to claim the benefit of receipts falling under Article 8.[666] Distinguishing it from *MISC Berhad*, the Tribunal held that in that case complete transportation under code sharing arrangement took place from origin to final destination in a single stretch. They were not interim destinations from which the passengers had to be further transported to final destination by the taxpayer's airlines

661. *Ibid.*
662. *Balaji Shipping* (n. 652).
663. *MISC Berhad* (n. 659) para. 29.
664. *ADIT v Delta Airlines* (2010) 124 ITD 114 (Mum).
665. India-USA Treaty, Art. 8 para. 2.
666. *Delta Airlines* (n. 664) para. 33.

so as to establish an inextricable link between voyage from India to interim destination by third parties under code sharing agreement and from interim destination to final destination by the taxpayer's owned, chartered or leased aircraft.[667] The taxpayer's alternative contention of this being a 'pool' arrangement in terms of paragraph 4 of Article 8 of the treaty was also negatived by the Tribunal, holding that a pool arrangement requires several persons coming together to contribute and combine their resources for a large business and then share the resources among them. A bilateral arrangement without commonality of funds and resources does not meet the principle of pool arrangement.[668]

In *Lufthansa German Airlines*,[669] the taxpayer was an international airline with headquarters and controlling offices in Cologne, Germany and Amsterdam, Netherlands and branch offices in India. They operated aircraft in international traffic business including India. As International Airlines Technical Pool (IATP) members, they extended minimal technical facilities (line maintenance facilities) to other IATP member airlines at Indian airport. The taxpayer claimed that amounts received from various IATP members airlines for aforesaid services rendered in India, were not taxable in India. Upholding the taxpayer's contention, the Tribunal held that taxpayer's profit due to participation in a pool was covered under Article 8(4) of the India-Germany Treaty and Article 8(1) of the Netherlands-India Treaty and, thus, such profit could not be brought to tax in India. The Delhi High Court upheld the conclusion of the Tribunal, holding that in terms of IATP manual, there was reciprocity in rendering and availing of services and there was clearly participation in pool, in terms of the two treaties and that profits from such participation were not taxable in India.

In *Apl Co Pte Ltd*,[670] the Revenue sought to deny the benefit of Article 8 in the context of Indo-Singapore Treaty,[671] which too incorporates a definition of the term 'profits from the operation of ships or aircraft in international traffic, on the ground that the entire leg of journey is undertaken by the taxpayer through charter arrangement or joint service arrangement and no part thereof has been undertaken on vessel owned or leased by it. Rejecting the Revenue's contention, the Tribunal held that once it is held that chartering includes slot charter/space charter and it falls within the ambit of 'operation of ships', then the benefit of Article 8 cannot be denied simply on the ground that a part of operation must be done on the vessel/aircraft owned or leased by the taxpayer. The transportation done either partly or fully through slot charter arrangement or joint charter arrangement fulfils the requirement of law.[672]

Further in terms of explanation contained in the OECD Commentary,[673] when the ship or aircraft is operated solely between places in the other contracting state, it will not constitute an international transaction. In some of the treaties, this exception has

667. *Ibid.*, para. 34.
668. *Ibid.*, para. 37.
669. *DIT v Lufthansa German Airlines* [2017] 392 ITR 218 (Del).
670. *APL Co Pte Ltd v ADIT (IT)* (2017) 185 TTJ 305 (Mum).
671. India-Singapore Treaty, Art. 8, para. 4.
672. *APL Co Pte Ltd* (n. 670), para. 17.
673. OECD MTC (2017) (n. 290) Commentary on Art. 3 para. 6.2.

been specifically mentioned.[674] However, some other treaties do not specify this exception.[675] The import of this exception came to be examined by the Gujarat High Court in *Taurus Shipping Services*,[676] where the taxpayer had acted as an agent of three vessels which had transported goods from Kandla Port to Visag. The freight beneficiary was a foreign company, which claimed benefit of the India-Singapore Treaty. The vessels had undertaken such freight transportation during the journey from Singapore to Dubai. The Revenue authorities held that transportation between Kandla to Visag could not be considered as international traffic as defined in the India-Singapore Treaty and, therefore, the taxpayer would not be entitled to benefit of Article 8 of the treaty. Rejecting the Revenue's contention, the High Court held that if the ship or aircraft, operating within a contracting state, is part of larger journey of vessels from one contracting state to the other, such transport would be covered under definition of 'international traffic' and the taxpayer would be entitled to benefit of Article 8. The following observations of the Court are significant:

> 5 If ships in question, therefore, were operated solely between Kandla and Visag, in the present case, such transport would be excluded from the definition of term 'international traffic'. Here, the word 'solely' is all important. It is not even the case of the Revenue that the journey being undertaken by such vessels in question were confined between the two ports in India either routinely or even in individual isolated case. Admitted facts, as noted above, are that such transportation was undertaken during a larger journey of the vessels from Singapore to Dubai. Under such circumstances, the requirement of such journey being solely between places in the other contracting state is not satisfied. The exclusion clause of the definition of term 'international traffic', therefore, would not apply.

Thus, jurisprudence, emerging from the above court decisions, may be summarised as follows:

(i) If the term 'operation of ship/aircraft' is not defined at all in the treaty, a broad interpretation of the article can be made in those cases, based on the rule of contemporaneous exposition. Thus, the words or expressions used in the treaty, if not defined in the treaty itself, should be understood in the sense in which the contracting states understood them at the time of execution of the treaty, which can be gathered from the provisions of domestic laws of the contracting states and in the absence thereof, from the OECD Commentary available at the time of such agreement.[677] Thus, the profits from such operations will include the direct profits from such operation as well as the indirect profits from the activities which are ancillary to such operations.[678]

(ii) The operation of ship/aircraft in the other contracting state will be excluded from the definition of international traffic, if it is operating solely

674. *See, e.g.*, India-Australia Treaty, Art. 8 para. 2; *see also* India-Armenia Treaty, Art. 8 para. 2 and India-Austria Treaty, Art. 8 para. 2.
675. *See, e.g.*, India's treaties with Belarus and Belgium.
676. *CIT v Taurus Shipping Services* [2015] 64 taxmann.com 64 (Guj).
677. *Balaji Shipping* (n. 652).
678. *Ibid.*

within that state. But where such intra-state operation is part of a larger journey of vessels from one contracting state to another, it will constitute international traffic.[679]

(iii) Similarly, transporting of goods within a state for the purpose of transporting it further to the destination in other state will be treated as part of international traffic and profit arising from such internal transport cannot be subjected to tax in terms of Article 8.[680]

(iv) Where the term 'operation of ship' is defined as transportation of goods in vessels owned, leased or chartered by the enterprise, the benefit of Article 8 can be extended only if the transportation is done by the enterprise by operation of ships that are owned, leased or chartered by it.[681] However, there is no requirement that the entire ship should be chartered by the taxpayer as even a part of a space or a slot charter or a voyage charter of a part of a ship for a particular journey is also sufficient to make the requirement of law.[682]

(v) Once it is held that chartering includes slot charter/space charter and it falls within the ambit of 'operation of ships', then there is no further requirement that a part of operation must be done on the vessel/aircraft owned or leased by the taxpayer. The benefit of Article 8 cannot be denied simply on the ground that the transportation has been done either partly or fully through slot charter arrangement or joint charter arrangement.[683]

(vi) In the case of transportation of cargo by feeder vessels belonging to other enterprise, if it is a part of main voyage by the mother ship i.e., owned or leased by the taxpayer's enterprise, it has to be taken as a part and parcel of the operation, which is inextricably linked with the completion of the entire voyage. Thus, a linkage between the transportation by feeder vessels and mother vessels of the ship owned by the taxpayer has to be established in order to claim benefit of Article 8.[684]

(vii) However, if the taxpayer only books, tickets under the court sharing agreement with a third party carrier and the actual transportation is done by the third party aircraft. The receipts attributable to the booking of tickets will not assume the character of profit from international transport.[685]

(viii) Profits from rendering of minimum technical facilities to IATP Members will be exempt under Article 8 as there was reciprocity in rendering and availing of these services and there was clear participation in pool in terms of Article 8.[686]

679. *Taurus Shipping Services* (n. 676).
680. *Safmarine Container Lines NV* (n. 657).
681. *MISC Berhad* (n. 659).
682. *Ibid.*
683. *Ibid.*
684. *Ibid.*, para. 29.
685. *Delta Airlines* (n. 664).
686. *Lufthansa German Airlines* (n. 669).

(ix) Where the term 'operation of ship' also covers 'any other activity directly connected with such transportation', the freight booked through feeder vessels will be eligible for DTAA benefit only when the goods transported through feeder vessels are further trans-shipped through mother vessels operated by the taxpayer. The taxpayer has to link the goods in the feeder vessels with mother vessels operated by it, to claim benefit.[687]

Thus, even though India has not accepted the UN prescription of taxing profits from international shipping and transport operations which are 'more than casual', the use of expression 'may be taxed in some of the Indian treaties, coupled with precise delineation of the scope of these activities in the relevant article itself, evinces a vivid recognition of the right of the source state to tax the profits from these activities.

3.4 RIGHTS TO TAX INVESTMENT INCOME: DIVIDEND, INTEREST AND ROYALTY

They are two methods prevalent for the taxation of investment income: *first*, to levy a withholding tax in the source state, wherein a flat rate of income tax is levied on the total amount, with the beneficial owner as the taxpayer and the payer as the withholding agent. Usually, the residence state will grant due credits for these taxes so paid in the final settlements. This is the reason why it is called a 'withholding tax'. *Second*, to levy an income tax with regard to business profits in the source state. This applies when the beneficial owner of the investment income, being a resident of a contracting state, carries on business in the other contracting state in which the investment income arises through a PE situated therein; and also when:

(i) the holding in respect which dividends are paid is effectively connected with such PE;[688] or
(ii) the debt claim in respect which interest is paid is effectively connected with such PE;[689] or
(iii) the right or property in respect which the royalties are paid is effectively connected with such PE,[690] as the case may be.

In such cases, the investment income shall be treated as business profits and taxed accordingly.

687. *APL Co Pte Ltd* (n. 670).
688. OECD MTC (2017) (n. 290) Art. 10 para. 4.
689. *Ibid.*, Art. 11 para. 4.
690. *Ibid.*, Art. 12 para. 3.

3.4.1 The Basic Principles of Allocating Rights to Tax Investment Income

Both the OECD Model[691] and the UN Model[692] have three special provisions respectively for dividends, interest and royalties. The UN Model gives the rights to tax to both states – i.e. both the source jurisdiction and residence jurisdiction. Unlike its OECD counterpart, no exception is made in the UN Model in respect of royalties,[693] which is subjected to tax exclusively by the residence state under the OECD provisions.[694] Granting rights to both states fully indicates the fact that income of franchising comes from the state of source, but the development of propriety rights such as patents and technical know-how results in large expenditures in the state of residence, making that state eligible to have a share of tax revenues. This distinction emphatically puts forth the economic nexus principle for tax rights allocation.

3.4.1.1 Dividend

Since both the source state and the residence state have rights to tax investment income, the two models put a limitation on the source state to tax in terms of tax rates. Since the source state is in an advantageous position to tax the income in advance, the state of residence would be left with nothing if there were no ceiling on the tax rates of source state. The customary practice, therefore, is to subject dividend income to a limited taxation in the source state in order to ensure that the fiscal interests between source and residence states are aptly balanced.

There is, however, considerable divergence in the two models on the extent of this limitation. The OECD Model prescribes a strict limitation on the withholding tax rates. It stipulates that 'the state of source must limit its tax to 5% of the gross amount of the dividends, where the beneficial owner is a company that holds directly at least 25% of the capital of the company paying the dividends, and to 15% of their gross amount in other cases'.[695] This article is, thus, beneficial to the residence state. The UN Model relaxes the limitation and lowers the shareholding of the company paying the dividend to 10% for a tax preference. Moreover, no specific ceilings are prescribed on the withholding tax rates with respect to investment income and the same is left subject to bilateral negotiations. This enables the source state to negotiate for higher-tax revenues.

691. *Ibid.*, Arts 10, 11 and 12.
692. UN MTC (2017) (n. 292) Arts 10, 11 and 12.
693. *Ibid.*, Art. 12, paras 1, 2.
694. OECD MTC (2017) (n. 290) Art. 12 para. 1.
695. OECD MTC (2010) (n. 538) Art. 10 para. 2.

3.4.1.1.1 *Recent Trends: BEPS and MLIs*

The BEPS Action 6 Final Report[696] noted the practice of engaging in transactions to increase the number of shares held at the time the dividend is legally available to the shareholder so as to obtain a lower rate of 5%. To address these concerns, the Report recommended that a minimum holding period of 365 days should be included in Article 10 of the OECD Model for shareholders seeking to avail the reduced 5% withholding rate on dividend payments. The Final Report also laid emphasis on additional anti-abuse rules to deal with cases where certain intermediary entities, set up in the source state, are employed to exploit the treaty provisions that lower the source taxation of dividends. For instance, the Final Report talks of an alternative provision provided in the Commentary to Article 10 to limit access to the 5% rate, where payments are made by domestic real estate investment trust (REITs)[697] to non-resident investors.[698] The 2017 OECD Model Convention has incorporated the minimum holding period.[699] The MLI also incorporates the holding period requirement.[700] Thus, the crucial consideration behind all these recent measures is to obviate tax evasion by circumventing the economic connection of the transaction by artificial measures.

3.4.1.1.2 *Indian Domestic Law and Treaty Practices*

Under the domestic law,[701] dividend paid by an Indian company outside India is deemed to accrue or arise in India and is subject to source taxation.[702] The domestic law[703] also contains provisions for withholding tax on dividend income at the rate of 20% of the total interest income.

In its tax treaties, India has followed the UN prescription and has negotiated the rates bilaterally with various countries. For instance, the India-US Treaty provides for a maximum rate of 15% of the gross amount of the dividends if the beneficial owner is a company which owns at least 10% of the voting stock of the company paying the dividends and of a maximum rate of 20% thereof in all other cases.[704] In tax treaties with Singapore[705] and Belarus,[706] the maximum rate is 10%, where shareholding is

696. OECD, *Preventing the Granting of Treaty Benefits in Inappropriate Circumstances, Action 6 - 2015 Final Report*, OECD/G20 Base Erosion and Profit Shifting Project (OECD Pub 2015) 70-71 (hereafter 'OECD, *Action 6 - 2015* Final Report').
697. A real estate investment trust (REIT) is a company that owns, and in most cases operates, income-producing real estate. REITs own many types of commercial real estate, viz., office, apartment buildings, warehouses, hospitals, shopping centres and hotels. Some REITs engage in financing real estate. REITs can be publicly traded on major exchanges, through non-listed, or private. It was introduced in India in 2014-2015 budget.
698. *Ibid.*, 71.
699. OECD MTC (2017) (n. 290) Art. 10 para. 2(b).
700. MLI (n. 403) Art. 8.
701. At (n. 302).
702. *Ibid.*, s. 9(1)(iv).
703. *Ibid.*, s. 195.
704. India-USA Treaty, Art. 10 para. 2.
705. India-Singapore Treaty, Art. 10 para. 2.
706. India-Belarus Treaty, Art. 10 para. 2.

20% and 15% in other cases. In Bangladesh, rates are similar, but shareholding threshold has been reduced to 10%.[707] Similarly, in India-Mauritius Treaty,[708] a rate of 5% with shareholding threshold of 10% and a rate of 15% in other cases have been agreed upon. In some treaties, shareholding threshold has been omitted altogether and a flat rate has been provided, for example, a rate of 15% with Australia, 10% with the UAE,[709] the UK,[710] South Africa,[711] Armenia[712] and Austria.[713]

With the recent signing of the MLI,[714] India has notified twenty-one of its covered tax treaties.[715] If the other contracting states also notify these provisions, the provisions of the covered tax treaties, dealing with dividend income shall stand replaced by Article 8 of the MLI, which provides for the minimum holding period of 365 days. India has reserved its right for non-applicability of Article 8 in respect of its tax treaty with Portugal (as it already has a twenty-four-month holding period condition).[716]

In a recent case,[717] an interesting question arose before the ITAT as to whether the rate of dividend distribution tax (DDT) as prescribed in section 115-O of the domestic law will also have to be restricted to the rate specified in the tax treaty. Although ITAT-Mumbai has not given its conclusion and has remanded this issue back for detailed examination, the issue needs to be understood in the correct context. It may be noted that the enactment of section 115-O was accompanied by the introduction of a new clause 34 in section 10, which excludes dividends from the scope of total income.

Therefore, the concept of dividend and DDT should not be confused. While dividend is a tax on shareholders, DDT is a tax on the company as a separate entity.[718] Article 10 of the tax treaty was designed to apply to cases where dividends are sought to be taxed in the hands of shareholders by the country where the company is tax resident. In the absence of express inclusion of DDT in the article, the same cannot be *ipso facto* extended to it. Wherever the contracting states have desired the article to be extended to DDT, they have expressly included the same into the provision, for instance, In the India-Hungary tax treaty,[719] it is expressly provided that any dividend

707. India-Bangladesh Treaty, Art. 11 para. 2.
708. India-Mauritius Treaty, Art. 10 para. 2.
709. India-UAE Treaty, Art. 10 para. 2.
710. India-UK Treaty, Art. 11 para. 2(b).
711. India-South Africa Treaty, Art. 10 para. 2.
712. India-Armenia Treaty, Art. 10 para. 2.
713. India-Austria Treaty, Art. 10 para. 2.
714. MLI (n. 403).
715. Bangladesh, Belarus, Canada, Croatia, Denmark, Italy, Lithuania, Montenegro, Nepal, Oman, Philippines, Qatar, Serbia, Singapore, Slovakia, Slovenia, Syria, Tajikistan, Ukraine, the United States and Zambia.
716. Global Tax Alert, 'India signs Multilateral Convention to Implement Tax Treaty Related Measures to Prevent BEPS' 6 July 2017, EY Global Tax Alert Library 4, https://www.ey.com/Publication/vwLUAssets/India_signs_Multilateral_Convention_to_Implement_Tax_Treaty_Related_Measures_to_Prevent_BEPS/%24FILE/2017G_04135-171Gbl_India%20signs%20MC%20to%20Implement%20Tax%20Treaty%20Related%20Measures%20to%20Prevent%20BEPS.pdf, accessed 22 January 2020.
717. *SGS India (P) Ltd v Addl CIT* (2017) 83 taxmann.com 163 (Mum).
718. *Godrej & Boyce Mfg Co Ltd v DCIT* (2010) 194 Taxman 203 (Bom); *see also Sunash Invest Co v ACIT* (2007) 14 SOT 80 (Mum); *Mohanlal v DCIT* (2007) 105 ITD 669 (Mum) and *ACIT v Delta Airlines* (2010) 124 ITD 114 (Mum) and *ACIT v Dakshesh Shah* (2004) 90 ITD 519 (Mum).
719. India-Hungary Treaty, Art. 10 para. 3.

which is paid by an Indian company and which is subjected to tax on distributed profits is deemed to be taxed in the hands of the shareholders and it shall not exceed 10% of gross amount of dividend. In the absence of a similar provision in other tax treaties, the DDT rate cannot be replaced with the tax treaty rate in the absence of the express intention of the contracting states.

A similar question of applicability of tax treaty to DDT was considered and rejected by the South African High Court in *Volkswagen*.[720] The issue before the High Court was whether 'secondary tax on companies' (STC) (akin to DDT) levied as per the South African domestic tax law could be regarded as a tax covered within the ambit of the South Africa-Germany tax treaty. Article 7 of the South Africa-Germany tax treaty provided for a withholding tax rate of 7.5% under the dividend article whereas the STC was levied at 12.5%. The High Court held that that STC was not a tax on dividends but was a tax imposed on the company declaring the dividends and hence outside the ambit of the tax treaty.

3.4.1.2 Interest Income

On the lines of dividend income, the OECD Model[721] provides for a 10% tax rate on interest income. The UN Model does not provide any withholding tax rates, for the same reasons as for dividends and leaves it to bilateral negotiations.[722]

3.4.1.2.1 Indian Domestic Law and Treaty Practices

The domestic law on taxability of interest income is contained in section 9(1)(v), according to which interest income is deemed to accrue or arise in India in three situations:

(a) if it is payable by the Government; or
(b) if it is payable by a resident, except where interest relates to debt incurred or money borrowed and used (i) for carrying business or profession outside India or (ii) for earning income from a source outside India; or
(c) if it is payable by a non-resident where interest relates to debt incurred or money borrowed and used for carrying business or profession in India.

The domestic law[723] also contains provisions for withholding tax on interest income at the rate of 20% of the total interest income.

In its treaties, India has negotiated the withholding tax rates in line with the UN Model. However, it has generally negotiated the 10% rate of withholding as spelt out

720. *Volkswagen of South Africa (Pty) Ltd v CIT*, International Tax 1700 STC Ruling January 2009 Issue 113, https://www.saica.co.za/integritax/2009/1700_STC_Ruling.htm accessed 23 January 2021.
721. OECD MTC (2017) (n. 290) Art. 11.
722. UN MTC (2017) (n. 292) Art. 11 para. 2.
723. At (n. 302), s. 195.

in the OECD Model, except in the case of a few countries, where a higher rate has been negotiated.[724]

3.4.1.3 Royalties

As stated in the preceding paragraphs, the UN Model recognises both residence and source jurisdiction in the case of royalty income. In contrast, the OECD Model confers an exclusive right to tax royalties on the residence state, to the exclusion of the source state.[725] Royalty income is recognised as emanating from the residence state where the beneficiary owner is a resident, since the propriety rights are normally developed there with an investment over a long period while assuming huge risks. A reasonable solution, therefore, would be to share the rights to tax: source state has the priority to tax royalties but at a low tax rate, while residence state may also gain some revenues. The priority to tax encourages the source state (mostly developing nations) to introduce the advanced technologies and achievements, which also entitles it to macro-regulate its economic development and selectively introduce technologies. The source state can also effectively counter tax avoidance. However, as the residence country does account for the production of propriety rights, provides public services and assumes risks for developing these rights, it too should also have due rights to tax.[726]

3.4.1.3.1 Indian Domestic Law and Treaty Practices

Section 9(1)(vi) of the Indian Income Tax Act deals with the taxability of royalty. The provisions are similar to the interest income. Royalty income is deemed to accrue or arise in India in three situations:

(1) if it is payable by the Government; or
(2) if it is payable by a resident, except where royalty relates to any rights, property, information or services used for: (i) the purposes of business or profession carried outside or (ii) earning income from a source outside India; or
(3) If it is payable by non-resident where royalty relates to any rights, property, information or services used for the purposes of business or profession carried in India.[727]

724. Tax Treaties with the UK, the USA, Italy, Singapore, Spain and Australia, for example, where a higher rate of 15% is agreed upon.
725. OECD MTC (2017) (n. 290) Art. 12, para. 1.
726. B Yang and C Ping Song, 'A Comparative Study of the OECD Model, UN Model and China's Treaties with Respect to Rights to Tax Income and Capital' (2011) 9(3) eJTR 254.
727. At (n. 302), s. 9(1)(vi) clauses (a), (b) and (c).

Explanation 2 to section 9(1)(vi) of the domestic legislation[728] defines the term 'royalty' in a fairly exhaustive manner. It means, *inter alia*, the transfer of any right or the granting of a licence in respect of a patent, design, process, secret formula or similar property. It also takes in the imparting of any information concerning technical, industrial, commercial or scientific knowledge or skill and the use of the patent, design, and so on. The domestic law[729] also contains provisions for withholding tax on royalty at the rate of 20% of the total royalty.

The practices of Indian tax treaties evince a general preference for a 10% withholding tax rate.[730] But with some countries, a higher rate of 15%–20% has been negotiated.[731]

3.5 RIGHTS TO TAX CAPITAL GAINS

The rules allocating rights to tax capital gains, stipulated in Article 13 of both the Models are, by and large, identical, even though the UN Model contemplates certain additional features. The rules in this regard are, however, broadly worded in view of the far-ranging variations in these rules across the states and are intended to cover all varying situations across jurisdictions. Although Article 13 does not provide a definition of the term 'gain' or 'alienation', the OECD Commentary addresses this concern by stating that 'alienation of property' should be read to include gains from a sale or exchange of property, a partial alienation, an expropriation, a transfer for share exchange, a sale of right, a gift or even a property transfer on death.[732] Under some domestic legislation, capital appreciation and the revaluation of business assets are also taxed, even if there is no alienation. The Commentary explains that such taxes are also covered under the article, and the same principle applies to gains on such capital appreciation and the revaluation of business assets.[733]

The taxing rights for capital gains generally follow a pattern similar to the one prescribed for the taxation of income arising from the holding of respective capital assets in both the models. Thus, income from the alienation of immovable property may be taxed in the state in which the immovable property is situated and also in the residence state on the lines of Article 6.[734] Thus, the primary taxing rights are assigned to the state where immovable property is situated and the residence state may also tax it under its domestic law subject to a relief granted for the tax paid in the source state.

728. At (n. 302), s. 9(1)(vi) expl 2.
729. At (n. 302), s. 195.
730. *See, e.g.*, Treaties with Hungary, Malaysia, Russia, Indonesia, Singapore, Sri Lanka and Sweden.
731. *See, e.g.*, India-Italy Treaty (with 20% rate), India-Nepal Treaty (with 15% rate), India-UK Treaty and India-USA Treaty (with 20% rate, which is reduced to 15% in case payer is the government).
732. OECD MTC (2017) (n. 290) Commentary on Art. 13 (General Remarks) para. 5.
733. *Ibid.*, para. 9.
734. OECD MTC (2017) (n. 290) Art. 13 para. 1; also, UN MTC (2017) (n. 292) Art. 13 para. 1.

Likewise, income from the alienation of movable property of a PE of an enterprise may be taxed in the state in which the PE is situated and also in the residence state.[735] For the application of this rule, it must first be established that the movable property, which is alienated forms part of the PE's business property. This rule, thus, aligns itself with Article 7. To determine whether the movable property forms part of the business property of the PE, the OECD Commentary prescribes that the principles outlined in the OECD's 2010 Report on the attribution of profits to PEs[736] should be used in this regard and if the economic ownership of the movable property is allocated to the PE, resulting in all benefits and risks in relation thereto being allocated to it, the movable property will form part of the business property of the PE. This may include the right to claim depreciation, exposure to risks relating to a decrease in the value of the property or the right to income derived from the use of the property.[737]

Similarly, gains from the alienation of ships or aircraft operating in international traffic or of movable property pertaining to such operations are exclusively taxed in the residence state of the enterprise on the lines of Article 8. It is important to note here that these provisions will hold good only if the enterprise operating the ship and aircraft must also be the one making the alienation. Thus, if the ship or aircraft that is alienated is operated by another enterprise, these provisions will not apply and the capital gains, in such a case, will either be taxed under Article 13(2) or under the residuary rule set out in Article 13(5) of the Model, which assigns taxing rights of any other type of property, not specifically addressed by Article 13, to the residence state of the alienator.[738]

The gains, derived by the resident of a contracting state, from the alienation of shares or comparable interests, may be taxed in the other contracting state, if, at any time during the 365 days preceding the alienation, these shares or comparable interests derived more than 50% of their value directly or indirectly from immovable property, situated in that other state. Thus, the taxing rights are assigned primarily to the state where immovable property is situated, and the residence state retains the residual rights, subject to a relief for the tax paid in the source state. The words 'comparable interests' are illustrated as 'interests in a partnership or trust'.

The BEPS Action 6 Final Report[739] noted the anomalies in the earlier version of Article 13(4) of the OECD Model and pointed out that there may be cases, where assets are contributed to an entity just before the sale of its shares or other interests in order to dilute the proportion of value of these shares or interests that is derived from immovable property situated in the other contracting state. In order to address these concerns, an amendment was recommended for considering the proportion of value of shares or interests derived from immovable property, not at the time of alienation, but

735. *Ibid.*, Art. 13 para. 2.
736. The OECD Attribution Report 2010 (n. 540).
737. OECD MTC (2017) (n. 290) Commentary on Art. 13(2) para. 27.1.
738. OECD MTC (2017) (n. 290) Art. 13 para. 5; UN MTC (2017) (n. 292) Art. 13 para. 6.
739. OECD, *Action 6 - 2015* Final Report (n. 696).

at any time during the 365 days preceding the alienation.[740] The 2017 OECD Model as well as the UN Model has incorporated these changes.[741]

The MLI also incorporates these suggestions.[742] Article 9 of the MLI sets out two options:

(1) The first option specifies that where the value threshold is met at any time during the 365 days preceding the transfer, the capital gains from the sale of shares or comparable interests shall be taxable in the country where the immovable property owned by the entity is situated. Contracting states can bilaterally negotiate the value threshold in their tax treaties.[743]
(2) The second option is similar to the first one, except that it fixes a value threshold of more than 50% for the trigger of source taxation in Article 9.[744]

The rule set out in Article 13(4) is intended to ensure that the state of the immovable property retains its source taxation in the case of an alienation, where a company, whose only assets are immovable property, is set up just for the purpose of disguising the disposal of the immovable property as a sale of shares, thereby shifting exclusive taxing rights to the residence state in terms of Article 13(5) of the OECD Model or Article 13(6) of the UN Model. The 50% threshold is to be determined by assessing the value of immovable property in the company, the shares of which are alienated, as compared to the value of all the property of that company, minus any debts or liabilities.[745]

The UN Model follows a similar approach, but it introduces an additional provision under which taxing rights to capital gains on the disposal of shares by a substantial shareholder is assigned primarily to the source state and the residence state retains the residual rights under its domestic law, subject to the relief for tax paid in the source state.[746] The provision sets out that capital gains, derived by the resident of one contracting state from the transfer of shares in a company or comparable interests in partnership or trust, resident in the other state, may be taxed in the other state, if the alienator, at any time during the 365 days preceding such alienation, had directly or indirectly at least a specified percentage of the capital of that company or entity.[747] The UN Commentary clarifies that even if a substantial shareholding is alienated through a number of transfers of smaller shareholdings, the taxing right granted by the paragraph will still apply if the shares transferred were alienated at any time during the twelve-month period.[748]

740. *Ibid.*, 71-72, paras 41-44.
741. OECD MTC (2017) (n. 290) Art. 13, para. 4, UN MTC (2017) (n. 292) Art. 13 para. 4.
742. MLI (n. 403) Art. 9.
743. *Ibid.*, Art. 9, para. 1.
744. *Ibid.*, Art. 9, para. 4.
745. OECD MTC (2017) (n. 290) Commentary on Art. 13(4) para. 28.4.
746. UN MTC (2017) (n. 292) Art. 13 para. 5.
747. *Ibid.*
748. UN MTC (2017) (n. 292) Commentary on Art. 13(5) para. 10.

The provision leaves the shareholding threshold to be established through bilateral negotiations. Despite huge variations in this regard, the most common threshold in practice is 25 % in this regard.[749] Some treaties even tend to give exclusive taxing rights to the source state.[750] As for the determination of interest held 'indirectly', the UN Commentary provides that interest held indirectly should be computed on the basis of the domestic law of the source state.[751]

Some states[752] extend their source rule under their domestic law to tax capital gains from an indirect transfer of shares, i.e., the transfer of shares of non-resident company, which holds indirectly, usually through a number of intermediaries, the shares of a company resident in the source state.

3.5.1 Indian Domestic Law and Treaty Practices

Under the domestic law of India, capital gains deemed to accrue or arise in India, comprise all income accruing or arising, whether directly or indirectly, through the transfer of a capital asset situated in India.[753] It is, thus, clear from a bare reading of the provisions that even if the gains actually arise outside India due to transfer occurring outside India, it is still deemed to arise in India if the capital asset transferred is situated in India.[754] Thus, where an Indian house property is transferred by one non-resident to another non-resident outside India, i.e., the contract for sale is executed outside India and full price is paid outside India, tax on gains would not be chargeable to tax in India in terms of section 5 of the Act as transfer take place outside India. However, as the property is situated in India, the gains would be deemed to arise in India by virtue of deeming fiction contained in section 9.[755]

It may also be noted here that in terms of Indian domestic law[756] even income accruing or arising, whether directly or indirectly, through any capital asset situated in India was taxable in India, which included within its ambit the indirect transfers of underlying assets of an Indian company by a non-resident. The Indian Supreme Court's decision did not, however, approve the taxability of capital gains arising on such indirect transfers in *Vodafone*.[757] In this case, the question arose whether Hutchison's sale of shares of a Cayman Islands company outside India, resulting in transfer of its entire Indian telecom business to Vodafone, would be liable to tax in India. Answering in the negative, the Court had held that in a transfer of an overseas asset outside India, one could not adopt a 'look through' approach to tax the underlying assets situated in India. The Indian Government came up with a slew of clarificatory amendments in

749. W Wijnen and J de Goede, 'The UN Model Practice 1997-2013' 68 Bull Int'l Tax'n 3 (2014) J IBFD.
750. *See, e.g.*, Singapore-Sweden Income and Capital Tax Treaty (1968) Art. X(5).
751. UN MTC (2017) (n. 292) Commentary on Art. 13(5) para. 10.
752. Canada, China, India, Peru and South Africa.
753. At (n. 302), s. 9(1)(i).
754. At (n. 302), s. 9(1)(i); also *see* JB Kanga, NA Palkhivala and BA Palkhivala, *The Law and Practice of Income Tax* (7th edn, Tripathi 1976) 205.
755. At (n. 302), s. 9(1)(i).
756. *Ibid.*, s. 9(1)(i).
757. *Vodafone International Holdings BV v Union of India* (2012) 341 ITR 1 (SC).

2012,[758] in order to further explain that an indirect transfer in terms of section 9(1)(i) would include a transfer of overseas assets if it results in transfer of an underlying Indian capital asset. These indirect transfers would, therefore, trigger taxation in India as clarified by the amendments. These amendments, which were clarificatory in nature, were made retroactive with effect from 1 April 1962.

The domestic law also contains provisions for withholding tax on capital gains,[759] which vary from 10% to 20% in respect of various types of long-term capital gains (LTCG) and is fixed at 15% in the case of short-term capital gains (STCG).

The question whether tax is required to be deducted under section 195 only on the capital gain, or on the whole amount of consideration paid to a non-resident has been extremely contentious in India. The law under section 195 is settled with sufficient clarity by two decisions of the Indian Supreme Court.

The *first* case is that of *Transmission Corporation*,[760] where the issue which fell for consideration was whether while making payment to non-residents towards trading receipts, against the purchase of machinery and equipment and also against the work executed by the non-residents in India of erecting and commissioning the machinery and equipment, the taxpayer corporation was liable to deduct tax under section 195. Answering in the affirmative, the Court elucidated the law thus:[761]

> The scheme of sub-sections (1), (2) and (3) of section 195 and section 197 leaves no doubt that the expression 'any other sum chargeable under the provisions of this Act' would mean 'sum' on which income-tax is leviable. In other words, the said sum is chargeable to tax and could be assessed to tax under the Act. Consideration would be - whether payment of sum to non-resident is chargeable to tax under the provisions of the Act or not? That sum may be income or income hidden or otherwise embedded therein. If so, tax is required to be deducted on the said sum. What would be the income is to be computed on the basis of various provisions of the Act including provisions for computation of the business income, if the payment is trade receipt. ...
>
> It has been contended that the sum which may be required to be paid to the non-resident may only be a trading receipt, and, may contain a fraction of sum as taxable income. It is true that in some cases, a trading receipt may contain a fraction of sum as taxable income, but in other cases such as interest, commission, transfer of rights of patents, goodwill or drawings for plant and machinery and such other transactions, it may contain large sum as taxable income under the provisions of the Act. Whatever may be the position, if the income is from profits and gains of business, it would be computed under the Act as provided at the time of regular assessment. The purpose of sub-section (1) of section 195 is to see that the sum which is chargeable under section 4 of the Act for levy and collection of income tax, the payee should deduct income tax thereon at the rates in force, if the amount is to be paid to a non-resident. The said provision is for tentative deduction of income tax thereon subject to regular assessment and by the deduction of income-tax, rights of the parties are not, in any manner, adversely affected. Further, the rights of payee or recipient are fully safeguarded under section 195(2),

758. The Finance Act 2012, ss 3 & 4.
759. IT Act 1961 s. 195.
760. *Transmission Corporation of AP Ltd v CIT* (1999) 239 ITR 587 (SC).
761. *Ibid.*

195(3) and 197. Only thing which is required to be done by them is to file an application for determination by the Assessing Officer that such sum would not be chargeable to tax in the case of recipient, or for determination of appropriate proportion of such sum so chargeable, or for grant of certificate authorising recipient to receive the amount without deduction of tax, or deduction of income-tax at any lower rates or no deduction.

...

Hence, in our view there is no substance in the contention of the learned Counsel for the Appellant that the expression 'any other sum chargeable under the provisions of this Act' would not include cases where any sum payable to the non-resident is a trading receipt which may or may not include 'pure income'. The language of section 195(1) for deduction of income tax by the payee is clear and unambiguous and casts an obligation to deduct appropriate tax at the rates in force.

In terms of the above holding of the Court, if the payment includes income embedded therein, the tax has to be deducted at the entire payment. However, it is open to the payee to take recourse to section 195(2) of the Act.[762]

The *second* case is that of *GE India Technology,*[763] where the question for determination was whether the payment for imported pre-packaged shrink wrapped standardised software by the distributor (the taxpayer) to Microsoft and other suppliers outside India attracted liability to deduct tax at source under section 195 of the Act.[764] The Revenue contended that since the sale of software included a licence to use the same, payments made by the taxpayer to the foreign suppliers constituted royalty, which was to be deemed to have accrued or arisen in India and, therefore, tax at source was liable to be deducted under section 195. On an appeal, the Tax Tribunal held that since the amount paid by the taxpayer to the foreign software suppliers was not royalty, the same did not give rise to any income taxable in India and, therefore, the taxpayer was not liable to deduct tax at source. Agreeing with the Tribunal's finding and negativing the Revenue's contention, the Supreme Court further expounded the law as follows:[765]

7. The most important expression in section 195(1) consists of the words 'chargeable under the provisions of the Act'. A person paying interest or any other sum to a non-resident is not liable to deduct tax if such sum is not chargeable to tax under the Income-tax Act. For instance, where there is no obligation on the part of the payer and no right to receive the sum by the recipient and that the payment does not arise out of any contract or obligation between the payer and the recipient but is made voluntarily, such payments cannot be regarded as income under the Income-tax Act. It may be noted that section 195 contemplates not merely amounts, the whole of which are pure income payments, it also covers composite payments which has an element of income embedded or incorporated in them. Thus, where an amount is payable to a non-resident, the payer is under an obligation to deduct TAS[766] in respect of such composite payments. The obligation

762. IT Act 1961.
763. *GE India Technology v CIT* (2010) 193 Taxman 234 (SC).
764. At (n. 302), s. 195, cl 1.
765. *GE India* (n. 763).
766. Tax at source (footnote added).

to deduct TAS is, however, limited to the appropriate proportion of income chargeable under the Act forming part of the gross sum of money payable to the non-resident. This obligation being limited to the appropriate proportion of income flows from the words used in section 195(1), namely, 'chargeable under the provisions of the Act'. It is for this reason that *vide* Circular No. 728 dated 30-10-1995 that the CBDT has clarified that the tax deductor can take into consideration the effect of DTAA in respect of payment of royalties and technical fees while deducting TAS. ... The application of section 195(2) presupposes that the person responsible for making the payment to the non-resident is in no doubt that tax is payable in respect of some part of the amount to be remitted to a non-resident but is not sure as to what should be the portion so taxable or is not sure as to the amount of tax to be deducted. In such a situation, he is required to make an application to the ITO(TDS) for determining the amount. It is only when these conditions are satisfied and an application is made to the ITO(TDS) that the question of making an order under section 195(2) will arise. ... This reasoning of ours is based on the decision of this Court in *Transmission Corpn of A.P. Ltd.'s* case (*supra*) in which this Court has observed that the provision of section 195(2) is a safeguard. From this it follows that where a person responsible for deduction is fairly certain then he can make his own determination as to whether the tax was deductible at source and, if so, what should be the amount thereof.

10. In *Transmission Corpn of AP Ltd's* case (*supra*) a non-resident had entered into a composite contract with the resident party making the payments. The said composite contract not only comprised supply of plant, machinery and equipment in India, but also comprised the installation and commissioning of the same in India. It was admitted that the erection and commissioning of plant and machinery in India gave rise to income-taxable in India. It was, therefore, clear even to the payer that payments required to be made by him to the non-resident included an element of income which was exigible to tax in India. The only issue raised in that case was whether TDS was applicable only to pure income payments and not to composite payments which had an element of income embedded or incorporated in them. The controversy before us in this batch of cases is, therefore, quite different. In *Transmission Corpn of AP Ltd's* case (*supra*) it was held that TAS was liable to be deducted by the payer on the gross amount if such payment included in it an amount which was exigible to tax in India. It was held that if the payer wanted to deduct TAS not on the gross amount but on the lesser amount, on the footing that only a portion of the payment made represented 'income chargeable to tax in India', then it was necessary for him to make an application under section 195(2) of the Act to the ITO(TDS) and obtain his permission for deducting TAS at lesser amount. Thus, it was held by this Court that if the payer had a doubt as to the amount to be deducted as TAS he could approach the ITO(TDS) to compute the amount which was liable to be deducted at source. In our view, section 195(2) is based on the 'principle of proportionality'. The said sub-section gets attracted only in cases where the payment made is a composite payment in which a certain proportion of payment has an element of 'income' chargeable to tax in India. It is in this context that the Supreme Court stated, 'If no such application is filed, income-tax on such sum is to be deducted and it is the statutory obligation of the person responsible for paying such 'sum' to deduct tax thereon before making payment. He has to discharge the obligation to TDS'. If one reads the observation of the Supreme Court, the words 'such sum' clearly indicate that the observation refers to a case of composite payment where the payer has a doubt regarding the inclusion of an amount in such payment which is exigible to tax in India. In our view, the above observations of this Court in *Transmission Corpn of AP Ltd's* case (*supra*) which is put in italics has been completely, with respect, misunderstood by

> the Karnataka High Court to mean that it is not open for the payer to contend that if the amount paid by him to the non-resident is not at all 'chargeable to tax in India', then no TAS is required to be deducted from such payment. This interpretation of the High Court completely loses sight of the plain words of section 195(1) which in clear terms lays down that tax at source is deductible only from 'sums chargeable' under the provisions of the Income-tax Act, *i.e.*, chargeable under sections 4, 5 and 9 of the Income-tax Act.

The law emerging from a conjoint reading of these two decisions may be summed up as follows:

(1) If the payment to non-resident includes income embedded therein, the tax has to be deducted at the entire payment, unless the payee takes recourse to section 195(2) of the Act and files an application for determination by the Revenue that such sum would not be chargeable to tax in the case of recipient, or for determination of appropriate proportion of such sum so chargeable, or for grant of certificate authorising recipient to receive the amount without deduction of tax, or deduction of income tax at any lower rates or no deduction.[767]
(2) If the payment does not at all include any sum chargeable to tax under the Income Tax Act, there is no liability to deduct tax at source at all.[768]

Thus, in the context of transfer of capital assets and accruing capital gains, unless the payee takes recourse to section 195(2), he is liable to deduct tax on the entire amount. In *Syed Aslam Hashmi*,[769] the Tax Tribunal was directly faced with this question whether an NRI (non-resident Indian) purchaser, having failed to take recourse to section 195(2), would be required under section 195(1) to deduct tax on the entire sale consideration payable to NRI seller. Relying on *Transmission Corporation*,[770] the Tribunal answered the question in the affirmative. A similar view was taken in *R Prakash*.[771]

Indian treaty practices are not uniform and evince differential approaches. Some treaties follow the UN Model, which requires that gains from the alienation of shares other than those mentioned in paragraph 4 representing a threshold participation in a company which is a resident of a contracting state may be taxed in that state. For example, while tax treaties with Belgium[772] and France[773] prescribe a participation threshold of 10%, the Korean agreement[774] contains a lower threshold of 5% share, with a holding period of twelve months, preceding the alienation. Some recent treaties apparently display an upward participation threshold. For instance, treaties with

767. *Transmission Corporation* (n. 760).
768. *GE India* (n. 763); *see also CIT v Creative Infocity Ltd* (2017) 82 Taxmann.com 356 (Guj).
769. *Syed Aslam Hashmi v ITO* (2013) 55 SOT 441(Bang).
770. *Transmission Corporation* (n. 760).
771. *R. Prakash v ITO* (2013) 38 taxmann.com 123 (Bang).
772. India-Belgium Treaty, Art. 13 para. 5.
773. India-France Treaty, Art. 14 para. 5.
774. India-Korea Treaty, Art. 13 para. 5.

Malaysia,[775] Indonesia[776] and Israel[777] prescribe a 50% of shares as a participation threshold.

Older treaties,[778] however, do not prescribe any participation threshold and allocate the taxing jurisdiction on gains of shares or similar rights to the residence state of the alienator. A few treaties, however, have allocated taxing rights in respect of capital gains to both states.[779] In the treaties with the UK[780] and the US,[781] each contracting state has been given rights to tax capital gains, other than the gains arising on the sale of aircrafts, ships, etc., in accordance with their respective domestic laws. With the recent signing of the MLI,[782] India has chosen to apply the second option,[783] and the look back period of 365 days, triggering the source taxation of the transfer of shares or comparable interest where such shares or comparable interest derive more than 50% of their value form immovable property situated in India. While India has notified sixty-one of its covered tax treaties which contain provisions dealing with source taxation of transfer of shares which derive their value from immovable property. It recently deposited its instrument of ratification along with its reservations, notifications and options on 25 June 2019. As a result, MLI has been in force in India since 1 October 2019. Its provisions will modify Indian DTAA (from FY 2020-2021 onwards) to address revenue loss through treaty abuse and profit shifting strategies by ensuring that profits are taxed in the jurisdiction where substantive economic activities are undertaken.

3.6 CONCLUSION

This analysis of the two treaty structures, therefore, clearly reveals that economic allegiance as the foundation of taxing rights has remained the guiding principle in the drafting of the treaty provisions. The divergence, however, in the two model structures is only due the competing ideologies of the theorists of residence and source taxation, who have been jostling with each other, since the League of Nation Double Taxation Reports,[784] to accord supremacy to the respective jurisdictional precepts – residence or

775. India-Malaysia Treaty, Art. 14 para. 4 (signed on 29 January 2013).
776. India-Indonesia Treaty, Art. 13 para. 4 (as amended vide Notification No. SO 1144(E) (No. 17/2016 (F.No. 503/4/2005-FTD-II)) dated 16 March 2016).
777. India-Malaysia Treaty, Art. 14 para. 4 (as amended vide Notification No. SO 441(E) (No. 10/2017 (F.No. 500/14/2004-FTD-II)) dated 14 February 2017).
778. *See, e.g.*, India-Australia Treaty, Art. 13 para. 5; India-South Africa Treaty, Art. 13 para. 5; India-Armenia Treaty, Art. 13 para. 5; India-Belarus Treaty, Art. 13 para. 5; India-Botswana Treaty, Art. 14 para. 5; India-Albania Treaty, Art. 13 para. 5; India-Austria Treaty, Art. 13 para. 5; India-Cyprus Treaty, Art. 13 para. 5; India-Georgia Treaty, Art. 13 para. 5; India-Germany Treaty, Art. 13, para. 5; India-Ireland Treaty, Art. 13 para. 5; India-Nepal Treaty, Art. 13 para. 5 and India-Mongolia Treaty, Art. 13 para. 5.
779. *See, e.g.*, India-Canada Treaty, Art. 13, para. 2.
780. India-UK Treaty, Art. 14 para. 1.
781. India-USA Treaty, Art. 13 para. 1.
782. MLI (n. 403).
783. *Ibid.*, Art. 9 para. 4.
784. GWJ Bruins, Luigi Einaudi, ERA Seligman and Sir Josiah Stamp, *Report on Double Taxation* (League of Nations 1923-1928).

source. However, whenever there is an agreed consensus, the provisions reflect a recognition of economic connection as the dominant determinant of tax allocation. BEPS proposals and the MLI provisions show these trends in ample measure as indicated in the foregoing analysis. Dietsch, although critical of various aspects of the BEPS project, agrees with the OECD that the primary goal of institutional reform should be the protection of fiscal self-determination and this aim may be secured in part by means of the implementation of the principle of economic allegiance (which he terms the 'membership principle'): 'we can restore fiscal self-determination by (among other things) ensuring that individuals and corporations pay taxes there where they employ economic activities'.[785]

785. P Dietsch, *Catching Capital: The Ethics of Tax Competition* (OUP 2015) 82-83.

CHAPTER 4
Strict Territorial Nexus and the Principles of International Law

Abstract

This chapter investigates whether the territorial nexus in the sense of physical presence in a state is an internationally accepted principle of tax allocation and if yes, what is the law regarding application of this principle vis-à-vis the municipal law in India? This chapter consists of five sections, in addition to the introduction. Sections 4.2 and 4.3 focus on the thematic divergence between the territoriality principle of public international law and that of tax law, followed by an analysis of the courts' decisions to see how mixing up of the two concepts influenced judicial reasoning over a period of time, distorting tax allocation. Sections 4.4 and 4.5 evaluate the hypothesis whether customary international law supports the requirements of a territorial presence in a state for its tax claims and if yes, whether such an international custom takes precedence over the municipal laws of states. The final section 4.6 concludes the chapter by analysing some of latest policy developments in context of this analysis.

4.1 INTRODUCTION

Despite the history and the theoretical basis of the source rule being rooted in the economic nexus doctrine, as explicated in Chapter 2 of this book, which runs through the treaty provisions, there have been a stubborn insistence by some tax lawyers on a strict territorial nexus in terms of a physical presence of the tax object in the state territory. This territorial insistence found support from some judicial pronouncements in India,[786] where the courts had stressed on the requirement of services being rendered in India so as to establish a territorial nexus between the income earned (fees received for services rendered) and the territory of India. According to the courts, mere

786. *Ishikawajima-Harima Heavy Industries Ltd v DIT* (2007) 288 ITR 408 (SC); *see also Jindal Thermal Power Company Ltd v DCIT (TDS)* (2010) 321 ITR 31 (Kar).

utilisation of services in India, sans their rendition in India, was not enough to confer jurisdiction.

Faced with these judicial holdings, India proceeded to amend its domestic law[787] in 2010 to nullify these court decisions. The amendment ordained the taxing of a non-resident's income from interest, royalty and fees from technical services, irrespective of whether there was a residence or place of business or business connection in India; or whether the non-resident's services were rendered in India. This amendment was criticised, *inter alia,* on the ground that it conflicted with the principles of international law and customs. It was argued that this amendment, which did away with the requirement of services being rendered in India, ran afoul of international law and customary principles, which allegedly mandated a strict territorial link with the source state for the assumption of tax jurisdiction.[788]

This criticism seems to have stemmed from certain observations in *Ishikawajima.*[789] In this case, Ishikawajima, a non-resident company incorporated in Japan, provided offshore services to persons resident in India. These services were rendered outside India, but they were utilised in India. Holding against its taxability in India, Sinha J, speaking for the court, observed as follows:

> Having regard to the internationally accepted principle and DTAA, it may not be possible to give an extended meaning to the words 'income deemed to accrue or arise in India' as expressed in Section 9 of the Act. ... Whereas a resident would come within the purview of Section 9(1)(vii) of the Act, a nonresident would not, as services of a non-resident to a resident utilised in India may not have much relevance in determining whether the income of the non-resident accrues or arises in India. It must have a direct live link between the services rendered in India, when such a link is established; the same may again be subjected to any relief under DTAA. A distinction may also be made between rendition of services and utilisation thereof.

Some tax theorists have also suggested the existence of a customary international law that limits states' taxing rights.[790] Frey and Schmid put it as follows:

---

787. The Finance Act 2010 s. 4. It inserted an expiation below s. 9 as follows:

> *Explanation* - For the removal of doubts, it is hereby declared that for the purposes of this section, the income of a non-resident shall be deemed to accrue or arise in India under clause (v) or clause (vi) or clause (vii) of sub-section (1) of section 9 and shall be included in his total income of non-resident, whether or not, -
>
> (a) the non-resident has a residence or place of business or business connection in India; or
> (b) the non-resident has rendered services in India.

788. N M Desai, 'Budget 2010-11: Non-Resident Services Outside India: Taxed Retroactively' (27 February 2010), http://www.nishithdesai.com/fileadmin/user_upload/pdfs/Budget_2010-11-_Non-resident_services_outside_India-_Taxed_retroactively.pdf, accessed 5 January 2019.
789. *Ishikawajima* (n. 786).
790. J Frey and F Schmid, 'Nexus Limitations on German-Source IP Taxation' (2020) vol. 100 Tax Notes Int'l, 1051-1057.

> These criteria comply with the generally accepted principle of territoriality. Territoriality principles require a significant (physical) presence in the taxing country. The right of a state to tax generally requires domicile, residence, property, or economic activity within the taxing country.[791]

This chapter, therefore, investigates the proposition whether the territorial nexus, in the sense it was understood in *Ishikawajima*,[792] is an internationally accepted principle of tax jurisdiction and if yes, what is the law regarding application of this principle vis-à-vis the municipal law in India? This chapter comprises six sections, including the introductory section. While section 4.2 focuses on the critical dichotomy between the concept of territorial jurisdictional nexus in public international law and that of territorial nexus in tax law, section 4.3 examines the municipal courts' decisions to see how judicial reasoning has been influenced by the territoriality principle of public international law; and how the nuances of connecting factors for tax nexus have been recognised only much later by the courts. Section 4.4 evaluates the hypothesis whether customary international law supports the requirements of a territorial presence in a state for its tax claims. Section 4.5 addresses the purely legal question of hierarchy of international custom vis-à-vis the municipal laws of India. Section 4.6 concludes this chapter by analysing some of the latest policy developments in the context of the new digital economy by analysing their economic rationale which forms the underlying basis of the source taxation principle.

4.2 TERRITORIAL NEXUS: CONCEPTUAL DIVERGENCE IN PUBLIC INTERNATIONAL LAW AND TAX LAW

It must be stated at the outset that in *Ishikawajima*,[793] the Court has not given any reasoning for its conclusion and has merely assumed that a strict territorial link (in the sense of a physical presence in the territory) is an accepted principle of international law and custom. This assumption in *Ishikawajima* seems to have emanated from the application of the public international law concept of territorial nexus, which, in turn, is based on the concept of sovereignty, to tax law.

The concept of territorial nexus in public international law determines the state's power to assert jurisdiction. For international lawyers – who do not necessarily possess tax law expertise, this territorial basis of states' taxing rights appears perfectly rational, since it is in accordance with the general understanding of state power to assert jurisdiction, i.e., to prescribe a rule regulating some social relationship and enforce this rule against a targeted subject.[794] Tax scholarship has widely used this notion of territoriality to describe practice of some states in determining the quantitative extent of taxpayer's income tax liability in such a way that only income from 'domestic

791. *Ibid.*, 1055, citing Juliane Kokott, Das Steuerrecht der Europäischen Union 143 (2018) 2.03 (2019).
792. *Ishikawajima* (n. 786).
793. *Ibid.*
794. P Capps, M Evans and S Konstadinidis, 'Introduction' in P Capps, M Evans and S Konstadinidis (eds), *Asserting Jurisdiction: International and European Legal Perspectives* (Hart 2003) xxi–xxii.

sources' is liable to tax.[795] The confusion between the two variants of jurisdictional nexus in public international law and tax law is brought out clearly by the following observations of Frey and Schmid:

> As Bernard Oxman explains, 'a State must be able to identify a sufficient nexus between itself and the object of its assertion of jurisdiction.'[796] The International Court of Justice (ICJ) provided important guidance on the nexus requirement in Nottebohm (Liechtenstein v Guatemala), 1955 ICJ 4 (Apr. 6), when it held that states' jurisdiction to prescribe rules applicable outside their own territory is limited. In so stating, the ICJ introduced the so-called genuine link requirement. In that case, the court ruled that a state's decision to grant diplomatic protection requires a 'genuine connection of existence, interests and sentiments, together with the existence of reciprocal rights and duties.' Because it is customary international law, the genuine link requirement also applies to a state's ability to impose tax on nonresidents.[797]

The application of this territoriality argument in the context of states' taxing rights, however, runs counter to the economic allegiance principle, upon which the four economists[798] grounded the states' tax claims over non-resident's income. Under tax law, what is relevant for a territorial nexus is an economic connection of the state territory with the tax object, and it is the extant of this economic link that forms the basis for tax claims.[799] As Mines puts it, 'nexus describes whether a taxpayer, property, or activity has sufficient connection with a state to be subject to that state's tax jurisdiction'.[800] In the words of Rohatgi, 'a country has the source taxing right only if there is an economic connection between a particular item of income and the country as a taxing jurisdiction'.[801]

Thus, the strict territoriality, in the sense it is used in public international law, is not a limiting factor for tax jurisdiction. As Arnold points out, apart from the countervailing interests of other governments and the practical difficulties of enforcement and collection, 'there are no limitations under international law on a nation's power to tax; and in most countries, there are no constitutional limitations'.[802] Qureshi explains it thus: 'substantive tax jurisdiction is limited by an international law requirement for a "reasonable connection" between the state and either the tax subject or tax object'.[803]

---

795. M Lang, *Introduction to the Law of Double Taxation Conventions* (IBFD and Linde 2013) 23-24.
796. Frey and Schmid (n. 790) 1054, citing BH Oxman, *Max Planck Encyclopedia of International Law* (1987).
797. *Ibid.*, citing W Schön, 'Neutrality and Territoriality – Competing or Converging Concepts in European Tax Law?' (2015) vol. 69 Bull. Int'l Tax'n 271, 3.2.
798. *See* the Four Economists' Report, 4031.
799. *Ibid.*
800. P Mines, 'Nexus' in JJ Cordes, RD Ebel and J Gravelle (eds), *The Encyclopedia of Taxation and Tax Policy* (The Urban Institute 2005) 269.
801. R Rohatgi, *Basic International Taxation* (2nd edn, Richmond Law & Tax 2005) 222.
802. BJ Arnold, *The Taxation of Controlled Foreign Corporations: An International Comparison* (CTF 1986) 1.
803. AH Qureshi, *The Public International Law of Taxation: Text, Cases and Materials* (Graham & Trotman 1994) 22, arguing that 'fiscal jurisdiction refers to a State's competence to tax persons, property and transactions, or events'.

The *Ishikawajima* decision,[804] thus, seems to have completely missed this fundamental distinction between territoriality paradigms in the public international law and tax law and has erroneously mixed up the two.[805] While the former perspective entails an exercise in establishing a link between the tax subject and personal and/or territorial sphere of a sovereign state, the latter entails an exercise in establishing whether economic ties of the tax subject with the state are strong enough to justify or legitimise pertinent taxing claim.[806] Needless to say that equating the two concepts or blurring the distinction thereof will have undesirable consequences inasmuch as it will relieve many taxpayers of liability to pay substantial taxes to the states from which they may have extracted considerable economic benefits. Thus, apart from territorial link based on residence and nationality, what is relevant for the purposes of tax claims of a state is an economic connecting factor between the state and the tax fact. Martha explains it thus:[807]

> The jurisdiction of a state to tax aliens (natural and juristic persons) is based on territorial sovereignty and takes the form of fiscal attachment on the basis of residence, fiscal attachment short of residence and economic fiscal attachment.

This economic nexus is based on factors aimed at measuring the existence and extent of the economic relationships between a particular state and the income or person to be taxed.[808]

---

804. *Ishikawajima* (n. 786).
805. Even otherwise, *Ishikawajima* was a case under section 9(1)(vii)(b) of the Act, but the Court erroneously based its decision on the wordings of section 9(1)(vii)(c), which was a provision applicable to a case where the payer is a non-resident. Sinha J expressed it thus:

> Section 9(1)(vii)(c) of the Act states that 'a person who is a non-resident, where the fees are payable in respect of services in a business or profession, carried on by such person in India, or for the purposes of making or earning any income from any source in India'. Reading the provision in its plain sense, it can be seen that it requires two conditions have [sic] to be met the services which are the source of the income that is sought to be taxed, has [sic] to be rendered in India, as well as utilised in India, to be taxable in India.
>
> Now a plain reading of section 9(1)(vii)(c) reveals that it applies to a case where the payer is a non-resident and services are utilised in India, which was not the case in *Ishikawajima*. The *Ishikawajima* decision, therefore, was rendered *per incuriam* in as much as it loses sight of section 9(1)(vii)(b) altogether, which unequivocally brings the payment of fees paid by a resident for services utilised in India within the legal fiction of deemed accrual/arising of income in India. Section 9(1)(vii)(c), which was not relevant to the facts and circumstances of the case. A *per incuriam* decision does not create a binding precedent; *see also AR Antulay v RS Nayak* (1988) 2 SCC 602 (SCCB); *N Bhargavan Pillai v State of Kerala* (2004) 13 SCC 217 (SC) and *Mayuram Subramanian v CBI* (2006) 5 SCC 752 (SC).

806. S Gadžo, 'The Principle of 'Nexus' or 'Genuine Link' as a Keystone of International Income Tax Law: A Reappraisal' (2018) vol. 46(3) Intertax 194, 205.
807. RSJ Martha, 'Extra-Territorial Taxation in International Law' in KM Meessen (ed), *Extraterritorial Jurisdiction in Theory and Practice* (Kluwer 1996) 19, 25.
808. OECD, 'Fundamental Principles of Taxation' in *Addressing the Tax Challenges of the Digital Economy* (OECD Pub 2014) 36.

4.3 JUDICIAL APPROACHES IN MUNICIPAL COURTS

Thus, the concept of economic allegiance, with its inherent regulation of taxing rights, sits uneasily with the idea of national sovereignty and territoriality principle.[809] This crucial distinction between the concepts of 'territorial nexus' in public international law and tax law has many a time been lost sight of by the municipal courts, giving rise to absurd conclusions.

4.3.1 Pakistan

In *Imperial Tobacco Co*,[810] which is one of the earliest cases, the Supreme Court of Pakistan, even though decided correctly on the facts of the case, mixed up the twin concepts of territoriality, while holding that Pakistan could not tax a company resident in India in respect of its India-sourced profits since, under the rules of (general) international law, 'a legislature has authority ... to tax foreigners only if they earn or receive income in the country for which that legislature has the authority to make laws'.[811] The following words of Munir CJ bring this out:[812]

> 'It is quite clear', said Lord Westbury in *Attorney General v. Campbell* 1872 LR 5 HL 524, 531 that 'you cannot apply an English Act of Parliament to foreign property while it remains foreign property.' This rule of law is 'the natural consequence' of the proposition of international jurisprudence, that 'every nation possesses an exclusive sovereignty and jurisdiction within its own territory ... For it would be wholly incompatible with the quality and exclusiveness of the sovereignty of all nations, that any one nation should be at liberty to regulate ... things not within its own territory. It would be equivalent to a declaration that the sovereignty' over a territory was never exclusive in any nation, but only concurrent with that of all nations, that each could legislate for all ... . The absurd results of such a state of things need not be dwelt on.

Thus, mainly guided by the principles of territorial sovereignty in public international law, the Court, at no point, examined the question of economic linkage between the income earned by the Indian company and the state of Pakistan. In this case, there was a clear absence of an economic linkage as not only transactions of the Indian company were carried out beyond Pakistan's territorial borders, but the profits of the company were also earned outside that country, which would automatically result in the denial of its taxing rights.

4.3.2 Germany

In a 1983 case, a German national was convicted for cigarette smuggling by the Austrian Supreme Court, and when the Austrian tax authorities sought assistance from

809. P Harris and D Oliver, *International Commercial Tax* (CUP 2010) 43.
810. *Imperial Tobacco Co of India v Commissioner of Income Tax* (1958) 27 ILR 103 (Pak SC).
811. *Ibid.*
812. *Ibid.*

their German counterparts with regard to the collection of ensuing tax receipts, fees and interest, the German national raised the issue before the Federal Constitutional Court (*Bundesverfassungsgericht, BVerfG*).[813] Here also, without going into the question of economic linkage for tax claims, the Court was solely guided by the norms of public international law in rejecting the tax claims of the Austrian tax authorities.[814] The following words of the Court illustrate the point:[815]

> (T)he imposition of taxes upon a foreigner living abroad, which is founded upon a set of facts wholly or partly implemented abroad requires sufficiently appropriate points of contact for taxation by the taxing State to prevent interference, contrary to the public international law, with the foreign State's claims to sovereignty. These points of contact and their factual closeness must, from the point of view of public international law, satisfy a minimum of reasonableness.

It is significant to note that apart from the obvious territoriality criteria for a sufficient nexus, viz., citizenship, residence, residual abode, or presence. the Court also referred to the criteria of realisation of a taxable event within Germany (the taxable event test) or the causation of a tax-significant outcome within Germany (the tax-significant outcome test),[816] although it failed to apply these economic tests. Had these tests been applied, tax receipts, fees and interests ensuing from cigarette smuggling in Austria would not have escaped taxation in Austria.

4.3.3 Austria

Similarly, in a 1998 decision of the Austrian Constitutional Court (*Verfassungsgerichtshof, VfGH*), which was not a case of any cross-border business or trade,[817] a similar approach was reflected in the judicial reasoning tendered by the Court. The case involved the legality of the exercise of taxing powers by the Municipality of Vienna. Under the federal legislation, Austrian municipalities were competent to impose a tax on commercial announcements and to regulate the main elements of this tax. The tax authorities of the Municipality of Vienna took the stand that the tax should be imposed on the value of income from commercial TV and radio announcements emitted from the studios located within its territory.[818] VfGH did not, however, approve of this action, basing its decision on the territoriality norms of public international law.[819] The Court reasoned that '(I)nternational custom permits the taxation of foreign economic

813. *BVerfGE* 63, 343 (1983) 48 Neue Juristische Wochenschrift, 2757.
814. *Ibid.*, 2760-2761.
815. *Ibid.*, 2758 (as translated in FA Mann, 'The Doctrine of International Jurisdiction Revisited After Twenty Years' in WM Reisman (ed) *Jurisdiction in International Law* (Ashgate 1999) 149).
816. *BVerfGE* (n. 813) 24 (as translated in FA Mann, 'The Doctrine of Jurisdiction in International Law' 110 (1964)).
817. Verfassungsgerichtshof G15/98, V9/98 (17 December 1998); *see* M Lang & L Paterno, 'Tax Coordination Between Regions in Austria – Role of the Courts' in M Lang et al. (eds), *Horizontal Tax Coordination* (IBFD 2012), for a synopsis of this case.
818. Lang & Paterno (n. 817) s. 3.2.
819. This VfGH decision underscores the similarity between the problems associated with the exercise of tax jurisdiction by the sovereign states and the problems associated with the

transactions when a sufficient connection exits between the taxpayer and the taxing state'.[820] Since the allocation of the taxing powers between states on an international plane and the allocation of taxing powers between sub-federal on an internal plane pursue the same objectives, the Court held that basic principles of international public law, such as the nexus norm, should be applied even in the exercise of tax jurisdiction by the Austrian municipalities.[821]

4.3.4 The United Kingdom

The UK courts also exhibited a similar trend initially. Instead of identifying an economic nexus, it was the international law concept of territoriality and sovereignty, which was recognised as the principal determinative factor for assertion of tax claims. The landmark judgment in *Ex Parte Blain*[822] is often cited to reinforce the territoriality principle of sovereignty in the domain of tax law. However, it may be noted at the outset that in *Ex parte Blain*, the question was related to an act of bankruptcy and not tax law, and the Court of Appeal was considering whether there was jurisdiction to make an adjudication order against a foreigner, domiciled and resident abroad, who had never been in England, but who was a member of an English firm upon which an execution had been levied by seizure and sale of the goods of the firm in England. It was in this context that the Court held that an act of bankruptcy must be a personal act or default, that it cannot be committed through an agent, nor by a firm as such, and that in such a case the Court ought not to make an order for service out of the jurisdiction of a bankruptcy petition on the foreigner. James LJ dwelt upon the territoriality principle of sovereignty in the following terms:[823]

> It appears to me that the whole question is governed by the broad, general, universal principle that English legislation, unless the contrary is expressly enacted or so plainly implied as to make it the duty of an English Court to give effect to an English statute, is applicable only to English subjects or to foreigners who by coming into this country, whether for a long or a short time, have made themselves during that time subject to English jurisdiction. ... But, if a foreigner remains abroad, if he has never come into this country at all, it seems to me impossible to imagine that the English Legislature could have ever intended to make such a man subject to particular English legislation.

However, the *Ex p Blain* ruling, delivered in the context of the territorial nexus principle of sovereignty, has often been misapplied to tax law as a fundamental nexus requirement. The confusion can be seen in the following words of Rao and Ajinkya:

---

exercise of taxing powers by the sub-units of composite states like federations or confederations. Thus, one could also rely on the extensive case law in the area of subnational taxation in attempting to prove existence of the nexus requirement under general international law; *see* FA Mann, *Studies in International Law* (Clarendon Press 1973) 95-96.

820. Lang & Paterno (n. 817) s. 3.3.
821. *Ibid.*
822. *Ex Parte Blain: In re Sawers* (1879) 12 Ch D 522, 528.
823. *Ibid.*

> Therefore, if the rule in international law is that a sovereign shall not act on the territory of another sovereign unless authorized, the presumption is that the Legislature would act within the boundaries of this rule unless specified to the contrary. This implies that our enforcement provisions relating to seizure, recovery etc. are limited to the territory of India, which suggests that the withholding provisions should also be considered applicable only to the extent that the Indian Revenue authorities can initiate recovery when there is failure to withhold.[824]

The limitation of the sovereignty principle in the context of taxing power, however, came to be distinctly recognised in *Oceanic Contractors Inc,*[825] where the House of Lords dealt with a case of a non-resident overseas company, engaged in laying of pipes and platform construction in the North Sea. The company employed 400 workers on its barges and other vessels to carry its on operations throughout the world, including the UK sector of the North Sea, which were designated areas under the Continental Shelf Act 1964. The Company deducted PAYE tax[826] in respect of its employees, who were employed at establishments in the UK. But those employed in the UK sector of the North Sea were paid in US Dollars free of tax. The Crown claimed that the company was required by its domestic law[827] to deduct PAYE tax from wages and salaries paid to the employees, who worked in the UK sector of the North Sea. The Court of Appeal, however, took the view that although statutory provision was general, it was to be presumed not to have extraterritorial effect as the Parliament could not have intended to cast on a foreigner who was not resident of the UK the role of tax collector for the Revenue. The Court placed reliance on its holding in *Ex p Blain*. Reversing the decision of the Court of Appeal, the House of Lords underlined the limitation of the *Ex p Blain* decision, and delineated the distinction between the territoriality principle of sovereignty and the economic nexus requirement of international tax law. Lord Scarman, adverting to the principles laid down in *Ex p Blain,*[828] observed that 'the principle is a rule of construction only' and that 'British tax liability has never been exclusively limited to British subjects and foreigners resident within the jurisdiction'. The Law Lord lucubrated it further:[829]

> Put into the language of today, the general principle being there stated is simply that, unless the contrary is expressly enacted or so plainly implied that the courts must give effect to it, United Kingdom legislation is applicable only to British subjects or to foreigners who by coming to the United Kingdom, whether for a short or long time, have made themselves subject to British jurisdiction. Two points would seem to be clear: first, that the principle is a rule of construction only

824. S Rao and B Ajinkya, 'Groping in the Dark: The Extending Arms of the Indian International Withholding Tax' (2020) vol. 22(1) NLS of India Rev 2010 97-122 (referring to *Ex Parte Blain* (n. 822)).
825. *Clark (Inspector of Taxes) v Oceanic Contractors Inc* (1983) 2 AC 130.
826. Pay-as-you-earn or pay-as-you-go tax. Devised by Sir Paul Chambers, PAYE was introduced into the UK in 1944, following trials in 1940-1941. The financial strain that World War II placed upon the country meant that the Treasury needed to collect more tax from many more people. This posed significant challenges to the government and to the many workers and employers who had previously never come into contact with the tax system.
827. The Income and Corporation Tax of 1970 s. 204 sch. E.117.
828. *Ex Parte Blain* (n. 822).
829. *Oceanic Contractors* (n. 825) 145.

> and, second, that it contemplates mere presence within the jurisdiction as sufficient to attract the application of British legislation. Certainly, there is no general principle that the legislation of the United Kingdom is applicable only to British subjects or persons resident here. Merely to state such a proposition is to manifest its absurdity. Presence, not residence, is the test.

Lord Scarman further observed that in the absence of any clear indications to the contrary, it does not necessarily follow that the Parliament has in its fiscal legislation intended any territorial limitation other than that imposed by such unenforceability. Having said this, Lord Scarman observed that the case was concerned with the territorial limitation to be implied into a section which establishes a method of tax collection. The method is to require the person paying the income to deduct it from his payments and account for it to the revenue. The only critical factor, so far as collection is concerned, is whether in the circumstances it can be made effective. The test which was applied by the House of Lords was that of a trading presence in the UK. A trading presence in the UK was held to suffice in order to attract the liability to deduct tax. On facts, it was held that the trading presence was made out.[830]

In *Agassi,*[831] the House of Lords reiterated the economic nexus rule for the allocation of taxing rights of non-residents. The case involved the famous tennis player Andre Agassi. Agassi, neither resident nor domiciled in the UK, came to play tennis tournaments in the UK (including Wimbledon). Agassi's company, again neither incorporated nor resident in the UK, carried on the business of entering into contracts with manufacturers of sports clothing and equipment. Agassi would sponsor or advertise the manufacturers' products in return for payments made to his company. This type of contract had been entered into with Nike Inc and Head Sport AG, which, too, were neither incorporated nor resident in the UK, nor did they carry on any business in the UK. Agassi played tournaments in the UK in the 1998-1999 tax year. In the same year, his company received payments from Nike and Head. The payments were not received in the UK. These payments were made between foreign companies, outside the UK. The UK tax administration argued that the payments had a prescribed connection with Agassi's activities in the UK and that Nike and Head should have deducted UK tax from the payments made to Agassi's company and remitted it to the UK tax administration. Agassi contended that the Parliament could not have intended to subject foreign individuals and companies with no residence or trading presence in the UK to such UK tax obligations.[832] The tax administration argued that if Agassi was right, it would mean that foreign entertainers and sportsmen, who earned money from commercial sponsorship contracts connected with their professional activities in the UK, could avoid liability to UK tax on that money. They could do this simply by ensuring that the payment was made to a foreign company with no trading presence or assets in the UK. The Special Commissioners and the judge at first instance held in favour of the tax administration. The Court of Appeal found in favour of the taxpayer.

830. *Ibid.*
831. *Agassi v Robinson* [2006] UKHL 23 (HL).
832. The Income and Corporation Taxes Act 1988 s. 555(2); now Income Tax Act 2007 s. 966.

The House of Lords, however, by a majority decision (4 to 1), found in favour of the tax administration. Lord Scott illustrated the principles thus:[833]

> 16. Counsel for Mr Agassi relies very heavily on well-known authorities such as *Re Sawers, ex p Blain*(1879) 12 Ch D 522 and, more recently, *Clark (Inspector of Taxes) v Oceanic Contractors Inc.* [1983] 2 AC 130. In *Ex p Blain*, James LJ referred at 526 to the
>
> > 'broad, general, universal principle that English legislation, unless the contrary is expressly enacted or so plainly implied as to make it the duty of an English Court to give effect to an English statute, is applicable only to English subjects or to foreigners who by coming into this country, whether for a long or a short time, have made themselves during that time subject to English jurisdiction ...'
>
> And in the *Oceanic Contractors* case, Lord Scarman, having cited the above passage with approval repeated at p. 145 the same principle. But Lord Scarman noted also that 'the principle is a rule of construction only' and that 'British tax liability has never been exclusively limited to British subjects and foreigners resident within the jurisdiction'. And Lord Wilberforce, at p. 152, referred to the 'territorial principle' as being 'really a rule of construction of statutes expressed in general terms'. The question to be asked, said Lord Wilberforce, is 'who ... is within the legislative grasp, or intendment, of the statute under consideration?'

Accordingly, it was held that foreign entertainers and sportsmen who, or whose controlled companies, receive payments in connection with their commercial activities in the UK should be subject to the section 18(1)(a)(iii) charge to tax and that the territorial principle cannot be implied so as to limit the effect of the clear language of the statute.

These decisions once again bring home the point that for invoking tax jurisdiction, what is required is not territorial presence but the presence of some factors connecting the subject of taxation to the taxing jurisdiction. Harris and Oliver have explored the relevant connecting factors in the context of income tax,[834] by drawing a distinction between a personal tax and an in-rem tax. The personal tax focuses on the person and, in particular, personal circumstances. The in-rem tax focuses on an activity or thing. In an international setting, a personal tax requires some connection between the person and the taxing jurisdiction and an in-rem tax requires some connection between the activity or thing and the taxing jurisdiction.[835] The composite tax principle recognises that, in an international setting, an income tax is both a personal tax and an in-rem tax.[836] The income tax often focuses on the activity or thing from which the income is derived and at the same time the person deriving the income. Since progressive taxation became popular more than a century ago, the focus of the income tax has been on the person but the in-rem element remains important in an international setting. In terms of economic allegiance, if a person who derives income

833. *Agassi* (n. 831) para. 16.
834. Harris and Oliver (n. 809) 45-46.
835. *Ibid.*
836. For further on the composite tax principle, *see* PA Harris, 'Corporate-Shareholder Income Taxation and Allocating Taxing Rights Between Countries: A Comparison of Imputation Systems' (IBFD 1996) 447-450.

or an activity or thing that generates income is within or sufficiently connected with a particular state, that state is entitled to a contribution towards public services.[837]

4.3.5 The United States

This dichotomy of a 'territorial presence' and an 'economic nexus' has also been the subject of fierce litigation in the US. The effect of the territoriality principle of sovereignty continued to guide the US Supreme Court, until very recently, in the determination of taxing rights of the federal states. In *National Bellas Hess*,[838] the US Supreme Court concluded that the taxpayer must have some physical presence in the taxing authority, before the corporation is subject to taxation. In this case, National Bellas Hess, a mailing order house, was licensed to do business only in Missouri and Delaware. It had no outlets or sales representative or any other place of business in Illinois. The entire business in Illinois was carried on via the US or common carrier. Twice a year catalogues were mailed to the company's active or recent customers to Illinois. This mailing was supplemented by advertising 'flyers' which were occasionally mailed to past and potential customers. Orders for merchandise were mailed by the customers to National Bellas and were accepted at its Missouri plant. The ordered goods were then sent to the customers either by mail or by common carrier. Illinois required National Bellas to collect and pay to the state the use tax imposed by its law.[839] The US Supreme Court ruled that a physical presence is an essential prerequisite to establishing nexus at least for sales tax purposes. With this ruling came the 'bright-line' rule that no 'substantial nexus' existed unless there was a physical presence within the state. The connection between the state and the foreign corporation must be more than just the transactions of using mail or common carrier services to connect them to state residents.

This trend continued for nearly five decades. In *Quill Corp*,[840] Quill Corp was an out-of-state mail-order office equipment vendor that solicited sales through a catalogue to potential customers in North Dakota. North Dakota charged that Quill should be applying a use tax to the goods it sold in the state. The North Dakota Supreme Court held that by selling its product to North Dakota customers, Quill established an economic presence in North Dakota, which created nexus for sales tax purposes. However, the US Supreme Court ruled in favour of Quill, saying that the business had no physical presence and that North Dakota could not tax Quill simply because it had customers within the state.

There had been considerable unease among states with the physical presence rule, enunciated in *National Bellas Hess* and *Quill Corp*. States' growing frustrations with the rule were due to the explosive growth of the Internet in the two decades since *Quill*, which expanded the pool of vendors that were protected by the physical presence rule from a relatively small group of retailers (principally mail-order vendors)

837. Harris and Oliver (n. 809) 46.
838. *National Bellas Hess v State of Illinois* (1967) 386 US 753.
839. Ill Rev Stat c 120 § 439.3 (1965).
840. *Quill Corp v North Dakota* (1992)504 US 298.

to a much larger group that is buoyed significantly by Internet retailers. This resulted in significant revenue losses for states across the nation. States responded to these losses by aggressively and continuously lobbying Congress to legislatively overturn the physical presence rule. Despite those efforts, however, Congress did not give states the reprieve that they sought and states responded to Congress' inaction in this area by taking steps aimed at mitigating the impact of Quill's physical presence directive, such as adopting statutory provisions attributing a physical presence to remote vendors, adopting unique information-reporting requirements that impose significant burdens on those vendors, and actively discussing challenging Quill's ongoing validity in courts.[841] Many state courts have, in fact, ruling in favour of an economic presence being sufficient for a state to impose tax on a foreign corporation, doing away with the requirement of a physical presence. In *Geoffrey Inc*,[842] for instance, Geoffrey, a foreign corporation, had no physical presence with South Carolina. Geoffrey, executed a licence agreement with its subsidiary Toys R Us, located in South Carolina, which gave them the right to use the 'Toys R Us' trade name. Geoffrey received royalty fees from Toys R Us stores located in South Carolina in exchange for services. On its South Carolina tax return, Toys R Us deducted the royalty fee payments. Thus, the South Carolina Tax Commission required that Geoffrey pay income tax and business licence fees, because the company was actively doing business within the state. However, Geoffrey's argument was that it did not have sufficient nexus within South Carolina and that the royalty income was derived from intangible means, and thus not taxable. The South Carolina Supreme Court decision addressed what is described as an economic relationship and not so much a physical presence issue. It was held that under the 'Due Process Clause', only 'minimum contacts' are required with the jurisdiction to create or establish a benefit from an economic market within the state. The South Carolina Supreme Court stated that 'any corporation that regularly exploits the markets of a state should be subject to its jurisdiction to impose an income tax even though not physically present' and that the presence of intangible property alone is sufficient to establish nexus. Also, the South Carolina Supreme Court stated that Geoffrey had 'purposefully directed its activity at the South Carolina's economic market by licensing intangibles for use in South Carolina and receiving income in exchange for their use'. As a result of its actions, Geoffrey created nexus, and the state can impose income tax and business tax on the company's activity.

Similarly, in *Orvis Co*,[843] Orvis Corporation, like Quill, had no physical presence within the state. However, its sales personnel visited their clients' wholesale and retail stores within New York State. According to the New York State Court of Appeals, this activity by Orvis' sales personnel created a direct solicitation of all its mail order and wholesale customers and satisfied the Commerce and Due Process Clauses. This ruling addressed economic nexus based on an out-of-state corporation whose activities are

841. A Thimmesch, 'The Fading Bright Line of Physical Presence: Did KFC Corporation v. Iowa Department of Revenue Give States the Secret Recipe for Repudiating Quill?' (2012) vol. 100 KY LJ 339-389, 339-340.
842. *Geoffrey Inc v South Carolina Tax Commission* (1993) 437 SE 2d 13 (SC).
843. *Orvis Co v Tax Appeals Tribunal* (1995) 654 NE2d 954.

similar to Orvis. New York's Court of Appeals also indicated that while physical presence is required, it need not be more than the 'slightest presence'.

In *Lanco,*[844] Lanco licensed intellectual property to a retailer in New Jersey in exchange for royalty payments. Lanco had no offices, employees, or tangible property in New Jersey, but the court stated the nexus premise thus:[845]

> [T]hat the physical presence of the taxpayer or its employee(s), agent(s), or tangible property in a jurisdiction has been and remains a necessary element for a finding of substantial nexus under the Commerce Clause of the United States Constitution. We respectfully disagree.

The Court explained that Lanco derived numerous benefits from the protection of New Jersey courts and police and fire department protection over the physical property utilising Lanco's trademarks, which was sufficient to create 'substantial nexus'.[846] The principal conclusion of the Lanco decision was that the Supreme Court in *Quill Corp* simply did not intend to 'create a universal physical presence requirement for state taxation under the Commerce Clause'.[847]

In *Amazon.com* and *Overstock.com,*[848] lawsuits were filed by Amazon.com and Overstock.com with the US Supreme Court to challenge the constitutionality of a 2008 state tax law of New York. It was argued that Amazon and Overstock did not have a physical presence in New York and the website owner (referred to as an 'Associate' under Amazon's programme), where their ads were placed, did not meet the nexus requirement standard of the Commerce Clause. Both companies' arguments were focused on the physical presence rule. In March 2013, however, the New York Court of Appeals ruled that the companies had a sufficient presence in the state because of affiliated independent sites that linked to the retailers in return for a commission. Lippman CJ, speaking for the majority, explained the nexus requirement in the following terms:[849]

> The bottom line is that if a vendor is paying New York residents to actively solicit business in this State, there is no reason why that vendor should not shoulder the appropriate tax burden. We will not strain to invalidate this statute where plaintiffs have not met their burden of establishing that it is facially invalid.
>
> ...
>
> The world has changed dramatically in the last two decades, and it may be that the physical presence test is outdated. An entity may now have a profound impact upon a foreign jurisdiction solely through its virtual projection via the Internet. That question, however, would be for the United States Supreme Court to consider. We are bound, and adjudicate this controversy, under the binding precedents of that Court, the ultimate arbiter of the meaning of the Commerce Clause.

844. *Lanco, Inc v NJ Div of Taxation* 879 A 2d 1234 (NJ Super Ct App Div 2005).
845. *Ibid.*, 1241.
846. *Ibid.*, 1237-1238.
847. *Lanco, Inc v NJ Div of Taxation* 908 A 2d 176 177 (NJ 2006).
848. *Amazon.com v NY Tax'n Dept & Fin* and *Overstock.com v NY Tax'n Dept & Fin*, Case Nos 33-34 NY Slip Op 02102 decided on 28 March 2013 (NY Court of Appeals).
849. *Ibid.*

> Subsequent to Quill, we further explained that, although an in-state physical presence is necessary, it 'need not be substantial. Rather, it must be demonstrably more than a slightest presence' (*Orvis, 86 NY2d* at 178, quoting *National Geographic Soc. v California Bd. of Equalization,* 430 US 551, 556 [1977]). The presence requirement will be satisfied if economic activities are performed in New York by the seller's employees or on its behalf (see *Orvis, 86 NY2d* at 178).

The Court of Appeals, thus, considered the issue of 'economic nexus' in these cases and held that Amazon and Overstock, even without a physical presence in New York State, had an economic presence by generating income from New York state residents with its affiliate programme through the Internet.[850] The US Supreme Court, in a writ petition filed by Amazon and Overstock, refused to review this ruling and let it stand.[851]

A recent ruling is the 2010 case of *KFC Corp v Iowa Department of Revenue.*[852] KFC, a Delaware corporation with its principal place of business in Kentucky, had licensed the KFC trademark and related systems to independent franchisees. All KFC locations in Iowa were owned by franchisees, and KFC had no property or employees located there.[853] KFC owned, managed, protected, and licensed all KFC materials and received a monthly 4% royalty from the franchises in Iowa. Franchisees were required to maintain specific KFC standards for menu items, advertising, marketing, and facilities. The licence also mandated the use of KFC approved vendors for procurement of equipment, supplies, and food.[854] The Supreme Court of Iowa held that the franchise right to operate in the state bestowed a direct connection to Iowa upon KFC, and taxing KFC's activity in Iowa did not place an undue burden on commerce, 'but rather a payment to government that provided the economic climate for the business to prosper'.[855] The Court noted as follows:

> [W]hile 'physical presence' may have been a significant feature, if not a requirement, in the Supreme Court's Dormant Commerce Clause analysis in early sales and use tax cases, 'physical presence' in the narrow sense does not appear as an important factor in cases involving state income taxation.[856]

The Court further suggested that a physical presence standard for income tax would create a huge loophole in tax structure and would provide incentive for 'entity isolation' where taxpayers would create affiliates without physical presence to avoid taxation.[857] A fundamental concept of law that the Court considered was the substance-over-form approach embraced by the Supreme Court in most modern cases involving the Dormant Commerce Clause.[858] The US Supreme Court denied a petition for a writ

850. *Amazon.com LLC v NY State Dep of Tax'n & Fin* (NY Sup Ct No. 601247 2008).
851. *Amazon.com v New York Tax'n Department, No. 13-259* and *Overstock.com v New York Tax'n Department, No 13-252,* vide order dated 2 December 2013 (US SC).
852. (2010) 792 NW 2d 308 (Iowa).
853. *Ibid.*, 310.
854. *Ibid.*, 311.
855. *Ibid.*
856. *Ibid.*, 314.
857. *Ibid.*, 328.
858. *Ibid.*, 313.

of certiorari against this decision as well vide its order dated 3 October 2011, with result that the Iowa Supreme Court decision stands. This decision, now final with the US Supreme Court's refusal to review, is the latest in a trend of state court decisions upholding income tax assessments against corporate taxpayers that have an economic presence.

A more recent case, *Jack Daniels Properties*,[859] furthered the arguments in *KFC Corp* and expanded nexus-creating activities for intangible holding companies. The facts were similar to *KFC Corp*, but Jack Daniels sought to differentiate its case from *KFC Corp* on three grounds: *first*, the appellant did not operate any stores in Iowa. *Second*, the activity in Iowa was negligible compared to the overall business of the company. *Third*, the appellant did not receive the benefit of 'orderly society' in Iowa.[860] The administrative law judge held the differentiation to be without distinction and reasoned that while Jack Daniels did not directly operate under agreements with locally owned businesses, the use of a wholly owned subsidiary was not sufficient to shield the entity from tax.[861] Additionally, merely having sales in Iowa afforded the company the benefits of 'orderly society' as the state provided infrastructure, a regulatory scheme, and legal protection, all of which supported the company and its ability to sell and conduct business in the state.[862]

In *ConAgra*,[863] ConAgra owned trademarks for a variety of food and drink products, which were licensed to numerous licensees in West Virginia. It manufactured all products and performed all business operations entirely outside West Virginia and did not maintain any offices, facilities, inventory, employees, or agents there. It never directed or dictated how licensees distributed the products bearing the ConAgra trademarks and trade names, nor did it purposefully direct its products to West Virginia. The West Virginia Supreme Court affirmed the finding that ConAgra did not have sufficient contacts with the state to satisfy the Due Process or Commerce Clause nexus requirements. The Court held that the Commerce Clause analysis centred on a 'significant economic presence' test,[864] which 'incorporates due process 'purposeful direction towards a state while examining the degree to which a company has exploited a local market'.[865] Further, a 'substantial economic presence analysis involves an examination of both the quality and quantity of the company's economic presence'.[866] The Court, thus, concluded that although physical presence is not a requirement for nexus, a significant economic presence must exist to subject an out-of-state taxpayer to West Virginia tax.[867]

859. *Jack Daniels Props, Inc v Iowa Dep't of Revenue*, Nos 09DORFC002:004 (Iowa Dep't of Inspections and Appeals, 7 March 2012).
860. *Ibid.*
861. *Ibid.*
862. *Ibid.*
863. *Griffith v ConAgra Brands, Inc* 728 SE 2d 74 (W Va 2012).
864. *Ibid.*, 76.
865. *Ibid.*, 81.
866. *Ibid.*
867. *Ibid.*, 84.

More recently in *Capital One Auto Finance*,[868] the Oregon Supreme Court held that two out-of-state financial institutions had substantial nexus in Oregon and were subject to the state's corporate income tax based on the economic activities of the financial institutions within the state. In this case, the Oregon Department of Revenue determined that the bank affiliates were subject to the corporate excise tax by reason of their lending and depository activities with Oregon customers and issued a notice of deficiency for the tax years at issue. The taxpayer appealed to the Oregon Tax Court, which found that the bank affiliates were subject to the corporate income tax rather than excise tax. The taxpayer appealed the decision to the Oregon Supreme Court. Rejecting the appeal, the Court held as follows:[869]

> We see no need to belabor the ordinary meaning of the phrase. A 'source' can be an 'individual, company, or corporation initiating a payment.' Webster's New Int'l Dictionary 2405 (2d ed. unabridged 1961). If customers located in Oregon are paying money to a taxpayer, then taxpayer would appear to have 'income derived from sources within this state,' within the ordinary sense of those words.

Based on the activities of the bank affiliates with respect to Oregon customers, the Court held that the bank affiliates derived income from sources within the state and therefore, the corporate income tax applied.

On the strength of these judicial rulings, the US states began exercising their rights to impose tax on foreign corporations conducting business within their borders. In times of fiscal crisis, where there were large budget deficits, state and local governments were even more diligent in developing innovative tax provisions and incorporating an economic nexus standard in their laws to ensure that the foreign corporations operating within the state's borders were subjected to tax.[870]

Thus, mist is being cleared, and the blurred distinction between the concept of territorial nexus in public international law and the concept of economic nexus in tax law has begun to crystallise gradually, with the result that the US Supreme Court finally affirmed the economic nexus doctrine in *Wayfair, Inc.*[871] In a 5-4 split decision, the majority overruled the state tax bright-line rules in overturning the standard of physical presence previously established in *National Bellas Hess*[872] and later upheld in *Quill.*[873] In *Wayfair*, South Dakota enacted a law requiring out-of-state retailers to collect and remit sales tax 'as if the seller had a physical presence in the state'.[874] South Dakota subsequently sued several online retailers with no employees or real estate in the state. The state sought a declaration that the sales tax was valid and applicable to the

868. *Capital One Auto Fin v Dept of Rev,* Oregon SC No. SC S064803, decided on 9 August 2018.
869. *Ibid.*
870. *See* L Schwartz and S Finkelstein, 'Nexus and the States' Jurisdictional Right to Tax' in WM Bergstein and JE Gold (eds), *Analysis* (Adelman Katz & Mond 2011) 6, http://akmcpa.com/wp-content/uploads/2011/10/AKM-Nexus-Report.pdf, accessed 14 January 2019.
871. *South Dakota v Wayfair*, No. 17-494 (21 June 2018) 585 US, https://www.supremecourt.gov/opinions/17pdf/17-494_j4el.pdf, accessed 15 January 2019.
872. *See National Bellas Hess* (n. 838).
873. *See Quill Corp* (n. 840).
874. The law only applied to retailers that made at least two hundred sales or sales totalling at least USD 100,000 in the state and required them to collect and remit 4.5% sales tax

retailers, along with an injunction requiring the retailers to register for licences to collect and remit the tax. A trial court dismissed the case before trial, and the state Supreme Court affirmed it, citing its obligation to follow US Supreme Court precedent - *Quill Corp,* which created the physical presence standard. Forty-one states, two territories, and the District of Columbia asked the Court to reject *Quill's* test. The US Supreme Court articulated that helping Wayfair's customers evade a lawful tax unfairly shifts an increased share of the taxes to those consumers who buy from competitors with a physical presence in the state. The Court further stated that it is essential to public confidence in the tax system that the Court avoid creating inequitable exceptions. The Court rejected its prior decision in *Quill.* It based its rejection on three key principles. *First,* the Court recognised how the physical presence rule has long been criticised as giving out-of-state sellers an advantage. The Court stated that each year, it becomes further removed from economic reality and results in significant revenue losses to the states. *Second,* the Court found that *Quill* creates market distortions - the Court calling it a judicially created tax shelter for businesses that limit physical presence. *Finally,* the Court said that *Quill* imposes an arbitrary, formalistic distinction that the Court's modern precedent do not approve. The Court said that the *Quill* decision treats economically identical actors differently for arbitrary reasons.

4.3.6 India

In Indian case law as well, while the sovereignty and territoriality principle of public international law has impacted judicial reasoning, the emerging economic nexus principle is gaining increasing recognition by the Indian courts in Indian tax jurisprudence.

In *RD Aggarwal & Co,*[875] for instance, two non-resident companies carried on the business of exporting worsted woollen yarn to the taxable territories, i.e., India. RD Aggarwal & Co, a partnership firm, canvassed orders for these non-resident companies and forwarded the same to them for acceptance. The option to accept the orders was solely with the non-resident companies. Any order that was complied with entitled the partnership firm to a commission. Sale contracts, payment for them and delivery of goods - all - occurred outside the taxable territories. The Revenue sought to tax the profits of non-residents at the rate of 5% of the net total value of sale, on the ground that there existed a business connection in India in the form of canvassing of orders by RD Aggarwal & Co. Finding in favour of the taxpayer firm, the Supreme Court of India adopted the territorial notion of jurisdiction and underlined the presence of some activity in the Indian territory. Shah J, speaking for a three-judge bench, observed thus:[876]

> A business connection in S.42 involves a relation between a business carried on by a non-resident which yields profits or gains and some activity in the taxable territories which contributes directly or indirectly to the earning of those profits or

875. *CIT v RD Aggarwal & Co* (1965) 56 ITR 20 (SC).
876. *Ibid.*

> gains. It predicates an element of continuity between the business of the non-resident and the activity in the taxable territories a stray or isolated transaction is normally not to be regarded as a business connection. In each case the question whether there is a business connection from or through which income, profits or gains arise or accrue to a non-resident must be determined upon the facts and circumstances of the case.
>
> A relation to be a 'business connection' must be real and intimate, and through or from which income must accrue or arise whether directly or indirectly to the non-resident. But it must in all cases be remembered that by S.42 income, profit or gain which accrues or arises to a non-resident outside the taxable territories is sought to be brought within the net of the Income-tax law, and not income, profit or gain which accrues or arises or is deemed to accrue or arise within the taxable territories.
>
> ...Turning to the facts of the present case, as found by the Revenue authorities, contracts for the sale of goods took place outside the taxable territories, price was received by the non-residents outside the taxable territories, and delivery was also given outside, the taxable territories. No operation such as procuring raw materials, manufacture of finished goods, sale of good or delivery of goods against price took place within the taxable territories: the assessees merely procured orders from merchants in Amritsar for purchase of goods from the non-resident companies. The orders were offers which the assessees had no authority to accept on behalf of the non-residents. Some commercial activity was undoubtedly carried on by the assessees in the matter of procuring orders which resulted in contracts for sale by the non-residents of goods to merchants at Amritsar. But on this account no business connection of the assessees with the non-residents within the taxable territories resulted.

The territoriality principle, thus, weighed heavily in the mind of the judges, and the Court could not unfortunately appreciate that canvassing orders through the taxpayer firm, the non-resident exporter had obtained regular sale orders and thus, a significant economic advantage, which clearly established a debt of economic allegiance with India and a consequent justification for the latter to invoke its tax jurisdiction. Since the non-resident was able to derive income through these sales in India, which were effected through the canvassing of the taxpayer firm, the precise criteria of economic allegiance were fully met. Vogel, quoting Georg van Schanz, has expressly opined that there exists an allegiance with the source state when a person is economically bound to the host state 'through business activities or by way of income arising in the other state' and that the physical presence in a jurisdiction is not a requirement in order to justify source taxation.[877] In the present case, the profits from sales to Indian dealers resulted in a significant economic advantage to the non-resident companies and created a business connection. *RD Aggarwal & Co,*[878] therefore, was not correctly decided.

In *Carborandum Co,*[879] the appellant, an American company, entered into an agreement with an Indian Company, Carborandum Universal Ltd, for rendering certain

877. K Vogel 'Worldwide vs Source Taxation of Income-A Review & Re-evaluation of Arguments' (Part I) (1988 vol. 8(9) Intertax 216, 219-220.
878. *RD Aggarwal & Co* (n. 875).
879. *Carborandum Co v CIT* (1977) 108 ITR 335 (SC).

technical and know-how services for the starting of a factory in India in the shape of examining the factory design and layout prepared by the latter and sending its advice by post. In lieu of the said services, the appellant received from the Indian company, an annual service fee equal to 3% of the net sale proceeds of the manufactured products manufactured.[880] The Revenue sought to tax this service fee on the reasoning that even though the technical information was supplied by the taxpayer company from outside India, the information received by the Indian company was put to use only in the taxable territory and the technical fee paid by it was mainly on account of such use. Rejecting the Revenue's contention, the Indian Supreme Court again invoked the territoriality principle to restrict the scope of the expression 'business connection' under the Indian Law.[881] The Court, through Untwalia J, observed thus:[882]

> The American company has made the services of the foreign personnel available to the Indian company outside the taxable territory. The latter took them as their employees, paid their salary and they worked under the direct control of the Indian company. The service rendered by the American company in that connection was wholly and solely rendered in the foreign territory. Even assuming, however, that there was any business connection between the earning of the income in the shape of the technical fee by the American company and the affairs of the Indian company, yet no part of the activity or operation could be said to have been carried on by the American company in India. And in absence of such a sustainable finding by the High Court the provision of section 42, either of sub-section (1) or of sub-section (3), were not attracted at all.

The Court, thus, completely missed the vivid economic nexus being established here by virtue of the user of services in the Indian territory and the consequent economic benefits derived by the non-resident company. The earning of service fee by the American company from rendition of technical services was dependent on their utilisation in India, which clearly established an unbreachable economic connection, conceived by the four economists in their Report.[883] The Court, thus, was solely guided by the international law doctrine of sovereignty and territoriality in interpreting the term 'business connection'.

Although decided in 1977, *Carborandum Co* was a case under the 1922 Act. Concerned with the erosion of its tax base and in keeping with its ideals of a welfare state to ensure economic justice, the Indian Government attempted to nullify the *Carborandum* holding by way of an amendment in 1976,[884] which modified and expanded the concept of nexus in section 9(1) of the Income Tax Act 1961. This amendment inserted three new clauses - clause (v), clause (vi) and clause (vii) in subsection (1) of section 9 which sought to remove the territorial contact paradigm altogether and rather replaced it with new parameters of economic connection.

The new law, thus, provided that certain types of income, such as interest, royalty, fees from technical services and so on shall be 'deemed to accrue or arise in

880. *Ibid.*
881. Income Tax Act 1922 s. 42.
882. *Carborandum Co* (n. 879).
883. The Four Economists' Report (n. 798).
884. The Finance Act 1976 s. 4.

India' on the basis of the residence of payer, location of debt, right or property concerned and the place of utilisation of services, irrespective of whether services were rendered in India or not. Thus, the mere utilisation of services, apart from the payer's residence, became sufficient for invoking the Indian tax jurisdiction, and there remained no further legal requirement for the rendition of services in India in terms of the new law.[885]

This legal position held the field until 2007, when the Supreme Court in *Ishikawajima*,[886] nullified the effect of the 1976 amendment by holding that despite the deeming fiction in section 9, for any such income to be taxable in India, there must be sufficient territorial nexus between such income and the territory of India and for establishing such territorial nexus, the services have to be rendered as well as utilised in India. The Government viewed this decision as being in conflict with the express legislative intent.[887] The Government, therefore, inserted an *Explanation* in section 9, by the Finance Act 2007,[888] clarifying that where income of a non-resident is deemed to accrue or arise in India under clauses (v), (vi) and (vii) of section 9(1), such income shall be charged to tax, regardless of whether the non-resident has a residence or place

885. Clauses (v), (vi) and (vii) of section 9(1), inserted in 1976, read as follows:

> 9(1) The following income shall be deemed to accrue or arise in India:
>
> ...
>
> (v) income by way of interest payable by--
> (a) the Government; or
> (b) a person who is a resident, except where the interest is payable in respect of any debt incurred, or moneys borrowed and used, for the purposes of a business or profession carried on by such person outside India or for the purposes of making or earning any income from any source outside India; or
> (c) a person who is a non-resident, where the interest is payable in respect of any debt incurred, or moneys borrowed and used, for the purposes of a business or profession carried on by such person in India;
>
> (vi) income by way of royalty payable by--
> (a) the Government; or
> (b) a person who is a resident, except where the royalty is payable in respect of any right, property or information used or services utilised for the purposes of a business or profession carried on by such person outside India or for the purposes of making or earning any income from any source outside India; or
> (c) a person who is a non-resident, where the royalty is payable in respect of any right, property or information used or services utilised for the purposes of a business or profession carried on by such person in India, or for the purposes of making or earning any income from any source in India:
>
> (vii) income by way of fees for technical services payable by--
> (a) the Government; or
> (b) a person who is a resident, except where the fees are payable in respect of services utilised in a business or profession carried on by such person outside India or for the purposes of making or earning any income from any source outside India; or
> (c) a person who is a non-resident, where the fees are payable in respect of services utilised in a business or profession carried on by such person in India or for the purposes of making or earning any income from any source in India:
> Provided that nothing contained in this clause shall apply in relation to any income by way of fees for technical services payable in pursuance of an agreement made before the 1 April, 1976, and approved by the Central Government.

886. *Ishikawajima* (n. 786).
887. The Finance Bill 2007 ExMemo.
888. The Finance Act 2007 s. 5.

of business or business connection in India. The amendment, too, had a retrospective effect from 1 June 1976.

However, the effect of this amendment, too, proved ephemeral. The territoriality doctrine of public international law, once again, coloured the reasoning of the Karnataka High Court in *Jindal Thermal Power Co,*[889] when it held that the 2007 *Explanation,* in its then form, did not do away with the requirement of rendering of services in India under section 9 as laid down in *Ishikawajima.*[890] The High Court did not notice that the Legislature had specifically introduced this amendment to do away with the requirement of territorial nexus or business connection for the purposes of clauses (v), (vi) and (vii) of section 9(1)[891] as was conceived and formulated in *Ishikawajima*. The Explanatory Memorandum to the Finance Bill 2007 clearly expressed this legislative intendment.[892] The High Court, however, ignored the Explanatory Memorandum, by assuming that 'when the purport of the explanation to Sec 9(2) is plain in its meaning, it is unnecessary and impermissible to refer to the Memorandum explaining the Finance Bill 2007'. The High Court should have read this Explanation along with clause (v), (vi) and (vii) of section 9(1), which, by themselves delineated the contours of income accruing or arising in India in the context of interest, royalty and fee for technical services and so viewed, the new explanation made it clear that there was no further need of any further territorial link such as residence or place of business or any other business connection. It was in the context of this construction that the Explanatory Memorandum assumed significance.

The use of Explanatory Notes to a Bill, offered by the Minister sponsoring the legislation, in statutory interpretation is a well-established practice in common law. For example, in *Pepper v Hart,*[893] while construing a taxation provision, the House of Lords held that clear statements made in the Parliament concerning the purpose of legislation in course of enactment may be used by the Court as a guide to the interpretation of

889. *Jindal Thermal Power Co* (n. 786).
890. *Ishikawajima* (n. 786).
891. Income Tax Act 1961, old s. 9(2) Expl; it reads as follows:

> For the removal of doubts, it is hereby declared that for the purposes of this section, where income is deemed to accrue or arise in India under clause (v) or clause (vi) or clause (vii) of sub-section (1) of section 9, such income shall be included in the total income of non-resident, whether or not the non-resident has a residence or place of business or business connection in India.

892. *See* the ExMemo (n. 887), which reads as follows:

> Legislative intent for introduction of clauses (v), (vi) and (vii) was to give legal sanctity to the source rule. This source rule is also recognised in India's Double Taxation Avoidance Agreements. For removal of doubts, an Explanation has now been inserted in section 9 to specifically reaffirm the source rule provided in that section, to clarify that where income is deemed to accrue or arise in India under clauses (v), (vi) or (vii) of sub-section (1) of section 9, such income shall be included in the total income of the nonresident, regardless of whether the non-resident has a residence or place of business or business connection in India. In such cases, it is not necessary to establish the territorial nexus between the income deemed to accrue or arise to the non-resident under the said clauses and the territory of India.

893. *Pepper v Hart* (1993) AC 593 HL.

ambiguous statutory provisions. In *National Asylum Support Service*,[894] Lord Steyn considered the Explanatory Notes admissible, even when the statute was unambiguous:

> Insofar as the Explanatory Notes cast light on the objective setting or contextual scene of the statute, and the mischief at which it is aimed, such materials are therefore always admissible as aids to construction.

The Supreme Court of India, in *R & B Falcon*,[895] has noted with approval the dicta laid down in *Pepper v Hart*[896] and observations of Lord Steyn in following terms:

> 23. Rules of executive construction in a situation of this nature may also be applied. Where a representation is made by the maker of legislation at the time of introduction of the Bill or construction thereupon is put by the executive upon its coming into force, the same carries a great weight.
> 24. In this regard, we may refer to the decision of the House of Lords in the matter of *R v National Asylum Support Service* [(2002) 1 WLR 2956] and its interpretation of the decision in *Pepper v Hart [(1993) AC 593]* on the question of 'executive estoppel.'

The *Jindal Thermal Power Co*,[897] therefore, was decided on an erroneous assumption of interpretative principles.

The 2007 amendment was correctly interpreted in terms of the Explanatory Memorandum by the Bombay High Court in *Siemens AG*,[898] where the question of taxability of amounts received as royalty, technical assistance fee and certain reimbursed expenses under section 9 of the Act[899] fell for consideration. Upholding its taxability on the basis of 2007 amendment, the Court invoked the Explanatory Memorandum and held that *Ishikawajima* was no longer a good law. Rebello J explained the law thus:[900]

> 28. Memorandum explaining the provisions, further notes that the source rule would mean that irrespective of the situs of the service, the situs of the payer and the situs of the utilisation of services will determine the tax jurisdiction. After noting the judicial opinion, it observed that:
>
> > 'Legislative intent for introduction of clauses (v), (vi) and (vii) was to give legal sanctity to the source rule. This source rule is also recognised in India's DTAAs.'
>
> 29. It then proceeds to observe as under:
>
> > 'For the removal of doubts, an Explanation has now been inserted in section 9 to specifically reaffirm the source rule provided in that section, to clarify that where income is deemed to accrue or arise in India under clause (v),

894. *R v National Asylum Support Service* (2002) UKHL 38.
895. *R & B Falcon v CIT* (2008) 7 SCR 804 (SC).
896. *Pepper v Hart* (n. 893).
897. *Jindal Thermal Power Co* (n. 786).
898. *CIT v Siemens Aktiongesellschaft* (2009) 310 ITR 320.
899. Income Tax Act 1961, s. 9.
900. *Seimens Aktiongesellschaft* (n. 898) 331-332.

> (vi) or (vii) of sub-section (1) of section 9, such income shall be included in the total income of the non-resident, regardless of whether the non-resident has a residence or place of business or business connection in India. In such cases, it is not necessary to establish the territorial nexus between the income deemed to accrue or arise to the non-resident under the said clauses and the territory of India.'
>
> 30. By the Explanation it appears that the ratio of the judgment in Ishikawajima-Harima Heavy Industries Ltd v Director of Income-tax, Mumbai (2007) 288 ITR 408 is sought to be overcome by providing that even if any non-resident has no permanent establishment the income from royalty accrued or paid by a resident would be deemed to be taxable in India.

The *Siemens AG* judgment[901] was pointed out to the Karnataka High Court in *Jindal Thermal Power Co,*[902] but the Court took the view that the tax liability clarified in Explanation is subject to the provisions of section 9(1)(vii)(c) and thus, the twin requisites laid down in *Ishikawajima*[903] still held the field. This reasoning was clearly erroneous as the tax liability clarified in the Explanation was not subject to the provisions of section 9(1)(vii)(c). The plain language of the Explanation[904] shows that it was the other way round, providing that where income is deemed to accrue or arise in India under clauses (v), (vi) or (vii) of section 9(1), such income shall be included in the total income of non-resident, irrespective of the non-resident having a residence or place of business or business connection in India. The reverse logic employed by the Court, therefore, in making the Explanation subject to section 9 is contrary to the plain wordings of the Explanation and the Explanatory Memorandum to the Finance Bill 2007.[905]

Further, reliance placed by the Karnataka High Court on a subsequent decision of the Bombay High Court in *Clifford Chace*[906] is also erroneous for two reasons: *first,* it was a decision subsequent to the Bombay High Court decision in *Seimens AG,*[907] but the later decision has not been referred to in *Clifford Chance.*[908] *Second,* the effect of the 2007 amendment, even though specifically referred to by the Revenue, was not dealt with by the Court and the Court simply proceeded on the basis of territoriality as laid down in *Ishikawajima,*[909] without considering the legislative intent of nullifying the territorial link as expressed in the Explanatory Memorandum.[910]

The following words of Daga J make the point clear:[911]

> 34. The territorial nexus doctrine, thus, plays an important part in assessment of tax. Tax is levied on one transaction where the operations which may give rise

901. *Seimens AG* (n. 898).
902. *Jindal Thermal Power Co* (n. 786).
903. *Ishikawajima* (n. 786).
904. Income Tax Act 1961, s. 9(1) explanation.
905. The ExMemo (n. 892).
906. *Clifford Chace v DCIT* (2009) 318 ITR 237.
907. *Seimens AG* (n. 898).
908. *Clifford Chace* (n. 906).
909. *Ishikawajima* (n. 786).
910. The ExMemo (n. 892).
911. *Clifford Chance* (n. 906) 249-250.

to income may take place partly in one territory and partly in another. The question which falls for our consideration is: whether the income that arises out of the said transaction would be required to be apportioned to each of the territories or not.

35. Income arising out of operations in more than one jurisdiction would have territorial nexus with each of the jurisdictions on actual basis. If that be so, it may not be correct to contend that the entire income 'accrues or arises' in each of the jurisdictions.

36. The apex court had occasion to consider the above question in the case of *Ishikawajima Harima* (2007) 288 ITR 408 (SC), wherein, while interpreting the provisions of section 9(1)(vii)(c) of the Act, the Supreme Court held as under (page 444):

> 'Section 9(1)(vii)(c) of the Act states that 'a person who is a non-resident, where the fees are payable in respect of services utilised in a business or profession carried on by such person in India, or for the purposes of making or earning any income from any source of India.'

37 Reading the provision in its plain sense, as per the apex court it requires two conditions to be met-the services which are the source of the income that is sought to be taxed, has to be rendered in India, as well as utilised in India, to be taxable in India. Both the above conditions have to be satisfied simultaneously. Thus, for a non-resident to be taxed on income for services, such a service needs to be rendered within India, and has to be part of a business or profession carried on by such person in India.

Thus, neither *Clifford Chance*[912] nor *Jindal Thermal Power Co*[913] laid down the correct law. The Government of India, therefore, moved to reaffirm the aforesaid source rule by the Finance Act 2010,[914] substituting the 2007 Explanation with a new Explanation, specifically stating that the income of a non-resident shall be deemed to accrue or arise in India under clauses (v), (vi) and (vii) of section 9(1) and shall be included in his total income, irrespective of whether the non-resident has a residence or place of business or business connection in India or of services being rendered in India.[915]

The amendment,[916] also taking effect retrospectively from 1 June 1976, completely removed the territorial nexus test in that sense of the term and its effect came to

912. *Ibid.*
913. *Jindal Thermal Power Co* (n. 786).
914. The Finance Act 2010 s. 4.
915. The Explanation reads as follows:

> For the removal of doubts, it is hereby declared that for the purposes of this section, the income of a non-resident shall be deemed to accrue or arise in India under clause (v) or clause (vi) or clause (vii) of sub-section (1) of section 9 and shall be included in his total income of non-resident, whether or not, -
>
> (a) the non-resident has a residence or place of business or business connection in India; or
> (b) the non-resident has rendered services in India.

916. The Finance Act 2010 (n. 914).

be eruditely illustrated by the ITAT in *Ashapura Minichem.*[917] In *Ashapura Minichem*, it was argued, on the basis of *Clifford Chance*,[918] that the fees paid to the Chinese company for services rendered in China was not taxable in the absence of a territorial nexus. Rejecting the argument, the Tribunal held as follows:[919]

> 8. It is thus clear that the judgment of Hon'ble Bombay High Court rests on the legal premises that, under section 9(1)(vii), 'services, which are source of income sought to be taxed in India, must be (i) utilised in India; and (ii) rendered in India' and the conceptual premises that 'territorial nexus for the purpose of determining the tax liability is an internationally accepted principle'. Learned Counsel has laid lot of emphasis on these two principles.
> 9. The legal proposition canvassed by the learned counsel, however, does no longer hold good in view of retrospective amendment w.e.f. 1st June 1976 in section 9 brought out by the Finance Act, 2010. Under the amended Explanation to Section 9(1), as it exists on the statute now, it is specifically stated that the income of the non-resident shall be deemed to accrue or arise in India under clause (v) or clause (vi) or clause (vii) of section 9(1), and shall be included in his total income, whether or not (a) the non-resident has a residence or place of business or business connection in India; or (b) the non-resident has rendered services in India. It is thus no longer necessary that, in order to attract taxability in India, the services must also be rendered in India. As the law stands now, utilisation of these services in India is enough to attract its taxability in India. To that effect, recent amendment in the statute has virtually negated the judicial precedents supporting the proposition that rendition of services in India is a sine qua non for its taxability in India.
> 10. The concept of territorial nexus, for the purpose of determining the tax liability, is relevant only for a territorial tax system in which taxability in a tax jurisdiction is confined to the income earned within its borders. Under this system, any foreign income that is earned outside of its border is not taxed by the tax jurisdiction, but then apart from tax heavens, the only prominent countries that are considered territorial tax systems are France, Belgium, Hong Kong and the Netherlands, and in those countries also this system comes with certain anti abuse riders. In other major tax systems, the source and residence rules are concurrently followed. On a conceptual note, source rule of taxation requires an income sourced from a tax jurisdiction to be taxed in this jurisdiction, and residence rule of taxation requires income, earned from wherever to be taxed in the tax jurisdiction in which earner is resident. In the US tax system, this residence rule is further stretched to cover US taxation of all its citizens - irrespective of their domicile, and the source rule is also concurrently followed. It is this conflict of source and residence rules which has been the fundamental justification of mechanism to relieve a taxpayer, whether under a bilateral treaty or under domestic legislations, of the double taxation - either by way of exclusion of income from the scope of taxability in one of the competing jurisdictions or by way of tax credits. Except in a situation in which a territorial method of taxation is followed, which is usually also a lowest common factor in taxation policies of tax heavens, source rule is an integral part of the taxation system and any double jeopardy, due to inherent clash of source and residence rule, to a taxpayer s relieved only through the specified relief mechanism under the treaties and the domestic

917. *Ashapura Minichem Ltd v ADIT* (2010) (40) SOT 220 (Mum).
918. *Clifford Chance* (n. 906).
919. *Ashapura Minichem* (n. 917).

> law. It is thus fallacious to proceed on the basis that territorial nexus to a tax jurisdiction being sine qua non taxability in that jurisdiction is a normal international practice in all tax systems. This school of thought is now specifically supported by the retrospective amendment to section 9.
>
> 11. It is thus clear that Hon'ble Bombay High Court's judgment in the case of Clifford Chance is no longer good law, as there have been amendments in law in consonance with the school of thought discussed above and the amendment unambiguously negate the principle of territorial nexus which is the under structure of line of reasoning adopted by the Hon'ble Courts above. It is no longer necessary that, in order to invite taxability under section 9(1)(vii) of the Act, the services must be rendered in the Indian tax jurisdiction. In our considered view, therefore, the income of the Chinese company, by way of impugned receipt of fees for technical services from an Indian company, is to be deemed to accrue or arise in India under Section 9(1)(vii) of the Act. It is accordingly liable to be taxed in India under the domestic tax law.

Despite these legal developments, the Indian Supreme Court, in *Vodafone,*[920] once again missed the economic nexus principle and displayed a strong influence of the international principle of territoriality in its reasoning. In this case, there was an offshore acquisition by Vodafone (a company resident in the Netherlands) of the entire share capital of CGP Investments (a company resident in the Cayman Islands), which, in turn, held 67% controlling interest in Hutchison Essar (a company resident in India). The Indian Revenue authorities sought to levy capital gains tax on this apparent offshore transaction on the ground that there was a transfer of underlying assets (i.e., 67% controlling interest in Hutchison Essar), which was situated in India. Negating the Revenue's claim, the Court gave a serious setback to the Indian source rule jurisprudence by holding that section 9(1)(i) of the Act cannot, by a process of interpretation, be extended to such indirect transfer of controlling interests in Hutchison, which had occurred in consequence of the transfer of the CGP shares outside India. According to the Court, the words underlying assets do not find place in section 9(1). Kapadia CJ, speaking for a three-judge Bench, gave the following reasoning:[921]

> 168. Substantial territorial nexus between the income and the territory which seeks to tax that income, is of prime importance to levy tax. Expression used in Section 9(1)(i) is 'source of income in India' which implies that income arises from that source and there is no question of income arising indirectly from a source in India. Expression used is 'source of income in India' and not 'from a source in India'. Section 9 contains a 'deeming provision' and in interpreting a provision creating a legal fiction, the Court is to ascertain for what purpose the fiction is created, but in construing the fiction it is not to be extended beyond the purpose for which it is created, or beyond the language of section by which it is created. [See *CIT v Shakuntala* AIR 1966 SC 719, *Mancheri Puthusseri Ahmed v Kuthiravattam Estate Receiver* [1996] 6 SCC 185.
>
> ...
>
> 171. Section 9(1)(i) covers only income arising or accruing directly or indirectly or through the transfer of a capital asset situated in India. Section 9(1)(i) cannot

920. *Vodafone International Holding BV v Union of India* [2012] 341 ITR 1 (SC).
921. *Ibid.*, paras 168-171.

> by a process of 'interpretation' or 'construction' be extended to cover 'indirect transfers' of capital assets/property situate in India.

The Supreme Court did not examine the issue in the context of an economic allegiance, which forms the bedrock of source rule taxation. In the present case, the offshore transfer of assets of CGP Investments' shares to Vodafone had resulted in the transfer of sizable business assets situated in India, which constituted a clear economic link, triggering the Indian tax jurisdiction. The words 'all income accruing or arising, whether directly or indirectly', appearing in the very opening sentence of section 9(1), were capable of embracing within its scope even the indirect transfer of Indian assets. Further, the distinction made by the Court between the income arising from a source of income in India and the income arising from a source in India is quite tenuous because if an income arises from a source in India, the source automatically partakes the character of a source of income. *Vodafone*,[922] thus, was not decided on the correct principles of source taxation.

The Indian Government, therefore, swiftly moved a slew of amendments to nullify this judgment. Vide the Finance Act 2012, three clarificatory amendments[923] were inserted with retrospective effect, to bring Vodafone-like transactions within the ambit of the Indian source rule. It added an Explanation to section 2(14) to define capital asset as including 'any rights in or in relation to an Indian company, including rights of management or control or any other rights whatsoever'. Another Explanation to section 2(47) clarified the definition of 'transfer' as inclusive of 'disposing of or parting with an asset or any interest therein, or creating any interest in any asset in any manner whatsoever, directly or indirectly, absolutely or conditionally, voluntarily or involuntarily, by way of an agreement (whether entered into in India or outside India) or otherwise, notwithstanding that such transfer of rights has been characterized as being effected or dependent upon or flowing from the transfer of a share or shares of a company registered or incorporated outside India'. Further, the expression 'through' in section 9(1) was clarified to mean and include 'by means of', 'in consequence of' or 'by reason of'.

A silver lining in judicial reasoning was, however, witnessed once again in *GVK Industries Ltd*,[924] where the Indian Supreme Court, while upholding the taxability of fees[925] received by a Switzerland-based company for certain services utilised in India, reiterated the economic nexus principle of the source rule, which was identified by the four economists in their Report.[926] The following reasoning of the Court is quite illuminative:

> The source rule is in consonance with the nexus theory and does not fall foul of the said doctrine on the ground of extra-territorial operation. The doctrine of source rule has been explained as a country where the income or wealth is physically or economically produced. [See League of Nations, Report on Double Taxation by

922. *Vodafone* (n. 920).
923. The Finance Act 2012 ss 3 and 4.
924. *GVK Industries Ltd v ITO* (2015) 371 ITR 453 (SC).
925. *See* s. 9(1)(vii)(b) (n. 891).
926. The Four Economists' Report (n. 798).

Bruins, Einaudi, Saligman and Sir Josiah Stamp (1923)]. Appreciated on the aforesaid principle, it would apply where business activity is wholly or partly performed is a source State, as a logical corollary, the State concept would also justifiably include the country where the commercial need for the product originated, that is, for example, where the consultancy is utilised.

Thus, despite vociferous resentment from the residence taxation theorists, the legal principles of the nexus rule are getting gradually settled to the effect that it is the economic nexus, and not a territorial link, which is determinative of taxing rights of states.

4.4 FINDING EVIDENCE OF INTERNATIONAL CUSTOM OF STRICT TERRITORIAL PRESENCE FOR TAX JURISDICTION

This brings us to the question whether customary international law lends support to the requirement of territorial presence in a state for its tax claims? Or, in other words, does international custom indeed prohibit taxation in the absence of a strict territorial nexus?

Even though, ascertaining both existence and precise content of customary international law is an extremely difficult task,[927] it can safely be stated that a norm can achieve status of international custom only if the two criteria are fulfilled: (1) the norm is manifested uniformly and consistently in the states' practice (objective element) and (2) the practice of the states is a result of the belief that they are legally obliged to do so (subjective or psychological element; *opinio juris sive necessitatis*).[928] These constitutive elements of customary law were repeatedly affirmed in the practice of international courts, thus acquiring the status of international custom themselves.[929] States' practice can be manifested in various ways. Domestic law, encompassing constitutional provisions, legislative acts, administrative practice and the case law of domestic courts and tribunals provide evidence of states' practice on the internal plane.[930]

While the preceding section presents a detailed analysis of the case law of domestic courts and tribunals, this section investigates domestic laws and practices to examine the existence of any uniform states' practice in this regard so as to indicate a customary law on the question of a territorial presence requirement for the states to exercise their tax jurisdiction.

Even a broad look at the states' practices would indicate that there is a considerable variance in basic source rules contained in the domestic laws of the states, depending on the nature or character of the income, and any broad convergence or

927. ME Villiger, *Customary International Law and Treaties: A Manual on the Theory and Practice of the Interrelation of Sources* (Kluwer 1997) 60.
928. T Treves, 'Customary International Law' in *Max Planck Encyclopedia of Public International Law* 8, http://opil.ouplaw.com/view/10.1093/law:epil/9780199231690/law-9780199231690-e1393?rskey = vlKjuK&result = 1&prd = EPIL, accessed 7 January 2019.
929. BD Lepard, 'Is the United States Obligated to Drive on the Right?: A Multidisciplinary Inquiry into the Normative Authority of Contemporary International Law Using the Arms' Length Standards as a Case Study' (1999) vol. 10(1) Duke J Comp & Intl L 155.
930. Villiger (n. 927) 17.

uniformity is conspicuously lacking in the states' practices. For example, intangible property rights are usually sourced either at the place of use or at the residence of the payer. In a sale of tangible goods, the source is generally the place where the ownership changes or title passes. It is usually the country of residence of the seller. However, these rules may specify the source as where the title passes, where the contract is signed, where the delivery takes place, or where the payment is made. Several jurisdictions regard income as sourced where the contractual offer is accepted. Thus, what emerges here is that the source rule, in every case, has been determined by selecting one economic connector or the other, and not by recourse to any territorial link.

Likewise, the income from an overseas sale transaction may also have a taxable source in the importing country. In the US, the production and selling profits may be split on cross-border transactions involving manufactured goods.[931] In Canada, a person is deemed to carry on a business and may be taxable if he or his agent solicits orders or offers anything for sale.

Similarly, the source of service income is not always the place where it is performed. Yu recognises the two alternative approaches[932] to determine the source of income from services, including employment income:

(1) the place where the services are performed;
(2) the location where the services are 'utilised', that is, where benefits from services are obtained.

Doernberg and Hinnekens suggest a third alternative, i.e., the place where the services are received (which may or may not be the place where services are utilised).[933] The source may also be the residence state of the payer or where the person is employed or the services are performed or where the payment is made.[934] The USA, the UK, France, Japan, and Canada adopt the first approach.[935] In Australia, the source rule for employment income can be either the place where the service is performed, or the place of the contract of employment or the place where the payment is made.[936] In Ireland, if the employment contract of a non-domiciled employee is negotiated and accepted abroad and the payments under it are made into a foreign bank account, the employment income is considered foreign-source even for work done in Ireland. It is

931. The title passage rule in the US applies to traded inventory and certain depreciable personal property. In other cases, the sales income is deemed to arise in the seller's country of residence, unless either (i) substantial sales activity is carried out in the country where the sale is made or (ii) the goods are sold for the use, consumption or disposition in the other country, and at least a significant amount of activity is carried out through a fixed place of business in that country. *See* Rohatgi (n. 801) 223, citing K Vogel, 'Worldwide v Source Taxation of Income' (1988) vol. 8(9) Intertax 225.
932. R Yu, 'E-Commerce: Relevance of Source and Residence Rules' (October 2001) 13, http://raymondyu.net/pub/papers/ecom_sr.pdf, accessed 11 January 2018.
933. *See generally* R Doernberg and L Hinnekens, *Electronic Commerce and International Taxation* (Kluwer 1999).
934. Rohatgi (n. 801) 224.
935. HJ Ault, *Comparative Income Taxation: A Structural Analysis* (Kluwer 1997) 442-443.
936. *Ibid.*, 443-444.

taxed on a remittance basis. Germany taxes employment if the services are carried out in Germany or by a German resident employer.[937] The practice of sourcing revenue, where the services are received can be seen in some US states, such as, Minnesota Georgia, Iowa and Michigan.[938] Thus, there is little consensus on the most appropriate jurisdiction criterion.[939]

Rosenbloom rightly argues that due to the varying socio-economic situation of states, it is impossible to imagine that all states will adopt the same rules of taxation.[940] The Business and Industry Advisory Committee to the OECD and the ICC, in a joint report, lament this absence of uniformity in jurisdictional approaches in the context of service income as follows:[941]

> The critical issue is not whether the predominant source rule of the OECD countries is the appropriate standard, but whether international harmony (i.e., consistency) can be achieved so as to avoid the potential for double taxation. As noted, most OECD countries use the place of performance test as a basis for sourcing services income. Developing countries, however, sometimes use a place of use test, which conflicts with the place of performance test. ... Inconsistency of tax treatment between countries is already creating the potential for double taxation. This situation will be exacerbated as the Internet makes the rendition of cross-border services from the resident country more effective and efficient. We urge that this issue be put on the agenda of international tax policy fora for further study. OECD's Project Outreach would be an appropriate additional forum for taking the discussion further.

Rules regarding dividend and royalty exhibit similar variation. Dividend distributed by a company may be deemed to have its source in the country of residence of the company distributing the dividend, or in the country or countries from which the company has derived its profits. Royalty may be deemed to have its source in the place where the underlying contract was signed, or in the place where any activities giving rise to the royalty were performed, or where the payer is resident.

Thus, there are wide variations in the basic source rules applied under the domestic law by various jurisdictions. It is, therefore, difficult to provide a single set of source or origin rules that is followed globally. Some commonly used source rules for various types or categories of income may be summed up as follows[942] to indicate the extent of divergence on the issue:

(1) Sale of tangible goods or services:

937. *Ibid.*
938. P Mata and MJ Smith, 'The Implementation of 'Market' Sourcing Rules: Practical Concerns'(6 September 2010) Tax Analysts 650, https://www.jdsupra.com/legalnews/a-pinch-of-salt-september-2010-the-imp-00487/, accessed 11 January 2018.
939. IFA, *Source and Residence: New Configuration of Their Principles* (vol. 90a, IFA: Cahiers de Droit Fiscal International 2005) 40.
940. HD Rosenbloom, 'International Tax arbitrage and the "International Tax System"' (2000) vol. 53 Tax L Rev 137, 166.
941. BIAC (OECD), Tax Analysts Report of Commission on Taxation jointly with BIAC, 'Tax Issues and Ramifications of Electronic Commerce' ICC (15 December 1999), http://www.iccwbo.org/policy/taxation/id414/index.html#source, accessed 25 March 2011.
942. Rohatgi (n. 801) 224-225.

(i) where the title passes;
(ii) where the payment is received or delivery made;
(iii) where the commercial cycle is completed;
(iv) where the sales contracts are concluded;
(v) where the business is carried on.

(2) Sale of employment services:
(i) where the service is performed or rendered;
(ii) where the results of the service are used;
(iii) where the payer is resident;
(iv) where the payment is received;
(v) where the service contract is made;
(vi) where the related sale takes place.

(3) Dividend income:
(i) where the paying company is resident;
(ii) where the underlying profits are sourced;
(iii) where the shares are registered.

(4) Interest income:[943]
(i) where the payer is resident;
(ii) where the debtor is resident;
(iii) where the loan contract is entered;
(iv) where the money is lent;
(v) where the borrowed funds are used;
(vi) where the income arises from which it is paid;
(vii) where the debt can be enforced;
(viii) where the collaterised assets are located;
(ix) where the interest is remitted from.

(5) Royalty income:
(i) where the payer is resident;
(ii) where the intangible rights are used;
(iii) where the inventor resides;
(iv) where the intangible rights are registered;
(v) where the intangible rights are transferable;
(vi) where the agreement is made.

(6) Equipment/movable property rentals:
(i) where the PE is situated;
(ii) where the assets are physically located;
(iii) where the payer is resident;
(iv) where the assets are used.

(7) Income from real/immovable property: where the property is situated.

(8) Capital gains:

943. *Westminster Bank Exec & Trustee Co v Natl Bank* (1970) 46 TC 472 (UK). Interest is sourced in the UK if there is sufficient nexus, depending on factors such as the place of the enforcement of debt claim, the place of interest payment or the source from which the debt is paid, how the debt is secured or the currency of the debt etc.

(i) immovable or real property: where the property is situated;
(ii) shares and securities: where they are registered;
(iii) ships and aircraft: where the effective management or residence of the enterprise is situated;
(iv) goodwill: where the trade, business or profession is carried out;
(v) copyrights, franchises, rights and licences: where the rights are exercisable or used;
(vi) judgment debt: where the judgment is recorded.

(9) Income from agriculture: where the asset generating the income is located.

Further, some countries that follow the territorial tax regime often treat certain foreign-source income as deemed domestic-source income. Similarly, certain countries tax foreign-source income of non-residents under a deemed-source provision. For example, such deeming provisions may extend their taxing rights over certain foreign-source income. In Namibia, for instance, the following foreign-source income is deemed as domestic-source: foreign interest income, foreign income derived from a domestic trading activity, and royalty and similar payments for the use of intellectual property in Namibia.[944]

Second, several countries with the worldwide tax regime have extended their source rules to tax certain foreign-source income of non-residents. The US, for instance, taxes foreign income as US source if there is a nexus with a trade or business conducted in the US. Prior to 2005, a pro rata share of the dividends paid by a foreign corporation was treated as US source, if 25% or more of its gross income in the three preceding years was effectively connected with a trade or business in the US. On the other hand, interest and dividends from a domestic company may be treated as foreign-source income if at least 80% of the gross income during the previous three years was active foreign business income. India treats certain overseas income of non-residents as taxable under its deeming provisions. They are deemed to accrue or arise in India.[945] For example, foreign income is subject to tax if it is derived directly or indirectly through, or from, a 'business connection' in India.[946] Foreign interest, royalties and technical services for use in India are deemed to arise in India, if an Indian tax resident pays them to non-residents. The income from unconnected activities undertaken by a non-resident entity may be taxable as business income under a 'force of attraction' principle, if it has a branch in that country (e.g., Japan, India, Indonesia, Latvia, the US). This principle usually involves an independent set of source rules.[947]

These diverse domestic practices, thus, indubitably point to a lack of uniform approach. However, a common denominator in all the source rules is the economic linkage with the source state. To elevate the physical presence as a jurisdictional requirement of taxation, therefore, does not seem to have any warrant in any principles

944. Rohatgi (n. 801) 226.
945. *Ibid.*
946. Similar provisions exist in India, Indonesia, Malaysia, Portugal, Singapore and the US; *see* H Govind, 'Business Connection and Permanent Establishment' (2001) vol. 7 APTB 195.
947. Rohatgi (n. 801) 226, citing HJ Ault, Comparative Income Taxation (Kluwer 2004) 395-415.

of international custom. It is, therefore, quite clear that no uniform international custom has so far emerged so as to require a territorial nexus or the rendition of services in the tax territory to be a mandatory test for invoking tax jurisdiction. It is a matter of policy best left to the governments of the day. The European Court of Justice (ECJ) in some of its decisions has reflected the same approach. According to the ECJ, for example in its *Gilly,*[948] *Compagnie de Saint-Gobain*[949] and *van Hilten-Van*[950] decisions, the Member States are free to unilaterally define the connecting factors for the allocation of taxation rights or to do so in tax treaties.

4.5 DOES INTERNATIONAL LAW OVERRIDE MUNICIPAL LAW?

Even assuming that there is such an international law or custom, the question arises: Can a principle of international law override municipal law? The law on this count appears fairly settled. Where the conflict is between a statute and customary international law, the statute prevails. In *Mortenson,*[951] a Scotch Court condemned a Danish subject for acts committed beyond the three-mile limit in accord with a statutory regulation of fisheries, thus extending its jurisdiction beyond that permitted by international law. Lord Dunedin said during the course of his opinion:

> In this court we have nothing to do with the question of whether the legislature has or has not done what foreign Powers may consider an usurpation in a question with them. Neither are we a tribunal sitting to decide whether an act of the legislature is ultra vires as in contravention of generally acknowledged principles of international law. For, as an Act of Parliament, duly passed by Lords and Commons and assented to by the King, it is supreme, and we are bound to give effect to its terms.

Some scholars, however, cite the decision of the judicial committee of the Privy Council in *The Zamora*[952] to assert the superiority of international law.[953] In this case, a British Court had informed its government in unmistakable terms that Orders in Council governing the conduct of war must be in accord with international law or they will not be regarded as law for the prize courts. It must be noted here that in *The Zamora*, the court was bound by the Prize Act of 1864, which specifically required it to apply international law, and hence the rule applied by the court owed its authority, not to international law, but to a parliamentary statute inherently superior to an Order in Council. Thus, the court did not apply international law per se, but only the rule of international law as mandated by the national law. *The Zamora* decision, therefore, does not present any inconsistency.

948. Case C-336/96 *R Gilly v Directeur* [1998] ECR I-2793.
949. Case C-307/97 *Compagnie de Saint-Gobain v Finanzamt* [1999] ECR I-6161.
950. Case C-513/03 *van Hilten-Van v Rijksbelastingdienst* (ECJ 23 February 2006).
951. *Mortensen v Peters* (1906) 14 Scots LTR 227.
952. *The Zamora*, LR (1916) 2 AC 77.
953. Q Wright, 'Conflicts of International Law with National Laws and Ordinances' (1917) vol. 11(1) Am J Intl L 1, 1.

In American law, also, the position is quite similar, that is, a statute must always be applied even though it conflicts with international law. For illustration, an Act of Congress of 3 March 1863,[954] permitting the requisition of neutral vessels before condemnation, was protested by Great Britain as in violation of international law. Attorney General Edward Bates rendered an official opinion[955] on the question, and while conceding the British contention that the Act, if strictly applied, might lead to the infringement of international law, stated that American officials would nevertheless be bound by it. Of course, such a conflict may lead to diplomatic reclamations, and possibly to war. But that cannot make the Act of Congress cease to be the law of the land, binding upon the people and their judges.

It has never happened, on the other hand, that in the case of a conflict of a statute with international law, the latter has been favoured. There have been decisions in both British[956] and American courts[957] to the effect that statutes in conflict with natural law are void, and British prize courts have sometimes gone pretty far in asserting their independence of statutes, but no case is known where statutes have been declared void as in conflict with international law.[958]

In the US, the courts have also held that statutes must always be interpreted if possible, so as not to conflict with international law. In *Charming Betsy*,[959] the Court held that the Non-intercourse Acts must not be interpreted as permitting extraterritorial seizures in time of peace, and frequently laws couched in universal terms have been interpreted as of only territorial application.[960]

India follows a similar trend. In 1954, in *Shri Krishna Sharma*,[961] the Calcutta High Court stated that if the language of the Indian Statutes is in conflict with any principle of international law, municipal courts of India have got to obey the laws passed by the Legislature of the country to which they owe their allegiance. The Court further explained the law thus:

> In interpreting and applying municipal law, these Courts will try to adopt such a construction as will not bring it into conflict with rights and obligations deducible from rules of international law. If such rules, or rights and obligations are inconsistent with the positive regulations of municipal law, municipal Courts cannot override the latter. It is futile in such circumstances to seek to reconcile, by strained construction, what are really irreconcilable.

In *Kesavananda Bharati*,[962] Sikri CJ referring to Article 51 held, in these terms:

---

954. Act of 3 March 1863 12 Stat 759 s. 2.
955. Edward Bates, Att Gen, 10 Op 519.
956. *Day v Savadge* (1614) Hobart 85, 87; *see also Thomas Bonham v College of Physicians* (1610) 8 Co Rep 107a, 118a.
957. *Goshen v Stonington* (1822) 4 Conn Rep 209, 225; *see also Bowman v Middleton* (1792) 1 Bay 252 (S Car); *Downes v Bidwell* (1901) 182 US 244, 282.
958. Wright (n. 953) 9.
959. *Murray v Schooner Charming Betsy* (1804) 6 US 2 Cranch 64; *see also Rose v Himely* (1808) 8 US (4 Cranch) 241.
960. Wright (n. 953) 10.
961. *Shri Krishna Sharma v State of West Bengal* AIR 1954 Cal 591.
962. *Kesavananda Bharati v State of Kerala* (1973) 4 SCC 225.

> It seems to me that, in view, of Article 51 of the Directive Principles, this Court must interpret language of the Constitution, if not intractable, which is after all a Municipal Law, in the light of the United Nations Charter and solemn declarations subscribed to by India.

The learned Chief Justice also relied on Lord Denning's observation in *Corocraft,*[963] to the effect that it is the duty of the courts to construe our legislation so as to be in conformity with international law and not in conflict with it. It is one thing to say that legislation may be interpreted in conformity with international principles but is entirely a different thing to give effect to a treaty provision in the absence of municipal laws.[964]

In *ADM Jabalpur,*[965] Khanna J, in his dissenting judgment explicated the law thus:

> Equally well established is the rule of construction that if there be a conflict between the municipal law on one side and the international law or the provisions of any treaty obligations on the other, the courts would give effect to municipal law. If, however, two constructions of the municipal law are possible, the court should lean in favour of adopting such construction as would make the provisions of the municipal law to be in harmony with the international law or treaty obligations. Every statute, according to this rule, is interpreted, so far as its language permits, so as not to be inconsistent with the committee of nations or the established rules of international law, and the court will avoid a construction which would give rise to such inconsistency unless compelled to adopt it by plain and unambiguous language. But if the language of the statute is clear, it must be followed notwithstanding the conflict between municipal and international law which results (see page 183 of Maxwell on the Interpretation of Statutes, Twelfth Edition.) As observed by Oppenheim's International law, although municipal courts must apply Municipal Law even if it conflicts with the law of Nations, there is a presumption against the existence of such a conflict. As the Law of Nations is based upon the common consent of the different States, it is improbable that an enlightened State would intentionally enact a rule conflicting with the Law of Nations. A rule of Municipal Law, which ostensibly seems to conflict with the Law of Nations, must, therefore, if possible, always be so interpreted as to avoid such conflict (see Vol. I, pages 45-46).

In *Jolly George Verghese,*[966] the question arose whether judgment debtor could be arrested in execution of money decree under section 51 CPC. Answering in the negative and harmoniously construing Article 11 of the International Covenant on Civil and Political Rights,[967] Krishnaiyer J expounded the law in the following words:

> Article 51(c) of the Constitution obligates the State to 'foster respect for international law and treaty obligations in the dealings of organized peoples with one another'. *Even so, until the municipal law is changed to accommodate the Covenant what binds the court is the former, not the latter.* AH Robertson in 'Human Rights-in

963. *Corocraft v Ram American Airways* (1969) All ER 82.
964. *Kesavananda Bharati* (n. 962).
965. *ADM Jabalpur v Shivkant Shukla* (1976) 2 SCC 521 (SC).
966. *Jolly George Verghese v Bank of Cochin* (1980) 2 SCC 360 (SC).
967. *See* the International Covenant on Civil and Political Rights, https://www.ohchr.org/en/professionalinterest/pages/ccpr.aspx, accessed 2 February 2019.

> National and International Law' rightly points out that international conventional law must go through the process of transformation into the municipal law before the international treaty can become an internal law.
>
> From the national point of view the national rules alone count. With regard to interpretation, however, it is a principle generally recognised in national legal system that, in the event of doubt, the national rule is to be interpreted in accordance with the State's international obligations.[968]

The law on the point came to be further explicated by a three-judge Bench in *Gramophone Company*.[969] Interpreting the term 'import' in section 53 of the Copyright Act in light of multilateral and bilateral conventions to mean 'bringing into India from outside' and not merely commercial importation, Chinnappa Reddy J observed thus:

> There can be no question that nations must march with the international community and the Municipal law must respect rules of International law even as nations respect international opinion. The comity of Nations requires that Rules of International law may be accommodated in the Municipal Law even without express legislative sanction provided they do not run into conflict with Acts of Parliament. But when they do run into such conflict, the sovereignty and the integrity of the Republic and the supremacy of the constituted legislatures in making the laws may not be subjected to external rules except to the extent legitimately accepted by the constituted legislatures themselves. The doctrine of incorporation also recognises the position that the rules of international law are incorporated into national law and considered to be part of the national law, unless they are in conflict with Act of Parliament. Comity of Nations or no, Municipal Law must prevail in case of conflict. National Courts cannot say yes if Parliament has said no to a principle of international law. National Courts will endorse international law but not if it conflicts with national law. National courts being organs of the National State and not organs of international law must perforce apply national law if international law conflicts with it. But the Courts are under an obligation within legitimate limits, to so interpret the Municipal Statute as to avoid confirmation with the comity of Nations or the well-established principles of International law. But if conflict is inevitable, the latter must yield.

Thus, three broad principles can be gleaned from these foreign and Indian judgments:

(1) In interpreting a municipal law, the courts must try to adopt such a construction that will not bring it into conflict with the rules of international law.
(2) If there is still a conflict between the two, the courts shall give effect to the municipal law.
(3) International law becomes binding if an appropriate municipal legislation is enacted to give effect to it. This is called the principle of dualism, incorporated in Article 253 of the Indian Constitution, which gives the Parliament the power to make laws that implement international law. Our tax treaties

968. *Jolly George Verghese* (n. 966).
969. *Gramophone Co of India v Birendra Bahadur* (1984) SCC 2 534 (SC).

acquire binding effects and override municipal laws because of their implementation by appropriate legislation.[970]

4.6 CONCLUSION AND RECENT TRENDS

Two inferences clearly emerge from the preceding discussion: *first*, there exists no such international customary law, which makes rendition of services in the territory of the source state mandatory for assertion of tax jurisdiction; and *second*, even if such an international custom exists, it is rendered nugatory, if the domestic statute in terms provides that it is the situs of the payer and the situs of utilisation of services, and not its rendition in India, which shall determine the taxability of fee for services. It is not open to the courts to hold otherwise to give effect to an 'internationally accepted principle', even if there is one. The dicta of a larger Bench in *Gramophone Co,*[971] was a binding authority for a division Bench,[972] which does not seem to have been pointed out to the Court in *Ishikawajima.*[973] *Ishikawajima* was, thus, decided on a wrong premise,

The emerging conceptual clarity on the economic nexus doctrine in tax law has resulted in the increased efforts on the part of various states to fine-tune their domestic laws to adapt to the principles of economic nexus recognised by international tax scholarship and explicated by the four economists in their 1923 Report.[974] China, for instance, issued a circular,[975] granting itself the authority to tax transactions between foreign entities taking place outside of China if the transactions effectively transfer interest in a domestic enterprise.[976] This is very much similar to the India's 2012 amendments, aimed at taxing Vodafone-like transactions.[977]

With the advancement in information and communication technology in the last few decades, new business models operating remotely through digital medium have emerged. The nexus based on physical presence, therefore, can no longer serve as proxy for economic allegiance of a non-resident. The US Supreme Court decision in *Wayfair*[978] has given a fresh impetus to the federal units to reassert the economic nexus principle.

---

970. *See*, for more information, G Singh, *International Law*, Ch. 4 p. 68 (3rd edn, Eastern Book Company 2015).
971. *Gramophone Co* (n. 969).
972. *See Bharat Petroleum Corp v Bombay Shramik Sangha* (2001) 4 SCC 460 (SCCB).
973. *Ishikawajima* (n. 786).
974. The Four Economists' Report (n. 798).
975. Circular No. 698 dated 10 December 2009, 'Circular on Strengthening the Management of Enterprise Income Tax Collection of Proceeds from Equity Transfers by Non-Resident Enterprises'.
976. W Shen and C Watters, 'Is China Creating a New Business Order? Rationalizing China's Extraterritorial Attempt to Expand the Veil-Piercing Doctrine' (2015) vol. 35(3) Nw J Intl L & Bus 469, 472.
977. Finance Act 2012 (n. 923).
978. *Wayfair, Inc* (n. 871).

Many states in the US have already jumped on the *Wayfair* bandwagon and have passed legislation setting out the economic nexus rule. Rhode Island, Ohio, Oklahoma, Pennsylvania, Hawaii, Maine, Massachusetts and Vermont are all states that have already enacted economic nexus laws. States like Pennsylvania have low economic presence threshold. Companies only need to sell USD 10,000 worth of goods into their state to exceed the economic threshold nexus standard. Mississippi introduced an economic nexus law with effect from 1 September 2018. The state requires retailers who sell USD 250,000 worth of goods into their state to start paying sales tax. Mississippi does not require a certain number of transactions, just a certain dollar amount. Alabama, Illinois, Indiana, Kentucky, Michigan, Minnesota, North Dakota, South Dakota, Washington and Wisconsin have brought in the economic nexus law with effect from 1 October 2018. North Carolina's effective date is 1 November 2018, while Georgia, Iowa and Louisiana and Nebraska all had 1 January 2019 as effective dates.

India, too, has reasserted the concept of 'significant economic presence' vide Finance Act 2012 for taxation of non-residents in India by inserting a clarificatory Explanation 2A to section 9(1)(i) of the Act[979] to the effect that a non-resident's significant economic presence in India shall constitute 'business connection' of the non-resident in India. The 'significant economic presence' for this purpose has been defined as:

(i) any transaction in respect of any goods, services or property carried out by a non-resident in India including provision of download of data or software in India if the aggregate of payments arising from such transaction or transactions during the previous year exceeds the amount as may be prescribed; or
(ii) systematic and continuous soliciting of its business activities or engaging in interaction with such number of users as may be prescribed, in India through digital means.[980]

It is further provided that the transactions or activities shall constitute significant economic presence in India, whether or not the agreement for such transactions or activities is entered into in India or the non-resident has a residence or place of business in India or renders services in India. Moreover, only so much of income as is attributable to the transactions or activities referred above shall be deemed to accrue or arise in India, as per the new provision. The CBDT has invited comments on 'revenue' and 'user' threshold for constituting significant economic presence for taxing non-residents.[981] On 29 February 2016, the Indian Government also introduced an equalisation levy of 6% on online advertising revenue by non-resident e-commerce companies earned in India. This has come into effect from 1 June 2016.

979. Income Tax Act 1961.
980. *Ibid.*, s. 9(1)(i), Expl. 2A.
981. CBDT Notification F.No. 370142/11/2018-TPL dated 13 July 2018, https://www.incometaxindia.gov.in/news/sep-rules-calling-stakeholder-comments-13-07-2018.pdf, accessed 23 January 2019.

The UK, on its part, is gearing up for a digital services tax (DST). On 29 October 2018, the UK Government announced a UK tax at a rate of 2% on any revenues which can be 'linked' to UK user participation, regardless of where the corporate owner of those revenues is located and irrespective of the physical presence that the corporate has in the UK. The 2% rate, which, at first look, sounds like a low rate, is applicable to revenue and not to profit. So, an entity with high turnover but relatively low profit, on the ground of being cost heavy, is not necessarily out of the regime. The DST is intended to be an 'interim measure' until the OECD comes up with an approach which enough countries worldwide can agree on. The UK Government has committed to a formal review in 2025 to check if the DST is still required once further international discussions have occurred, and to disapply the DST if an 'appropriate international solution' is in place prior to that date. However, given the difficulties faced by the OECD in trying to reach an international solution, the DST may just continue for some time yet, and the UK Government has left itself room to manoeuvre in what they do or do not consider 'appropriate'.[982] Additionally, the UK has also introduced a Diverted Profits Tax (DPT), a distinct tax levied at a rate of 20%. The tax is limited in scope to profits that are considered to be artificially diverted from the UK. It is based on a twelve-month review period during which a dialogue needs to take place between the taxpayer and the tax authorities to determine the final tax liability. Profits diverted from the UK are identified according to two basic rules: an avoided PE rule and an alternative provision rule. These rules potentially cover a broad range of BEPS arrangements and are not confined to structures used by highly digitalised businesses.[983] It is designed to target a very specific type of trade structure: the use of an overseas company (so-called billing company), supported by locally based personnel (typically a local subsidiary), with the aim of remotely supplying goods and services to final customers located in the UK.

Australia too has come up with similar measures. Its Multinational Anti-Avoidance Law (MAAL) is an anti-abuse rule for corporate tax purposes adopted in the context of a significant debate in Australia on the level of taxes paid by MNEs. It replicates aspects of the UK's DPT related to PE avoidance and shares common policy objectives with the recent changes proposed to the PE definition under BEPS Action 7.[984]

France has finalised its own GAFA tax[985] on large internet and technology companies by preparing a bill that would be retroactive from 1 January 2019. Economy and Finance Minister Bruno Le Maire told the weekly newspaper Journal du Dimanche that they were working on a tax that would affect internet service companies with

982. E Walker, 'How Will the UK's Upcoming Digital Services Tax Impact You?' posted 22 November 2018, https://www.out-law.com/en/articles/2018/november/how-will-the-upcoming-digital-services-tax-impact-you/, accessed 23 January 2019.
983. OECD, 'Chapter 4: Relevant Tax Policy Developments' in *Tax Challenges Arising from Digitalisation – Interim Report 2018: Inclusive Framework on BEPS, OECD/G20 Base Erosion and Profit Shifting Project* (OECD *Pub* 2018) 149, http://dx.doi.org/10.1787/9789264293083-en, accessed 18 February 2019.
984. *Ibid.*, 153.
985. It is so named after Google, Apple, Facebook and Amazon.

global sales of more than EUR 750 million (USD 850 million) and EUR 25 million in France. If these two criteria were not met, the tax would not be imposed. The tax is effective from 1 January 2019 and its rate would vary according to the level of sales, with a maximum of 5%, a level that would represent 'around five hundred million euros' annually for France. Le Maire called the question 'a major issue in the twenty-first century', as Paris has been driving hard for it to ensure the global internet giants pay a fair share of taxes on their huge European business operations.[986]

In the 2018 Budget Law, Italy enacted a new concept of Fixed Place PE in the context of tax measures for the digital economy. In time, the new definition may impact other businesses as well. Under the amended text of Article 162(2) of the Italian Income Tax Code, a foreign entity's significant and continuous economic presence in Italy may constitute a fixed base that could give rise to an Italian PE even if it does not result in a substantial physical presence. This new PE definition is based on the nexus rules proposed for the digital economy by BEPS Action 1 and, in particular, on the notion of 'significant economic presence', so that non-resident digital companies can trigger taxable presence in a country in ways that are not uncommon in the digital economy. These include: (i) the earning of revenues from customers situated in the country, (ii) the presence of a local digital platform, (iii) the frequency of digital transactions, and (iv) the number of users.[987] Italy has also introduced a 3% levy on digital transaction (LDT) in 2017, which is effective from 1 January 2019, somewhat on the lines of equalisation levy.[988]

Hungary amended its advertisement tax law, effective from 2017, which applies to the net sales revenue (exclusive of VAT) of both resident and non-resident enterprises arising from the sale of advertisement time or space in Hungary. The taxable transactions include a broad list of advertising services defined by reference to the various media used for their broadcast to the public (e.g., TV and radio, printed newspapers, outdoor billboards, vehicles, real estate, and internet websites). In terms of establishing nexus with Hungary, the legislation is focused on the destination of the advertisement and the location of the targeted public. Different proxies apply depending on the type of advertisement concerned. Looking at the particular case of online advertising, for example, nexus is established when the advertisement is displayed predominantly in the Hungarian language, irrespective of the location of the publisher and of the advertiser.[989]

The EU is also seriously contemplating an EU-wide digital levy of 3% on digital revenues of large firms that would be introduced before a global overhaul of tax rules. However, there was a deadlock in December 2018 when Finance Ministers from across the EU failed to reach a consensus on the DST plans, with a number of Member States including Ireland, Sweden, Denmark, and Finland opposing the plans. The opposition

986. Phys.org, 'France Nears Implementation of Digital Tax' (Paris, 20 January 2019), https://phys.org/news/2019-01-france-nears-digital-tax.html, accessed 23 January 2019.
987. S Loconte and L Favi, 'A New Definition of Permanent Establishment in Italian Domestic Income Tax Law', http://publications.ruchelaw.com/news/2018-03/Italy-Permanent-Establishment.pdf, accessed 23 January 2019.
988. OECD 2018 Interim Report (n. 983) 143.
989. *Ibid.*, 145.

came, despite a last-ditch attempt by France and Germany to lessen the impact of the levy by making it applicable only to companies' online advertising revenue.[990]

In 2016, Israel issued a circular,[991] clarifying that online services provided by a non-resident enterprise from a remote location to in-country customers may create a taxable presence in Israel if these activities constitute a 'significant economic presence' (SEP). This domestic law measure applies only outside the scope of double tax treaties, when the supplier of the online services is resident in a country with no double tax agreement with Israel. The SEP test may be satisfied absent any physical activities in Israel, and is broadly defined by reference to factors of 'digital presence' which include, but are not limited to:

(i) Online contract conclusion: a significant number of contracts are concluded online between the foreign company and Israeli customers.
(ii) Use of digital products and services: the foreign company offers online services/products that are used by a significant number of Israeli customers.
(iii) Localised web site: the foreign company employs a website with localised features targeted at the Israeli market (e.g., Hebrew language, local discounts and marketing, local currency and payment options).
(iv) Multi-sided business model: the company generates significant revenue that is closely related to the volume of online activities performed by users located in Israel.

This circular indicates that the listed 'digital presence' criteria can be applied separately or cumulatively, with no revenue threshold requirement based on local sales. Where the test is satisfied, for the purpose of attributing profits, the circular merely refers to the domestic rules based on the arm's length principle (i.e., analysis of functions performed, assets used and risks assumed).[992]

Thus, the continued globalisation of world economies, and the related developments in information and communications technologies have further intensified the jurisdictional polemics and brought into sharper focus the question whether maintaining the existing international tax principles provides an effective way of taxing international transactions. The digital commerce poses a lot of complex issues today as compared to traditional commerce, as the national borders of a country no longer matter. Businesses may be carried out in a country with minimal presence in that particular country, making the tax authorities go haywire in determining their jurisdictional right to tax the income from such transactions.

The tax policy decisions, therefore must comport with these new realities. The OECD Policy Note,[993] released on 29 January 2019, is a pointer in that direction. The Policy Note recognises 'that the digitalisation of the economy is pervasive, raises

990. S Stolton, 'Le Maire Renews Push for EU-Wide Digital Services Tax', Euractive.com, posted 21 January 2019, https://www.euractiv.com/section/digital/news/le-maire-renews-push-for-eu-wide-digital-services-tax/, accessed 19 February 2019.
991. Administrative Circular No. 04/2016 (11 April 2016).
992. OECD 2018 Interim Report (n. 983) 137.
993. OECD, *Addressing the Tax Challenges of the Digitalisation of the Economy – Policy Note* (OECD Pub 2019).

broader issues, and is most evident in, but not limited to, highly digitalized businesses'.[994] The OECD webcast noted explicitly that the proposals may go beyond the arm's length principle and also consider innovative types of nexus that would not require a physical presence.[995] Thus, the concept of physical nexus as a jurisdictional foundation does not accord with the idea of a fair tax allocation paradigm, which is one of the accepted normative principles of source taxation as noted in Chapter 2 of this book.

994. *Ibid.*, 1.
995. *See* webcast, http://www.oecd.org/tax/tax-talks-webcasts.htm, accessed 18 February 2019.

CHAPTER 5
Territorial Nexus and Constitutionality

Abstract

This chapter delves into the constitutional question whether tax jurisdiction based on an economic nexus, *sans* physical presence, breaches the constitutional doctrine of extraterritoriality or due process. This chapter has five sections. Section 5.1 introduces this extraterritoriality-based constitutional challenge, incessantly mounted on the economic nexus principle, whenever there is no physical presence of the entity or the tax object in a state. Section 5.2 surveys the historical setting of the extraterritoriality doctrine and examines, in the process, the linkages among the concepts of sovereignty, territoriality and comity. Sections 5.3 and 5.4 evaluate the question whether the extraterritorial operation of law is circumscribed by constitutional imperatives, and this is done by analysing the existing legal and constitutional framework in different part of the world, along with some recent judicial trends. The final section 5.5 scrutinises the expansive concepts of 'nexus' appearing in Article 245(1) of the Indian Constitution to underscore the tenuous reasoning, employed in *Ishikawajima* and *Vodafone* to restrict the contours of this constitutional concept.

5.1 INTRODUCTION

The assumption of tax jurisdiction in the absence of physical presence of the tax object in the source state has also been attacked, many a time, by some tax lawyers and scholars, both in India and abroad, on the grounds of constitutionality and due process. The 2010 amendment[996] in Indian domestic law,[997] which substituted the existing Explanation with a new Explanation[998] and specifically clarified that the income of a non-resident shall be deemed to accrue or arise in India under clauses (v), (vi) and (vii)

996. The Finance Act 2010 s. 4.
997. The Income Tax Act 1961.
998. The Explanation reads as follows:

> For the removal of doubts, it is hereby declared that for the purposes of this section, the income of a non-resident shall be deemed to accrue or arise in India under clause (v) or

of section 9(1) and shall be included in his total income, irrespective of whether the non-resident has a residence or place of business or business connection in India or of services being rendered in India, was specifically assailed on the ground of its extraterritorial operation.[999] It was argued that the assumption of taxing jurisdiction merely on the basis of the situs of the payer or the utilisation of services in India, without their rendition in the Indian territory, would be hit by the constitutional restraint of extraterritoriality.

This constitutional critique in India is apparently grounded in the language of Article 245(1) of the Indian Constitution, which provides: 'Subject to the provisions of this Constitution, Parliament may make laws for the whole or any part of the territory of India … .' Similar objections,[1000] based on the Due Process and Commerce Clauses of the US Constitution, are recently being raised in the US against the US Supreme Court decision in *Wayfair*,[1001] which recently affirmed the economic nexus doctrine as the basis of tax allocation, thereby reversing the physical presence standard previously established in *National Bellas Hess*[1002] and later reaffirmed in the Quill.[1003] Although this holding is in the context of a law of a US state, the principles laid down hold true in the international context as well.[1004] The Due Process Clause of the Fourteenth Amendment to the US Constitution mandates that no state may 'deprive any person of life, liberty, or property without due process of law'. As a deprivation of property, state taxation is subject to the constraints of the Due Process Clause. It is argued that the Due Process Clause requires that a company must have at least minimal contacts with the state that seeks to impose a tax. The US Supreme Court had explicated the Due Process Clause in *Miller Bros*,[1005] where a Delaware merchandising corporation sold directly to customers at its store in Delaware. Residents of nearby Maryland came to the store and

---

clause (vi) or clause (vii) of sub-section (1) of section 9 and shall be included in his total income of non-resident, whether or not, -

(a) the non-resident has a residence or place of business or business connection in India; or

(b) the non-resident has rendered services in India.

999. NM Desai, 'Budget 2010-11: Non-resident Services Outside India: Taxed Retroactively' (27 February 2010), http://www.nishithdesai.com/fileadmin/user_upload/pdfs/Budget_2010-11-_Non-resident_services_outside_India-_Taxed_retroactively.pdf, accessed 2 February 2019; *see also* N Singh and D Gitte, 'Constitutionality of Extra-Territorial Taxation of Off-Shore Services of Non-residents under Income Tax Act 1961' (2014) vol. 1(10) IJR 236; and K Gautam, 'Taxing Offshore Transactions in India and the Territoriality Clause: A Case for Substantial Constitutional Limitations on Indian Parliament's Power to Retrospectively Amend the Income Tax Act' (2014) vol. 40(4) Intl Tax J 19, 24.

1000. EA Zelinsky, 'The Siren's Song of "Amazon" Laws: The Colorado Example' (2011) vol. 59 STN 695; SP Kranz, DL Smith and B Freeman, 'Colorado's End Run: Clever, Coercive, and Unconstitutional' (2010) vol. 56 STN 55; *see also* C Alert, 'US Supreme Court Overturns Physical Presence Requirement in Sales Tax Case', https://www.cooley.com/news/insight/2018/2018-06-25-us-supreme-court-overturns-physical-presence-requirement-in-sales-tax-case, accessed 2 February 2019.

1001. *South Dakota v Wayfair, Inc*, No. 17-494, decided 21 June 2018, 585 US (2018).

1002. *National Bellas Hess v State of Illinois* (1967) 386 US 753.

1003. *Quill Corp v North Dakota* (1992) 504 US 298.

1004. RS Avi-Yonah, 'The International Implications of Wayfair' (2018) 160 Tax Notes 215.

1005. *Miller Bros Co v Maryland* (1954) 347 US 340.

made purchases which they either took away or which were delivered to them in Maryland by common carrier or by the store's own truck. Maryland imposed on its residents an excise tax on 'the use, storage, or consumption' in the state of such articles, and it required every vendor to collect and remit the tax to the state. The Delaware store did not do this, and a truck belonging to it was seized in Maryland and held liable for the use tax on all goods sold to Maryland residents. The Court held that the Maryland taxing act, as applied to this Delaware store, violated the Due Process Clause of the Fourteenth Amendment, which required some definite link, some minimum connection, between a state and the person, property or transaction it seeks to tax.[1006]

It is, accordingly, sought to be canvassed in some quarters that the Supreme Court decision in *Wayfair* obviates the constitutional requirements under the Due Process Clause.[1007] The American Catalogue Mailers Association (ACMA) and the catalogue marketers and other remote merchants it represented were quite outraged that the Supreme Court upended well-established precedent that has served the country well for more than half a century.[1008] 'Given the lack of restraint historically shown by regulators and tax administrators willing to impose virtually any burden on companies outside their borders', ACMA President and Executive Director Hamilton Davison called the Court's decision 'sobering and troubling'.[1009]

This chapter, therefore, investigates this constitutional debate and examines whether the economic nexus-based tax jurisdiction and absence of a physical presence breaches the constitutional doctrine of extraterritoriality or due process. This chapter consists of five sections. This section presents a brief introduction to this extraterritoriality-based constitutional challenge, which is being mounted on the principle of tax allocation on the basis of economic nexus, where there is no physical presence of the entity or the tax object in a state's territory. The next section 5.2 focuses on a historical overview of the doctrine of extraterritoriality and, in the process, examines the linkages among the concepts of sovereignty, territoriality and comity which offer justification for the continuing extraterritorial operation of law. Section 5.3 investigates whether the extraterritorial operation of law is limited by constitutional restraints. This is done by scrutinising the existing legal and constitutional framework in different parts of the world, more particularly the UK, the US, Canada, Australia and India. Section 5.4 examines some recent judicial trends in India in order to assess the extraterritorial operation of law on the anvil of the constitutional principles. Section 5.5 concludes the chapter by analysing and summarising the broad and expansive concepts of 'nexus' appearing in Article 245(1) and by underscoring the tenuous

1006. *Ibid.*, 341-347.

1007. Foster Swift Collins and Smith PC, 'The Post-Wayfair Future of SALT Controversies: The Due Process Clause', Tax Law Blog (USA 26 July 2018), https://www.lexology.com/library/detail.aspx?g=31f0b2ce-b2d7-4856-9e26-3d70e1d8260c, accessed 10 February 2019.

1008. S Wiercinski, 'Catalog Mailers Infuriated by Supreme Court's Wrong Decision in South Dakota v Wayfair Case' Catalogs Blogs, http://www.sheridan.com/catalogs-blog/catalog-mailers-supreme-court, accessed 6 February 2019.

1009. *Ibid.*

reasoning, which has been employed in *Ishikawajima*[1010] and *Vodafone*[1011] to delineate the contours of this constitutional concept.

5.2 THE EXTRATERRITORIALITY PRINCIPLE: ITS HISTORICAL SETTING

5.2.1 The Early Phase

The notion of strict territoriality that a nation-state and its governmental organs, must always be associated only with persons, property, things, phenomenon, acts or events within its own territory emerged in the context of development of nation-states in an era when external things, phenomenon, acts and events were not considered much significant. Likewise, sovereignty, in its early forms, which emerged along with nation-states, conceptualised internal sovereignty as being absolute and vested in one or some organs of governance. Similarly, external sovereignty was viewed in terms of co-equal status and absolute non-interference with respect to aspects or causes, pertaining to other territories. German jurist Oppenheim articulated it thus:[1012]

> The concept of sovereignty was introduced and developed in political theory in the context of the power of the ruler of the state over everything within the state. Sovereignty was, in other words, primarily a matter of internal constitutional power … . The twentieth century has seen the attempt, particularly through the emergence in some instances of extreme nationalism, to transpose this essentially internal concept of sovereignty on to the international plane. In its extreme forms such a transposition is inimical to the normal functioning and development of international law and organisation. It is also inappropriate … . no state has supreme legal power and authority over other states in general, nor are states generally subservient to the legal power and authority of other states. Thus, the relationship of states on the international plane is characterized by their equality, independence, and in fact, by their interdependence.

This classical sovereignty model restricts the state's 'monopoly' of power within its borders[1013] and shows the traditional paradigm of prescriptive jurisdiction as exclusively territorial.[1014] This paradigm not only limited the reach of state authority but also mutually reinforced the absolute power of every state within its own territory. Thus, a state's extension of its law-making authority into the territory of another state would contravene the second state's sovereignty – a point that only becomes clearer in the context of jurisdiction to enforce.

1010. *Ishikawajima-Harima Heavy Industries Ltd v DIT* (2007) 288 ITR 408 (SC).
1011. *Vodafone International Holding BV v Union of India* [2012] 341 ITR 1 (SC).
1012. *Oppenheim's International Law*, vol. I, *Peace* 2 vols (Jennings Sir Robert and Watts Sir Arthur eds, 9th edn, Longman 1992) 125.
1013. JH Jackson, 'Sovereignty-Modern: A New Approach to an Outdated Concept' (2003) vol. 97 Am J Intl L 782,786.
1014. *The Schooner Exchange v McFaddon* (1812) 11 US 7 Cranch 116, 136.

Moreover, compared with its civil counterpart, criminal law has viewed jurisdiction in conservatively territorial terms,[1015] and until very recently, it came quite close to Blackstone's famous formulation that '[c]rimes are in their nature local, and the jurisdiction of crimes is local'.[1016] For a sovereign to have exercised criminal jurisdiction within this early common law view, the subject harm must have occurred within its territory.[1017] In fact, so strong was this jurisdictional assumption that courts apparently viewed the extraterritorial application of law to individuals later brought before them as a prima facie due process violation, deeming such an application retroactive since only the locus of the conduct could determine the governing law.[1018]

Increasing scientific and technological progress, however, gave rise to a considerable increase in cross-border social, political and economic transactions and interactions which began eroding the rigid territorial paradigm,[1019] posing a challenge to the early notion of strict territoriality. The jurisdictional rules began evolving to meet these emerging developments. They started recognising the territorial jurisdiction of a nation state over acts that occur within its territory but that may have effects outside its territory – or what is called subjective territoriality,[1020] as well as conduct that occurs outside, but has, or is intended to have, effects within its territory - or what is called objective territoriality.[1021] Colangelo put it thus:[1022]

> In sum, both national and international jurisdictional rules have evolved to account for the growing reality that crime is no longer strictly local, and presently provide for the extraterritorial extension of criminal law to foreign actors abroad where the state has some objective interest in protecting itself against their potentially harmful acts. This objective interest typically takes the form of a territorial or national link, or 'nexus' – whether to the conduct itself, its perpetrators, or its victims.

This change in view and concept of territoriality often led to conflicting claims of jurisdiction among nation-states, which began engaging the jurists' attention.

1015. L Brilmayer and J Corre, *An Introduction to Jurisdiction in the American Federal System* (Michie Company 1986) 329.
1016. William Blackstone, 2 Commentaries, 1055, 1058 (quoted in *Huntington v Attrill* (1892) 146 US 657, 669).
1017. Brilmayer and Corre (n. 1015) 323.
1018. ES Stimson, *Conflict of Criminal Laws* 3-8 (Foundation Press 1936) 7, citing J Beale, *A Treatise on the Conflict of Laws* s. 75 (first published 1916, Lawbook Exchange 2004).
1019. Brilmayer and Corre (n. 1015) 324.
1020. *See, e.g.*, Restatement (Third) of Foreign Relations Law of the United States s. 402(1)(a) (1987).
1021. *Ibid.*, s. 402(1)(c).
1022. AJ Colangelo, 'Constitutional Limits on Extraterritorial Jurisdiction: Terrorism and the Intersection of National and International Law' (2007) vol. 48(1) Harv Intl LJ 121,129.

5.2.2 Huber's Formulations

In 1689, a Dutch jurist, Ulrich Huber, wrote the shortest treatise ever written on the conflict of laws (only 5 quarto pages) known as *De Conflictu Legum*[1023] which had a considerable influence on English and American laws more than any other foreign jurist. He enunciated three axioms to resolve the difficulty of this particularly complex issue:

(1) The laws of sovereign nation-states have force within, but not beyond, states' boundaries, i.e., *the doctrine of territorial operation.*
(2) Only those individuals found within a nation-state's boundaries - regardless of whether they are there permanently or temporarily - are subject to the nation-state's authority.
(3) Sovereign authority must be exercised by way of comity, and the laws of every nation-state should retain their effect everywhere as long as they do not prejudice the powers or rights of another state or its subjects, i.e., *the doctrine of comity.*[1024]

Huber, thus, theorised that the doctrine of territorial operation is balanced by the doctrine of comity which explains why laws still have extraterritorial operation.[1025] Huber's formulations can be seen to have been adopted in AV Dicey's *Conflict of Laws.*[1026]

5.2.3 The *Lotus* Principles

Similar views also came to be reflected by the Permanent Court of International Justice (hereafter 'the PCIJ') in *the Lotus.*[1027] In this case, a collision occurred on the high seas between a French vessel, Lotus, and a Turkish vessel, Boz-Kourt. The Boz-Kourt sank and killed eight Turkish nationals on board the Turkish vessel. The survivors of the Turkish vessel were taken to Turkey on board the Lotus. In Turkey, Demons, the officer in charge of the Lotus, was charged with manslaughter and sentenced to eighty days of imprisonment and fine. France protested against the exercise of jurisdiction by Turkish Court over a crime committed by a French national outside Turkey. By mutual agreement, the matter was taken to the PCIJ. The question before the PCIJ was whether Turkey violated international law when Turkish courts exercised jurisdiction over a

---

1023. U Huber, 'De Conflictu Legum Diversarum in Diversis Imperiis' in Ulrich Huber, *Praelectiones Juris Romani et Hodierni* (First published 1689), translated in DJ Llewelyn Davies, 'The Influence of Huber's *De Conflictu Legum* on English Private International Law' (1937) 18 BYBIL 49; *see also* EG Lorenzen, 'Huber's De Conflictu Legum' in EG Lorenzen (ed), *Selected Articles on the Conflict of Laws* (Yale 1947) 136.
1024. Davies (n. 1023) 56-57; also *see* Lorenzen (n. 1023) 162.
1025. MD Mc Clean, *The Conflict of Laws* (5th edn, Sweet and Maxwell 2000) 533.
1026. FE Noronha, *Private International Law in India: Adequacy of Principles in Comparison with Common Law and Civil law Systems* (Universal 2010) 75.
1027. *SS 'Lotus', France v Turkey* (1927) PCIJ Series A No. 10, ICGJ 248 (PCIJ).

crime committed by a French national beyond the Turkish territory. Answering in the negative, the PCIJ laid down two important principles: *first*, a state cannot exercise its jurisdiction outside its territory unless an international treaty or customary law permits it to do so. This is known as the first principle of *the Lotus*. The Court expressed it thus:[1028]

> [T]he first and foremost restriction imposed by international law upon a State is that-failing the existence of a permissive rule to the contrary-it may not exercise its power in any form in the territory of another State. In this sense jurisdiction is certainly territorial; it cannot be exercised by a State outside its territory except by virtue of a permissive rule derived from international custom or convention.

Second, within its territory, a state may exercise its jurisdiction, in any manner, even if there is no specific rule of international law permitting it do so. In these instances, states have a wide measure of discretion, which is only limited by the prohibitive rules of international law. This is called the second principle of *the Lotus*. The PCIJ set out this principle in the following words:[1029]

> It does not, however follow that international law prohibits a State from exercising jurisdiction in its own territory, in respect of any case which relates to acts which have taken place abroad, and in which it cannot rely on some permissive rule of international law. Such a view would be tenable if international law contained a general prohibition to States to extend the application of their laws and the jurisdiction of their courts to persons, property and acts outside their territory, and if, as an exception to this general prohibition, it allowed States to so in certain specific cases. But this is certainly not the case under international law as it stands at present. Far from laying down a general prohibition to the effect that States may not extend the application of their laws and the jurisdiction of their courts to persons, property and acts outside their territory, it leaves them in this respect a wide measure of discretion which is only limited in certain cases by prohibitive rules; as regards other cases, every State remains free to adopt the principles which it regards as best and most suitable.
>
> This discretion left to States by international law explains the great variety of rules which they have been able to adopt without objections or complaints on the part of other states; it is in order to remedy the difficulties resulting from such variety that efforts have been made for many years past, both in Europe and America, to prepare conventions the effect of which would be precisely to limit the discretion at present left to States in this respect by international law, thus making good the existing lacunae in respect of jurisdiction or removing the conflicting jurisdictions arising from the diversity of the principles adopted by the various States. In these circumstances all that can be required of a State is that it should not overstep the limits which international law places upon its jurisdiction; within these limits, its title to exercise jurisdiction rests in its sovereignty.

The Court further held that if the existence of a specific rule was a prerequisite to exercise jurisdiction, then 'it would therefore in many cases result in paralysing the

1028. *Ibid.*, para. 45.
1029. *The Lotus* (n. 1027) paras 46, 47.

actions of the court, owing to the impossibility of citing a universally accepted rule on which to support the exercise of their jurisdiction'.[1030]

There is some apprehension in international law scholarship that *the Lotus* judgment gives unbridled powers to the states.[1031] A close look at *the Lotus* decision, however, easily dispels this apprehension and reveals that the PCIJ has, in fact, cautioned against overstepping of limits, which international law places on the states' jurisdiction.[1032] The limits of international law are duly recognised in the first principle of the *Lotus* that the state cannot exercise its power in the territory of another state.[1033]

However, the PCIJ has rightly set out the normative principle that within its territory, the state can exercise its jurisdiction extraterritorially, on the given facts of the case, in the absence of any express prohibition in international law. In the given case, the object of the crime are the Turkish nationals and therefore, the trial in respect thereof within the Turkish territory has a distinct territorial link for the exercise of jurisdiction by Turkish courts.

The Lotus holding must, therefore, be construed on the facts of the given case and should not be treated as proffering arbitrary and excessive extraterritorial powers to the states even in the absence of a territorial link or nexus.[1034] In this case, the crime against the Turkish national constitutes a valid jurisdictional link for the assumption of jurisdiction by the Turkish courts. It is for this reason that Professor Jean d'Aspremont cautions against conflating the *Lotus* dictum 'with radical voluntarism and unbridled sovereignty as far as it is concerned with jurisdiction'.[1035]

5.3 EXTRATERRITORIALITY AND THE CONSTITUTIONAL QUESTIONS

5.3.1 The International Scenario

5.3.1.1 The United Kingdom

The Common Law in England does no longer recognise any constitutional limitation on the extraterritorial operation of English Law. The early doctrine of extraterritorial powers of Dominion Legislature, stated by Lord Halsbury in *Macleod*,[1036] has widely been criticised. In this case Macleod appealed against his conviction in New South Wales for bigamy. He had married originally in New South Wales, but then a second time in Missouri in the US. It was held that the court in New South Wales did not have jurisdiction. The crime alleged occurred on the second marriage which was not within

1030. *Ibid.*, para. 48.
1031. *See generally* C Ryngaert, 'Public International Law Approaches to Jurisdiction', in C Ryngaert, *Jurisdiction in International Law* (2nd edn, OUP 2015) 29.
1032. *The Lotus* (n. 1027) para. 47.
1033. *Ibid.*, para. 45.
1034. *See generally* An Hertogen, 'Letting Lotus Bloom' (2015) vol. 26(4) EJIL 901.
1035. J d'Aspremont, 'Multilateral Versus Unilateral Exercises of Universal Criminal Jurisdiction' (2010) vol. 43 Israel L Rev 301, 315.
1036. *John Macleod v AG, NSW* (1891) AC 455, 458-459.

the jurisdiction of the New South Wales court. This holding was finally cast aside by the Statute of Westminster.[1037] The principle was duly recognised by Lord Macmillan in *Croft v Dunphy*,[1038] establishing the principle, which was declared and established by the Statute of Westminster, that the parliaments of the self-governing dominions had full power to make laws having extraterritorial operation.[1039] The Dominion legislation challenged in *Craft v Dunphy* is to be found in sections 151 and 207 of the Customs Act of Canada. This legislation authorises, *inter alia*, the seizure of any vessel registered in Canada found hovering within twelve marine miles of the coast and having on board goods dutiable under the Act. The 'Dorothy M Smart', a schooner registered in Nova Scotia, sailed from the French island of St Pierre for 'the high seas' with a cargo of rum and other liquors. Three days later the schooner was seized at a distance of eleven and a half miles from the Nova Scotia coast, under the Canadian customs legislation referred to above. Dunphy, the owner of the schooner, brought an action against Croft, the customs officer making the seizure. Lord Macmillan took note of the doctrine laid down as early as *The Queen v Burah*[1040] and *Hodge v The Queen*[1041] and observed in the following terms:

> Once it is found that a particular topic of legislation is among those which the Dominion Parliament may competently legislate as being for the peace, order and good government of Canada or as being one of the specific subjects enumerated in s. 91 of the British North America Act, their Lordships see no reason to restrict the permitted scope of such legislation by any other consideration than is applicable to the legislation of a fully Sovereign State.

In *Cain and Gilhula*,[1042] the case concerned expulsion of two US citizens from Canada. The expulsion involved not only expulsion from Canada but also their entry on to American territory under restriction by officers of the Crown. It was argued that the Crown had no power to continue to effect the expulsion beyond the Canadian frontiers. Lord Atkinson, delivering the opinion of the judicial Committee of the Privy Council, held that the Crown had the power of expulsion and was not limited by the territorial scope of the statute.[1043]

In *Trustees Executors*,[1044] the question was asked whether Australian estate duty could be levied on movables situated abroad. Answering in the affirmative, Evatt J severely criticised *Macleod*,[1045] and elucidated the principles in the following terms:

1037. The Statute of Westminster (11 December 1931) was a British law clarifying the powers of the Canadian Parliament and those of the other Commonwealth Dominions. It granted these former colonies full legal freedom except in those areas where they chose to remain subordinate to Britain.
1038. *Croft v Dunphy* (1933) AC 156, 163.
1039. B Cahill, *The Thousandth Man: A Biography of James McGregor Stewart* (Osgoode Society for Canadian Legal History (Toronto 2000)) 56.
1040. *The Queen v Burah* (1878) 3 AC 889.
1041. *Hodge v The Queen* (1883) 9 AC 117.
1042. AG *v Cain and Gilhula* (1906) AC 542 (PC).
1043. C Vincenzi, *Crown Powers, Subjects and Citizens* (Pinter 1998) 98.
1044. *Trustees Executors v Fed Comm'r of Tax'n* (1933) 49 Com LR 220.
1045. Macleod (n. 1036).

> Contentions based upon theories which deny the Legislature's power upon 'territorial' grounds are becoming so frequent that it may, perhaps, be useful to consider their general validity. It is well known that the modern theory of the necessary invalidity of any Dominion law, so far as it attempted to deal with matters, persons and things outside its borders, is based upon certain obiter dicta of Lord *Halsbury* in *Macleod* v. *Attorney-General for New South Wales*. The theory was very convincingly criticised by Professor *H. A. Smith (Canadian Bar Review* (1923), vol. 1, p. 338). He said:
>
> > 'If Courts were always guided by principle the question of extra-territorial legislation would never have presented any difficulties. Unfortunately, the application of the principle has been quite needlessly confused by the interference of an undefined and imperfectly analysed idea, which has some times been expressed in the old Latin tag, *Extra territorium jus dicenti impune non paretur*. Like most maxims of its kind the phrase is of little practical help in the solution of actual legal problems. If it means that laws may be disobeyed with impunity where the executive power to enforce them does not extend, the statement is perfectly true but somewhat obvious. If it is meant that a legislature could never attach legal consequences to acts taking place beyond its own territory, the maxim would be palpably absurd and would be clearly contrary to the practice of every legislature in the world. In its original context (*Digest* 11.1.20), it is used quite properly in relation to the jurisdiction of Courts and their power to enforce their decrees. The maxim has nothing whatever to do with the question of legislative competence' (pp. 349, 350).

Later the same distinguished authority said (*Law Quarterly Review* (1927), vol. 43, pp. 380, 381):

> It seems clear from the decision in *Ashbury* v. *Ellis* (2) that there is nothing to prevent a colony from attaching civil consequences within its jurisdiction to acts transacted beyond its borders, and I have elsewhere given my reasons for thinking that there is no logical reason for denying the competence of colonial legislatures to attach penal consequences within their own territories to criminal acts committed abroad, subject to the restrictions which are in practice observed by the Imperial Parliament in dealing with such matters. This view is supported by the much higher authority of the late Sir *John Salmond.*
>
> Professor *Smith's* reference is to the fact that in 1917 Sir *John Salmond,* after a close consideration of the leading authorities dealing with the presence of extra-territorial elements or features in Dominion legislation, came to the conclusion that there was no legal restriction of legislative power merely upon the so-called extra-territorial ground.[1046]

The statement of Lord Halsbury in *Macleod* has also been called unsound by Jennings[1047] and Dicey.[1048]

This question of legislative power to make extraterritorial operation of law came in for consideration before the Privy Council in *British Columbia Electric Railway Co*,[1049] where the constitutionality of section 9B-(2) of the Income War Tax Act of

1046. *Trustees Executor* (n. 1044).
1047. W Ivor Jennings and CM Young, *Constitutional Laws of the British Empire* (Clarendon Press 1938) 34.
1048. AV Dicey and ECS Wade, *Introduction to the Study of the Law of the Constitution* (9th edn, Macmillan 1939) 103.
1049. *British Columbia Electric Railway Co v King* (1946) 1 AC 527.

Canada, which imposed an income tax of 5% on non-residents in respect of dividend and interest received from Canadian citizens, was challenged on the ground of extraterritorial operation. The Supreme Court of Canada rejected the plea. On an appeal to the Privy Council, Viscount Simon gave a clear and unambiguous dictum regarding the extraterritorial operation of law in the following words:[1050]

> A legislature which passes a law having extraterritorial operation may find that what it has enacted cannot be directly enforced, but the Act is not invalid on that account, and the courts of its country must enforce the law with the machinery available to them.

Thus, Simon's dictum is a clear authority for the extraterritorial operation of law and the same cannot be invalidated on the grounds of sovereignty principle of non-enforcement of law beyond the territorial limits of a sovereign state.

In a more recent case,[1051] the House of Lords gave a strong disapproval of the territorial limits in the context of the UK Income Tax Act. The facts of the case are rather straightforward. Agassi, the tennis player, received substantial sponsorship amounts from companies (Nike and Head) which were not based in the UK. The payments were made to his company, which was resident in the US. Hence the payments never entered into or through the UK territory. The UK Inland Revenue claimed an amount of UK tax on the share of these sponsorship payments that was proportionate to the fact that Agassi participated in *inter alia* the Wimbledon tournament in the UK. Agassi argued that Parliament could not have intended to subject foreign individuals and companies with no residence or trading presence in the UK to such UK tax obligations.[1052] The House of Lords, by a majority of 4:1, rejected the taxpayer's contentions. It was observed that, if Agassi was right, the ease with which the tax liability under the UK tax law could be avoided simply by ensuring that the potentially taxable payments were made by foreign entities with no residence or trading presence in this country would render payment of the tax to all intents voluntary. Lord Scott, delivering the leading speech, considered that the territoriality principle, which was only a rule of construction, could not be implied to limit the effect of the clear language of section 555(2) of the UK legislation. In the course of his judgment, Lord Scott noted the broad, general, universal principle, laid down in *Re Sawers, ex p Blain*,[1053] to the effect that English legislation, unless the contrary is expressly enacted or so plainly implied as to make it the duty of an English court to give effect to an English statute, is applicable only to English subjects or to foreigners who, by coming to England, have made themselves subject to English jurisdiction, but he also agreed with the views expressed in *Oceanic Contractors Inc*[1054] that the 'territorial principle' as being 'really a rule of construction of statutes expressed in general terms' and the question to be asked is: '[W]ho ... is within the legislative grasp, or intendment, of the statute under consideration?'[1055]

1050. Ibid.
1051. *Agassi v Robinson* (2006) UHKL 23 (HL).
1052. The Income and Corporation Taxes Act 1988 s. 555(2); now *see*, Income Tax Act 2007 s. 966.
1053. *Ex Parte Blain: In re Sawers* (1879) 12 Ch D 522, 526.
1054. *Clark v Oceanic Contractors Inc* (1983) 2 AC 130,145.
1055. *Agassi* (n1051) para. 16.

Thus, the discussion in the House of Lords revolved principally around the interpretive question, with the majority taking an approach to the legislative framework that placed much reliance on notions of parliamentary intention, and if the alleged extraterritorial object was within the 'grasp' or 'intendment of the legislature', the law was valid and there was no constitutional infringement.

5.3.1.2 The United States

Traditionally, US understandings of the constitutional application abroad were shaped by the nineteenth-century international law principles of jurisdiction, which largely restricted the authority of a sovereign state to its geographic territory. Both international law and constitutional law since have moved significantly away from strictly territorial understandings of governmental authority. Recent trends in international law principles of jurisdiction and state responsibility now recognise that states lawfully may exercise power in a number of extraterritorial contexts, and that legal obligations may apply to situations aboard over which state exercise 'effective control'. International bodies, including the European Court of Human Rights, have applied the principle of effective control to constrain state conduct aboard.[1056]

The principle of extraterritoriality is explicitly and implicitly embedded in the US Constitution, which grants the Congress the enumerated powers: 'To define and punish Piracies and Felonies committed on the high Seas, and Offences against the Law of Nations ...,'[1057] 'To regulate commerce with foreign Nations',[1058] 'To make all laws which shall be necessary and properly for carrying into Execution the foregoing Powers', and 'all other Powers vested by this Constitution in the Government of the United States, or in any Department or Officer thereof'.[1059] In US law, therefore, questions of extraterritoriality are not, for the most part, questions of constitutionality.[1060] No reported federal court decision has held an extraterritorial application of substantive US law unconstitutional.[1061] It is, therefore, a given that Congress has the constitutional authority to enact extraterritorial legislation.[1062]

However, having power is one thing and exercising that power is another. Some statutes are clearly extraterritorial, and some are clearly not.[1063] In most cases, though, Congress does not clearly express its intent. To disambiguate such statutes, the Supreme Court has enunciated two canons of statutory interpretation: the *Charming*

1056. SH Cleveland, 'Embedded International Law and the Constitution Abroad', Symposium in Honour of Henry Paul Monaghan (2010) vol. 110(2) Colum L Rev 225.
1057. US Constitution, Art. I s. 8 cl. 10.
1058. US Constitution, Art. I s. 8 cl. 3.
1059. US Constitution, Art. I s. 8 cl. 18.
1060. Some courts have discussed potential substantive due process constraints on the extraterritorial application of US law. *See, e.g.*, *US v Davis*, 905 F 2d 245, 248 (9th Cir 1990).
1061. GB Born & PB Rutledge, *International Civil Litigation in US Courts* (4th edn, New York: Aspen Publishers 2007) 579.
1062. *See, e.g.*, *EEOC v Arabian Amer Oil Co* (1991) 499 US 244, 248; *see also Lauritzen v Larsen* (1953) 345 US 571, 579.
1063. C Doyle, 'Extraterritorial Application of American Criminal Law' Cong Research Serv, CRS Rep (26 March 2010) 94, 37-60.

Betsy canon and the *presumption against extraterritoriality*. These two separate rules guide courts in determining whether an ambiguous statute applies extraterritorially.

The *Charming Betsy* canon is named after the Supreme Court decision in *Charming Betsy*.[1064] This case was concerned with the scope of the Non-intercourse Act, which restricted trade with France and its dependencies. In this case, the Charming Betsey, an American merchant vessel, was sold to Jared Shattuck (JS), who was born in the US and while an infant moved to St. Thomas, where he carried on trade as a merchant, got married, and later took an oath of allegiance to Denmark. The vessel, initially captured by a French privateer, was recaptured by an American frigate and was brought to the US. The vessel was considered as having violated the US law prohibiting intercourse between the US and France, and the sale to JS was asserted to be a cover to evade the law. Holding the recapture as illegal, Marshall CJ concluded that the Non-intercourse Act did not apply to these facts. Citing the principle that 'an act of Congress ought never to be construed to violate the law of nations if any other possible construction remains', Marshall held that the Non-intercourse Act could not apply to JS because his capture would violate international norms on the capture of neutrals. An American citizen may acquire in a foreign country the commercial privileges attached to his domicile and be exempted from the operation of an act of Congress expressed in general terms.[1065] The *Charming Betsy*, thus, directs courts to choose a reasonable construction of an ambiguous statute consistent with international law.[1066]

The rule of presumption against extraterritoriality, on the other hand, provides that ambiguous statutes are presumed not to apply extraterritorially. As the court has often stated, 'legislation of Congress, unless a contrary intent appears, is meant to apply only within the territorial jurisdiction of the United States'.[1067] This presumption is primarily grounded in the desire to avoid potential conflicts with foreign laws and the assumption that Congress attends primarily to domestic issues.[1068]

In practice, this presumption works in two ways: *first*, it requires an enquiry if Congress has not indicated that the statute applies extraterritorially. If the litigant can show that Congress so indicated, it overcomes the presumption. Recently, the Supreme Court has set a high bar to obviate the presumption, requiring either a 'clear statement'[1069] or at least a 'clear indication'[1070] of congressional intent to legislate extraterritorially. *Second*, it is to be seen whether the presumption applies in the first place, i.e., to see if the purportedly extraterritorial case is in fact territorial in some meaningful way, in which case the presumption against extraterritoriality would be irrelevant. Scalia J noted this in the *Morrison* decision:[1071]

1064. *Murray v Schooner Charming Betsy* (1804) 6 US (2 Cranch) 64.
1065. *Ibid.*, 118.
1066. *See, e.g., Hartford Fire Insurance Co v California* (1993) 509 US 764, 815.
1067. *EEOC* (n. 1062) 248, citing *Foley Brothers Inc v Filardo* (1949) 336 US 281, 285; *see also Sale v Haitian Centers Council Inc* (1993) 509 US 155.
1068. *EEOC* (n. 1062) 248, citing *McCulloch v Sociedad Nacional de Marincros de Honduras* (1963) 372 US 10, 20-22.
1069. *Ibid.*, 258.
1070. *Morrison v National Australia Bank Ltd* (2010) 130 S Ct 2869, 2883.
1071. *Ibid.*, 2884.

> [I]t is a rare case of prohibited extraterritorial application that lacks all contact with the territory of the United States. But the presumption against extraterritorial application would be a craven watchdog indeed if it retreated to its kennel whenever some domestic activity is involved in the case.

In the context of this presumption, courts always followed the Second Circuit's *conduct-and-effects* test, i.e., whether there was any conduct or effect in the US that would qualify the case as territorial.[1072] In *Morrison*, however, the court announced a new test, that is, the presumption against extraterritoriality would apply only when the activity that represents the 'focus' of the statute occurs outside the US.[1073] In *Morrison*, for example, the 'focus' of section 10(b) of the Securities Exchange Act 1934 was the allegedly fraudulent securities transaction, and thus the presumption only applied to cases where the relevant transaction was abroad, even if significant aspects of the case had territorial connections to the US.[1074] In sum, Congress can legislate extraterritorially, and the courts will enforce expressly extraterritorial statutes.

Following the same line of reasoning, the US Supreme Court, in a recent decision,[1075] though delivered in the context of a US state legislation, repelled a constitutional challenge based on the Due Process Clause, while laying down the economic nexus doctrine. In this case, South Dakota enacted a law requiring out-of-state retailers to collect and remit sales tax 'as if the seller had a physical presence in the State'.[1076] South Dakota subsequently sued several online retailers with no employees or real estate in the state. The state sought a declaration that the sales tax was valid and applicable to the retailers, along with an injunction requiring the retailers to register for licences to collect and remit the tax. A trial court dismissed the case before trial, and the State Supreme Court affirmed, citing its obligation to follow US Supreme Court precedent – *Quill Corp v North Dakota,* which created the physical presence standard. Forty-one states, two territories, and the District of Columbia asked the Court to reject *Quill's* test.

Rejecting the long-standing precedent on the subject, the Supreme Court clarified that due process is merely concerned with whether the person's activities with a state are substantial enough to justify the state's exercise of jurisdiction or power over him. It is, at the bottom, a fairness concern.[1077] Kennedy J, speaking for the majority, explained that '*Quill* is flawed on its own terms'. The Court advanced three reasons: *First,* the physical presence rule is not a necessary interpretation of the requirement that a state tax must be 'applied to an activity with a substantial nexus with the taxing State'. *Second, Quill* creates rather than resolves market distortions. *Third, Quill*

1072. *Ibid.*, 2878-2881, discussing *Schoenbaum v Firsibrook* 268 F Supp 385 (2d Cir. 1967) 392 and *Leasco Data Processing Equip Corp v Maxwell* 468 F 2d 1326 (2d Cir. 1972).
1073. *Ibid.*, 2884-2886.
1074. *Ibid.*, 2884, citing 15 USC s. 78j(b).
1075. *Wayfair inc* (n. 1001).
1076. The law only applied to retailers that made at least 200 sales or sales totalling at least USD 100,000 in the state and required them to collect and remit a 4.5% sales tax.
1077. TM Todd, 'Supreme Court's Quill and Wayfair Cases Explained', posted in Forbes on 27 June 2018, https://www.forbes.com/sites/timtodd/2018/06/27/supreme-courts-quill-and-wayfair-cases-explained/#63737fdd72a4≥ accessed 6 February 2019.

imposes 'the sort of arbitrary, formalistic distinction that the Court's modern Commerce Clause precedents disavow'.[1078] Thus, the Court concluded that, 'that the physical presence rule of *Quill* is unsound and incorrect',[1079] and that 'such a nexus is established when the taxpayer [or collector] avails itself of the substantial privilege of carrying on business in that jurisdiction'.[1080]

5.3.1.3 Canada

In the early years of the Dominion, there was some uncertainty in Canada about the Legislature's power to enact extraterritorial legislation.[1081] The doubt was removed in 1931, when the Statute of Westminster declared that 'the Parliament of a Dominion has full power to make laws having extra-territorial operation'.[1082] Relying on this pronouncement, Canadian courts have affirmed the Government's power to legislate extraterritorially,[1083] and many a time the Canadian Parliament has chosen to include expressly extraterritorial provisions in Canadian laws.[1084]

Canada, too, has a principle similar to the *Charming Betsy* canon of the US. 'Parliament is not presumed to legislate in breach of a treaty or in any manner inconsistent with the comity of nations and the established rules of international law.'[1085] This rule of construction, like the *Charming Betsy* rule, applies only when the statute is ambiguous. Parliament, otherwise, has the power to violate international law if it so indicates.[1086] Canadian courts have also approved the notion that this presumption incorporates the international law of legislative jurisdiction.[1087]

Canadian law also entails a presumption against extraterritoriality. The Supreme Court of Canada explained it thus: 'While the Parliament of Canada ... has the legislative competence to enact laws having extraterritorial effect, it is presumed not to intend to do so, in the absence of clear words or necessary implication to the contrary.'[1088] Like its US equivalent, the presumption recognises the power to legislate extraterritorially but requires expressed or implied intent to do so. This common law presumption was also codified in the Canadian Criminal Code.[1089]

1078. Wayfair (n. 1001) 10.
1079. *Ibid.*, 22.
1080. *Ibid.*, citing *Polar Tankers Inc v City of Valdez* 557 US 1 11 (2009).
1081. S Zucker, 'Extraterritoriality and Canadian Criminal Law' (1975) vol. 17 CRIM LQ 146, 148-151; *see also Libman v The Queen* (1985) 2 SCR 178.
1082. Statute of Westminster, Chapter 4 of the Statutes of the United Kingdom, 22 George V (11 December 1931), s. 3; *see Croft v Dunphy* (1933) AC 156 (PC) 163.
1083. *R v Hape* (2007) 2 SCR 292 para. 66; *see also Society of Composers, Authors & Music Publishers of Canada v Canada Ass'n of Internet Providers* (2004) 2 SCR 427, paras 142-43.
1084. RJ Currie and S Coughlan, 'Extraterritorial Criminal Jurisdiction: Bigger Picture or Smaller Frame?' (2007) vol. 11 Can Crim L Rev 141.
1085. *Daniels v White* (1968) SCR 517, 541 (Can).
1086. *Hape* (n. 1083) para. 54; also *see R v Cook* (1998) 2 SCR 597 (Can) para. 129.
1087. *Hape* (n. 1083) paras 57-65; also *see Cook* (n. 1086) paras 131-38.
1088. *Society of Composers* (n. 1083) para. 54.
1089. Revised Statutes of Canada, 1985 Act c C-46, s. 6(2).

As for the meaning of extraterritoriality, *Libman v The Queen* may be seen as the Canadian equivalent of *Morrison*, although they produced different conclusions.[1090] Libman was charged with a fraud scheme in which calls were made from Canada to the US, convincing Americans to send money to Libman's co-schemers in Costa Rica in exchange for shares in a sham mining company. The court succinctly described the case as 'both here and there'.[1091] The court concluded that such 'here-and-there conduct' should be treated as territorial only if there was 'a real and substantial link between an offence and this country'.[1092] The presumption against extraterritoriality applies only if there is no such link.[1093]

Thus, since *Libman*, 'real and substantial connection' test is the threshold enquiry in determining whether the presumption against extraterritoriality may be avoided in criminal and civil cases.[1094] Notably, this test calls upon courts to assess the overall factual circumstances of the case and determine whether those facts sufficiently engage the Canadian legal system. It does not require courts to focus on the statute in question. In this way, Canada offers a different threshold for extraterritoriality than the US, although both apply the same presumptions once a case is determined to be extraterritorial.

5.3.1.4 Australia

In Australia too, the Constitution empowers Parliament to 'make laws for the peace, order, and good government of the Commonwealth with respect to ... external affairs'.[1095] It is this clause that gives Parliament the power to legislate extraterritorially, subject to the 'peace, order, and good government' limitation, which is said to be hardly constituting a limit.[1096] The High Court of Australia has construed this external-affairs power broadly, including not only all matters which are geographically external to Australia but also seemingly all internal matters that are, in some way, subject to

1090. *Libman* (n. 1081); also *see* Currie and Coughlan (n. 1084) paras 151-152.
1091. *Ibid.*, para. 63.
1092. *Ibid.*
1093. Professor Currie refers to *Libman* as a test of 'qualified territoriality'; *see also* RJ Curie and J Rikhof, *International and Transnational Criminal Law* (2nd edn, Irwin Law Canada 2014) 409-424.
1094. *See, e.g., Society of Composers* (n. 1083) para. 60.
1095. The Australian Constitution s. 51 (xxix).
1096. *R v Foster, Exparte E & Austrl* SS Co (1959) 103 CLR 256 (Austl) para. 4; *see also Polyukhovich v Com* (1991) 172 CLR 501(Austl) para. 169.

international concern.[1097] The Statute of Westminster, as applied to Australia, offers a resounding confirmation of this authority.[1098]

In terms of statutory interpretation, the Australian position is considerably nebulous as compared to the American or Canadian position in this regard.[1099] Three canons of interpretations are clearly discernible here. *First*, Australia has a *Charming Betsy* equivalent. Australian courts presume that statutes do not violate international law,[1100] although they recognise that the Government has the power to do so. In *Lipohar v R*,[1101] for instance, questions concerning the operation, within the Australian Federation, of common law principles of territoriality in relation to the crime of conspiracy to defraud came in for consideration. In this case, a South Australian company owned an office building in Melbourne, Victoria, and was looking for tenants. The letting agents for the building were in Melbourne. At the relevant time, it was a common practice for owners of commercial premises to offer substantial inducement payments in order to attract suitable tenants to occupy their buildings. The appellants, who were residents of Queensland and Victoria, devised a fraudulent scheme in order to induce the South Australian company to make a large incentive payment to a sham tenant. They negotiated with the letting agents of the South Australian company for a lease of part of its premises, seeking to obtain a cash incentive. They were required to provide security for the obligations of the proposed lessee. They falsely represented that the Krung Thai Bank would provide such security in the form of a promissory note. The conspiracy went no further. Some people involved in dealings with the bank were arrested, and the negotiations for the lease and the incentive payment were terminated. Subsequently the South Australian authorities prosecuted the appellants for a common law offence. The appellants raised a contention that their conduct did not constitute an offence that was punishable under the law of the forum. Dismissing the appeal, the court observed as follows:

> 94. In modern times, with respect to crimes created by statute, where it is specified as sufficient for liability that some or all of the elements are located outside the territory of the enacting legislature, two questions arise. The first is one of construction. With respect to the United Kingdom, it was described as follows by Lord Diplock in Treacy:[1102]

1097. DR Rothwell, 'International Law and Legislative Power' in BR Opeskin and D Rothwell (eds), *International Law and Australian Federalism* (Melbourne 1997) 104, 105. (Categorising external-affairs decisions as approving the Parliament's authority to make laws with respect to matters: (a) geographically external to Australia, (b) implementing an international treaty, (c) subject to international concern, (d) generally regulated and subject to international law under either customary international law or under general principles of international law, and (e) that has[ve] been the subject of recommendations by international bodies, agencies or organisations; *see also Polyukhovich* (n. 1096); *Victoria v Com* (1996) 187 CLR 416 (Austl).)

1098. Statute of Westminster, Chapter 4 of the Statutes of the United Kingdom, 22 George V (11 December 1931) s. 3. The Australian states also may legislate extraterritorially; *see* Australia Act 1986 c. 2, s. 2(1).

1099. ZD Clopton, 'Extraterritoriality and Extranationality: A Comparative Study' (2013) vol. 23 Duke J Comp & Intl L 217, 228.

1100. *See, e.g., Minister for Immigr'n & Ethnic Affairs v Teoh* (1995) 183 CLR 273, para. 27 (Austl).

1101. *See, e.g., Lipohar v R* (1999) vol 200 CLR. 485 paras 94-95.

1102. *Treacy v DPP* [1971] AC 537, 561.

> 'The Parliament of the United Kingdom has plenary power, if it chooses to exercise it, to empower any court in the United Kingdom to punish persons present in its territories for having done physical acts wherever the acts were done and wherever their consequences took effect. When Parliament, as in the Theft Act 1968, defines new crimes in words which, as a matter of language, do not contain any geographical limitation either as to where a person's punishable conduct took place or, when the definition requires that the conduct shall be followed by specified consequences, as to where those consequences took effect, what reason have we to suppose that Parliament intended any geographical limitation to be understood?'

95. His Lordship answered that question by stating, now that the technicalities of venue had long been abolished, the 'only relevant reason' was to be found in the municipal rules of international comity which 'in the absence of express provision to the contrary, it is presumed that Parliament did not intend to break.'[1103] Lord Diplock added:[1104]

> 'It would be an unjustifiable interference with the sovereignty of other nations over the conduct of persons in their own territories if we were to punish persons for conduct which did not take place in the United Kingdom and had no harmful consequences there. But I can see no reason in comity for requiring any wider limitation than that upon the exercise by Parliament of its legislative power in the field of criminal law.'

Second, Australia, too, has a presumption against extraterritoriality,[1105] which may be overcome by express or implied legislative intent.[1106] In addition to the common law version of this rule, Parliament and numerous state legislatures have codified the presumption against extraterritoriality in interpretation acts.[1107]

Third, courts, in Australia, have also devised a presumption that statutes do not extend to cases governed by foreign law.[1108] There is some debate as to whether this rule is an independent presumption,[1109] or merely a 'specific application' of the presumption against extraterritoriality.[1110]

The meaning of territoriality, however, is still not very clear in Australia. It is sometimes said that Australia has yet to have its *Morrison* or *Libman* moment.[1111] *Lipohar* is said to be the closest to a *Morrison* or *Libman* decision, but that decision did more to muddy the waters than clarify the law.[1112] Although 'interstate', 'criminal', and

1103. *Ibid.*
1104. *Ibid.*
1105. *Morgan v White* (1912) 15 CLR I (Austl).
1106. *Meyer Heine Pty v China Navigation Co* (1966) 115 CLR 10, para. 7 (Austl).
1107. DC Pearce and RS Geddes, *Statutory Interpretation in Australia* (5th edn, Butterworths 2001) 175-176.
1108. *See, e.g.*, *Akai Pty Ltd v People's Insurance Co* (1996) vol 188 CLR 418 (Austl).
1109. *See, e.g.*, G Hill, 'Resolving a True Conflict Between State Laws: A Minimalist Approach' (2005) 29 MULR 39, 42-43; *see also* S Dutson, 'The Conflict of Laws and Statutes: The International Operation of Legislation Dealing with Matters of Civil Law in the United Kingdom and Australia' (1997) 60 MLR 668, 674-76.
1110. Pearce & Geddes (n. 1107) 135-136.
1111. Clopton (n. 1099) 230.
1112. *Ibid.*

'conspiracy' bring with them specific issues, the confusion with respect to territoriality in this case is generalised.[1113] Six judges issued four separate opinions and tried to offer several theories of territoriality. Gleeson CJ would apply the law only where a 'real connection' to the state existed.[1114] Gaudron, Gummow, and Hayne JJ evaded the tricky theoretical question and simply went by the premise that steps in furtherance of the conspiracy had occurred in the forum state.[1115] Callinan J merely looked for a 'real link'.[1116] And Kirby J criticised 'the unsatisfactory state of legal authority' and presented five different, reasonable proposals: (i) adopting a strict requirement of locality; (ii) treating conspiracy as an exception; (iii) looking to the location of the victim; (iv) citing common law as a basis of jurisdiction across all states; and (v) adopting *Libman*'s 'real and substantial connection' test before advocating a strict territoriality rule.[1117] In short, the meaning of territoriality is still an open question in Australian law, and therefore the question of how to avoid the presumption against extraterritoriality is open as well.[1118]

5.3.2 The Indian Scenario

5.3.2.1 The Government of India Act, 1935

In India, the concept of extraterritorial operation of law emerged with the Government of India Act, 1935 (hereafter 'the 1935 Act'). This Act was made by British Parliament with a view to granting certain degree of autonomy to the provinces of British India. The 1935 Act empowered the Federal Legislature to make laws for the whole or part of British India or any Federated State.[1119] Section 99(2) of the 1935 Act provided that 'without prejudice to the generality of the powers conferred by the preceding subsection, no Federal law shall, on the ground that it would have an extra-territorial operation, be invalid so far as it applies to certain persons and things'. Although India was not a sovereign country at that point of time, the 1935 Act was made under the sovereign function of British Parliament which empowered the Federal Legislature to make extraterritorial operation of law – beyond the territorial boundary of Federation of India.

1113. *Ibid.*
1114. *Lipohar* (n. 1101) para. 38.
1115. *Ibid.*, paras 112-113.
1116. *Ibid.*, paras 269-273.
1117. *Ibid.*, paras 133-136, 173-200.
1118. Clopton (n. 1099) 231.
1119. The Government of India Act 1935 ss 99(1) and 100, http://www.legislation.gov.uk/ukpga/1935/2/pdfs/ukpga_19350002_en.pdf, accessed 6 February 2019.

5.3.2.1.1 *Raleigh Investment Co*

A constitutional dispute under the 1935 Act, however, arose before the Federal Court[1120] in *Raleigh Investment Co.*[1121] The Raleigh Investment Co (RIC) was a company incorporated in England, holding bulk of shares in nine sterling companies, which, though incorporated in England, carried on business in British India. These companies declared and paid their dividends in England. The RIC, as a person non-resident in British India, was assessed to income tax and super-tax under section 4(1)(c) and Explanation 3 to section 4(1) the Indian Income Tax Act 1922 in respect of dividends received in England from sterling companies. The legislative competence of the Indian Legislature to enact the aforesaid provisions of the Act[1122] was challenged before the Federal Court on the ground of extraterritoriality in terms of section 99 of the 1935 Act. Rejecting the argument, Spens CJ explained the law thus:[1123]

> Under s. 99 of the Constitution Act the Indian Legislature has power to make laws having extraterritorial operation. The only limitation is that the law must be 'for British India'. The Constitution Act must be construed liberally and so as to give the widest possible amplitude to the powers: In re Central Provinces Motor Spirits Act ([1939] FCR 18); British Coal Corporation v The King ([1935] AC 500). No limitations other than those expressly imposed should be invoked if the matter is within the words used in the Act: The Queen v Burah ([1878] 3 AC 889). 'For British India' are words of very wide import. They do not indicate any territorial limit. Sub-section (2) of s. 99 only emphasises this. It does not cut down sub-section (1). Certain extra-territorial matters are only particularised for abundant caution in view of the provisions contained in s. 65 of the Government of India Act of 1915 and to prevent any doubt that those provisions were repealed. The doctrine of limitation of extra-territorial powers of Dominion Legislatures, stated by Lord Halsbury in *Macleod*'s case ([1891] AC 455), has been criticised and was discarded once for all by the Statute of Westminster. There are several items in List I involving extra-territorial powers, e.g., items 3, 22, 23. It is not necessary to go into the powers of the Dominion Legislatures. There is no rule of law which compels us to put a limitation. Extra-territorial powers were recognised in *Croft v Dunphy*. ([1933] AC 156) and *Attorney General of Canada v Cain and Gilhula* ([1906] AC 542). In *Trustees Executors and Agency Co Ltd v Federal Commissioner of Taxation* ([1933] 49 Com LR 220) it was held that 'property' included personal property outside Australia. Evatt J deals with the question in detail. *Macleod*'s case ([1891] AC 455) is strongly criticised in this case. The statement of Lord Halsbury is also criticised as unsound in Jennings' Constitutional Laws of the British Empire, at p. 34, Dicey's Conflict of Laws, 9th edn by Wade, at p. 103, and Clement's Canadian Constitution, 3rd edn, at p. 85, 114. This old and exploded doctrine should not be applied in construing our Constitution Act especially after the

1120. After Indian Independence in 1947 and coming into being of the Constitution of India in 1950, the Federal Court came to be replaced by the Supreme Court of India; but under Article 13 read with Art. 374(2) of the Constitution, the decisions of the Federal Court shall have the same effect as if they had been delivered by the Supreme Court, unless they are in conflict with the express provision of the Constitution or reversed by the Supreme Court; *Director of Rationing & Distrib v Corp of Calcutta* (1960) AIR 1355 (SCCB).
1121. *Governor General in Council v Raleigh Investment Co Ltd* (1944) FCR 229.
1122. The Income Tax Act 1922 s. 4(1)(c).
1123. *Raleigh Investment Co* (n. 1121) 235.

Statute of Westminster. The Calcutta High Court has given undue importance to previous practice, Revenue and income-tax laws have to be altered and widened in their scope according to economic conditions.

It was further held:[1124]

It is a matter for each State to decide what revenue should be raised and how to raise it. This depends on its economic and other conditions. The argument that such taxation is not levied in England or other countries is not relevant. The existence of numerous Indian States and foreign companies in India creates an acute economic problem here. The Privy Council has repeatedly laid down that the principles applicable to English revenue law should be applied with extreme caution in construing the Indian Income-tax Act. The English and Indian Acts are not in pari materia. Nothing can be gained by reasoning from the one to the other. The Indian Legislature has power to define what shall be deemed to be 'income' and what income shall be deemed to accrue in India. In the present case the source of the revenue is in British India. The profits were initially earned in British India. The business is in fact carried on in this country. This country affords protection and business facilities. These circumstances are sufficient to give territorial jurisdiction.

Thus, the Federal Court unequivocally expounded in *Raleigh Investment*[1125] that the expression 'for British India', appearing in section 99 of the 1935 Act, was an expression of wide import, and it did not connote any constitutionally devised territorial limit on the state's right to taxation. It was held that as long as business was carried on in India and profits were earned in India, the country provided protection and business facilities and these factors were sufficient to constitute a territorial link and mere fact that dividend was declared and paid in England would not affect the tax jurisdiction of British India.

5.3.2.1.2 Wallace Brothers

The question about the scope of powers conferred by sections 99 and 100 of the 1935 Act[1126] on the Central Legislature once again arose before the Privy Council in *Wallace Brothers*.[1127] Wallace Brother and Co was a company incorporated in the UK. The control and management of its affairs were situated exclusively in the UK. It was a member of the firm of Wallace and Co, which carried on business in Bombay. In the previous year, for the purposes of income tax, the income of the company arising in British India was INR 1,785,831 and its income arising without British India was INR 7,48,427. There was no connection between the Company and British India excepting the derivation from British India of the major part of the income during the previous year and the question in issue in appeal was whether the provisions of the Indian Income Tax Act 1922-1939 by virtue of which the whole income of the company, including that which arose without British India, was subjected to income tax, was hit

1124. *Ibid.*, 233.
1125. *Ibid.*
1126. The Government of India Act 1935.
1127. *Wallace Brothers and Co v CIT* (1948) FCR 1 (Privy Council).

by the extraterritoriality principle. Answering in the negative, the Privy Council rejected the contention that the legislation in regard to income tax having an extraterritorial operation was 'ultra vires' of the Central Legislature. Lord Uthwatt explicated the law in the following words:[1128]

> Their Lordships do not approach the matter on the formal lines embodied in these contentions. There is no rule of law that the territorial limits of a subordinate legislature define the possible scope of its legislative enactments or mark the field open to its vision. The ambit of the powers possessed, by a subordinate legislature depends upon the proper construction of the statute conferring those powers. No doubt the enabling statute has to be read against the background that only a defined territory has been committed to the charge of the legislature. Concern by a subordinate legislature with affairs or persons outside its own territory may therefore suggest a query whether the legislature is in truth minding its own business. It does not compel the conclusion that it is not. The enabling statute has to be fairly construed.

It was further observed:[1129]

> The result is that the validity of the legislation in question depends on the sufficiency for the purpose for which it is used of the territorial connection set forth in the impugned portion of the statutory test. Their Lordships propose to confine themselves to that short point and do not propose to lay down any general formula defining what territorial connection is necessary. In their view, the derivation from British India of the major part of its income for a year gives to a company as respects that year a territorial connexion sufficient to justify the company being treated as at home in British India for all purposes relating to taxation on its income for that year from whatever source that income may be derived. If it is so at home in British India it is a person properly subject to the jurisdiction of the Central Indian Legislature. Unlike an individual, a company has an economic existence only. No activities other than the making and spending of money are open to it. When a company in any particular year derives the major portion of its income from a country, it is a legitimate conclusion that the company has rooted itself there for that year. The connection that results is at least as solid as the connection given by the place of central control; and in a search for a home for income-tax purposes as respects that year that connection might well be thought more pertinent than the connection, readily changeable and often changed, given by the place of central control. In such a search the place where commercial activities yield the result is at least as relevant as the pace where they are conceived. A company which in substance lives on a country may rationally be treated as living in it.

Thus, ignoring the factors of the company's incorporation in England and its place of central control, etc., *Wallace Brothers*[1130] enunciated that the constitutional validity of a legislation depended on the sufficiency of purpose for which it was used for the territorial connection. Lord Uthwatt aptly noted that unlike an individual, a company had an economic existence only and no activities other than the making and spending of money were open to it. When a company in any particular year, therefore,

1128. *Ibid.*, 15.
1129. *Wallace Brothers* (n. 1127) 17.
1130. *Ibid.*

derived the major portion of its income from a country, the company legally rooted itself there for that year. This constituted a territorial connection 'as solid as the connection given by the place of central control'.[1131]

5.3.2.1.3 AH Wadia

In *AH Wadia*,[1132] the Gwalior Durbar, a princely state outside British India, was advancing large sums on mortgage of debentures over property in British India. The question was whether interest received by the Durbar at Gwalior was assessable to income tax. The taxpayer contended before the Federal Court that section 42(1) of the Income Tax Act 1922 under which the assessment was sought to be made was extraterritorial in its operation and therefore, ultra vires of the Indian Legislature in the absence of sufficient territorial connection. Rejecting the contention, Kania CJ, held as follows:[1133]

> The short question to be decided is whether income arising out of a transaction with these incidents establishes some real territorial connection between the person and British India or not. In my opinion the answer is in the affirmative because the source, i.e., the source from which the income accrues to the lender, is known to be going into British India in cash or in kind and this incident is an integral part of the money-lending transaction. As mentioned above, the extent of the connection, if it is real, is not relevant to be discussed in considering the validity of the legislation. That is a matter of policy to be considered by the Legislature.
>
> In the view I have taken, it is unnecessary to discuss in detail the second contention of the respondent against the legislation being ultra vires, although in my opinion it is well founded. Generally, States can legislate effectively only for their own territories, but for purposes of taxation and similar matters, a State makes laws designed to operate beyond its territorial limits. In the case of a sovereign Legislature like the British Parliament the question of extraterritoriality of any enactment can never be raised in the municipal courts as a ground for challenging its validity. The legislation may offend the rules of International Law, may not be recognised by foreign courts or there may be practical difficulties in enforcing them, but these are questions of policy with which the domestic tribunals are not concerned. This was recognised in Ashbury v Ellis (1893 AC 339) and Croft v Dunphy (1933 AC 156).
>
> Having regard to the fact that the Indian Legislature is supreme within the ambit of the legislative heads mentioned in the Government of India Act, 1935, I am unable to consider that the legislation in question is ultra vires. As mentioned above, the aspect of it affecting persons who are beyond the jurisdiction of the municipal courts cannot be considered sufficient for the Court to hold it ultra vires. The municipal courts are bound to enforce the law. Whether after obtaining the opinion or decree the same is enforceable against the other side or not, is not a matter for the Court's consideration. The Court has only to see that the legislation is within the ambit of the powers of the Legislature.

1131. *Ibid.*, 17.
1132. *AH Wadia v CIT* (1948) FCR 121 (FC).
1133. *Ibid.*, 141, 142.

Thus, the Federal Court found a clear territorial link in the interest paid outside British India, since the source of the interest was sums advanced on mortgage of debentures of property situated in British India, which constituted a connection, which was real and the extent of this connection was not relevant in determining the *vires* or validity of legislation.

5.3.2.2 Position under the Indian Constitution

The Draft Constitution, prepared by Sir Benegal Narsinga Rau, the Constitutional Advisor to the Constituent Assembly, comprised seven clauses (179-185) prescribing the distribution of legislative power.[1134] The provision of the extraterritorial operation of law was included in clause 179 of the Draft Constitution.[1135] Clause 179 possessed all the features of section 99(1) and 99(2) of the 1935 Act, except that it did not subject the extraterritorial jurisdiction of Federal Parliament to any qualification. The drafting Committee of the Constituent Assembly redrafted Clause 179, split it into two parts and incorporated it as Article 216(1) and 216(2) in the new Draft Constitution.[1136] Article 216(1) and 216(2) of the draft Constitution were adopted on 13 June 1949 as such in the Constitution of India, as Article 245(1) and 245(2) which paved the way for the principle of extraterritorial operation of existing law and future Indian legislation.

The very first line of the preamble of the Constitution of India declares that India is a 'Sovereign' country. Chapter 1 of the Part XI of the Constitution of India provides distribution of legislative powers. Article 245 provides for the extent of laws made by Parliament and by legislatures of states subject to the provisions of the Constitution. Article 245(1) of the Constitution states: 'Subject to the provisions of this Constitution, Parliament may make laws for the whole or any part of the territory of India … .' Article 245(2) however adds: 'No law made by Parliament shall be deemed to be invalid on the ground that it would have extraterritorial operation.'

Article 245, thus, lays down the principle of territoriality and the Parliament's power to transcend it. Article 245 actually enacts the doctrine of territoriality of laws, from private international law. Article 245(2), notwithstanding the rule, provides an exception thereto signifying that a municipal court cannot refuse to give effect to a law made by the Parliament because it has extraterritorial operation.[1137] A conjoint reading of Article 245(1) and 245(2), thus, makes it clear that what the Indian Constitution bars is extraterritorial legislation, and not its extraterritorial operation.

1134. B Shiva Rao, *The Framing of India's Constitution: A Study* (Tripathi 1964) 614.
1135. Clause 179 reads as follows: 'Subject to the provisions of this Constitution, the Federal Parliament may make laws, including laws having extraterritorial operation, for the whole or any part of the territories of the Federation … .'
1136. The Drafting Committee of the Government of India, *Draft Constitution of India* (Government of India Press, New Delhi 1948) 100.
1137. HM Seervai, *Constitutional Law in India: A Critical Commentary* (3rd edn, Universal Law Publishing 1986) vol. I 1893.

5.3.2.2.1 *Rungta Engineering*

In *Rungta Engineering,*[1138] which was one of the earliest cases under the Indian Constitution 1950, notices for assessment years 1945-1946, 1946-1947 and 1947-1948, issued under section 34(1A) of the Income Tax Act 1922, inserted vide IT (Amendment Act) XXXIII of 1954, were assailed before the Calcutta High Court on the ground of extraterritoriality. The plea taken was the tax payable by the appellant in respect of these three assessment years, including the tax in respect of the income, if any, which escaped assessment, became due from the appellant as and when the Finance Act for each of those years were passed. The tax became then vested in His Britannic Majesty for the purposes of the Governor General in Council. Subsequently the Indian Independence Act 1947 was passed, the Dominions of India and Pakistan were brought into existence, and by virtue of section 7 of the Indian Independence (Rights, Properties and Liabilities) Order, 1947, which provided for the distribution of the property, the tax so due became vested on the appointed day in His Majesty for the joint purposes of both the Dominions of India and Pakistan. However, the tax so due never became vested in the Dominion of India exclusively, and the Dominion of India had no power to make laws with respect to such tax. Accordingly, it was argued that the Income Tax Amendment Act XXXIII of 1954 which introduced subsection (1A)-(1D) in section 34 of the Indian Income Tax Act being a law with respect to tax vested in His Majesty for the joint purposes of the two Dominions is not a law 'for the whole or any part of the territory of India', and such law is invalid, as under Article 245, the Parliament has power only to make laws for the whole or any part of the territory of India. Rejecting the argument, Bachawat J explained the law in the following terms:[1139]

> The Indian Income Tax Amendment Act (XXXIII of 1954) has no extra-territorial operation. Even, if that law had extra-territorial operation, by the express words of Article 245(2) of the 'Constitution, the law cannot be pronounced to be invalid on the ground that it would have extraterritorial operation.'
>
> Assuming for a moment that the Act XXXIII of 1954 is a law with respect to income tax which is still vested in His Majesty for the purposes of the two Dominions, Article 245 of the Constitution can in no sense be said to be a limitation on the legislative power of the Union of India to legislate with regard to such tax. Article 245 of the Constitution defines the geographical extent of the laws made by the Parliament. That Article is in no sense a limitation of the subject-matters with regard to which the Parliament can legislate.

Rungta Engineering,[1140] thus, affirmed the view that Article 245 of the Constitution does not limit the legislative power of the Indian State to legislate with regard to the subject matters allocated to it under the constitutional scheme.

1138. *Rungta Engineering v ITO* (1962) 44 ITR 315 (Cal).
1139. *Ibid.*, 321.
1140. *Ibid.*

5.4 RECENT TRENDS IN INDIA

5.4.1 *Electronics Corporation*

More recently, an identical question of constitutionality and extraterritorial operation of section 9(1)(vii) of the Income Tax Act 1961 arose before a three-judge Bench of the Supreme Court in *Electronics Corporation*,[1141] where a Norwegian company was paid fees in Norwegian currency by a resident company, Electronics Corporation, for services rendered in the nature of training abroad to its employees. A question arose whether these fees were taxable under section 9(1)(vii), so as to oblige the resident company to deduct tax at source under section 195(2) of the Act. A writ petition filed by the resident company, assailing the constitutionality of section 9(1)(vii) on the ground of its extraterritoriality and absence of territorial nexus, was dismissed by the High Court. On a special leave to the Supreme Court, Pathak CJ expressed the law in these terms:[1142]

> Now it is perfectly clear that it is envisaged under our constitutional scheme that Parliament in India may make laws which operate extra-territorially. Article 245(1) of the Constitution prescribes the extent of laws made by Parliament. They may be made for the whole or any part of the territory of India. Article 245(2) declares that no law made by Parliament shall be deemed to be invalid on the ground that it would have extra-territorial operation. Therefore, a Parliamentary statute having extra-territorial operation cannot be ruled out from contemplation. The operation of the law can extend to persons, things and acts outside the territory of India. The general principle, flowing from the sovereignty of States, is that laws made by one State can have no operation in another State. The apparent opposition between the two positions is reconciled by the statement found in *British Columbia Electric Railway Company Limited v The King*, [1946] AC 527:
>
>> A legislature which passes a law having extra-territorial operation may find that what it has enacted cannot be directly enforced, but the Act is not invalid on that account, and the courts of its country must enforce the law with the machinery available to them.
>
> In other words, while the enforcement of the law cannot be contemplated in a foreign State, it can, nonetheless, be enforced by the courts of the enacting State to the degree that is permissible with the machinery available to them. They will not be regarded by such courts as invalid on the ground of such extra-territoriality.
>
> But the question is whether a nexus with something in India is necessary. It seems to us that unless such nexus exists Parliament will have no competence to make the law. It will be noted that Article 245(1) empowers Parliament to enact law for the whole or any part of the territory of India. The provocation for the law must be found within India itself. Such a law may have extra-territorial operation in order to subserve the object, and that object must be related to something in India. It is inconceivable that a law should be made by Parliament in India which has no relationship with anything in India. The only question is then whether the ingredients in terms of the impugned provision indicate a nexus. The question is one of substantial importance, especially as it concerns collaboration agreements

1141. *Electronics Corporation of India v CIT* (1990) 183 ITR 43 (SC Const. Bench).
1142. *Ibid.*, 54, 55.

> with foreign companies and other such arrangements for the better development of industry and commerce in India. In view of the great public importance of the question, we think it desirable to refer these cases to a Constitution Bench, and we do so order.

Before the Constitution Bench could decide the question relating to the ingredients of nexus in terms of Article 245(1) of the Constitution, the appellant withdrew its appeal, pursuant to an agreement with the Government.

However, it may be noted here that the use of expression 'provocation' in *Electronic Corporation*[1143] suggests that the test of nexus for the purposes of Article 245(1) postulates a real connection between the source of income and India. It does not necessarily require either the performance of any business activities or rendering of services in India to constitute the necessary nexus. For example, in the context of fees from technical services, the situs of payer being in India and the situs of services being utilised in Indian business provide sufficient connection for the Indian State to levy tax on the fees paid and it is not necessary that services should have been rendered in India. The extent and degree of connection is held to be irrelevant, relying on *AH Wadia,*[1144] where Kania CJ referred to the following dicta of Spens CJ in *Raleigh Investment Co*:[1145]

> If some connection exists the legislature is not compelled to measure the taxation by the degree of benefit received in particular cases by the tax payer. This affects the policy and not the validity of the legislation. ... All the four heads of income mentioned in Section 42(1) show a real connection between the person receiving income under the particular head and India. Once such connection is held to exist it is unnecessary to ascertain the extent of the connection.

The principle, therefore, is well established that so long as the statute selects some facts or circumstances which provide some relation, the extent and amplitude of that connection is not really material.

5.4.2 *GVK Inds Ltd*

In another case,[1146] decided on 1 March 2011, a Constitution Bench of the Indian Supreme Court had to deal with the question of constitutionality of section 9(1)(vii)(b) of Indian Income Tax Act 1961, a provision which was invoked by the Revenue to bring to tax fees[1147] received by a Switzerland-based company for certain services utilised but not rendered in India. Since the rendition of services was carried out outside India, the Swiss company invoked the constitutional doctrine of extraterritoriality to assail the tax provision.

Rejecting the constitutional assail, the Court held that the only limitation on the legislative power of Parliament to make law flows from the use of expression 'for' in

1143. *Ibid.*, 55.
1144. *AH Wadia* (n. 1132) 138.
1145. *Raleigh Investment Co* (n. 1121) 253.
1146. *GVK Inds Ltd v ITO* (2011) 332 ITR 130 (SC Const. Bench).
1147. Income tax Act 1961, s. 9(1)(vii)(b).

Article 245(1), which has been used as a preposition and signifies 'a range of meanings' between the preceding and succeeding words.[1148] It was held that the range of senses in which the word 'for' is ordinarily used would suggest that Parliament under Article 245(1) is empowered to enact all laws, 'in the interest of, to the benefit of, in defence of, in support of or favour of, suitable or appropriate to, in respect of or with reference to the whole or any part of territory of India'.[1149] This means that as long as the law made has or is expected to have some impact on, or effect in, or consequences 'for' the territory of India or the interests of the inhabitants of India and Indians, the Parliament is competent to legislate even with respect to extraterritorial aspects. Explaining the law, Sudershan Reddy J observed thus:[1150]

> [T]he Parliament may exercise its legislative powers with respect to extra-territorial aspects or causes, events, things, phenomena (howsoever commonplace they may be), resources, actions or transactions, and the like -,that occur, arise or exist or may be expected to do so, naturally or on account of some human agency, in the social, political, economic, cultural, biological, environmental or physical spheres outside the territory of India, and seek to control, modulate, mitigate or transform the effects of such extra-territorial aspects or causes, or in appropriate cases, eliminate or engender such extra-territorial aspects or causes, only when such extra-territorial aspects or causes have, or are expected to have, some impact on, or effect in, or consequences for: (a) the territory of India, or any part of India; or (b) the interests of, welfare of, wellbeing of, or security of inhabitants of India, and Indians.
>
> It is important for us to state and hold here that the powers of legislation of the Parliament with regard to all aspects or causes that are within the purview of its competence, including with respect to extra-territorial aspects or causes as delineated above, and as specified by the Constitution, or implied by its essential role in the constitutional scheme, ought not to be subjected to some a-priori quantitative tests, such as 'sufficiency' or 'significance' or in any other manner requiring a pre-determined degree of strength. All that would be required would be that the connection to India be real or expected to be real, and not illusory or fanciful. Whether a particular law enacted by Parliament does show such a real connection, or expected real connection, between the extra-territorial aspect or cause and something in India or related to India and Indians, in terms of impact, effect or consequence, would be a mixed matter of facts and of law. Obviously, where the Parliament itself posits a degree of such relationship, beyond the constitutional requirement that it be real and not fanciful, then the courts would have to enforce such a requirement in the operation of the law as a matter of that law itself, and not of the Constitution. ... Any laws enacted by Parliament with respect to extraterritorial aspects or causes that have no impact on or nexus with India would be ultra-vires, as answered in response to Question 1 above, and would be laws made 'for' a foreign territory.

Reddy J further clarified that the ratio of *Electronic Corporation*[1151] must not be read to mean that both the 'provocations' and 'objects' of law enacted by Parliament, pursuant to Article 245, must arise solely 'in' or 'within' the territory of India. Such a

1148. *GVK Inds Ltd* (n. 1146) para. 33.
1149. *Ibid.*, para. 34.
1150. *Ibid.*
1151. *Electronics Corporation* (n. 1141).

narrowing of the ambit of Clause (1) of Article 245 would arise by substituting 'in' or 'within', as prepositions, in the place of 'for' in the text of Article 245. The word 'in', used as a preposition, has a much narrower meaning, expressing inclusion or position within limits of space, time or circumstance, than the word 'for'. The consequence of such a substitution would be that Parliament could be deemed to not have the powers to enact laws with respect to extraterritorial aspects or causes, even though such aspects or causes may be expected to have an impact on or nexus with India, and laws with respect to such aspects or causes would be beneficial to India.[1152]

Explicating the rationale of this holding, the Constitution Bench recognised the emerging significance of economic nexus in the modern world due to a mammoth increase in cross border travel and transactions on account of scientific developments. The following observations of Reddy J are instructive in this regard:[1153]

> On account of scientific and technological developments the magnitude of cross border travel and transactions has increased tremendously. Moreover, existence of economic, business, social and political organisations and forms, of more or less determinate structure, and both recognised and unrecognised, that operate across borders, implies that their activities, even though conducted in one territory may have an impact on or in another territory. Externalities arising from economic activities, including but not limited to large scale exploitation of natural resources, and consequent pressure on delicate global environmental balance, are being recognised to be global in scope and impact. Global criminal and terror networks are also examples of how events and activities in a territory outside one's own borders could affect the interests, welfare, well-being and security within. Many other examples could also be adduced. For instance, the enablement, by law, of participation of the State in many joint, multilateral or bilateral efforts at coordination of economic, fiscal, monetary, trade, social, law enforcement activities, reduction of carbon emissions, prevention or mitigation of war in another region or maintenance of peace and security, etc., may be cited as additional examples of such inter-territorial dependence.

However, the Constitution Bench cautioned that 'an exercise of legislative powers by Parliament with regard to extraterritorial aspects or causes that did not have any, or may be expected to not have nexus with India' would be constitutionally impermissible in terms of Article 245(1), which lays down the fundamental condition of 'benefit to' or 'of India'.[1154]

The Court noted that Article 245(1) uses the verb 'make' with respect to laws, indicating Parliament's power to make laws. The subject of Article 245(2), on the other hand, is the law made by Parliament, pursuant to Article 245(1). The opening clause of Article 245(2) with the phrase 'No law made by the Parliament' clarifies that Article 245(2) is not an independent source of legislative powers. It is dependent on Article 245(1) because power to make law is enumerated in the article.[1155] This distinction between the phrases 'make laws' and 'extraterritorial operation of law' is important to

1152. *GVK Inds Ltd* (n. 1146) para. 37.
1153. *Ibid.*, para. 39.
1154. *Ibid.*, para. 43.
1155. *Ibid.*, para. 52.

understand the constitutional scheme envisaged under Article 245(1) and 245(2) of the Constitution of India.

The Court observed that the conflict between 'Principle of Sovereignty of States' that reflects in the phrase 'make law' (the laws made by one state can have no operation in another state) and 'extraterritorial operation of law' reflected in Article 245(2) was noted in *Electronics Corporation.*[1156] In that case, a three-judge Bench of Apex Court relied on the ratio of *British Columbia Railway Company Limited v King*[1157] that the problems of inability to enforce the laws outside the territory of a nation state cannot be grounds to hold such laws invalid.

The Court further observed that such laws, in breach of the fundamental condition of 'benefit to' or 'of India', may not be invalidated on the singular ground of extraterritorial operation, but on other grounds, they can be subjected to judicial review as 'the power of the judiciary to invalidate laws that are ultra-vires flows from its essential functions, constitutional structure, values and scheme, and indeed to ensure that the powers vested in the organs of the state are not being transgressed, and that they are being used to realise a public purpose that subserves the general welfare of the people. It is one of the essential defences of the people in a constitutional democracy'.[1158]

5.4.3 *Raj Shipping*

In *Raj Shipping,*[1159] Raj Shipping, the petitioner, was engaged in 'Bunker Supplies' which mainly consisted of supply of high-speed diesel oil (HSD) to various incoming and outgoing vessels within or beyond the port limits of Mumbai port. The petitioner did not pay sales tax on supply of HSD to ships or vessels on the ground that since the ships and vessels were located beyond 1.5 nautical miles on the high seas beyond the territorial limits of the state, the Maharashtra Value Added Tax Act (MVAT Act) was not applicable. The Revenue had claimed that sales tax was leviable on the supply of HSD as MVAT Act was applicable.

The Hon'ble High Court of Bombay relying upon *Tata Iron & Steel Company v State of Bihar*[1160] held that for levying tax, it was not necessary that the sale should take place within the territorial limits of the state. The tax could be levied if all the ingredients of sale like the agreement to sale, the passing of title, delivery of goods have a territorial connection. In the instant case, the goods were manufactured or refined within the state and the petitioner was situated at Mumbai. Thus, the place of business of the petitioner was at Mumbai. Also, the goods were supplied to the petitioner at Mumbai from where it was carried in furtherance of contract through vessels. Therefore, there was sufficient territorial nexus for applicability of MVAT Act. Hence,

1156. *Electronics Corporation* (n. 1141).
1157. *British Columbia* (n. 1049).
1158. *Ibid.*, para. 53.
1159. *Raj Shipping v State of Maharashtra* (2015) 62 Taxmann.com 309 (Bom).
1160. *Tata Iron & Steel Company v State of Bihar* AIR 1958, SC 452.

the goods were transported within the State of Maharashtra and, thus, the MVAT Act was applicable.

5.5 CONCLUSION

Thus, the legislature of a country is presumed to formulate laws applicable to its own territory. However, such a presumption of sovereignty may be rebutted and certain laws may operate extraterritorially.[1161] The sovereign legislature is not prohibited from expanding its tax net as 'good government demands a solution to the problems of a state attempting to collect revenue beyond its borders ... and cooperation among the states should help to effect a more equitable distribution of the tax burden'.[1162] Thus, a taxing statute, like any other statutes, necessitates a nexus requirement to overcome the presumption of extraterritoriality. This nexus requirement cannot be reduced to a mere physical presence of the entity or the activities in the territory of a state.

The nexus has a broader connotation than a physical contact and envisages and entails all externalities or extraterritorial aspects or matters, which have an impact or effect on the territory of the state so as to clothe it with legislative jurisdiction in respect of thereof. Further, the extraterritorial aspects or matters must have a bearing on or consequences for the state or they must be for the interests or wellbeing of the state or its populace. Michael Lang explains it thus:[1163]

> [I]n International law practice, there are no significant limits on the tax sovereignty of states. In designing the domestic personal tax law, the national legislator can even tax situations when, for example, only a 'genuine link' exists. It is only when neither the person nor the transaction has any connection with the taxing state that tax cannot be levied.

In granting the Parliament the powers to legislate 'for' India under Article 245(1) of the Indian Constitution, and consequently also with respect to extraterritorial aspects or matters under Article 245(2), the architects of our Constitution certainly envisaged that there be restrictions as to the manner in which, and the extent to which, the organs of the state, including Parliament, may take cognizance of extraterritorial aspects or matters. Thus, the extraterritorial aspect or matter, which has an effect or consequence on India or is for the benefit or interest of India, would constitute a territorial nexus and would fall within the constitutional parameters of Article 245(1).[1164]

The *Ishikawajima*[1165] and *Vodafone*[1166] decisions completely ignore this constitutional scheme as delineated in *GVK Inds Ltd.*[1167] In *Ishikawajima*, the services of a

1161. *See generally* SD Sharma, 'Applicability of the Doctrine of Extraterritoriality to Legislation by Indian Legislature' (1946) vol. 28(3-4) J Comp Leg 91.
1162. CF Midkiff, 'Extraterritorial Enforcement of Tax Claims' (1970) 12 Wm & Mary L Rev 111.
1163. M Lang, *Introduction to the Law of Double Taxation Conventions* (IBFD and Linde 2013) 441.
1164. *GVK Inds Ltd* (n. 1146) para. 33
1165. *Ishikawajima* (n. 1010).
1166. *Vodafone* (n. 1011).
1167. *GVK Inds Ltd* (n. 1146).

non-resident, though rendered outside India, were utilised in India; this utilisation in India along with payment for them having been made by an Indian resident clearly had an 'effect' or 'consequence' in India, and this clearly met the constitutional standards of 'nexus' as conceived in Article 245(1). The quest for 'a direct live link' of rendition of services in India, apart from its utilisation, by Sinha J in *Ishikawajima*, unduly restricted the scope of the expression 'for India' in Article 245(1). A restrictive construction of the Constitution must always be avoided. The observations of McKenna J of the US Supreme Court are quite illuminating in this regard:[1168]

> Legislation, both statutory and constitutional, is enacted, it is true, from an experience of evils, but its general language should not, therefore, be necessarily confined to the form that evil had therefore taken. Time works changes, brings into existence new conditions and purposes. Therefore, a principle, to be vital, must be capable of wider application than mischief which gave it birth. This is peculiarly true of Constitutions. They are, to use the words of Chief Justice Marshall, 'designed to approach immortality as nearly as human institutions can approach it.' The future is their care, and provisions for events of good and bad tendencies of which no prophecy can be made. In the application of a Constitution, therefore, our contemplation cannot be only of what has been, but of what may be. Under any other rule a Constitution would indeed be as easy of application as it would be deficient in efficacy and power. Its general principles would have little value, and be converted by precedent info impotent and lifeless formulas. Rights declared in the words might be lost in reality. And this has been recognised. The meaning and vitality of the Constitution have developed, against narrow and restrictive construction.

Bhagwati J in *Francis C Mullin*,[1169] noting the aforesaid observations of McKenna J with approval, expounded the rule of liberal constitutional construction in the following words:[1170]

> This principle of interpretation which requires that a Constitutional provision must be construed, not in a narrow and constricted sense but in a wide and liberal manner so as to anticipate and take account of changing conditions and purposes so that the Constitutional provision does not get atrophied or fossilized but remains flexible enough to meet the newly emerging problems and challenges, applies with greater force in relation to a fundamental right enacted by the Constitution.

Thus, the nexus based on the utilisation of services in India and the payment by an Indian resident, as specified in section 9(1)(vii) of the Indian Income Tax Act 1961, satisfied the requirement of law being 'for India' and was constitutionally valid. *Ishikawajima* was, therefore, an erroneous decision and the amendment,[1171] introduced by the Indian Legislature, to overrule it, was definitely in order.

Likewise, in *Vodafone*,[1172] while stating that substantial territorial nexus between income and the territory, which sought to tax that income, was of prime importance,

1168. *Weems v United States* (1910) 217 US 349.
1169. *Francis C Mullin v Administrator* AIR 1981 SC 746.
1170. *Ibid.*, 752.
1171. The Finance Act 2007 s. 5 and the Finance Act 2010 s. 4.
1172. *Vodafone* (n. 1011).

the Supreme Court completely missed the constitutional scheme of Article 245(1) in holding that that section 9(1)(i) of the Act cannot, by a process of interpretation, be extended to such indirect transfer of Indian assets (i.e., controlling interests in Hutchison), which had occurred in consequence of the transfer of CGP shares outside India. This reasoning is clearly tenuous as the transfer of CGP shares had its effect on the Indian assets, which stood transferred as a result of the overseas transfer of CGP shares. Thus, there was a clear territorial link with India in terms of Article 245(1) of the Indian Constitution, triggering the Indian tax jurisdiction. The legislature, therefore, had to again intervene and introduce certain clarificatory amendments[1173] to nullify the effect of this holding, which was constitutionally way off the mark. A legislature has, in fact, power to define the contours of territorial connection and what income shall be deemed to accrue or arise in India. The extent, degree or amplitude of this connection, if it is real, is not relevant in considering and determining the validity of a legislation. That is a matter of policy to be considered by the legislature.[1174]

It is being increasingly recognised all over the world that modern constitutional requirement of territoriality or modern due process jurisprudence allows states to reach out-of-state actors who 'purposefully avail' themselves of the state's economic market.[1175] This 'purposeful availment test' was vociferated by Brennan J in the following terms:[1176]

> [I]t is essential in each case that there be some act by which the defendant purposefully avails itself of the privilege of conducting activities within the forum State, thus invoking the benefits and protections of its laws.
>
> This 'purposeful availment' requirement ensures that a defendant will not be haled into a jurisdiction solely as a result of 'random,' 'fortuitous,' or 'attenuated' contacts, [*Keeton v Hustler Magazine*, Inc, 465 US, at 774; *World-Wide Volkswagen Corp v Woodson*, supra, at 299,] or of the 'unilateral activity of another party or a third person,' [*Helicopteros Nacionales de Colombia, SA v Hall*, supra, at 417]. Jurisdiction is proper, however, where the contacts proximately result from actions by the defendant himself that create a 'substantial connection' with the forum State. [*McGee v International Life Insurance Co*, supra, at 223; see also Kulko v California Superior Court, supra, at 94, n. 7]. Thus where the defendant 'deliberately' has engaged in significant activities within a State, [*Keeton v Hustler Magazine, Inc, supra*, at 781], or has created 'continuing obligations' between himself and residents of the forum, [*Travelers Health Assn v Virginia*, 339 US, at 648] he manifestly has availed himself of the privilege of conducting business there, and because his activities are shielded by 'the benefits and protections' of the forum's laws it is presumptively not unreasonable to require him to submit to the burdens of litigation in that forum as well [quoting *Hanson v Denckla*, 357 US 235, 253 (1958)].

This deliberate 'availment' of economic market of the source state by an entity or its activity is the real determinant of the economic nexus in terms of the constitutional requirement of nexus. Therefore, insistence upon a physical presence is not the correct

1173. The Finance Act 2012 ss 3 and 4.
1174. *AH Wadia* (n. 1132) 141.
1175. *Burger King Corp v Rudzewic* (1985) 471 US 462.
1176. *Ibid.*, 474-475.

exposition of the constitutional law of territorial nexus. Hellerstein and Hellerstein are, therefore right when they draw the distinction between the two distinct concepts of nexus in a constitutional context, viz., nexus with the person or the entity paying the tax and nexus with the income, transaction, activity, or property sought to be taxed.[1177] The first concept of nexus connotes the minimum connection between the state and a person that is required in order for the state to have the jurisdiction to impose a tax on him - within the context of the constitutional due process. The second concept entails a sufficient connection between the state and the income, transaction, activity, or property it seeks to tax,[1178] which means that as long as the income, transaction, activity, or property are connected with the state, it creates a debt of economic allegiance and a corresponding rationale for invoking taxing rights. This is why, Swain calls it a fair tax apportionment issue.[1179] The territoriality debate, therefore, is essentially about equity, fair tax allocation and the scourge of tax avoidance.

1177. JR Hellerstein and W Hellerstein, *State Taxation* (3rd edn, Thomson Reuters 1998) para. 6.01.
1178. *Ibid.*
1179. JA Swain, 'State Income Tax Jurisdiction: A Jurisprudential and Policy Perspective' (2003) 45 Wm & Mary L Rev 319, 328-329.

CHAPTER 6

Conclusion: Retrospective Amendments, Fairness and More Politics

Abstract

This concluding chapter analyses the contrived territoriality debate initiated by the residence taxation theorists in the context of India's retrospective legislative changes introduced in 2012 to tax capital gains arising on indirect transfer of Indian assets through tortuous structural changes by non-residents, which have been dubbed as unfair and discriminatory. India losing the *Vodafone* and *Cairn* arbitration cases has again sparked a heated debate recently. This chapter assesses international principles and practices in this regard, and evaluates the argument whether retrospective legislative amendment by India resulted in an unfair and discriminatory treatment to Vodafone and Cairn. This chapter concludes that tax politics, competing concerns of states and the issues of fairness and tax justice must be factored in, in all tax policy formulations.

6.1 CONTRIVED DEBATE: FAIRNESS IN TAX ALLOCATION

The avoidance of taxes is the only intellectual pursuit that carries any reward, Keynes once remarked. The analyses presented in the preceding chapters of this book clearly demonstrate that the territorial nexus debate, based on a strict physical presence, is essentially a contrived polemic initiated by the theorists of residence taxation and some interested tax lawyers, aimed at helping the multinational companies (MNCs) in their profit-shifting venture and preventing an equitable tax allocation among the developing nations. Thakurta and Jain have illustrated these political manoeuvres in their recent book,[1180] pointing out how 'the BEPS consultations were dominated by the representatives of MNCs, tax lawyers and special industry groups, who outnumbered members of the civil society, representatives of labour groups, academics and various

1180. P Guha Thakurta and S Jain, *Thin Dividing Line: India, Mauritius and Global Illicit Financial Flows* (Penguin Random House 2017) ch IX.

country representatives'.[1181] They specifically note that in the BEPS consultations on the taxation of digital economy, the leading US and European technology companies, whose Governments act as staunch allies to protect the competitiveness of these MNCs, stood united against any discussion of tax rules that would consider the concept of digital presence in the tax nexus rules, 'while their home countries extolled the need for traditionally accepted and durable principles such as physical presence'.[1182]

It has been argued right through this book that the physical presence standard distorts a fair and equitable allocation of tax. The doctrine of economic allegiance, on the contrary, posits that a part of the total tax paid by the taxpayer 'ought to reach the competing authorities according to his economic interest under each authority'.[1183]

These issues of fairness in tax allocation and what is of late being referred to as 'global tax justice' have assumed considerable significance today. The TJN[1184] released its pledge *The Fair Share Commitment* in connection with World Public Services Day (23 June), which highlighted the anger felt across civil society about the failure of corporations and the world's rich to pay their fair share in taxes, and the urgent need for tax justice.[1185] The TJN has reported on the OECD's BEPS projects and conducted its own research to conclude that the scale of corporate taxes being avoided by multinationals was an estimated USD 660 billion in 2012 (a quarter of US multinationals' gross profits), which is equivalent to 0.9% of World GDP.[1186]

The deficiencies in the international taxation regime have also come to share G20 agenda and communiqué space. The recent tax haven exposé by the International Consortium of Investigative Journalists[1187] has amply displayed that tax is no longer a technical issue. It has now become a global political concern, which cannot really be ignored.[1188] All countries need tax revenue in order to reduce poverty and inequality by funding vital public services such as healthcare and education. There is increasing understanding that tax dodging by MNCs undermines public spending, and that the

1181. *Ibid.*
1182. *Ibid.*
1183. K Holmes, *International Tax Policy and Double Tax Treaties: An Introduction to Principles and Application* (IBFD 2007) 21, citing M Bruins et al., '1923 Report', EFS 73 / F19 in *Report and Resolutions Submitted by the Technical Experts to the Financial Committee of the League of Nations*, Geneva, 1925, Document F. 212, 9.
1184. The Tax Justice Network (TJN) is an independent advocacy group consisting of a coalition of international researchers and activists with a shared concern about tax avoidance, tax competition, tax evasion, and tax havens. It has a particular focus on offshore financial centres that behave as corporate tax havens.
1185. War on Want News, 'A Global Tax Justice Movement Rises: The New Fight to End Inequality' (19 June 2013), https://waronwant.org/media/global-tax-justice-movement-rises-new-fight-end-inequality accessed 19 February 2019.
1186. B Stupples, Tax Avoidance Costing US USD 189 Billion: Tax Justice Network, Tax Justice Network, Bloomberg News, 23 March 2017, https://www.bna.com/tax-avoidance-costing-n57982085579/ accessed 19 February 2019.
1187. M Forsythe, 'Paradise Papers Shine Light on Where the Elite Keep Their Money' *New York Times* (5 November 2017).
1188. War on Want News (n. 1185).

same actors and unsustainable ideologies are at work in both developed and developing countries. A number of well-known development economists have recently called for urgent and drastic action to deal with the crises in world poverty and inequality.[1189]

6.2 *VODAFONE* AND *CAIRN* ARBITRATION CASES

This fairness debate has recently assumed intensified momentum, not only in India, but across the world, with India losing the *Vodafone* and *Cairn* arbitration cases in the international arbitration tribunals. The arbitral awards in *Vodafone* and *Cairn* cases raise two significant concerns which, in fact, form the bases for the tribunal's arbitral decisions. The first concern relates to the question whether an arbitration tribunal can adjudicate a tax dispute under an investment treaty. The tribunals in both the cases held that they had the jurisdiction to entertain a tax dispute under bilateral investment treaties. This holding was despite a specific stipulation in the treaties that admission of all investments shall be subject to the laws and policies of the contracting party in whose territory the investment is made.[1190] The second question, which is far more fundamental, is whether retrospective legislative amendment by India resulted in an unfair and discriminatory treatment to Vodafone and Cairn.

Delving into the questions, whether a BIT can entail tax disputes or whether a sovereign legislation can be brought to naught by an arbitration tribunal set up under an investment treaty is outside the scope of this book, as these are the questions which India is deeply concerned about and is contesting them in the appropriate court in terms of Article V of the New York Convention.[1191] However, the tribunal's conclusion regarding discriminatory and unfair treatment given to Vodafone and Cairn by way of retrospective legislative amendments introduced by India does not appear to be well founded and raises serious concern about fair tax allocation among the states. The arbitration tribunals, at no occasion, seems to have considered the fact that Indian source rule, right from its inception, provided for taxing of income arising or accruing in India, whether *directly or indirectly*, through the transfer of a capital asset situated in India. The existing domestic law,[1192] prior to 2012 amendments, read as follows:

> 9(1). The following incomes shall be deemed to accrue or arise in India:
> (*i*) all income accruing or arising, whether directly or indirectly, through or from any business connection in India, or through or from any property in India, or through or from any asset or source of income in India, [* * *] or through the transfer of a capital asset situate in India.

In *Vodafone*, its offshore acquisition of the entire share capital of CGP Investments (a Cayman Islands company), which, in turn, held 67% controlling interest in Hutchison Essar (a Indian company), resulted in indirect transfer of Indian assets, and

1189. K Brooks, 'Tax Treaty Treatment of Royalty Payments from Low-Income Countries: A Comparison of Canada and Australia's Policies' (2007) vol. 5(2) eJTR (Mich Issue) 169, 171.
1190. *See, e.g.*, the Netherlands-India Bilateral Investment Treaty, Art. 3.
1191. United Nations Convention on the Recognition and Enforcement of Foreign Arbitral Awards, Art. V (New York, 10 June 1958).
1192. Income Tax Act 1961 s. 9(1)(i).

the capital gains arising on such indirect transfer of Indian assets were clearly covered by the expression 'income accruing or arising, whether directly or indirectly, through the transfer of a capital asset situated in India', appearing in section 9(1)(i) of the Income Tax Act.[1193]

The Indian Supreme Court, despite the express mention of this source rule in the domestic law, got persuaded by the territoriality principle of public international law by holding that substantial territorial nexus between the income and the territory, which seeks to tax that income, is of prime importance to levy tax and that section 9(1)(i) of the Act cannot, by a process of interpretation, be extended to such indirect transfer of controlling interests in Hutchison, which had occurred in consequence of the transfer of the CGP shares outside India. In so construing, the Court missed two important aspects of the matter: *first*, it ignored the expression 'indirect' appearing in section 9, which clearly takes within its ambit all incomes arising from the indirect transfer of Indian assets. *Second*, it gave a complete go-by to the economic nexus doctrine, enunciated by the four economists in their Report.[1194] In the present case, the offshore transfer of assets of CGP Investments' shares to Vodafone had resulted in the transfer of sizable business assets situated in India, which constituted a clear economic link, triggering the Indian tax jurisdiction. In a subsequent judgment, the Indian Supreme Court duly recognised the economic nexus principle, thus:[1195]

> The source rule is in consonance with the nexus theory and does not fall foul of the said doctrine on the ground of extra-territorial operation. The doctrine of source rule has been explained as a country where the income or wealth is physically or economically produced. [See League of Nations, Report on Double Taxation by Bruins, Einaudi, Saligman and Sir Josiah Stamp (1923)]. Appreciated on the aforesaid principle, it would apply where business activity is wholly or partly performed is a source State, as a logical corollary, the State concept would also justifiably include the country where the commercial need for the product originated, that is, for example, where the consultancy is utilised.

Thus, the Supreme Court completely misconstrued the underlying rationale of the source rule in *Vodafone*[1196] and rendered otiose the expression 'indirectly' appearing in the statute.

6.3 LEGISLATIVE CHANGES: RETROSPECTIVE OPERATION AND DISCRIMINATION

The Indian Government, therefore, had to swiftly move to introduce three clarificatory amendments[1197] in 2012 with retrospective effect, to bring Vodafone-like transactions within the ambit of the Indian source rule. It added an Explanation to section 2(14) to define capital asset as including 'any rights in or in relation to an Indian company,

1193. *Ibid.*
1194. *See* the Four Economists' Report, 4031.
1195. *GVK Industries Ltd v ITO* (2015) 371 ITR 453 (SC).
1196. *Vodafone International Holding BV v Union of India* [2012] 341 ITR 1 (SC).
1197. The Finance Act 2012 ss 3 and 4.

including rights of management or control or any other rights whatsoever'. Another Explanation to section 2(47) clarified the definition of 'transfer' as inclusive of 'disposing of or parting with an asset or any interest therein, or creating any interest in any asset in any manner whatsoever, directly or indirectly, absolutely or conditionally, voluntarily or involuntarily, by way of an agreement (whether entered into in India or outside India) or otherwise, notwithstanding that such transfer of rights has been characterized as being effected or dependent upon or flowing from the transfer of a share or shares of a company registered or incorporated outside India'. Further, the expression 'through' in section 9(1) was clarified to mean and include 'by means of', 'in consequence of' or 'by reason of'. These amendments, therefore, merely clarified the intent of law and attempted to prevent the mischief arising therefrom

In *Cairn*, too, the issues were similar. The Indian assets of CUH were held by CIHL, a Channel Islands-based[1198] subsidiary of CUH that, in turn, was fully owned by Cairn Energy PLC. Cairn Energy wanted to exit its stake in the Indian exploration operations by listing its Indian assets. To enable that, the Indian assets held by CIH had to be transferred to a company registered in India. This was achieved by creating CIL, a group company registered in India. By way of a subscription and share purchase agreement, shares, constituting the entire issued share capital of CIHL, were transferred to CIL, the consideration for which was partly paid in cash and partly in the form of shares of CIL. CIL then divested 30.5% of its shareholding by way of an IPO. As a result of divesting approximately 30% of its stake in the subsidiaries and part of IPO proceeds, CUH received approximately INR 6,101 crore (approximately USD 931 million). India sought to levy capital gains tax on this receipt.

Thus, the decision of the international arbitration tribunal in *Vodafone* and *Cairn* is, therefore, flawed on two counts. First, it did not notice that India has always sought to tax income even arising or accruing 'indirectly' from the transfer of Indian assets and the 2012 amendments were merely clarificatory in nature and were aimed at explaining the expression 'arising or accruing, whether directly or indirectly' appearing in Indian domestic law.

6.3.1 Context of Retrospectivity

Second, the tribunal erroneously assumed that a retrospective amendment of law by itself incorporates an element of discrimination or lack of fairness. An aversion towards retrospective legislation is understandable when an altogether new law altering the status quo is enacted because the function of the law is to provide a stable framework by which people can be fairly confident of the effects of their actions on their legal rights and liabilities. Retrospective laws are fatal to their ability to plan their financial lives. There is risk in operating any business, and decision-makers must live with the uncertainties of the future, but they ought to be able to rely on the past remaining

1198. A tax haven country.

stable.[1199] But a newly enacted law, which is merely clarifying an earlier provision or is curative in nature, can operate retrospectively as it merely explicates the existing law or cures the mischief therein. According to Bland, one or more of the following four factors must be present for a newly enacted law to qualify as clarifying or curative:

(1) The law inadvertently failed to expressly cover a particular issue.
(2) The earlier law contained a manifest error or was ambiguous in its coverage and therefore needed language refinement.
(3) The existing law contained general language that was later found to need more specificity.
(4) The courts have misinterpreted the construction of the existing law.[1200]

6.3.2 The *Carlton* Standard

These principles are being followed the world over. In *United States v Carlton*,[1201] the Supreme Court upheld the retrospective application of a 1987 amendment to the Internal Revenue Code. In this case, Carlton, the executor of an estate, sought to take advantage of the new section 2057. In December 1986, he bought shares of MCI Communications Corporation for over USD 11 million, and two days later, sold them to the MCI ESOP for approximately USD 10.5 million. He claimed a deduction under section 2057 in his return, reducing the estate's tax liability by approximately USD 2.5 million. The IRS in January 1987 introduced an amendment that the deduction for these sales will be admissible only if the decedent directly owned the stocks immediately before death. The amendment applied retrospectively. Carlton contested the retrospective amendment on the ground that it violated the Fifth Amendment's Due Process Clause. The Court permitted Congress to change section 2057 retrospectively in order 'to correct what it reasonably viewed as a mistake in the original 1986 provision that would have created a significant and unanticipated revenue loss'.[1202] The Court held that such a change does not violate Due Process because it is a rational means to further a legitimate legislative purpose. The Court admonished that 'tax legislation is not a promise, and a taxpayer has no invested right in the Internal Revenue Code', and quoted the following passage from its prior decision in *Welch*:[1203]

> Taxation is neither a penalty imposed on the taxpayer nor a liability which he assumes by contract. It is but a way of apportioning the cost of government among those who in some measure are privileged to enjoy its benefits and must bear its burdens. Since no citizen enjoys immunity from that burden, its retroactive imposition does not necessarily infringe due process … .

1199. Roxanne Bland, No Love for Retroactive Tax Legislation, Tax Notes, https://www.forbes.com/sites/taxnotes/2020/07/14/no-love-for-retroactive-tax-legislation/?sh=2ee8058a3278, accessed 15 February 2021.
1200. *Ibid.*
1201. *United States v Carlton* 114 S Ct 2018 (1994).
1202. *Ibid.*, 2023.
1203. *Welch v Henry*, 305 US 134 (1938).

The Court also quoted from its decision in *Milliken*:[1204] 'A taxpayer should be regarded as taking his chances of any increase in the tax burden which might result from the carrying out the established policy of taxation.'

6.3.3 The *Huitson* Principles

In the UK, the landmark case is *Huitson*.[1205] The case concerned an electrical engineering consultant resident in the UK. He sought to avoid tax on his income through a scheme by setting-up an Isle of Man Trust in which he was the settler and had a right to income. This trust had become a partner in an Isle of Man partnership, which in turn had entered into a contract with Huitson to provide his services. Under the contract, Huitson was entitled to an annual fee, apart from a share of the partnership profits as a beneficiary under the trust. Under the terms of the Double Tax Treaty between the UK and the Isle of Man, income tax was due on Huitson's annual fee, but not on the profits he received as beneficiary of the trust. Huitson had used the scheme for seven years and had avoided huge income tax. The UK Government, therefore, introduced section 858 of the Income Tax (Trading and Other Income) Act 2005 with retrospective effect to counteract such schemes. The provision stated that 'for the purposes of this section, the members of a firm include any person entitled to a share of income of the firm'. Huitson sought a judicial review of this new legislation claiming that the retrospective legislative changes failed to achieve a balance between the interests of individual taxpayer and the general public and that the measures were disproportionate and violated his rights under the European Convention on Human Rights. Rejecting the plea, the High Court held that it was a legitimate aim of the UK to ensure that its DTA did no more than relieve double taxation and should not be permitted to avoid tax completely by those both resident and conducting business in the UK, and that this public policy was of such importance that it was expected that Parliament would introduce legislation to stop any such abuse identified. The Court held that the purpose of a DTA was to prevent double taxation and not to extinguish tax in both jurisdictions. The Court, thus, deemed the use of retrospective tax legislation lawful.

The abuse of tax treaty, the artificiality of the scheme and the amount of tax at stake are significant factors in the UK, which justify retrospective legislation. In March 2011, the UK Government, in fact, published a protocol on the unscheduled announcement of changes to tax law, stating as follows: 'The protocol will explicitly recognise that changes to tax legislation, where the change is effective from a date earlier than the date of announcement, will be wholly exceptional.'

Again, in February 2012, David Gauke, then Exchequer Secretary to the UK Treasury, declared in his Ministerial Statement that the Government would introduce legislation to block Barclays buyback arrangements created to avoid corporation tax on buybacks of corporate debt. The relevant legislation would apply to debt purchases

1204. *Milliken v United States*, 283 US 15 (1931).
1205. *Robert Huitson v HMRC* [2015] UKFTT 448.

that took place from December 2011, some three months prior to the announcement, meaning that it had retrospective effect. The Ministerial Statement reiterated that the potential tax loss from this scheme and the history of previous abuse in this area justified the action to change the legislation with full retrospective effect to ensure that the system was fair for all and that those who sought to benefit from this aggressive avoidance did not get an unfair advantage.

In the same year, the UK Government introduced retrospective legislation to counter stamp duty avoidance scheme (SDLT scheme) on property bought in Britain and used for residential purposes. The legislation was challenged before the High Court in *St Mathews*[1206] on the ground of its breach of Human Rights. Rejecting the plea, the High Court upheld the retrospective legislation, stating that the changes were lawful and were not arbitrary and that it was equally compelling justification for retrospective tax legislation that it would have the desirable effect that the relevant provisions would operate in the manner Parliament intended.

In April 2019, the UK once again introduced a simple PAYE charge on the users of so-called disguised remuneration schemes, which would apply retrospectively to any loan taken out and not repaid since 1999.

6.3.4 The Australian Position: *Chevron*

In Australia too, there is a significant history of retrospective tax legislation, and it is generally done where there is a significant risk to revenue that is inconsistent with the Parliament's intention.[1207] During the 1970s and 1980s, the tax avoidance industry in Australia evolved and flourished because of disproportionate increase in tax collection. One method used to avoid tax was to strip a company of its assets and accumulated profits before tax was payable and transfer those assets to another company which would continue the business operations. The stripped company would then be transferred to the ownership of someone who did not have the means to pay the tax and was also disinterested in the activities of the company. With a view to checking this scheme, the Government finally had to take recourse to allow the retrospective collection of tax which had been avoided under the schemes from 1 January 1972 to 4 December 1980. The Taxation (Unpaid Company Tax) Assessment Act 1982 was, thus, enacted, applying it to schemes entered into on or after 1 January 1972 and before 4 December 1980. The retrospective nature of this legislation passed muster because of large-scale use of schemes and the huge effect on the revenue.[1208]

A capital gain tax (CGT), introduced in Australia, was also retrospective as it taxed the gain which arose on the giving of a lease on a property which a taxpayer had

1206. *St Mathews (West) Ltd and Others v HMRC* (2014) EWHC 1848 (Admin).

1207. R Loiacono and C Mortimer, 'Retrospective Tax Law: Has Pandora's Box Opened Never to Be Shut Again?' (2017) vol. 15(1) eJournal Tax Res 105-118, 109.

1208. L Xynas, 'Tax Planning, Avoidance and Evasion in Australia 1970-2010: The Regulatory Responses and Taxpayer Compliance' (2011) vol. 20(1) R L J, citing the Asprey Report: W Asprey and R Parsons, 'Taxation Review Committee' (University of Sydney Library, 1975) ch 11, [11.1].

owned prior to the introduction of the tax. The matter was raised in *Gray v FCT,*[1209] which effectively endorsed the taxation of such lease premiums and the grant of an easement.

However, the most important case was *Chevron,*[1210] which was the first case to consider the validity of the transfer pricing rules in sub-div 815-A of the Income Tax Assessment Act (ITAA) 1997 because of their retrospective nature. These rules operated concurrently with existing transfer pricing rules in div 13 of the ITAA 1936. From 1 July 2013, both div 13 and sub-div 815-A were replaced with sub-div 815-B of the ITAA 1997. Chevron, *inter alia*, submitted that sub-div 815-A was retroactive as it applied, by virtue of section 815-1 of the Income Tax (Transitional Provisions) Act 1997, to the income years commencing on or after 1 July 2004 and, therefore, was invalid because it imposed an arbitrary exaction and therefore did not answer the description of a law with respect to taxation for the purposes of section 51(ii) of the Constitution. Chevron also submitted that an unduly retrospective tax could, in the circumstances of its imposition, be arbitrary in character and thus beyond legislative power. Robertson J, speaking for the Court, rejected Chevron's arguments in the following words:[1211]

> In my opinion, the contentions on behalf of the applicant in this respect misconceived the nature of the amendments made by s 815-1 of the Income Tax (Transitional Provisions) Act. The provision had the effect, according to its terms, that Subdiv 815-A of the ITAA 1997 applied to income years starting on or after 1 July 2004. I accept the respondent's submission that the Income Tax Act did not impose tax only for the particular year in which it was enacted and did not impose tax limited to the form of the Assessment Act as it stood at the time the Income Tax Act was enacted. Section 7 of the Income Tax Act provided that the tax imposed by s 5(1) 'is levied, and shall be paid, for the financial year commencing on 1 July 1986 and for all subsequent financial years until the Parliament otherwise provides'.

Thus, the Court upheld the power of Parliament to legislate retrospectively in matters of taxation. The general principle against retrospectivity advanced by Chevron, namely, the inability of a taxpayer to comply with a law that did not exist at the time of a particular transaction, was also dismissed by the Court.

6.3.5 China, Canada and South Africa

China has also taken recourse to extraterritorial and retroactive tax and disclosure rule relating to share transfers by non-resident enterprises.[1212] In December 2009, it introduced a new law (Circular 689) to retrospectively tax sale of offshore holding

1209. *Gray v FCT* 3 (1989) 20 ATR 649.
1210. *Chevron Australia Holdings Pty Ltd v Commissioner of Taxation* [No 4] [2015] FCA 1092.
1211. *Ibid.*, 553.
1212. Ubilla & Cia, 'China Adopts Controversial Extraterritorial & Retroactive Tax and Disclosure Rule Relating to Share Transfers by Non-Resident Enterprises', http://www.ub-co.com/country/china/china-adopts-controversial-extraterritorial-retroactive-tax-and-disclosure-rule-relating-to-share-transfers-by-non-resident-enterprises/, accessed 16 February 2021.

companies having underlying Chinese interests by disregarding the intermediary entity in specific circumstances. The law seeks to capture abusive structures aimed at tax avoidance.

In Canada, the position is similar. In *British Columbia,*[1213] the Supreme Court of Canada held that it was fully within the power of Parliament and the provincial and territorial legislatures to enact retroactive legislation - even if it overturns the settled expectations of those affected by the law. Retroactive tax legislation is in fact a fairly common phenomenon in Canada, and there have been numerous examples over the years. For example, in 1994 the Department of Finance enacted section 141.01 of the Excise Tax Act, RSC 1985, c. E-15, as amended, retroactive to 17 December 1990, i.e., the date on which the goods and services tax (GST) legislation received royal assent.

Retrospective amendments in tax law were held to be lawful in a recent South African judgment in *Pienaar Brothers (Pty) Ltd.*[1214] In this case, the Taxation Laws Amendment Act, 2007 inserted section 44(9A) into the Income Tax Act, 1962, which provided that section 44 (9A) of the Act shall be deemed to have come into operation on 21 February 2007 and to be applicable to any reduction or redemption of the share capital or share premium of a resultant in company, including the acquisition by that company of its shares in terms of section 85 of the Companies Act, on or after that date. Pienaar Brothers approached the court seeking a declaration that the Amending Act was inconsistent with the Constitution on the ground of its retrospective operation. Rejecting the contention, the Court pointed out that the Constitution itself did not contain a provision prohibiting retrospective legislation. The court accepted that Parliament may not legislate with retrospective effect as it pleases, but to do so must meet the standard required for the constitutional validity of retrospective amendments. It indicated that reference must be made to the rationality test and the second standard relating to reasonableness or proportionality. The Court came to the conclusion that it was not necessary that exceptional circumstances must exist for Parliament to pass retrospective legislation. The Court decided that there was no overriding duty to give notice of intended legislation.

6.3.6 The Indian Position

In India, the common law practice of retrospective tax legislation has always been upheld. In *Tata Iron and Steel Company,*[1215] a question of retrospective imposition of sales tax fell for consideration before a Constitution Bench. It was pleaded that sales tax, being an indirect tax on the purchaser, cannot be imposed retrospectively after the conclusion of sale transaction because it cannot, at that stage, be passed on to the purchaser. Das CJ negatived the contention in following words:[1216]

1213. *British Columbia v Imperial Tobacco Canada Ltd* 2005 SCC 49.
1214. *Pienaar Brothers (Pty) Ltd v Commissioner for the SARS* [2017] 4 All SA 175 (GP).
1215. *Tata Iron & Steel Company v State* [1958s] AIR 452 (SC).
1216. *Ibid.*

> This also makes it clear that the sales tax need not be passed on to the purchasers and this fact does not alter the real nature of the tax which, by the express provisions of the law, is cast upon the seller. The buyer is under no liability to pay sales tax in addition to the agreed sale price unless the contract specifically provides otherwise. See Love v. Norman Wright (Builders) Ltd. LR (1944) 1 KB 484. If that be the true view of sales tax then the Bihar Legislature acting within its own legislative field had the powers of a sovereign legislature and could make its law prospectively as well as retrospectively. We do not think that there is any substance in this contention either.

In *Chhotabhai,*[1217] wherein, through a retrospective amendment, the government imposed a duty on manufactured tobacco from the date of the introduction of the Bill and not from the date in which the law came into force. The Supreme Court validated the act on the principle that retrospective amendments were brought into effect to correct earlier flaws which defeated the purpose of the legislation in the first place. The Court also followed and cited with approval the decision of the Privy Council in *Colonial's Sugar Refining Co,*[1218] which had laid down the proposition that if there was a power to impose tax conferred by a constitution, the Legislature could equally make the law retroactive and impose the duties from a date earlier than that from which it was imposed.

In *Lohia Machines Ltd,*[1219] the case revolved around a certain exemption to new industrial undertakings on the amount of capital employed by these undertakings. The amount of borrowed monies was being excluded in the calculation of the capital employed, owing to the rule that disentitled the taxpayers from claiming tax relief on long-term borrowings. This rule was declared by the High Courts to be ultra vires. Parliament passed a retrospective amendment through which the substance of the rule was made a part of the Act itself. A challenge was brought to the said retrospective amendment before the Supreme Court, which gave the ruling by majority in favour of the government, stating that the amendment was merely clarificatory in nature. Therefore, the power of the legislature of passing retrospective amendments along with the amendment itself was upheld by the Court.

In *Empire Industries Ltd,*[1220] the Court upheld the validity of the Central Excises and Salt and Additional Duties of Excise (Amendment) Act, 1980, which had retrospective effect, stating that the same was not unreasonable or harsh and that there was no scope for arbitrariness or discrimination. It merely aimed at making 'small repairs'. The Court highlighted that the Legislature should be allowed to cure the inadvertent defects in legislations by making such small repairs.

In *J & K Cotton Spg and Wvg Mills,*[1221] the validity of the substance of the circular issued by the Central Board of Excise was challenged, for it interpreted Rules 9 and 49 of the Central Excise Rules, 1944 to the prejudice of the taxpayer. Meanwhile, the Government amended the two aforesaid rules through a Notification and provided

1217. *Chhotabhai v Union* 1962 Supp 2 SCR 1.
1218. *The Colonial Sugar Refining Company Ltd v Irving* (1905) AC 369.
1219. *Lohia Machines Ltd v Union of India* [1985] 152 ITR 308 (SC).
1220. *Empire Industries Ltd v Union of India* [1985] taxmann.com 426 (SC).
1221. *J&K Cotton Spg and Wvg Mills Ltd v Union of India* AIR 1988 SC 191.

retrospective effect to the same from the date of enforcement of the Excise Rules. The taxpayer challenged this retrospective amendment by amending their written submissions. Disregarding the appeal, the Court upheld the retrospective amendment to the rules.

In view of such overwhelming international practices and judicial trends, the arbitration tribunals in *Vodafone* and *Cairn* made erroneous assumption of unfairness and discrimination. The object of the 2012 amendments was to merely clarify that Indian legislation has always sought to tax capital gains arising indirectly on the transfer of Indian assets and the legal provision of a sovereign state could not be permitted to the circumvented by structural schemes, artifices and arrangements employed by the taxpayers. In *Vodafone* and *Cairn*, structures were created to indirectly transfer Indian assets to give it a colour of an offshore transaction to bypass the domestic law of India and it was quite legitimate for the Indian Legislature to retrospectively alter the law to thwart such tax avoidance schemes. The Carlton and Huitson standards laid down by the US and the UK Courts respectively are squarely applicable in the given circumstances. The international arbitration tribunal made an egregious blunder in assuming a lack of fairness in India's retrospective law.

The theoretical premise of the source rule, as has been argued in the preceding chapters of this book, is the debt of economic allegiance, which is duly established in *Vodafone* and *Cairn* by the effective transfer of assets located in India, albeit 'indirectly' and the creation of artificial structures to disguise it as a transaction occurring beyond the territorial frontiers of India cannot be permissible on the pretext of supposed fairness. The arbitral awards in *Vodafone* and *Cairn* are, therefore, erroneous, fail to pass muster in terms of international practices with regard to retrospective laws, and reflect the long-entrenched prejudice of residence taxation theorists.

Viewed thus, the significance of the present work lies in establishing and reiterating the economic nexus doctrine as a fair and equitable normative principle of tax allocation to the developing countries, which, historically, have been in the vanguard of source taxation ideology. This tax politics, competing concerns of the developed and developing nations and the issues of fairness and tax justice must be taken into consideration in all tax policy decisions, more particularly by the developing nations.

Bibliography

Books

American Law Institute, *Proposals on United States Taxation of Foreign Persons and of the Foreign Income of United States Persons* (ALI 1987).

Arnold Brion J. and McIntyre Michael J., *International Tax Primer* (Kluwer 2002).

Arnold Brion J., Sasseville J. and Zolt Eric M. (eds), *The Taxation of Business Profits Under Tax Treaties* (CTF 2003).

Arnold Brion J., *The Taxation of Controlled Foreign Corporations: An International Comparison* (CTF 1986).

Asprey K.W. and Parsons R.W., *Asprey Report*: Taxation Review Committee (University of Sydney Library, 1975).

Ault Hugh J., *Comparative Income Taxation: A Structural Analysis* (Kluwer 1997).

Baker, P. Q.C., *Double Tax Conventions: A manual on the OECD Model Tax Convention.*

Bastable Charles F., *Public Finance* (first published 1892, 3rd ed. Macmillan 1932).

Beale J., *A Treatise on the Conflict of Laws* s 75 (first published 1916, Lawbook Exchange 2004).

Bobbit P.C., *The Shield of Achilles: War, Peace and the Course of History* (Penguin, 2003).

Born Gary B. and Rutledge Peter B., *International Civil Litigation in US Courts* (4th ed. Aspen Publishers 2007).

Brilmayer L. and Corre, J., *An Introduction to Jurisdiction in the American Federal System* (Michie Company 1986).

Bruins, G.W.J., Einaudi, Luigi, Seligman, E.R.A. and Stamp, Sir Josiah, *Report on Double Taxation* (League of Nations 1923-1928).

Cahill B., *The Thousandth Man: A Biography of James McGregor Stewart* (Osgoode Society for Canadian Legal History (Toronto 2000).

Carroll M.B., *Double Taxation Relief: Discussion of Conventions Drafted at International Conference of Experts, 1927, and Other Measures,* (Washington: US GPO 1928).

Carroll M.B., *Prevention of International Double Taxation and Fiscal Evasion: Two Decades of Progress under the League of Nations* (League of Nations 1939).

Curie R.J. and Rikhof J., *International and Transnational Criminal Law* (2nd ed. Irwin Law Canada 2014).

Dicey A.V. and Wade E.C.S., *Introduction to the Study of the Law of the Constitution.* (9th ed. Macmillan 1939).

Dietsch P., *Catching Capital: The Ethics of Tax Competition* (OUP 2015).

Doernberg R.L. and Hinnekens L., *Electronic Commerce and International Taxation* (Kluwer 1999).

Durst M.C., *Taxing Multinational Business in Lower Income Countries: A Problem of Economics, Politics and Ethical Norms* (Institute of Dev Stud, ICTD 2018).

Gerston L.N., *Reviving Citizen Engagement: Policies to Renew National Community* (CRC Press 2015).

Harding A.L., *Double Taxation of Property and Income: A Study in the Judicial Determination of the Conflicting Claims of Taxing Jurisdictions Advanced by the American States* (Harvard 1933).

Harris P.A., *Corporate-Shareholder Income Taxation and Allocating Taxing Rights Between Countries: A Comparison of Imputation Systems* (IBFD 1996).

Harris P. and Oliver D., *International Commercial Tax* (CUP 2010).

Hellerstein J.R. and Hellerstein W., *State Taxation* (3rd ed. Thomson Reuters 1998).

Hobbes T., *Leviathan* (first published 1651, London Pelican Classics 1968).

Holmes K., *International Tax Policy and Double Tax Treaties: An Introduction to Principles and Application* (IBFD 2007).

Huber U., 'De Conflictu Legum Diversarum in Diversis Imperiis' in Ulrich Huber, *Praelectiones Juris Romani et Hodierni* (First published 1689), translated in DJ Llewelyn Davies, 'The Influence of Huber's *De Conflictu Legum* on English Private International Law' (1937) 18 BYBIL 49.

IFA., *Source and Residence: New Configuration of Their Principles* (vol 90a, IFA: Cahiers de Droit Fiscal International 2005).

Jeffery R.J., *The Impact of State Sovereignty on Global Trade and International Taxation* (Kluwer 1999).

Jennings W.I. and Young C.M., *Constitutional Laws of the British Empire* (Clarendon Press 1938).

Kanga J.B., Palkhivala N.A. and Palkhivala B.A., *The Law and Practice of Income Tax* (Tripathi 7th ed. 1976).

Keen M., *The Welfare Economics of Tax Coordination in the European Community: A Survey* (Institute of Fiscal Studies 1993).

Knechtle Arnold A., *Basic Problems in International Fiscal Law* (Kluwer 1979).

Kobetsky M., *International Taxation of Permanent Establishments: Principles and Policy*, (CUP 2011).

Lang M., et al (eds), *Source Versus Residence* (Kluwer 2008).

Lang M., *Introduction to the Law of Double Taxation Conventions* (IBFD and Linde 2013).

Lang M., *Introduction to the Law of Double Taxation Conventions* (IBFD and Linde 2013).

Li J., *International Taxation in the Age of Electronic Commerce: A Comparative Study* (CTF 2003).

Mann Francis A., *Studies in International Law* (Clarendon Press 1973).

Martha R.S.J., *The Jurisdiction to Tax in International Law: Theory and Practice of Legislative Fiscal Jurisdiction* (Springer 1989).

McClean D. and Morris J.H.C., *The Conflict of Laws* (5th ed. Sweet and Maxwell 2000).

Mehta A., *Permanent Establishment in International Taxation* (Taxmann 2012).

Miller A. and Oats L., *Principles of International Taxation* (3rd ed., Bloomsbury 2012).

Model Tax Convention on Income and on Capital (Condensed version, OECD Pub 1998).

Musgrave P.B., *United States Taxation of Foreign Investment Income* (Harvard 1969).

Musgrave R.A., *Fiscal Systems* (Yale 1969).

Musgrave P.B., *Taxation of Foreign Investment Income – An Economic Analysis* (John Hopkins Press 1963).

Musgrave R.A. and Musgrave P.B., *Public Finance in Theory and Practice* (5th ed. McGraw-Hill 1989).

Noronha F.E., *Private International Law in India: Adequacy of Principles in Comparison with Common Law and Civil law Systems* (Universal 2010).

Oats L., Miller A. and Mulligan E., *Principles of International Taxation* (Bloomsbury 6th ed. 2017).

OECD 1993 Report, *Attribution of profits to Permanent Establishments.*

OECD Model Tax Convention (OECD Pub 1993) full version vol II R (13)-1.

OECD, 'Issues in International Taxation' in *2002 Reports Related to the OECD Model Tax Convention* No. 8 (OECD Pub 2003).

OECD, *2010 Report on The Attribution of Profits to Permanent Establishments* (OECD Pub 2010).

OECD, *Additional Guidance on the Attribution of Profits to Permanent Establishments*, BEPS Action7 (OECD Pub 2018).

OECD, *Addressing Base Erosion and Profit Shifting* (OECD Pub 2013).

OECD, *Addressing the Tax Challenges of The Digitalisation of The Economy – Policy Note* (OECD Pub 2019).

OECD, Centre for Tax Policy and Administration, *Interpretation and Application of Article 5 (Permanent Establishment) of The OECD Model Tax Convention* (OECD Pub 2011).

OECD, *Discussion Draft on the Attribution of Profits to Permanent Establishments* (OECD Pub 2001).

OECD, *Draft Double Taxation Convention on Income and Capital* (OECD Pub 1963).

OECD, *Explanatory Statement: OECD/G20 Base Erosion and Profit Shifting Project* (OECD Pub 2015).

OECD, *Model Double Tax Convention on Income and on Capital* (OECD Pub 1977).

OECD, *Model Tax Convention on Income and on Capital* (Condensed version, OECD Pub 2008).

OECD, *Model Tax Convention on Income and on Capital* (Condensed version, OECD Pub 2010).

OECD, *Model Tax Convention on Income and on Capital* (Condensed version, OECD Pub 2014).

OECD, *Model Tax Convention on Income and on Capital* (OECD Pub 2000).

OECD, *Model Tax Convention on Income and on Capital* (OECD Pub 2005).

OECD, *Model Tax Convention on Income and on Capital* (OECD Pub 2017).

OECD, *New Discussion Draft on Action 7: Prevent the Artificial Avoidance of PE Status* (OECD Pub 2015).

OECD, *Report on the Attribution of Profits to Permanent Establishments* (OECD Pub 2008).

OECD, *Taxation and Electronic Commerce-Implementing the Ottawa Framework Conditions* (OECD Pub 2001).

OECD, *Transfer Pricing Guidelines for Multinational Enterprises and Tax Administrations*, (OECD Pub 1995).

OECD, *Transfer Pricing Guidelines for Multinational Enterprises and Tax Administrations* (OECD Pub 2017).

OECD, *Preventing the Artificial Avoidance of Permanent Establishment Status, Action 7 - 2015 Final Report, OECD/G20 Base Erosion and Profit Shifting Project* (OECD Pub 2015).

OECD, *Preventing the Granting of Treaty Benefits in Inappropriate Circumstances, Action 6 - 2015 Final Report*, OECD/G20 Base Erosion and Profit Shifting Project, (OECD Pub 2015).

OEEC, *The Elimination of Double Taxation: Report of The Fiscal Committee of the OEEC* (OEEC 1961), Annexures A-E, reprinted in Legislative History.

Olivier L. and Honibal M., *International Tax, A South African Perspective* (Siber Ink CC 5th ed. 2011).

Oppenheim's International Law, vol. I, Peace 2 vols (Jennings Sir Robert and Watts Sir Arthur eds, 9th ed., Longman 1992).

Oxman Bernard H., *Max Planck Encyclopedia of International Law* (1987).

Pearce Dennis C. and Geddes Robert S., *Statutory Interpretation in Australia* (5th ed., Butterworths 2001).

Peters C., *On the Legitimacy of International Tax Law* (IBFD 2014).

Petty W., 'A Treatise of Taxes and Contributions' in Charles Henry Hull (ed) *The Economic Writings of Sir William Petty* (CUP 1899).

Pires M., *International Juridical Double Taxation of Income* (Kluwer 1989).

Qureshi Asif H., *The Public International Law of Taxation: Text, Cases and Materials* (Graham & Trotman 1994).

Ramon J.J., *The Impact of Sovereignty on Global Trade and International Taxation* (Kluwer 1999).

Rao B.S., *The Framing of India's Constitution: A Study* (Tripathi 1964).

Rawal R., *The Taxation of Permanent Establishments: An International Perspective* (Spiramus 2006).

Rawls J., *The Law of Peoples* (Harvard 1999).

Reimer E., Orell M. and Schmid S., *Permanent Establishment: A Domestic Taxation, Bilateral Tax Treaty and the OECD Perspective* (Wolters Kluwer 3rd ed. 2014).

Rohatgi R., *Basic International Taxation* (2nd ed. Richmond Law & Tax 2005).

Rohatgi R., *On International Taxation, Volume 1: Principles* (IBFD 2018).

Schofield R., *Taxation Under the Early Tudors, 1485-1547* (Blackwell 2004).

Rothwell D.R., 'International Law and Legislative Power' in Brian R. Opeskin and Donald Rothwell (eds), *International Law and Australian Federalism* (Melbourne 1997) 104.

Schön W., *Persons and Territories: On the International Allocation of Taxing Rights* (British Tax Review 2010).

Seervai H.M., *Constitutional Law in India: A Critical Commentary* (3rd ed. Universal Law Publishing 1986).

Seligman E.R.A., *Double Taxation and International Fiscal Cooperation* (Macmillan 1928).

Seligman E.R.A., *Progressive Taxation in Theory and Practice* (2nd ed. Princeton 1908).

Simons H.C., *Personal Income Taxation* (1st ed. Chicago 1938).

Singh G., *International Law*, Ch 4 p. 68 (Eastern Book Company 3rd ed. 2015).

Skaar A.A., *Permanent Establishment: Erosion of a Tax Treaty Principle* [1991] Series on International Taxation (Kluwer Law and Taxation 1991).

Smith A., *An Inquiry in to the Nature and Causes of the Wealth of Nations* (first published 1776, Regnery Publishing 1998).

Stimson E.S., *Conflict of Criminal Laws* 3–8 (Foundation Press 1936).

Tanzi V., *Taxation in an Integrating World* (Brookings Institution 1995).

Technical Experts, Double Taxation and Tax Evasion Report and Resolutions submitted by the Technical Experts to the Financial Committee Document F 212 vol. 4 sec 1 (League of Nations 1925).

Thakurta P.G. and Jain S., *Thin Dividing Line: India, Mauritius and Global Illicit Financial Flows* (Penguin Random House 2017).

The US Treasury Dept, *The Deferral of Income Earned Through U.S. Controlled Foreign Corporations: A Policy Study* (Office of Tax Policy Department of the Treasury 2000).

Treasury Dept, 'United States Model Convention on Income and Capital' (1976), (reprinted in 10 Walter H Diamond and Dorothy B Diamond) *International Tax Treaties of All Nations* 417.

Treasury Dept, *Model Income Tax Treaty of June 16, 1981*, reprinted in 1 Tax Treaties (CCH) 211.

Treasury Dept, *Model Income Tax Treaty of May 17, 1977*, reprinted in 1 Tax Treaties (CCH) 212.

UN, *United Nations Model Double Taxation Convention Between Developed and Developing Countries* (UN Pub 2001).

UN, *United Nations Model Double Taxation Convention between Developed and Developing Countries* (UN Pub 2017).

UNCTAD, *World Investment Report 2015: Reforming International Investment Governance* (UN Pub 2015).

United States Model Income Tax Convention of Nov. 15, 2006, reprinted in 1 Tax Treaties (CCH).

United States Model Income Tax Convention of Sept. 20, 1996, reprinted in 1 Tax Treaties (CCH).

Villiger M.E., *Customary International Law and Treaties: A Manual on the Theory and Practice of the Interrelation of Sources* (Kluwer 1997).

Vincenzi C., *Crown Powers, Subjects and Citizens* (Pinter 1998).

Vogel K., *'Worldwide vs. Source Taxation of Income: A Review and Re-Evaluation of Arguments'* in *Influence of Tax Differentials on International Competitiveness: Proceedings of the Munich Symposium on International Taxation* (Kluwer Law and Taxation 1990).

Vogel K., *Klaus Vogel on Double Taxation Conventions* (Kluwer Law International 4th ed. 2015).

Chapters in Edited Collections

Arnold B.J., 'Threshold Requirements for Taxing Business Profits under Tax Treaties', in B.J. Arnold, J. Sasseville and E.M. Zolt (eds), *The Taxation of Business Profits under Tax Treaties* (Canadian Tax Foundation, 2003) 55.

Auerbach A., 'The Theory of Excess Burden and Optimal Taxation' in A. Auerbach and M. Feldstein (eds), *Handbook of Public Economics* (vol. 1 ch. 2, Elsevier 1985) 61.

Ault H.J. and Bradford D.F., 'Taxing International Income: An Analysis of the U.S. System and Its Economic Premises' in A. Razin and J. Slemrod (eds), *Taxation in The Global Economy* 11, 31 (Chicago 1990).

Bird R.M. and Wilkie J.S., 'Source- vs. Residence-Based Taxation in the European Union: The Wrong Question?'' in S. Cnossen (ed.), *Taxing Capital Income in the European Union* (OUP 2000).

Brooks K., 'Canada's Evolving Tax Treaty Policy toward Low-Income Countries' in A.J. Cockfield (ed.), *Globalization and The Impact of Tax on International Investments* (Toronto 2009).

Brooks K., 'Inter-Nation Equity: The Development of an Important but Underappreciated International Tax Value' in R. Krever and J.G. Head (eds), *Tax Reform in The Twenty First Century* (Kluwer 2008).

Capps P., Evans M. and Konstadinidis S., 'Introduction' in P. Capps, M. Evans and S. Konstadinidis (eds), *Asserting Jurisdiction: International and European Legal Perspectives* (Hart 2003).

Cerioni L. and Herrera P.M., 'The Nexus for Taxpayers: Domestic, Community and International Law' in M. Lang, P. Melz and L. Kristoffersson (eds), *Value Added Tax and Direct Taxation: Similarities and Differences* (IBFD 2009).

Jones F.R., 'History of Taxation in Connecticut: 1636-1776' in *Johns Hopkins University Studies in Historical and Political Science* 14th Series (no. 8) 15.

Kobetsky M., 'History of Tax Treaties and The Permanent Establishment Concept', in *International Taxation of Permanent Establishments: Principles and Policy* 106-151 (CUP 2011).

Lang M. & Paterno L., 'Tax Coordination Between Regions in Austria - Role of the Courts' in M. Lang et al (eds), *Horizontal Tax Coordination* (IBFD 2012).

Lorenzen E.G., 'Huber's De Conflictu Legum' in E.G. Lorenzen (ed.), *Selected Articles on the Conflict of Laws* (Yale 1947) 136.

Mann F.A., 'The Doctrine of International Jurisdiction Revisited After Twenty Years' in W.M. Reisman (ed.) *Jurisdiction in International Law* (Ashgate 1999) 149.

Martha R.S.J., 'Extra-Territorial Taxation in International Law' in K.M. Meessen (ed.), *Extraterritorial Jurisdiction in Theory and Practice* (Kluwer 1996).

Musgrave P.B. and Musgrave R.A., 'Fiscal Coordination and Competition in an International Setting' in L. Eden, (ed.), *Retrospectives on Public Finance* (Duke 1991).

Musgrave P.B. and Musgrave R.A., 'Inter-Nation Equity' in R.M. Bird and J.G. Head (eds), *Modern Fiscal Issues* (Toronto 1972).

Musgrave P.B. 'Combining Fiscal Sovereignty and Coordination: National Taxation in a Globalizing World' in I. Kaul and P. Conceicao (eds), *The New Public Finance Responding to Global Challenges* (OUP 2006).

Musgrave P.B., 'Interjurisdictional Equity in Company Taxation: Principles and Applications to the European Union,' in S. Cnossen, (ed.), *Taxing Capital Income in the European Union: Issues and Options for Reform* (OUP, 2000).

OECD, 'Fundamental Principles of Taxation' in *Addressing the Tax Challenges of the Digital Economy* (OECD Pub 2014).

OECD, 'Chapter 4: Relevant Tax Policy Developments' in *Tax Challenges Arising from Digitalisation – Interim Report 2018: Inclusive Framework on BEPS, OECD/G20 Base Erosion and Profit Shifting Project* (OECD Pub 2018).

OECD, 'Fundamental Principles of Taxation' in *Addressing the Tax Challenges of the Digital Economy* (OECD Pub 2014).

Paul Mines, 'Nexus' in J.J. Cordes, R.D. Ebel and J. Gravelle (eds), *The Encyclopedia of Taxation and Tax Policy* (The Urban Institute 2005).

Roosevelt F.D., 'Public Papers and Addresses of Franklin D Roosevelt', S.I. Rosenman (ed.), (Address in Worcester, Massachusetts, 21 October 1936) vol. 5 (Random House 1938).

Ryngaert C., 'Public International Law Approaches to Jurisdiction', in C. Ryngaert, (ed.) *Jurisdiction in International Law* (2nd ed. OUP 2015) 29.

Schwartz L. and Finkelstein S., 'Nexus and the States' Jurisdictional Right to Tax' in W.M. Bergstein and J.E. Gold (eds), *Analysis* (Adelman Katz & Mond 2011) 6, http://akmcpa.com/wp-content/uploads/2011/10/AKM-Nexus-Report.pdf.

Shah V.J., Sheth S. and Mehta K., 'India' in E. Reimer, S. Schmid and M. Orell (eds), *Permanent Establishments: A Domestic Taxation, Bilateral Tax Treaty and OECD Perspective* (Wolters Kluwer 6th ed. 2018).

Slemrod J., 'Effect of Taxation with International Capital Mobility' in H.J. Aaron, H. Galper and J.A. Pechman (eds), *Uneasy Compromise: Problems of a Hybrid Income-Consumption Tax* (Brookings Institution 1988).

Vogel K., 'The Search for Compatible Tax Systems' in H. Stein (ed.), *Tax Policy in the 21st Century* (Wiley 1988).

Journal Articles and Academic Papers

Alert C., 'US Supreme Court Overturns Physical Presence Requirement in Sales Tax Case'. https://www.cooley.com/news/insight/2018/2018-06-25-us-supreme-court-overturns-physical-presence-requirement-in-sales-tax-case.

Andersson K., 'An Economist's View on Source Vs Residence Taxation: The Lisbon Objectives and Taxation in European Union' (2006) vol. 60(10) BIFT 395.

Ault H.J., 'Corporate Integration, Tax Treaties and the Division of the International Tax Base: Principles and Practice' (1992) vol. 47 Tax L Rev 565.

Avi-Yonah R.S., 'All of a Piece Throughout: The Four Ages of U.S. International Taxation.' (2005) vol. 25(2) Va Tax Rev 313.

Avi-Yonah R.S., 'International Taxation of Electronic Commerce' (1997) vol. 52(3) Tax L Rev 507.

Avi-Yonah, R.S., 'The International Implications of Wayfair' (2018) 160 Tax Notes 215.

Avi-Yonah, R.S., 'The Structure of International Taxation: A Proposal for Simplification' (1996) vol. 74(6) Tex L Rev 1301.

Avi-Yonah R.S. and Lahave Y., 'The Effective Tax Rate of the Largest US and EU Multinationals', University of Michigan Law School, Program in Law and Economics, WPN 41 (2011).

Baker, P. Q.C., 'CBDT Draft Report on PE Profit Attribution- Treading the Unbeaten Path?' https://www.taxsutra.com/content/cbdt-draft-report-pe-profit-attribution-treading-unbeaten-path.

Barker W.B., 'A Comparative Approach to Income Tax Law in the United Kingdom and the United States' (1996) vol. 46(1) Cath UL Rev 7.

Barker W.B., 'An International Tax System for Emerging Economies, Tax Sparing, and Development: It is All About Source' (2007) vol. 29(2) U Pa J Intl L 349.

Barker W.B., 'Optimal International Taxation and Tax Competition: Overcoming the Contradictions' (2002) vol. 22(2) Nw J Intl L and Bus 161.

Basu S., *Global Perspectives on E-Commerce Taxation Law* (Ashgate 2007) 47.

BIAC (OECD), Tax Analysts Report of Commission on Taxation jointly with BIAC, 'Tax Issues and Ramifications of Electronic Commerce' ICC (15 December 1999) http://www.iccwbo.org/policy/taxation/id414/index.html#source.

BJ Arnold, 'An introduction to tax treaties', p 5, https://www.un.org/esa/ffd//////wp-content/uploads/2015/10/TT_Introduction_Eng.pdf.

Bland, R., No Love for Retroactive Tax Legislation, Tax Notes https://www.forbes.com/sites/taxnotes/2020/07/14/no-love-for-retroactive-tax-legislation/?sh = 2ee8058a3278.

Bradford D.F., and US Treasury Dept., *Blueprints for Basic Tax Reform* (2nd ed., US Dept. of Treasury 1984), https://www.treasury.gov/resource-center/tax-policy/Documents/Report-Blueprints-1977.pdf.

Brooks K., 'Tax Treaty Treatment of Royalty Payments from Low-Income Countries: A Comparison of Canada and Australia's Policies' (2007) vol. 5(2) eJTR (Mich Issue) 169.

Cavelti L.U., Jaag C. and Rohner T.F., 'Why Corporate Taxation Should Mean Source Taxation: A Response to the OECD's Actions Against Base Erosion and Profit Shifting' (2017) vol. 9(3) WTJ (IBFD) 352.

Clausing K.A. and Avi-Yonah, R.S., 'Reforming Corporate Taxation in a Global Economy: A Proposal to Adopt Formulary Apportionment' (2007) The Hamilton Project, Brookings Institution 12.

Cleveland S.H., 'Embedded International Law and the Constitution Abroad', Symposium in Honour of Henry Paul Monaghan (2010) vol. 110(2) Colum L Rev 225.

Clopton Z.D., Extraterritoriality and Extranationality: A Comparative Study (2013) vol. 23 Duke J Comp & Intl L 217.

Cockfield A.J., 'Reforming the Permanent Establishment Principle Through A Quantitative Economic Presence Test' (2003) vol. 38 CBLJ 400.

Colangelo A.J., 'Constitutional Limits on Extraterritorial Jurisdiction: Terrorism and the Intersection of National and International Law' (2007) vol. 48(1) Harv Intl LJ 121.

Currie R.J. and Coughlan S., 'Extraterritorial Criminal Jurisdiction: Bigger Picture or Smaller Frame?' (2007) vol. 11 Can Crim L Rev 141.

d'Aspremont, J., 'Multilateral Versus Unilateral Exercises of Universal Criminal Jurisdiction', (2010) vol. 43 Israel L Rev 301.

Desai M.A. and Hines J., 'Evaluating International Tax Reform' (2003) vol 56(3) Natl Tax J 487.

Desai N.M., 'Budget 2010-11: Non-resident Services Outside India: Taxed Retroactively,' http://www.nishithdesai.com/fileadmin/user_upload/pdfs/Budget_2010-11-_Non-resident_services_outside_India-_Taxed_retroactively.pdf.

Doyle C., 'Extraterritorial Application of American Criminal Law', Cong Research Serv, CRS Rep (26 March 2010) 94.

Duff DG., 'Benefit Taxes and User Fees in Theory and Practice' (2004) vol. 54((4) UTLJ 391.

Durst M.C., 'Poverty, Tax Competition, and Base Erosion' (2018) vol. 89(12) Tax Notes Intl 1189.

Dutriez, J-F., 'Attribution of Profits to a Permanent Establishment of a Company Engaged Online Sales of Goods through a Local Warehouse' (2018) vol. 25(3) Int'l TP J 185.

Dutson S., 'The Conflict of Laws and Statutes: The International Operation of Legislation Dealing with Matters of Civil Law in the United Kingdom and Australia' (1997) vol. 60 MLR 668.

Fingar C., 'India Grabs Investment League Pole Position,' FT Report 29 September 2015, https://www.ft.com/content/fdd0e3c2-65fc-11e5-97d0-1456a776a4f5#axzz3n8D9cCEN.

Fleming Jr, J.C., Peroni R.J. and Shay S.E., 'Fairness in International Taxation: The Ability-to-Pay Case for Taxing Worldwide Income' (2001) vol. 5(4) Fla Tax Rev 299.

Forsythe M., 'Paradise Papers Shine Light on Where the Elite Keep Their Money', *New York Times* (5 November 2017).

Foster Swift Collins and Smith PC., 'The Post-Wayfair Future of SALT Controversies: The Due Process Clause', Tax Law Blog (USA 26 July 2018) https://www.lexology.com/library/detail.aspx?g=31f0b2ce-b2d7-4856-9e26-3d70e1d8260c.

Frey J. and Schmid F. 'Nexus Limitations on German-Source IP Taxation' (2020) vol. 100 Tax Notes Int'l 1051.

Friedlander L. and Wilkie S., 'Policy Forum – The History of Tax Treaty Provisions and Why It Is Important to Know About It', (2006) vol. 54 Canadian Tax J 4.

Fuest C. and Riedel N., 'Tax Evasion and Tax Avoidance in Developing Countries: The Role of International Profit Shifting' (2010) Oxford University Centre for Business Taxation WPN 1012/2010 https://assets.publishing.service.gov.uk/media/57a08b3de5274a31e0000a66/60670_TaxEvasionReportDFIDFINAL1906.pdf.

Gadžo S., 'The Principle of 'Nexus' or 'Genuine Link' as a Keystone of International Income Tax Law: A Reappraisal' (2018) vol. 46(3) Intertax 194.

Gautam K., 'Taxing Offshore Transactions in India and the Territoriality Clause: A Case for Substantial Constitutional Limitations on Indian Parliament's Power to Retrospectively Amend the Income Tax Act' (2014) vol. 40(4) Intl Tax J 19.

Gelineck M.S., 'Permanent Establishments and the Offshore Oil and Gas Industry – Part 1' (2016) vol. 70(4) BIT 206.

Geu T.E., 'Professor TS Adams (1873-1933) on Federal Taxation: Déjà vu All Over Again' (1993) vol. 10 Akron Tax J 29.

Gordon R.H., 'Taxation of Investment and Savings in a World Economy' (1986) vol. 76(5) Am Econ Rev 1086.

Govind H., 'Business Connection and Permanent Establishment' (2001) 7 APTB 195.

Graetz M.J. and O'Hear, M.M., 'The "Original Intent" of US International Taxation (1997) vol. 46 Duke LJ 1021.

Graetz M.J., 'Taxing International Income: Inadequate Principles, Outdated Concepts, and Unsatisfactory Policies' (2001) vol. 54 (3) Tax L Rev 261.

Green R.A., 'The Future of Source-Based Taxation of the Income of Multinational Enterprises' (1993) vol. 79 Cornell L Rev 18.

Guruli E.L., 'International Taxation: Application of Source Rule to Income from Intangible Property' (2005) vol. 5 HBTLJ 205.

Hakelberg L. and Schaub M., 'The Redistributive Impact of Hypocrisy in International Taxation' (2018) vol. 12(3) Regulation and Governance 353.

Harris PA., 'Corporate-Shareholder Income Taxation and Allocating Taxing Rights Between Countries: A Comparison of Imputation Systems' (IBFD 1996) 447.

Harris PA., Income Tax in Common Law Jurisdictions: From the Origins to 1820 vol. 1 (Cambridge 2006) 44.

Hearson M., 'The Challenges for Developing Countries in International Tax Justice' (2018) vol. 54(10) J Dev Stud 1932.

Hellerstein W., 'Jurisdiction to Tax in the New Economy: International, National, and Subnational Perspectives' (2003) vol. 38(1) Ga L Rev 1.

Hertogen, An, 'Letting Lotus Bloom' (2015) vol. 26(4) EJIL 901.

Hill G., 'Resolving a True Conflict Between State Laws: A Minimalist Approach' (2005) vol. 29(1) Melb U L Rev 39.

Houseman N. & Condoleon G., 'Attribution of Profit to Permanent Establishments: Asia Overview' (PWC 2014) 5, https://www.pwc.com/jp/en/tax-focus-on/assets/attribution-of-profit-to-permanent-establishments-asia-overview.pdf.

Jackson J.H., 'Sovereignty-Modern: A New Approach to an Outdated Concept' (2003) vol. 97 Am J Intl L 782.

Kane M.A., 'A Defense of Source Rules in International Taxation' (2015) vol. 32(2) Yale J Reg 315.

Kaufman N.H., 'Equity Considerations in International Taxation' (2001) vol. 26(4) Brooklyn J Intl L 1466.

Kaufman, NH., 'Fairness and the Taxation of International Income' (1998) vol. 29(2) L & Pol Int Bus 145.

Kemmeren, E., *Principles of Origins in Tax Conventions: A Rethinking of Models* (PijnenburgVormgevers/Uitgevers 2001) 20.

Knoll M.S., 'Reconsidering International Tax Neutrality' (2011) vol. 64 Tax L Rev 99.

Kobetsky M., 'Article 7 of the OECD Model: Defining the Personality of Permanent Establishments' (2006) vol. 60(10) BFIT 411.

Kofler G. and Thiel S. van, 'The "Authorised OECD Approach" and EU Tax Law' (2011) vol. 51(8) Euro Tax 327, 328.

Kokott J. Das Steuerrecht der Europäischen Union 143 (2018) 2.03 (2019).

Kopits G.F., 'Taxation and Multinational Firm Behavior: A Critical Survey' (1976) vol. 23(3) IMF Staff Papers 624.

Kragen A.A., 'Double Income Taxation Treaties: The OECD Draft' (1964) vol. 52(2) Calif L Rev 306.

Kranz S.P., Smith D.L. & Freeman B., 'Colorado's End Run: Clever, Coercive, and Unconstitutional' (2010) vol. 56 State Tax Notes 55 (5 April 2010).

Lang M. and Brugger F., 'The Role of the OECD Commentary in Tax Treaty Interpretation' (2008) vol. 23 ATF 95.

Lepard B.D., 'Is the United States Obligated to Drive on the Right?: A Multidisciplinary Inquiry into the Normative Authority of Contemporary International Law Using the Arms' Length Standards as a Case Study' (1999) vol. 10(1) Duke J Comp & Intl L 155.

Loconte S. and Favi L., 'A New Definition of Permanent Establishment In Italian Domestic Income Tax Law' http://publications.ruchelaw.com/news/2018-03/Italy-Permanent-Establishment.pdf.

Loiacono R. and Mortimer C., 'Retrospective Tax Law: Has Pandora's Box Opened Never to Be Shut Again?' eJournal Tax Res. (2017) vol. 15(1) 105.

Ma'ilei S. and Brown J., 'PE Issues in Global Insurance Distribution', Int'l Tax Rev, 3 August 2015, https://www.internationaltaxreview.com/article/b1f9jp8z6l4rpz/pe-issues-in-global-insurance-distribution.

Mata P. and Smith M.J., 'The Implementation of "Market" Sourcing Rules: Practical Concerns' (6 September 2010) Tax Analysts 650 https://www.jdsupra.com/legalnews/a-pinch-of-salt-september-2010-the-imp-00487/.

Midkiff C.F., 'Extraterritorial Enforcement of Tax Claims,' (1970) vol. 12 Wm & Mary L Rev 111.

Musgrave P.B., 'International Tax Base Division and the Multinational Corporation', (1972) vol. 27(4) Public Finance 394.

Musgrave P.B., 'Sovereignty, Entitlement, and Cooperation in International Taxation' (2001) vol. 26(4) Brooklyn J Intl L 1335.

Nouel L., 'The New Article 7 of the OECD Model Tax Convention: The End of the Road?' (2011) vol. 65(1) BFIT 5.

Parekh J.V., 'Foreign Direct Investment in Indian Retail Sector', http://www.fnbnews.com/FB-Specials/Foreign-Direct-Investment-in-Indian-retail-sector.

Pechman, J.A., 'The Future of the Income Tax' (1990) vol. 80(1) Am Ec Rev 6 (1990).

Peroni R.J., 'Back to the Future: A Path to Progressive Reform of the U.S. International Income Tax Rules' (1997) vol. 51(4) U Miami L Rev 975.

Pinto D., 'Exclusive Source or Residence Based Taxation: Is A New and Simpler World Tax Order Possible?' (2007) July BIT 277.

Pinto D., *E-Commerce and Source-Based Taxation*, vol. 6 Doctoral Series (IBFD 2002) 17.

Preston J., 'Shaping the Tax System; http://www.pwc.com/en_GX/gx/tax/publications/assets/pwc-global-tax-policy-trends.pdf.

Rajadhyaksha S., Reghuvaran G. and Chatterjee B., 'The Curious Case of Extraterritorial Taxation in India', The Hindu, (New Delhi, 2 April 2012) https://www.lexology.com/library/detail.aspx?g=9f54a7b2-0e08-4e3f-a1fa-6b66fc91b786.

Ram V., 'Vodafone Serves Arbitration Notice on Indian Govt Over New Tax Plan', The Hindu Business Line (London, 17 April 2012) https://www.thehindubusinessline.com/info-tech/vodafone-serves-arbitration-notice-on-indian-govt-over-new-tax-plan/article20422749.ecel.

Rao S. and Ajinkya B., 'Groping in the Dark: The Extending Arms of the Indian International Withholding Tax,' (2020) vol. 22(1) NLS India Rev 2010 97.

Ring, Diane M., 'International Tax Relations: Theory and Implications' (2007) vol. 60 Tax L Rev 83.

Rosenbloom, H.D., 'International Tax Arbitrage and the "International Tax System"' (2000) vol. 53 Tax L Rev 137.

Schadewald M.S. and Kaye T.A., 'Source of Income Rules and Treaty Relief from Double Taxation Within the NAFTA Trading Bloc' (2001) vol. 61(2) La L Rev 353.

Schäfer A. and Spengel C., 'ICT and International Corporate Taxation: Tax Attributes and Scope of Taxation' (2002) Centre for European Economic Research (ZEW) and University of Mannheim DPN 02-81, 32, http://ftp.zew.de/pub/zew-docs/dp/dp0281.pdf.

Schanz, G. Von, 'ZurFrage Der Steuerpflicht' (1892) vol. 9(II) FinanzArchiv 1.

Schindel A. and Atchabahian A. 'General Report', in *Source and Residence: A New Configuration of Their Principles* (vol. 90a, IFA Cahiers de droit fiscal international 2005) 21.

Schön W., 'Neutrality and Territoriality — Competing or Converging Concepts in European Tax Law?'(2015) vol. 69 Bull. Int'l Tax'n 271.

Schoueri L.E., 'Arm's Length: Beyond the Guidelines of the OECD' (2015) vol. 69(12) BFIT 690.

Schwarz J., 'Model Treaty 2016: What Does it Say about the US and BEPS?' 21 February 2016 http://kluwertaxblog.com/2016/02/21/us-model-treaty-2016-what-does-it-say-about-the-us-and-beps/?_ga=2.103386121.846281485.1544359381-449772679.1544359381.

Sharma S.D., 'Applicability of the Doctrine of Extraterritoriality to Legislation by Indian Legislature' (1946) vol. 28 (3-4) J Comp Leg 91.

Shay S.E., Fleming Jr, J.C. and Peroni, R.J., 'What's Source Got to Do With It: Source Rules and U.S. International Taxation' (2002) vol. 56 Tax L Rev 81.

Shen W. and Watters C., 'Is China Creating A New Business Order? Rationalizing China's Extraterritorial Attempt to Expand the Veil-Piercing Doctrine' (2015) vol. 35(3) Nw J Intl L & Bus 469.

Singh N. and Gitte D., 'Constitutionality of Extra-Territorial Taxation of Off-Shore Services of Non-residents under Income Tax Act 1961' (2014) vol. 1(10) IJR 236.

Stolton S., 'Le Maire Renews Push For EU-Wide Digital Services Tax', Euractive.com, posted 21 January 2019, https://www.euractiv.com/section/digital/news/le-maire-renews-push-for-eu-wide-digital-services-tax/.

Stupples B., 'Tax Avoidance Costing US USD 189 Billion: Tax Justice Network, Tax Justice Network', Bloomberg News, 23 March 2017, https://www.bna.com/tax-avoidance-costing-n57982085579/.

Swain J.A., 'State Income Tax Jurisdiction: A Jurisprudential and Policy Perspective' (2003) vol. 45 Wm & Mary L Rev 319.

Thimmesch A., 'The Fading Bright Line of Physical Presence: Did KFC Corporation v. Iowa Department of Revenue Give States the Secret Recipe for Repudiating Quill?' (2012) 100 KY LJ 339.

Thornton G., 'International Tax CRA Relief on International Tax Issues Caused by COVID-19 Extended,' 20 July 2020, https://www.grantthornton.ca/insights/coronavirus-covid-19/cra-relief-on-international-tax-issues-caused-by-covid-19-extended/.

Todd T.M., 'Supreme Court's Quill and Wayfair Cases Explained', posted in Forbes on 27 June 2018, https://www.forbes.com/sites/timtodd/2018/06/27/supreme-courts-quill-and-wayfair-cases-explained/#63737fdd72a4.

Treves T., 'Customary International Law' in *Max Planck Encyclopedia of Public International Law* 8, http://opil.ouplaw.com/view/10.1093/law:epil/9780199231690/law-9780199231690-e1393?rskey=vlKjuK&result=1&prd=EPIL.

Valderrama I.J.M., 'BEPS Principal Purpose Test and Customary International Law' (2020) vol. 33 Leiden J Int'l L 745.

Vann R.J., 'Do We Need 7(3)? History and Purpose of the Business Profits Deduction Rules in Tax Treaties' Paper presented at the Tax History Conference, Cambridge 2010.

Vogel K., 'Double Tax Treaties and Their Interpretation' (1986) vol. 4(1) Berk J Intl L 7.

Vogel K., 'Worldwide v Source Taxation of Income' (1988) vol. 8(9) Intertax 225.

Vogel K., 'Worldwide Vs Source Taxation of Income: A Review and Revaluation of Arguments (Part II)' (1988) vol. 10 Intertax 310.

Vogel K., 'Worldwide Vs Source Taxation of Income: A Review and Revaluation of Arguments' Part III (1988) vol. 11 Intertax 393.

Vogel K., 'Worldwide Vs Source Taxation of Income-A Review & Re-evaluation of Arguments' (Part I) (1988) vol. 8(9) Intertax 216.

Walker E., 'How Will the UK's Upcoming Digital Services Tax Impact You?' posted 22 November 2018, https://www.out-law.com/en/articles/2018/november/how-will-the-upcoming-digital-services-tax-impact-you/.

Weisbach D.A., 'The Use of Neutralities in International Tax Policy' (2014) University of Chicago, Coase-Sandor Inst for Law and Econ Research Paper 697/2014 3, https://ssrn.com/abstract = 2482624.

Well B. and Lowel C.H., 'Income Tax Treaty Policy in the Twenty First Century: Residence vs. Source' (2013) vol. 5(1) Colum J Tax L 1.

Wiercinski S., 'Catalog Mailers Infuriated by Supreme Court's Wrong Decision in South Dakota v Wayfair Case' Catalogs Blogs, http://www.sheridan.com/catalogs-blog/catalog-mailers-supreme-court.

Wijnen W. and Goede J. de, 'The UN Model Practice 1997-2013' 68 Bulletin for International Taxation 3 (2014) Journals IBFD.

Wilson J. and Hill D.C., 'Relationship Between Tax Treaties and Domestic Tax law: Scenario Involving the Canada-India Tax Treaty', https://www.lexology.com/library/detail.aspx?g = fab88c7f-8b54-43f7-8eb0-d7e0bbe27afd.

Wright Q., 'Conflicts of International Law with National Laws and Ordinances' (1917) vol. 11(1) Am J Intl L 1.

Xynas L, 'Tax Planning, Avoidance and Evasion in Australia 1970–2010: The Regulatory Responses and Taxpayer Compliance' (2011) vol. 20(1) Revenue L J, Article 2, 1.

Yang B. and Song C.P., 'A Comparative Study of the OECD Model, UN Model and China's Treaties with Respect to Rights to Tax Income and Capital' (2011) vol. 9(3) eJTR 254.

Yang J.G.S. and Metallo V.N.A., 'The Emerging International Taxation Problems' (2018) vol. 6(1) Int J Fin Stud 6.

Yu R., 'E-Commerce: Relevance of Source and Residence Rules' (2001) 13, http://raymondyu.net/pub/papers/ecom_sr.pdf.

Zelinsky E.A., 'The Siren's Song of 'Amazon' Laws: The Colorado Example' (2011) vol. 59 STN 695.

Zucker S., 'Extraterritoriality and Canadian Criminal Law' (1975) vol. 17 CRIM LQ 146.

Miscellanea

Cabinet Approves Non-binding Conciliation to Resolve Vodafone Tax Issue, India Today (New Delhi, 4 June 2013), https://www.indiatoday.in/business/corporate/story/vodafone-tax-dispute-british-telecom-major-vodafone-tax-issue-hutchison-essar-finance-minister-p-chidambaram-cabinet-165589-2013-06-04.

CBDT, 'Report on Profit Attribution to Permanent Establishments' dated 18 April 2019, https://www.incometaxindia.gov.in/Lists/Press%20Releases/Attachments/757/CBDT_stakeholder_comments_Permanent_Establishment_18_4_19.pdf.

Committee of Experts on International Cooperation in Tax Matters, 'Revision of the Manual for the Negotiation of Bilateral Tax Treaties' (Seventh Session' Geneva, 24-28 October 2011) Item 5(h) of the provisional agenda, http://unpan1.un.org /intradoc/groups/public/documents/un/unpan008579.pdf.

Global Tax Alert, 'India Signs Multilateral Convention to Implement Tax Treaty Related Measures to Prevent BEPS' 6 July 2017, EY Global Tax Alert Library 4.

GOI, *High Power Committee Report* (Ministry of Fin 2001) [2001] 251 ITR 118.

History of the United Nations, http://www.un.org/en/sections/history/history-united -nations/.

India Joins the Multilateral Competent Authority Agreement (MCAA) on Automatic Exchange of Information (AEOI), PTI News, https://pib.gov.in/newsite/PrintRe lease.aspx?relid = 122256.

India loses tax arbitration case against Cairn; told to pay Rs 8,000 cr (BusinessToday.In, December 23, 2020), https://www.businesstoday.in/current/corporate/breakin g-india-loses-tax-arbitration-case-against-cairn-told-to-pay-rs-8000-cr/story/425 747.html.

India's Non-signing of Automatic Info Exchange agreement- 'Confidentiality' vs 'Disclosure' Crossfire, http://www.taxsutra.com/content/indias-non-signing-autom atic-info-exchange-agreement-%E2%80%98confidentiality%E2%80%99-vs-dis closure.

International Chamber of Commerce, Congress of London 1921, brochure 11, 3 (Brochures 1-16, ICC Paris Archives).

International Tax Glossary (IBFD 2001).

IT Department Sells Part of Cairn's Energy Shares in Vedanta to Recover Its Dues, The Hindu Business Line (New Delhi, 9 July 2018).

Joint Committee on Taxation, *Factors Affecting the International Competitiveness of the United States* (US Govt Printing Office 1991) (hereafter called the JCT 1991Report).

Joint Committee on Taxation, *Study of Present-Law Taxpayer Confidentiality and Disclosure Provisions as Required by Section 3802 of the Internal Revenue Service Restructuring and Reform Act Of 1998* (US Govt Printing Office 2000) vol II: Study of Disclosure Provisions Relating to Tax-Exempt Organizations, http://www.jct .gov/s-1-00vol2.pdf.

McLure Jr, Charles E., 'Source-Based Taxation and Alternatives to the Concept of Permanent Establishment' *Report of the Proceedings of the World Tax Conference: Taxation Without Borders* (CTF 2000).

Nokia Says It Paid 202 Million Euro To Settle Tax Row With India, The Economic Times (New Delhi, 27 April 2018) https://economictimes.indiatimes.com/tech/hardw are/nokia-paid-202-million-euro-to-settle-tax-row-with-india/articleshow/63942 891.cms.

Osborne Raises Vodafone Tax Issues with Pranab, The Hindu (New Delhi, 2 April 2012), https://www.thehindu.com/business/osborne-raises-vodafone-tax-issue -with-pranab/article3273229.ece.

Phys.org, 'France Nears Implementation of Digital Tax' (Paris, 20 January 2019), https://phys.org/news/2019-01-france-nears-digital-tax.html.

Report on Profit Attribution to PEs submitted by the Committee to Examine the Issues related to Profit Attribution to Permanent Establishment (PE) in India and Amendment of Rule 10 of Income-tax Rules. 1962, http://incometaxindia.gov.in/News/Public_consultation_Notice_18_4_19.pdf#search = cbdt%20draft%20report%20on%20profit%20attribution.

Solicitor General Tushar Mehta Recommends Indian Government to Challenge PCA Award in Vodafone Tax Case, Bar and Bench, (27 October 2020), https://www.barandbench.com/news/sg-tushar-mehta-urges-centre-challenge-award-vodafone-tax-case.

Tax from Vodafone-Like Deals May Fetch Government Rs 40,000 Crore, The Economic Times (New Delhi, 25 April 2012), http://articles.economictimes.indiatimes.com/2012-04-25/news/31399045_1_tax-havens-income-tax-amendment.

The 2005 Update to The Model Tax Convention: Public Discussion Draft dated 15 March 2004, https://www.oecd.org/ctp/treaties/34576874.pdf.

The Drafting Committee of the Government of India, *Draft Constitution of India*, (Government of India Press, New Delhi 1948).

The President's Tax Proposals to the Congress for Fairness, Growth, and Simplicity 383 (May 1985), https://www.treasury.gov/resource-center/tax-policy/documents/report-reform-proposal-1985.pdf.

The US Department of Treasury Report (1996), *Selected Tax Policy Implications of Global Electronic Commerce*, https://www.treasury.gov/resource-center/tax-policy/Documents/Report-Global-Electronic-Commerce-1996.pdf.

TNN: *'India Pips China, US to Emerge as Favourite Foreign Investment Destination'* TOI, http://timesofindia.indiatimes.com/articleshow/49160838.cms?utm_source = contentofinterest&utm_medium = text&utm_campaign = cppst.

Ubilla & Cia, 'China Adopts Controversial Extraterritorial & Retroactive Tax and Disclosure Rule Relating to Share Transfers by Non-Resident Enterprises', http://www.ub-co.com/country/china/china-adopts-controversial-extraterritorial-retroactive-tax-and-disclosure-rule-relating-to-share-transfers-by-non-resident-enterprises/.

UN Committee of Experts on International Cooperation in Tax Matters, E/C.18/2017/CRP.7 *Proposed Base Erosion and Profit Shifting Related Changes to the UN Model Double Tax Convention Between Developed and Developing Countries*, 3-37, https://www.un.org/development/desa/financing/document/proposed-base-erosion-and-profit-shifting-related-changes-united-nations-model-double.

UN Committee of Experts on International Cooperation in Tax Matters, *Report on the Fifth Session'* Economic and Social Council Official Records.

UN Economic and Social Council Committee of Experts on International Cooperation in Tax Matters, 'Proposal for Amendments of the United Nations Model Double Taxation Convention between Developed and Developing Countries: Further Issues Relating to Permanent Establishment', 4th session Geneva, 20-24 October 2008, https://www.un.org/esa/ffd/wp-content/uploads/2014/10/4STM_EC18_2008_CRP3.pdf.

War on Want News, 'A Global Tax Justice Movement Rises: The New Fight to End Inequality' (19 June 2013), https://waronwant.org/media/global-tax-justice-movement-rises-new-fight-end-inequality.

Webcast, http://www.oecd.org/tax/tax-talks-webcasts.htm.

Table of Cases

Table of Statutes

Table of Treaties and Conventions

Index

O

P

SERIES ON INTERNATIONAL TAXATION

1. Alberto Xavier, *The Taxation of Foreign Investment in Brazil,* 1980 (ISBN 90-200-0582-0).
2. Hugh J. Ault & Albert J. Rädler, *The German Corporation Tax Law with 1980 Amendments,* 1981 (ISBN 90-200-0642-8).
3. Paul R. McDaniel & Hugh J. Ault, *Introduction to United States International Taxation,* 1981 (ISBN 90-6544-004-6).
4. Albert J. Rädler, *German Transfer Pricing/Prix de Transfer en Allemagne,* 1984 (ISBN 90-6544-143-3).
5. Paul R. McDaniel & Stanley S. Surrey, *International Aspects of Tax Expenditures: A Comparative Study,* 1985 (ISBN 90-654-4163-8).
6. Kees van Raad, *Nondiscrimination in International Tax Law,* 1986 (ISBN 90-6544-266-9).
7. Sijbren Cnossen (ed.), *Tax Coordination in the European Community,* 1987 (ISBN 90-6544-272-3).
8. Ben Terra, *Sales Taxation. The Case of Value Added Tax in the European Community,* 1989 (ISBN 90-6544-381-9).
9. Rutsel S.J. Martha, *The Jurisdiction to Tax in International Law: Theory and Practice of Legislative Fiscal Jurisdiction,* 1989 (ISBN 90-654-4416-5).
10. Paul R. McDaniel & Hugh J. Ault, *Introduction to United States International Taxation* (3rd revised edition), 1989 (ISBN 90-6544-423-8).
11. Manuel Pires, *International Juridicial Double Taxation of Income,* 1989 (ISBN 90-6544-426-2).
12. A.H.M. Daniels, *Issues in International Partnership Taxation,* 1991 (ISBN 90-654-4577-3).
13. Arvid A. Skaar, *Permanent Establishment: Erosion of a Tax Treaty Principle,* 1992 (ISBN 90-6544-594-3).
14. Cyrille David & Geerten M.M. Michielse (eds), *Tax Treatment of Financial Instruments,* 1996 (ISBN 90-654-4666-4).
15. Herbert H. Alpert & Kees van Raad (eds), *Essays on International Taxation,* 1993 (ISBN 90-654-4781-4).
16. Wolfgang Gassner, Michael Lang & Eduard Lechner (eds), *Tax Treaties and EC Law,* 1997 (ISBN 90-411-0680-4).
17. Glória Teixeira, *Taxing Corporate Profits in the EU,* 1997 (ISBN 90-411-0703-7).
18. Michael Lang et al. (eds), *Multilateral Tax Treaties,* 1998 (ISBN 90-411-0704-5).
19. Stef van Weeghel, *The Improper Use of Tax Treaties,* 1998 (ISBN 90-411-0737-1).

20. Klaus Vogel (ed.), *Interpretation of Tax Law and Treaties and Transfer Pricing in Japan and Germany,* 1998 (ISBN 90-411-9655-2).
21. Bertil Wiman (ed.), *International Studies in Taxation: Law and Economics; Liber Amicorum Leif Mutén,* 1999 (ISBN 90-411-9692-7).
22. Alfonso J. Martín Jiménez, *Towards Corporate Tax Harmonization in the European Community,* 1999 (ISBN 90-411-9690-0).
23. Ramon J. Jeffery, *The Impact of State Sovereignty on Global Trade and International Taxation,* 1999 (ISBN 90-411-9703-6).
24. A.J. Easson, *Taxation of Foreign Direct Investment,* 1999 (ISBN 90-411-9741-9).
25. Marjaana Helminen, *The Dividend Concept in International Tax Law: Dividend Payments Between Corporate Entities,* 1999 (ISBN 90-411-9765-6).
26. Paul Kirchhof, Moris Lehner, Kees van Raad, Arndt Raupach & Michael-Rodi (eds), *International and Comparative Taxation: Essays in Honour of Klaus Vogel,* 2002 (ISBN 90-411-9841-5).
27. Krister Andersson, Peter Melz & Christer Silfverberg (eds), *Liber Amicorum Sven-Olof Lodin,* 2001 (ISBN 90-411-9850-4).
28. Juan Martín Jovanovich, *Customs Valuation and Transfer Pricing: Is It Possible to Harmonize Customs and Tax Rules?,* Second Edition, 2018 (ISBN 978-90-411-6134-5).
29. Stefano Simontacchi, *Taxation of Capital Gains under the OECD Model Convention: With Special Regard to Immovable Property,* 2007 (ISBN 978-90-411-2549-1).
30. Michael Lang, Josef Schuch, & Claus Staringer (eds), *Tax Treaty Law and EC Law,* 2007 (ISBN 978-90-411-2629-0).
31. Duncan Bentley, *Taxpayers' Rights: Theory Origin and Implementation,* 2007 (ISBN 978-90-411-2650-4).
32. Sergio André Rocha, *Interpretation of Double Taxation Conventions: General Theory and Brazilian Perspective,* 2008 (ISBN 978-90-411-2822-5).
33. Robert F. van Brederode, *Systems of General Sales Taxation: Theory, Policy and Practice,* 2009 (ISBN 978-90-411-2832-4).
34. John G. Head & Richard Krever (eds), *Tax Reform in the 21st Century: A Volume in Memory of Richard Musgrave,* 2009 (ISBN 978-90-411-2829-4).
35. Jens Wittendorff, *Transfer Pricing and the Arm's Length Principle in International Tax Law,* 2010 (ISBN 978-90-411-3270-3).
36. Marjaana Helminen, *The International Tax Law Concept of Dividend,* Second Edition, 2017 (ISBN 978-90-411-8394-1).
37. Robert F. van Brederode (ed.), *Immovable Property under VAT: A Comparative Global Analysis,* 2011 (ISBN 978-90-411-3126-3).
38. Dennis Weber & Stef van Weeghel, *The 2010 OECD Updates: Model Tax Convention & Transfer Pricing Guidelines - A Critical Review,* 2011 (ISBN 978-90-411-3812-5).
39. Yariv Brauner & Martin James McMahon, Jr. (eds), *The Proper Tax Base: Structural Fairness from an International and Comparative Perspective— Essays in Honour of Paul McDaniel,* 2012 (ISBN 978-90-411-3286-4).
40. Robert F. van Brederode (ed.), *Science, Technology and Taxation,* 2012 (ISBN 978-90-411-3125-6).

41. Oskar Henkow, *The VAT/GST Treatment of Public Bodies*, 2013 (ISBN 978-90-411-4663-2).
42. Jean Schaffner, *How Fixed Is a Permanent Establishment?*, 2013 (ISBN 978-90-411-4662-5).
43. Miguel Correia, *Taxation of Corporate Groups*, 2013 (ISBN 978-90-411-4841-4).
44. Veronika Daurer, *Tax Treaties and Developing Countries*, 2014 (ISBN 978-90-411-4982-4).
45. Claire Micheau, *State Aid, Subsidy and Tax Incentives under EU and WTO Law*, 2014 (ISBN 978-90-411-4555-0).
46. Robert F. van Brederode & Richard Krever (eds), *Legal Interpretation of Tax Law*, 2014 (ISBN 978-90-411-4945-9).
47. Radhakishan Rawal, *Taxation of Cross-border Services*, 2014 (ISBN 978-90-411-4947-3).
48. João Dácio Rolim, *Proportionality and Fair Taxation*, 2014 (ISBN 978-90-411-5838-3).
49. Paulo Rosenblatt, *General Anti-avoidance Rules for Major Developing Countries*, 2015 (ISBN 978-90-411-5839-0).
50. Gaspar Lopes Dias V.S., *Tax Arbitrage through Cross-Border Financial Engineering*, 2015 (ISBN 978-90-411-5875-8).
51. Geerten M.M. Michielse & Victor Thuronyi (eds), *Tax Design Issues Worldwide*, 2015 (ISBN 978-90-411-5610-5).
52. Oktavia Weidmann, *Taxation of Derivatives*, 2015 (ISBN 978-90-411-5977-9).
53. Chris Evans, Richard Krever & Peter Mellor (eds), *Tax Simplification*, 2015 (ISBN 978-90-411-5976-2).
54. Reuven Avi-Yonah & Joel Slemrod (eds), *Taxation and Migration*, 2015 (ISBN 978-90-411-6136-9).
55. Alexander Bosman, *Other Income under Tax Treaties: An Analysis of Article 21 of the OECD Model Convention*, 2015 (ISBN 978-90-411-6610-4).
56. John Abrahamson, *International Taxation of Manufacturing and Distribution*, 2016 (ISBN 978-90-411-6664-7).
57. Frederik Boulogne, *Shortcomings in the EU Merger Directive*, 2016 (ISBN 978-90-411-6713-2).
58. Angelika Meindl-Ringler, *Beneficial Ownership in International Tax Law*, 2016 (ISBN 978-90-411-6833-7).
59. Andreas Waltrich, *Cross-Border Taxation of Permanent Establishments: An International Comparison*, 2016 (ISBN 978-90-411-6832-0).
60. Sergio André Rocha & Allison Christians (eds), *Tax Sovereignty in the BEPS Era*, 2017 (ISBN 978-90-411-6707-1).
61. Peter Antony Wilson, *BRICS and International Tax Law*, 2018 (ISBN 978-90-411-9435-0).
62. Louise Otis, Brigitte Alepin & Blanca Moreno-Dodson (eds), *Winning the Tax Wars: Tax Competition and Cooperation*, 2018 (ISBN 978-90-411-9460-2).
63. Marta Castelon, *International Taxation of Income from Services under Double Taxation Conventions: Development, Practice and Policy*, 2018 (ISBN 978-90-411-9594-4).

64. D.M. Broekhuijsen, *A Multilateral Tax Treaty: Designing an Instrument to Modernise International Tax Law*, 2018 (ISBN 978-90-411-9872-3).
65. John Abrahamson, *International Taxation of Energy Production and Distribution*, 2018 (ISBN 978-90-411-9101-4).
66. Leopoldo Parada, *Double Non-taxation and the Use of Hybrid Entities: An Alternative Approach in the New Era of BEPS*, 2018 (ISBN 978-90-411-9991-1).
67. Richard Snoeij, *International Tax Aspects of Sovereign Wealth Investors: A Source State Perspective*, 2018 (ISBN 978-90-411-9431-2).
68. Aleksandra Bal, *Taxation, Virtual Currency and Blockchain*, 2019 (ISBN 978-94-035-0103-1).
69. Werner Haslehner, Georg Kofler, Katerina Pantazatou & Alexander Rust (eds), *Tax and the Digital Economy: Challenges and Proposals for Reform*, 2019 (ISBN 978-94-035-0361-5).
70. Eva Escribano, *Jurisdiction to Tax Corporate Income Pursuant to the Presumptive Benefit Principle: A Critical Analysis of Structural Paradigms Underlying Corporate Income Taxation and Proposals for Reform*, 2019 (ISBN 978-94-035-0640-1).
71. Jérôme Monsenego & Jan Bjuvberg (eds), *International Taxation in a Changing Landscape: Liber Amicorum in Honour of Bertil Wiman*, 2019 (ISBN 978-90-411-9234-9).
72. Kasper Dziurdz´, *Non-discrimination in Tax Treaty Law and World Trade Law: The Impact of Formal, Substantive and Subjective Approaches*, 2019 (ISBN 978-94-035-0904-4).
73. Félix Daniel Martínez Laguna, *Hybrid Financial Instruments, Double Nontaxation and Linking Rules*, 2019 (ISBN 978-94-035-1074-3).
74. Jan Gooijer, *Tax Treaty Residence of Entities*, 2019 (ISBN 978-94-035-1301-0).
75. John Abrahamson, *International Taxation of Banking*, 2020 (ISBN 978-94-035-1094-1).
76. Richard Krever & François Vaillancourt (eds), *The Allocation of Multinational Business Income: Reassessing the Formulary Apportionment Option*, 2020 (ISBN 978-94-035-0614-2).
77. Ajit Kumar Singh, *Exploring the Nexus Doctrine in International Tax Law*, 2021 (ISBN 978-94-035-3363-6).